Theology and Human Flourishing

Theology
and
Human Flourishing

Essays in Honor of Timothy J. Gorringe

Edited by
Mike Higton,
Christopher Rowland,
and
Jeremy Law

2011

 CASCADE *Books* • Eugene, Oregon

THEOLOGY AND HUMAN FLOURISHING
Essays in Honor of Timothy J. Gorringe

Copyright © 2011 Wipf and Stock Publishers. All rights reserved. Except for brief quotations in critical publications or reviews, no part of this book may be reproduced in any manner without prior written permission from the publisher. Write: Permissions, Wipf and Stock Publishers, 199 W. 8th Ave., Suite 3, Eugene, OR 97401.

Cascade Books
An Imprint of Wipf and Stock Publishers
199 W. 8th Ave., Suite 3
Eugene, OR 97401

www.wipfandstock.com

ISBN 13: 978-1-60899-755-8

Cataloging-in-Publication data:

Theology and human flourishing : essays in honor of Timothy J. Gorringe / edited by Mike Higton, Christopher Rowland, and Jeremy Law

x + 312 p. ; 23 cm. —Includes bibliographical references.

ISBN 13: 978-1-60899-755-8

1. Gorringe, Timothy. I. Gorringe, Timothy. II. Higton, Mike. III. Rowland, Christopher, 1947– IV. Law, Jeremy. V. Title.

BX4827.G69 T54 2011

Manufactured in the U.S.A.

Contents

Contributors

Zoë Bennett, Director of Postgraduate Studies in Pastoral Theology at Anglia Ruskin University and the Cambridge Theological Federation.

Nigel Biggar, Regius Professor of Moral and Pastoral Theology at the University of Oxford.

Walter Brueggemann, Professor Emeritus of Old Testament at Columbia Theological Seminary.

Dhyanchand Carr, pastor in the Church of South India and teacher at the Tamilnadu Theological Seminary.

Paul S. Fiddes, University Research Professor of Systematic Theology at the University of Oxford.

Duncan Forrester, Professor Emeritus of Christian Ethics and Practical Theology at the University of Edinburgh.

Elaine Graham, Grosvenor Research Professor of Practical Theology at the University of Chester.

John W. de Gruchy, Robert Selby Taylor Professor of Christian Studies at the University of Cape Town.

Stanley Hauerwas, Gilbert T. Rowe Professor of Theological Ethics at Duke Divinity School.

Mike Higton, Academic Co-Director of the Cambridge Inter-faith Programme and Senior Lecturer in Theology at the University of Exeter.

David G. Horrell, Professor of New Testament Studies at the University of Exeter.

Louise J. Lawrence, Lecturer in New Testament Studies at the University of Exeter.

Jeremy Law, Dean of Chapel at Canterbury Christ Church University.

Rachel Muers, Senior Lecturer in Christian Studies at the University of Leeds.

Christopher Rowland, Dean Ireland's Professor of the Exegesis of Holy Scripture at the University of Oxford.

Francesca Stavrakopoulou, Senior Lecturer in Hebrew Bible at the University of Exeter.

Adrian Thatcher, Professor Emeritus of Theology at the University of Exeter.

Graham Ward, Professor of Contextual Theology and Ethics at the University of Manchester.

John Webster, Professor of Systematic Theology at the University of Aberdeen.

Mark Wynn, Senior Lecturer in the Philosophy of Religion at the University of Exeter.

Preface

The essays in this book are presented with affection and gratitude to Timothy Gorringe, on the occasion of his retirement. We have tried to celebrate Tim's work and influence in the most appropriate way, by pursuing the task that his own work has set out for us: a serious theological exploration of the forms in which our societies imagine, betray, and pursue human flourishing—and, by the grace of God, sometimes embody it.

Tim's work is astonishingly diverse, because it is driven by a delighted and critical engagement with the diversity of human social life, and a passionate concern for engagement with the Bible and the Christian tradition in pursuit of human flourishing. The built environment, politics, education, agriculture, crime, art: his work asks what it means for Christian theology to concern itself with, to immerse itself in, to risk critical commentary on, each of these and more. We have gathered a similarly diverse set of essays from Tim's friends and colleagues, in the hope that Tim will see a reflection of some of his own passionate concerns, and find fuel to feed ongoing conversation and engagement.

We have tried to follow the same rhythm that shapes Tim's work: insistent attention to the Christian tradition in the light of the particular contexts where human flourishing is imagined, fought for, and achieved, and a critical, constructive, and celebratory examination of those contexts in the light of the Christian tradition. The essays treat everything from city life to human curiosity, but they are united by a passion to make theological sense of human life, for the sake of human flourishing—and we offer them to Tim as a token of our immense gratitude for all that he has taught us, for his support, and for his friendship.

The Theology of Tim Gorringe

MIKE HIGTON

EUCHARIST

If you turn to the bibliography of Tim Gorringe's work at the back of this book and look down the list of titles, one of the first things that might strike you is the astonishing diversity. There are books on farming, on crime, on the built environment, on capitalism, on punishment, on culture, on art; there are books on the eucharist, on providence, on atonement, and on pneumatology. Delve deeper into the books themselves, however, and you will discover that the diversity is held together by a consistent theological vision—a vision already clear in the earliest books on the list, but then elaborated, refined, and improvised upon in each of the titles that follows.[1]

Tim's work proclaims that the whole world, in all its real historical complexity and social and environmental interconnectedness, is the arena of God's redeeming work, so that to be caught up in that work is

1. For those beginning an exploration of Tim's work, I'd recommend *The Sign of Love*, his brief book of reflections on the eucharist—and the best taster for his work as a whole. Then move on to *Redeeming Time* and *Discerning Spirit*, which between them will give the best guide to the overall structure of his thinking, especially *Redeeming Time*. Most of the other books can then be read as "journeys of intensification," pursuing one or another of the lines of inquiry opened up in those central works—with the exception of *Karl Barth* and *Alan Ecclestone*, which display two of the most important apprenticeships by which Tim learnt his theological trade.

1

necessarily to be caught up in the world. Theology must engage with society, culture, politics, economics, and the environment because it serves a God who so engages, and because to do less would be to risk bowing to a "non-engaged God"—which is to say no God at all.[2]

Tim's engagement with the world, displayed in all those books, is indeed complex and varied, but that complexity and variety are held within a simple and coherent pattern that can best be described as *eucharistic*. That is certainly not a characterization that should bring with it any whiff of priestly exclusivism, or of an ecclesial enclave protected from the pollution of the world. Rather, Tim's work is eucharistic because of the way the eucharist "intersects with our daily life—the whole fabric of our social, political and economic reality";[3] his is a eucharist that cries out to be celebrated in the market square, in the midst of ordinary life, not hidden from view in a chancel. In fact, for Tim, the eucharist can and should be a school in which Christians are trained to live in the world—to live fully, wholeheartedly, unreservedly in the world. It can and should provide a context within which the people of God are reshaped and reoriented for life in the world, and so caught up "into the stream of God's continuing and liberating activity" in the world.[4] It can and should stand at "the heart of the Christian education of desire," opening the worshipping community's eyes and hearts to more of the world.[5] Tim's theology is eucharistic because it is worldly, and worldly because it is eucharistic.

Jesus' instruction to his disciples to "do this in remembrance of me" should not, in Tim's eyes, be understood simply to refer to Jesus' handling of bread and wine on the night before he died, nor exclusively in relation to the death that he was about to die. Jesus was, rather, calling the disciples to recognize and to remember the whole pattern of his table-fellowship—his profligate, decorum-snubbing, purity-endangering habit of sharing of bread and wine with sinners.[6] The first

---

2. *Discerning Spirit*, 1.

3. *Sign of Love*, 4.

4. Ibid., 15.

5. *Education of Desire*, 105.

6. *Sign of Love*, chap. 2. In this light, the disciples at Emmaus, a little later in the story, should be read as recognizing the risen Christ when he breaks bread with them not simply because it recalls the Last Supper, but because it recalls an action that they have seen Jesus perform again and again.

eucharistic note that we may recognize in Tim's theology is therefore not sacrifice but *welcome*—or *grace*, where "[g]race is God's love reaching out to us absolutely irrespective of our worthiness, restoring us, making us more human, by acceptance and forgiveness."[7] This first note of Tim's eucharistic theology is therefore an alarmingly, disarmingly indiscriminate *yes* to the world. It is a theology of God's free welcome of sinners to God's table, God's lavish and irrepressible mercy. A eucharistic theology is a theology for Zacchaeus (see Luke 19:1–10), and for all his many contemporary brothers and sisters.

That mention of Zacchaeus, whose meal with Jesus led to a redistribution of rapaciously accumulated wealth, recalls a second way in which Tim's theology is eucharistic. One cannot extend an indiscriminate welcome to the world's crowd without running up against the question of how that crowd's very uneven needs can be met. Tim therefore notes that Jesus' actions at the Last Supper recall the stories of the great feedings—or the great *sharings*, as he would have it. The story as he sees it is not one of the supernatural multiplication of scant resources, but of a crowd awoken by the uncalculating generosity of a small boy to the possibility of sharing rather than hoarding the food they had brought with them,[8] but which they had hidden from fear of others' needs.[9] Tim quotes Gandhi to the effect that there was enough for everyone's need, but not for everyone's greed. "The eucharist comes out of the great feedings: it is a sign act of a need to share what we have."[10]

The eucharist, then, is a feast focused not just on grace, but on *justice*. We are welcomed to Jesus' table, and are to welcome others indiscriminately to that table—but what we and they are welcomed to is a *shared* feast. The invitation to such a feast is a call out of hoarding and defensiveness, and a call to share what each of us has been given, for the sake of all, and especially for the sake of those who have least. Paul's eucharistic instructions to the church in Corinth (1 Cor 11) bear out the centrality of this question of justice, or of fair sharing, and witness to the fact that, unless we have managed to hide the nature of this feast under a blanket of piety, questions of fair sharing are bound to arise when rich and poor are invited to feast at the same table. The indiscriminate

---

7. Ibid., 20–21.

8. *Education of Desire*, 110.

9. Ibid., 109; cf. *Sign of Love*, chap. 3.

10. *Education of Desire*, 110.

welcome that God offers and calls us to offer is not a welcome to a shape-less throng, but to a life with a particular shape: it is an invitation to a common feasting.

When we note, however, that this sharing is not simply of elements that "earth has given," but of products that "human hands have made," "we remember that these products represent the 'life' of those who made them, their time and creativity"[11]—and there turns out to be no safe way of isolating the eucharistic call to share from deep questions about economic justice and the political order within which the eucharist is celebrated. And that brings us to the third route into the interpretation of the eucharist that Tim offers: it is indeed connected to the death that Jesus was about to die. The call to live in the light of God's unfettered welcome, and the just order that such a welcome demands, is a call to live against the grain of the present world order.[12] It is a call to live by "a truly alternative order," one characterized by "the refusal of all arbitrary and tyrannical power"—and in such a contest "for fullness of life, for the right to feast and drink, as Jesus loved to do, it may be necessary to take on the powers that be, and to die."[13] The eucharist does speak of sacrifice, in other words—but it is sacrifice for the sake of liberation and life.

It is here that the theology of indiscriminate welcome becomes also a theology of discriminating protest. By displaying what happens to the life of grace and justice in a world like ours, the cross exposes the death-dealing nature of that world, and by proclaiming the death of Christ, the eucharist acts as "a protest, its function to prevent our accepting injustice and oppression as 'normal.'"[14] It is, in words that Tim uses to describe Barth's theology, a protest "against hegemony, and understands Christian life as a constant struggle against hegemony. But it is against hegemony because it understands the vividness, joy, celebration and for-giveness of human life as this is promised to us in Christ. It is the gospel of freedom for life."[15] This, then, is the basic shape of Tim's eucharistic

---

11. *Sign of Love*, 43. I quoted from one of the "Prayers at the Preparation of the Table" from *Common Worship*, 291: "Blessed are you, Lord God of all creation: through your goodness we have this bread to set before you, which earth has given and human hands have made. It will become for us the bread of life."

12. *Sign of Love*, chap. 4.

13. Ibid., 47; *Redeeming Time*, 68; *Sign of Love*, 59.

14. *Redeeming Time*, 56; see also *Sign of Love* 72.

15. *Karl Barth*, 290.

theology. It is a theology of grace, of justice, and of sacrifice—and of all three for the sake of fullness of life.

CREATION

The eucharist speaks of grace, of justice, and of sacrifice—but it speaks of these by narrating a drama acted out in the midst of the ordinary: a community of people gathered with bread and with wine. The drama does not take place in a rarefied religious realm, but on the everyday earth where ordinary human life is lived out. "What the eucharist signifies is not the existence of a sacred world set over against the profane, requiring its own sacral space and time, but rather the hallowing of the ordinary—of bread, wine, labour and community."[16] Tim's eucharistic theology involves a marked "preference for the everyday, the modest, humble and ordinary";[17] it is focused on "the beauty, depth and mystery of the trivial and ordinary,"[18] or, in words he used of Alan Ecclestone's theology, it is a "celebration of the mystery of supposedly ordinary things, of ordinary lives and events which to the eye of faith disclose the divine."[19]

This celebration of the ordinary is, in Tim's work, focused in part upon living with creation—that is, on living with the natural world, with its materiality and its ecological interconnectedness. He recognizes, for instance, that the eucharistic elements do not simply appear, fully formed, on the shelves of ecclesiastical suppliers, but that they are the products of processes that emerge from basic activities of digging, sowing, and harvesting, of pruning and picking, of responding to the weather and the seasons. Such a recognition is characteristic of his work more widely. He writes in a world where it is often difficult to remember the forms of labor and the kinds of natural resources consumed in the making of the objects that surround us, but writes in such a way as to remind us that the connections are still there, and that beneath the slick consumer economy we see, there is a deeper economy, in which the husbanding of the natural world remains basic. Whether we realize it or not,

---

16. *Built Environment*, 18.

17. Ibid., 8.

18. *Sign of Love*, 80.

19. *Alan Ecclestone*, xx.

our lives are enmeshed with the patterns and cycles, the fragilities and resistances, that structure the natural world.

The deepest mystery of creation revealed in the eucharist is that it is God's *gift*, and a gift given for us all to share—a "common treasury," to quote Gerrard Winstanley.[20] To live in response to God's grace is therefore first of all "to live by gratitude" for the world God has given us,[21] and a eucharistic theology is above all things, as the word *eucharist* suggests, a theology of delighted thankfulness.

To live in response to God's gift is also, however, to live with a sense that holding things in common is a more fundamental pattern of human life than holding things as private property. "If creation is grace . . . then self-evidently life is not there to appropriate the benefits for myself, to hoard things over against others."[22] It is simply nonsense to think that I can own some resource that for me is a luxury but that another needs for her survival. In what sense could that resource be said to be proper to me, and not to her—or in what sense could I be said to have rights to it that she does not? It is a mark of how deeply we have internalized the ideology of property that we do not see the absurdity here, nor the depth of the hole into which that ideology has tipped us. "If we are to understand how to live gracefully in creation, then, everything hinges on the idea of *koinonia*, on what is due to humans in common, as a result of their common right to the gift of creation, and on what is due to the rest of creation. The issue is not academic. The fate of whole communities and cultures, and indeed possibly of the whole planet, depends on it."[23]

To understand creation as God's gift also, however, means recognizing that we are a part of the natural world that is a gift, and therefore that our own creatureliness is a divine gift. And that means that Tim's work rings with an affirmation of our own materiality, as well as the materiality of the economy within which we live—a recognition that "[f]lesh (matter, the material) is patent of glory."[24] The wide-open welcome of Tim's theology is therefore also a wide-open welcome to the body—to a kingdom in which "all the senses are passionately, and sometimes wildly affirmed." "In and through bodies, and through the exercise

---

20. *Harvest*, chap. 1; cf. *Sign of Love*, 4.

21. *Harvest*, 130.

22. *Built Environment*, 20.

23. *Harvest*, 8.

24. *Education of Desire*, 2.

of our senses, God moves towards the creation of a new world, a world of the celebration and affirmation of bodies, and therefore of the creator who imagined them and gave us them materially, as the consummate sign of the grace of God's essential nature."[25] The passion for a godly ordering of life, and the protest against forms of life that militate against such ordering, therefore takes the form not just of a protest in favor of the "common treasury" of creation, but of what Tim calls a "body-friendly asceticism"[26]—a pattern of life in which we learn to live together gracefully and delightedly within the constraints and possibilities given to us by the wise husbanding of the natural world. The eucharist in which we can learn such forms of life is both a "school of celebration" and "a school of asceticism,"[27] and what we need to learn is a form of life that is something like a *craft*, a skill at working with the real interconnections, the real limitations and possibilities of things—at delighting in those connections, limitations, and possibilities and discovering what it is possible to say in their meter and rhythm.

HISTORY

If Tim's eucharistic theology is in part a theology of creation, however, it is even more a theology of history, for God's "assumption of flesh is the assumption of history."[28] If the eucharist is a school in which we learn to recognize creation as a gift, it is also a school in which the community "receives its interpretation of historical existence"[29]—and what it learns in this school is, fundamentally, a belief in providence, which Tim calls "the very structure of religious life": "belief that God acts, that he has a purpose not simply for the whole of creation but for me, that this purpose can be discerned and that, through prayer, I can put myself in the way of it."[30]

In other words, history for Tim is not one damn thing after another—and to settle for any view of history that can see no more than this is to stop short of the task to which word and sacrament call us.

25. Ibid., 27.

26. Ibid., 101.

27. Ibid., 104.

28. *Sign of Love*, 52.

29. *Redeeming Time*, 21.

30. *God's Theatre*, 1.

However difficult it may be in the face of the horrendous evils of history, we are called to look for the patterns of the Spirit's work in history, seeking in prayer to see "the lines of God's emergent work in what appear[s] to be formless."[31]

What we need to learn to see, first of all, is "the openness and fundamental hopefulness of human history under God's pedagogy"—the existence of "long historical processes which make for mutuality and real humanity" and in which we discern "the slow and patient pedagogy of God's Spirit," and the thousand smaller-scale movements and opportunities of which such large-scale processes are composed.[32] The church learns, for instance, to see "in the women's movement or in the programme to combat racism, small signs at least of the possibility of a more human future, and in these signs it discerns the pedagogy of God's Spirit realising a solidarity in redemption to break the hold of, and set people free from, solidarity in sin."[33] What the church sees when it sees all this is God's redemption at work. History is the medium—the only medium—in which God's redemptive work takes place, and that redemption takes the form of an education towards human flourishing, working so that "human beings should have life and have it more abundantly, that through the educational process persons may be more fulfilled and therefore more creative, more free and therefore more loving, more loving and therefore more free. The ultimate aim . . . is the becoming of human being."[34]

The fundamental axis involved in plotting our understanding of history, therefore, is provided by the attempt to judge (fallibly but seriously) whether any given event, any given process or structure, makes for more fully human life, or militates against it. History simply *is* the story of God's education of the human race for full humanity, and of the various ways in which that education has been ignored, undermined, resisted, and distorted; it simply is the arena of the God who "woos, inspires and elicits men and women towards freedom, co-operation, righteousness and rest," and in which human beings in freedom are either caught up into that movement, or resist it.[35]

31. *Alan Ecclestone*, 147.

32. *Sign of Love*, 12; *Redeeming Time*, xv.

33. *Redeeming Time*, 56.

34. Ibid., 7.

35. Ibid., 110; cf. *God's Theatre*, 87, 104.

To say that human beings are "caught up" by this pedagogy highlights the fact that the point of eucharistic discernment is not simply understanding: it is *participation*—our doing whatever is needed "to cup hands round the small flame of human dignity and creativity and freedom wherever it is found, in whatever cultural or religious context."[36] Discernment is the catalyst that transforms us from passive recipients of history, moved by its apparently random currents in a historical Brownian motion, into agents within history, working in whatever fragile and limited ways might be available to us to drive forward the pedagogy in which we have been caught up, and by which we have been shaped precisely for this discernment and participation. The point of discernment is not to understand history, but to become part of the way in which the God of Jesus Christ is changing it.

COMMUNITY

Such participation in God's work is not, however, an individual matter; it "proceeds only through relationship."[37] It is first of all a task for the church: Tim insists that "[h]earing God speak, discerning God's will, consists in large part of living within a community, steeping oneself in its tradition and praying within that tradition" in an "ongoing conversation both with the present community and with the past."[38]

In fact, for Tim, the church simply *is* the community in which this discernment and participation should be nurtured. The church exists for the sake of "fashioning a more human community"; it exists "where human desire is educated, disciplined, by word and sacrament."[39] "The community we call 'church' is not primarily an institution but something which is continually coming into being, an event within the reading of the Word and the celebration of the eucharist . . . and the personal, political and social practice which follows from this."[40]

The church, then, should fundamentally be a school—a school of divine pedagogy. It is not simply that the church should provide a practical context *within which* this process of education can take place.

36. *Redeeming Time*, 222.
37. Ibid., 8.
38. *Discerning Spirit*, 22.
39. *Sign of Love*, 68; *Education of Desire*, 103.
40. *Discerning Spirit*, 88.

Rather, the church should *itself* be the form that this education takes. The members of the church learn discernment of God's ways with the world by learning how to live as a eucharistic community together in the midst of the world, and for the sake of the world. They learn to live a corporate life that makes sense in the light of the gospel proclaimed to them in word and sacrament—the gospel of grace, justice, and sacrifice for the sake of the world—and they learn to make sense of that gospel by discovering how to live this kind of life together. Their corporate life, to the extent that they discover how to live in the light of the gospel of Jesus Christ, becomes the icon by which they learn to recognize more clearly the face of God—until "[t]hey understand their corporate existence as bound up with the self-revelation of God, and they know God present in and through the community as the 'people of God' or 'the body of Christ.'"[41] Therefore Tim can say that "community is the most fundamental condition of our knowledge of God . . . the concrete community which exists in the dialectic of rich and poor," and that "[k]nowledge of God . . . consists in the practical interactions of persons, 'doing justice' in the community."[42]

As I have said, however, Tim never focuses on the church for its own sake, but on the church in the world and for the sake of the world. Christians learn the nature of God, and the nature of the life to which God is calling the world, through word and sacrament and the concrete community that gathers around them—but that word and sacrament call for a community that is salt and light to the world, and the church only *is* the church to the extent that it is becoming salt and light. "Theology is always primarily addressed to the Church, but it is addressed to the Church at a particular time, seeking to understand itself and what in faith it has to contribute to the world of which it is an indissoluble part."[43]

POLITICS

Tim's discussions of divine pedagogy, of the discernment learned in and as the church, always therefore end up in the world of which the church is "an indissoluble part." In the broadest sense, his theology is always thoroughly *political*. When discussing the eucharist, for instance,

41. *Redeeming Time*, 21.
42. *Discerning Spirit*, 76, 78.
43. *Built Environment*, 25.

he says that "I do not come to the eucharist to escape from sordid political reality and get in touch with some quite different spiritual reality, but to find the one reality which frames my whole life interpreted, refracted and made more hopeful."[44] The eucharist as he has presented it ought therefore to be "the seedbed of political imagination and creativity."[45]

The church can be such a seedbed precisely because it is a school in which we discover (or should be discovering) that "another world is possible"[46]—the world of the just feast—and discover that this other world is the end for which this world of ours was made. The just feast is the proper, natural form of our world, and it is the forces that oppose and deny it, the forces exposed as death-dealing by Christ's death on the cross, that are properly understood as unreal and unnatural. The imagination to which we are called by the eucharist, and by divine pedagogy more generally, is therefore a deep form of realism, according to Tim—a realism "concerned with looking beyond the appearance of things as they are, bound by all kinds of 'iron laws,' to the way things might be in a more human future where such laws no longer prevail."[47] It is the realism of the real alternative. "Part of the ideology of the market is that there is no alternative, but this is false. There *are* realistic alternatives"[48]—and our problem is not that such alternatives lack reality, but that we lack the truthful imagination that can see such alternatives, and the will to pursue that imagination.[49]

The realism to which we are called by the eucharist and by divine pedagogy more generally is also realistic in another sense. It is (or needs to be) an imagination that sees how the just feast might be played out in all the concrete structures and patterns of ordinary human life, and that sees, and protests against, all the ways in which that future is denied or rejected in those concrete structures and patterns. It is, therefore, a matter of "the awkwardness of families, places of work, churches, across sexual, racial and class divides, full of tensions, dislikes and misunderstandings";[50] it is a matter of economics—of money,

44. *Sign of Love*, 67.

45. Ibid., 72.

46. *Harvest*, 133; *Redeeming Time*, 131; *Discerning Spirit*, 66.

47. *Redeeming Time*, 133.

48. *Capital and the Kingdom*, 164, my emphasis.

49. Ibid., 168.

50. *Discerning Spirit*, 79.

taxation, and debt; it is a matter of "sanitation, shelter, clean water, bodily integrity";[51] it is a matter of farming, of penal policy; it is a matter of the homes we live in and the cities, towns, and villages that we inhabit; it is a matter of art, and a matter of culture—high culture, mass popular culture, and folk culture.

Take culture, for instance. Tim insists that attention to culture is not a secondary or dispensable task for a theologian (or for a church), but is an urgent and a demanding task. "Culture" is not, for him, a neutral descriptive category, as if one could simply say that all human communities have culture, and then proceed to a patient and detached cataloging of the forms that culture takes. We orient ourselves to the study of culture more truly, and see the centrality of engagement with culture to the task of Christian life, if we recognize that "culture" is properly the name "of that whole process in the course of which God does what it takes . . . to make and keep human beings human"[52]—and that "culture" is therefore "the nourishing of life in all its fullness." Whatever does not nourish such life is not culture because it is not formation and it is not a community's habitable pattern of meanings; it is anti-culture, deformation, and is ultimately uninhabitable. Tim's theology of culture therefore becomes a critical search for what is life-affirming in the patterns of meaning that human communities weave. So, for instance, he sets out an imaginative vision of "a popular culture . . . which is concerned with fineness of living, and which to that extent leads into and lays the groundwork for 'the best which has been thought and said,' all the achievements of high culture."[53] Elsewhere, he distinguishes the real art that "is born of that rigorous attention which enables us to see the real beyond the dense obfuscation of self-interested fantasy" from the bad art that "is essentially dishonest art."[54]

As anyone who delves into the books I've mentioned will discover, they are full of bold, opinionated, argumentative, and controversial claims about where the line between humanizing and dehumanizing is to be drawn, and about the possibilities for human culture and society that we need to pursue, as well as those we need to avoid or deny. He sets out good and bad ways to build houses, good and bad ways to handle

51. *Karl Barth*, 273.
52. *Furthering Humanity*, 4.
53. Ibid., 102.
54. *Discerning Spirit*, 114, 121.

money, good and bad forms of public art, good and bad farming practices, good and bad forms of town planning, good and bad forms of land
ownership—and so on. He is not timid about engagement, of risking
judgment and decision, and he does not believe that the theological task
handed to us by the gospel *allows* us to be timid.

THE POOR

Tim is well aware, of course, that there is one serious danger that besets
theological engagement: the risk that we will end up simply identifying
God's pedagogic work with some inevitably ambivalent and ambiguous
human project. He is well aware, that is, that he might be suspected of
a return to some kind of culture Protestantism (even if one that has a
decidedly different tenor from the *Kulturprotestantismus* against which
Barth protested). He insists, though, that what we need is not a retreat
from the risk of judgment—from the task of tracing the ways of God in
culture—but a dialectic between such serious and affirmative attention
to culture and a seriousness about the ways in which divine revelation
stands *over against* our understandings and aspirations.

On the one hand, then, he insists that "God is active in the entire
course of world history, creating and redeeming 'from the inside' *so that
our acts are his acts, our story his story*"[55]—and he insists that we may rely
upon God's promise to be present "on the path of historical liberation in
the future."[56]

On the other hand, he insists that we be aware of "our daily idolatries," because "God and his purposes may be ignored and rejected, so
that our acts are not at all what God wills. In this case God as Spirit
reveals his will to us in ways which may cut across our deepest social
and cultural aspirations and contradict the ways we have learned to see
our world."[57] Hence divine revelation—divine pedagogy—is both an
affirmation of the deepest, truest currents of our social, cultural, and
economic life, and an event that knocks us off course,[58] in response to
which we must say that "[t]o know God's revelation is to be a *displaced*

---

55. Ibid., 6, my emphasis.

56. *Redeeming Time*, 20.

57. *Discerning Spirit*, 2.

58. Ibid., 24. Hence, for instance, he can say that "[t]he inspiration of scripture is
the fact that this collection of documents ticks like a bomb in the hold of the church"
(ibid., 85).

person, to be made homeless, driven beyond the self-contained set of assumptions which constitute a totality, be it our egoism, our world view, or the culture of the day."[59]

Tim nevertheless holds the two sides of this insistence indissolubly together. The gospel "is completely part of culture, but a foreign element within as well, an irritant, an immanent critique."[60] The two sides are held together not by a harmonizing theory, however, nor by insistence upon some abstract concept such as "paradox" or even "dialectic," but in two deeply concrete ways. In the first place, and fundamentally, they are held together in Jesus of Nazareth, who confronts the church in word and sacrament, and in affirmation and judgment. "The criteria for what constitutes truly human behaviour, and therefore for discernment of the Spirit, are to be found *essentially* in a history, essentially set in, arising out of, and bearing upon the dust and blood of Palestine, upon the lives of men and women in their concrete historical situations."[61] The story of Jesus of Nazareth is "a permanent catalyst within human history."[62]

In the second place, affirmation and denial are held together when we turn to those who are given to us by this Jesus as his brothers and sisters. We are kept from idolatry by loving attention to our brothers and sisters in and beyond the church, and openness to the challenge that they represent—the difficulties of discovering how to live with them the life of feasting to which Jesus calls us. "The one who is other to me, whom I cannot ultimately colonise, who resists me and interrogates and so stands outside my totality, is always the potential place of revelation—what I cannot tell myself."[63] Jesus calls us, in particular, to a just feast in which *all* participate, and since if we are on the way to that feast we most need to be interrupted by those who are excluded from it by our existing practices and ideologies, we will find discernment by turning especially to the poor—not because we romanticize them as pure and noble, and as the bearers of unsullied natural wisdom, but precisely because we have excluded them, and we know that God wants them included. The preferential option for the poor, whom Jesus gives us as our brothers and sisters, is therefore our best guard against idolatry.

59. Ibid., 9.
60. *Furthering Humanity*, 102.
61. *Discerning Spirit*, 31.
62. Ibid., 25.
63. Ibid., 74–75.

CODA

Tim's work can be described in the same words that he used to describe Alan Ecclestone's. It is an "attempt to address every area of human life, to discern God at work there, to measure everything by the revelation of the true 'Yes to God' of Jesus of Nazareth."[64] Or, in the words with which he closed *Furthering Humanity*, it is a call "to tell the story, trust in God, pray in the darkness, act for justice as the prophets commanded, and cheerfully wait to see what happens . . . It depends on our cultural imagination, on our creativity, on the search for the best which both has been and will be thought and known. But it depends even more on hope in the God who calls the dead to life."[65] His is a eucharistic theology of divine pedagogy and human flourishing—and it calls its readers to risk discernment and engagement in the world, for the sake of life.

Bibliography

For works by Tim Gorringe, see the bibliography at the end of the book.

Common Worship: Services and Prayers for the Church of England. London: Church House, 2000.

64. *Alan Ecclestone,* 154.
65. *Furthering Humanity,* 266.

2

Prophetic Imagination toward Social Flourishing

Walter Brueggemann

"Part of the ideology of the market," Tim Gorringe has written, "is that there is no alternative, but this is false. There are realistic alternatives."[1] To see that "another world is possible,"[2] however, requires an act of imagination: emancipatory imagination.

I

The procurement of "surplus value" requires a sustained strategy for accumulation and adequate institutions for sustaining that strategy. In a state economy that strategy is through law that continually transfers wealth from labor to capital or, in Old Testament categories, from "peasants" to "urban elites." In a corporate economy the strategy is the vigorous enactment of market ideology that squeezes production schedules and arranges the social infrastructure for the sake of maximum profits. In the Western world, most particularly in the United States, that strategy is a combination of state and corporate economy in which the government is tilted, if not controlled, by lobbyists who act in the interest of corporate power by ensuring a minimum of public regulation. The outcome either way—state economy, corporate economy, or a combina-

1. Gorringe, *Capital and the Kingdom*, 164.
2. Gorringe, *Harvest*, 133.

tion of the two—is a sustained and effective process of accumulation of surplus value, not without high social cost.

The course of surplus value requires, in addition to a friendly government, centralized institutions that are unembarrassed about the ends of privilege that they serve. On the one hand, such accumulation requires an effective military establishment, because surplus value inevitably levies a high cost from some in society who may eventually act forcefully against centralized privilege. On the other hand, such social entitlement requires a central bank for protection, investment, and growth of surplus value for the stakeholders who constitute a small minority of the population.

II

In the world of ancient Israel, the strategy for accumulation and maintenance of surplus value was enacted and epitomized by King Solomon, who is the quintessential accumulator.[3] Indeed, one need only read of the extravagance of the royal apparatus (1 Kgs 4:22–28), the monopoly of learning (4:29–34), the extravagance of his building projects (7:1–12), the ostentatious display of gold in his new temple (6:20–22; 7:48–51), and the gain of his international commerce (10:14–25) in order to see that he was a most successful accumulator, ending with material accumulation matched by his accumulation of women, no doubt in the interest of a network of powerful alliances (11:3). This narrative report of accumulation is so over the top as to suggest that it may be offered as a mocking caricature of the ways of surplus wealth.

Almost in passing it is reported that Solomon had a standing army, no doubt for purposes of exhibit and intimidation: "So Solomon rebuilt Gezer, Lower Beth-horon, Baalath, Tamar in the wilderness, within the land, as well as all of Solomon's storage cities, the cities for his chariots, the cities for his cavalry, and whatever Solomon desired to build in Jerusalem, in Lebanon, and in all the land of his dominion . . . Solomon gathered together chariots and horses; he had fourteen hundred chariots and twelve thousand horses, which stationed in the chariot cities and with the king in Jerusalem" (1 Kgs 9:17–19; 10:26). His military capacity, moreover, was reinforced by his success as an arms dealer who

---

3. See Brueggemann, *Solomon*.

apparently controlled the flow of armaments in the international arena due to his strategic geographical location (1 Kgs 10:28).

The matter of a central bank is not obvious for Solomon. But the detailed description of his tax-collecting apparatus suggests the constant flow of internal revenue to the central government (4:7–19) that was matched by the immense flow of international tribute (10:23–25). We are not told where all of that revenue was kept and invested or from where it was dispensed; but we do know that the temple functioned as such a financial center in that ancient world. Thus we may "double-read" the narrative about the temple (1 Kgs 5–8) that was designed to be not only a "royal chapel" but also as an ostentatious gathering point for unimaginable wealth. If we equate temple with bank, we may better understand why the temple became a target of protest and judgment.[4] Thus Solomon has all the necessary equipment to procure and maintain surplus value.

The matter is not different in the economy of the United States that operates with a central bank and central bankers who are practitioners of outrageous wealth. The recent "stimulus package" gives ample evidence of how the government is in collusion with the managers of surplus wealth, a collusion that did not evoke protest until the Republican Party—by any read the party of big wealth—caught on to the potential of populist resentment.

Clearly, the military establishment of the current lone superpower indicates that a broad military strategy is required to maintain economic advantage in the pursuit of natural resources and in the development of amenable markets.[5] Chalmers Johnson has well chronicled the way in which US militarism is now world-defining and, given market ideology, has its way in public imagination with almost no protest.[6]

Alongside military capacity and a central bank, a third prerequisite for surplus value is cheap labor or, as given in the Solomonic narrative, "forced labor": those not able to receive or enjoy the full fruit of labor. In ancient Israel, forced labor is identified as an important component

---

4. The most direct and telling critique of the temple is in Jer 7:1–15 where the temple is attacked and a bid is made for justice for widows and orphans. The two accounts are intimately connected to each other.

5. The claim of the United States as the only and final superpower is a quite provisional claim; see Jacques, *When China Rules the World*.

6. Johnson, *Blowback*; *Nemesis*; *Sorrows of Empire*.

of Solomon's economy (5:13–18; 9:20–23), a component that undoubtedly reflects the exodus narrative in which more-ancient Hebrews are remembered as building store cities for Pharaoh's surplus wealth (see Gen 47:13–26; Exod 1:11–14; 5:4–21). On the storage cities, see 1 Kgs 9:19, surely an allusion back to that chilling exodus memory. In the US market economy we of course do not practice or speak of "forced labor"—except that what passes for health care policy keeps working people fearfully attached to their jobs, lest they "lose coverage."

What strikes one about this complex power arrangement—ancient or contemporary—is that it is a totalizing system that intends to contain all possible social options, that allows for no deviation from ideological orthodoxy concerning "God and Country." That power arrangement, moreover, precludes any initiative outside this totality. It is, for some, a soft velvet totalitarian system that makes promises to all but keeps promises only to some.

III

When we come to Tim Gorringe's category of "flourishing," it is clear that such an exploitative system that coercively transfers wealth from the weak to the strong cannot, in the long run, "flourish." Social flourishing depends upon passion for and commitment to the common good. It is axiomatic that coercive exploitation—whether by the state, corporation, or market economy—cannot create an environment for such flourishing. That much is clear upon any serious reflection, for such exploitation produces social hostility and a refusal, if not an inability, to act humanely toward the common good. And if our reflection is not to be trusted, then the facts on the ground lead to the same conclusion. It is clear in the United States that we are at a near stalemate between centralized interests and what people perceive as the common good. If we take "safety and happiness" as shorthand measures of the common good, then it is clear that a combination of state-corporate interests have not made us safe. Indeed, such aggressive militarism contributes to a lack of safety, both because of the production of external enemies and the generation of internal hostility. Nor has that combination made us happy by any social index. It was, of course, not different in the regime of Solomon that ended with (*a*) a dire judgment against the regime voiced in theological terms (2 Kgs 11:1–12), (*b*) a series of rebellions (11:14–22, 23–25, 26–40), (*c*) a prophetically instigated coup (11:31–39) and, (*d*) eventually, a tax revolt that divided the state (12:1–24). Many opponents of Solomon—religious, political, and economic—clearly saw that such a power arrangement would never generate "flourishing."

IV

If the totalizing purview of military capitalism—a combination of state and corporate interests propelled by an ideology of acquisitiveness—cannot keep its promises, then it is required to think "outside the box" of such totalizing claims. It is by no means clear that such thinking is possible (leave alone permitted), and Slavoj Žižek judges that such thought in contemporary context is not possible.[7] It may well be that our circumstance of totalism is unprecedented and for the first time such thought is impossible. More likely, every such context, ancient and modern, has led to the same judgment about the practical impossibility of an alternative to the "facts on the ground" or better, to the ideology that voices those "facts on the ground."

It is for that reason that such thoughts turn, finally, perhaps inevitably, to the Hebrew Bible and to the odd, inexplicable "voice" that speaks in that enigmatic, unsettled, unsettling tradition. All the way back to the exodus narrative, this tradition imagines and stages a dialogical transaction that constitutes a subversion of the monologue of military acquisitiveness. In the exodus narrative the dialogic transaction that produces daring revolutionary energy is an exchange between *the cry of the oppressed* and *the responses of Holy Resolve* that dwells outside the totalizing system of Pharaoh: "After a long time the king of Egypt died. The Israelites groaned under their slavery, and cried out. Out of the slavery their cry for help rose up to God. God heard the groaning, and God remembered his covenant with Abraham, Isaac, and Jacob. God looked upon the Israelites, and God took notice of them" (Exod 2:23–25). The cry, the voice of the oppressed, broke the silence of totalism; the slaves went public with their pain that was imposed by the exploitative system and thereby honored and owned their suffering. This act of *speaking pain*

7. Žižek, *Universal Exception*, 159: "It is practically impossible effectively to call into question the logic of Capital: even a modest social-democratic attempt to redistribute wealth beyond the limit acceptable to Capital 'effectively' leads to an economic crisis, inflation, a fall in revenues and so on. Nevertheless, one should always bear in mind the way that the connection between 'cause' (rising social expenditure) and 'effect' (economic crisis) is not a direct, objective causal one; it is always-already embedded in a situation of social antagonism and struggle."

had to wait until a propitious moment when "the king of Egypt died." When that moment came, it is impossible to over-appreciate the transforming energy set in motion by that daring, subversive act of bringing imposed pain to public speech.

IC
Sphased

And of course, the response of Holy Resolve is equally stunning. The slaves who cried out did not address anyone; they only "groaned under their slavery and cried out." Unbeknownst to them, there was a Listener who attended to the cry and who answered in a resolve to transform (see also Exod 3:7–10). That exchange, before which Pharaoh is helpless, set in motion a revolutionary history that created an opening for covenantal politics and covenantal economics wholly precluded by Pharaoh.[8]

The same dynamic is assumed and enacted in Psalm 10,[9] which, like the exodus narrative, relentlessly insists that there are three rather than two actors in the human drama. There are *the exploiters* who say:

> God will not seek it out . . .
> There is no God . . .
> We shall not be moved;
> Throughout all the generations we shall not meet adversity . . .
> God has forgotten,
> He has hidden his face, he will never see it . . .
> You will not call us to account. (Ps 10:4, 6, 11, 13)[10]

There are *the exploited* who here speak as they cannot elsewhere in the public domain. Most surprisingly, they can not only describe the unbearable situation in which they find themselves, they can also muster the courage to speak an imperative that is not elsewhere permitted them. The imperative is not addressed to the exploiters from whom they expect nothing. It is addressed, rather, to the same Holy Resolve that answered back in the narrative. That is, subsequent dialogic discourse replicates that ancient memory, only now the groan and cry know whom to address:

> Rise up, O Lord; O God, lift up your hand;
> do not forget the oppressed . . .
> But you do see! Indeed, you note trouble and grief,

8. See Walzer, *Exodus*.

9. On this psalm, see Brueggemann, "Psalms 9–10."

10. To be sure, the "exploiters" are presented through the lens of the exploited; there is no suggestion that this is "objective" characterization.

that you may take it into your hands;
the helpless commit themselves to you;
you have been the helper of the orphan.
Break the arm of the wicked and evildoers;
seek out their wickedness until you find none. (vv. 12, 14, 15)

The speech culminates in (a) a doxology that assigns legitimate power to YHWH and away from Pharonic agents (v. 16) and (b) a confident expectation for justice (vv. 17–18):

The Lord is king forever and ever;
the nations shall perish from his land.
O Lord, you will hear the desire of the meek;
you will strengthen their heart, you will incline your ear
to do justice for the orphan and the oppressed,
so that those from earth may strike terror no more. (vv. 16, 17–18)

The third party, YHWH, does not speak here. In the tradition, however, there is divine answer. It is the reality of divine answer, all the way back to Exod 2:24–25, that is the ground for continued trust in YHWH beyond the power of the system. Clearly this psalm is uttered on the assumption of such a responsive holiness.

The characteristic divine answer, so well described by Patrick Miller, is a salvation oracle, wherein God speaks, acknowledges the cry for help, and promises active, transformative engagement:

There are many indications that the prayers are heard and answered. Sometimes this is a matter of direct testimony, particularly in the psalm prayers where there is no context to discover the outcome of the prayer except as it is conveyed within the prayer itself or in the song of thanksgiving that follows the prayer. Indeed it is in such testimony that the close connection of the song of thanksgiving to the prayer for help is indicated. One such song, Psalm 34, provides a kind of paradigm of the structure of prayer in Scripture and enables us to see the movement that is initiated in the relationship between God and the person in need when a cry for help goes up, when prayer is uttered:

I sought the Lord, and he answered me,
and delivered me from all my fears.
Look to him, and be radiant;
so your faces shall never be ashamed.
This poor soul [i.e., afflicted] cried,
and was heard by the Lord,

and was saved from every trouble. (vv. 4–6)

The one who prayed is identified as an "afflicted" person. The term may have to do with humility and meekness, but, in the context of the prayer for help, it is also to be understood as an indication of the distress of the suppliant—literally poor and weak, afflicted or oppressed.[11]

The clearest example, cited by Miller, is found in the poetry of Lamentations that seeks divine help after the destruction of Jerusalem:

I called on your name, O Lord,
from the depths of the pit;
you heard my plea . . .
You came near when I called on you;
you said, "Do not fear!" (Lam 3:55–57)

The "do not fear" of the divine answerer is an act that intends to override the awesome, intimidating, threatening power of monological coercion. It is to be noticed that in the first instance, such divine resolve does not "do" anything, but only aims to dissolve fear. Surely the intent is that the "fearless" will not cede reality over to the ideological claims of the acquisitive engine of oppression.

V

Our focus in what follows is upon the divine resolve that is evoked by the subversive public voicing of pain. Scholars suggest that this stylized answer is given by a designated human agent, a priest or an elder. That human agency opens, of course, the question of what traction such a theological-liturgical claim has in the midst of *Realpolitik*, and whether it is necessary to be a "believer" in order to enact such dramatic force. No doubt those who generated and trusted such a textual tradition and practice "believed" in the reality of such a dialogic transaction. But even short of that, one can see that what is performed is an instance of "guerilla theatre" whereby the dominant claims of coercive power are exposed as inadequate and less than compelling.[12] Clearly, performing "outside the box" is a characteristic strategy against monological power for which we have many twentieth-century examples. Such "theological performance" serves to deabsolutize the claims of the regime. Thus, in

11. Miller, *They Cried to the Lord*, 136.
12. I take the phrase from Wilder, *Theopoetic*, 28.

The Teachings of Jesus   method of Jesus' teaching style

Exodus 2, Pharaoh is exposed as penultimate by the cries of the slaves and the divine response. In the prophetic oracle of 1 Kings 11:31–39, Solomon and his claim are placed in deep jeopardy. And in Psalm 10, the poetry imagines a "resurrection" ("Rise up") of power from outside the zone of the wicked exploiters.

In all three cases the textual utterance, no doubt performed in some public venue (Passover?), attests to a reality (or a reality in waiting in Psalm 10) that is beyond the control or intimidation of the acquisitive enterprise. All three cases of narrative, oracle, and psalm constitute *acts of imagination* that expose the imagination of the regime as faulty, inadequate, and eventually false.[13] Regime imagination is displaced and overridden (in the performance) by an act of imagination that digs deeper into a claim for holiness. For after all, a regime that traffics in exploitation can only make a very thin claim for grounding in God's holiness. Whether and to what extent the alternative performance is persuasive remains open in each new usage, for to be persuaded by the alternative imagination is to embrace an immediate and concrete risk; but the tradition attests that it does happen.

VI

I focus now on the divine response (to the cry) that is voiced in prophetic oracle. It is my thesis that *prophetic oracles of promise* imagine a social reality in which there can be social flourishing; put negatively, where there is no such promissory imagination, social flourishing is all but impossible. A sub-note to this claim is the fact that we have all too often thought of "prophetic ministry" as critique, as an act of righteous indignation against established power. There is, to be sure, such a component to the prophets in ancient Israel. Here, however, I focus on a neglected theme in prophetic utterance: promises that are indeed responses to situations of unbearable dismay that are voiced as protest and petition.

Micah 4:1–5

This text, well known on its own, is placed in the book of Micah as a response to the harsh oracle of 3:9–12 that anticipates the destruction of

13. On out-imagining the imagination of the regime, see Cavanaugh, *Torture and Eucharist*, 278–81 and passim.

Jerusalem, due precisely to the acquisitive exploitation of that city and its leadership. We may, for our purposes, imagine a pause between 3:12 and 4:1, a pause that allows for the implementation of the threat of 3:9–12, namely, the destruction of the city, which in turn evokes the lament of those who witness the demise of the city. Of itself the move from 3:12 to 4:1 is abrupt and makes little sense. But if we "fill in" the space between the two, we may see that the promise of 4:1–5 is a divine response to a lament over the failed city, the same dramatic sequence that we see in the book of Lamentations.

While Micah's listeners may imagine a city still engaged in injustice (3:9–11) or a city now in ruins (v. 12), this new oracle in 4:1–5 imagines out beyond both acquisitiveness and destruction. The new imagination of *a newly organized city* is given in *a human oracle* that purports to be *divine intentionality* (see Isa 2:1). That is, in the promise of God, the potential of Jerusalem is not confined to the scope of dominant imagination nor is it defined by destruction, anticipated or enacted. It is rather characterized by a new resolve on God's part. That resolve is that:

- Jerusalem will be the new center and rallying point for the assembly of the world's peoples (4:1–2).[14]

- They will assemble in Jerusalem for Torah instruction (v. 2).

- YHWH will be established and recognized as the umpire of justice between the nations (v. 3).

- The nations, in response to Torah teaching, will undertake disarmament (v. 3).

- The new adherents to Torah will settle for a modest standard of living (vine and fig-tree), in recognition of the fact that a self-indulgent standard of living evokes war (v. 4).

- There will be acknowledgement of the reality and legitimacy of "other gods," without yielding on Israel's loyalty to YHWH (v. 5).

It is evident that this poetic scenario contradicts everything about the established reality of Jerusalem either in its acquisitiveness or in its destruction:

- That Jerusalem, unlike this imagined one, does not welcome the nations.

14. On the text, see Gottwald, *All the Kingdoms*, 196–203.

- That Jerusalem, unlike this imagined one, gives others no access to Torah.

- That Jerusalem, unlike this imagined one, keeps YHWH as Israel's patron, thus never as arbiter.

- That Jerusalem, unlike this imagined one, is fully armed with no energy for disarmament.

- That Jerusalem, unlike this imagined one, craves an extravagant standard of indulgence.

- That Jerusalem, unlike this imagined one, gives no credit or legitimacy to any other god.

The poem offers the stunning reality (a) that the listeners are placed in deep contradiction between the city given by dominant ideology and the one announced in this promissory oracle and (b) that the contradiction is sponsored and vouched for by YHWH, who is the source of the alternative. That contradiction, then, invites the listeners to choose, and to affirm that an alternative choice is possible. Thus the intent of the prophetic "performance" is that the listeners might sign on to an alternative imagination and act accordingly. At the very least, this oracle challenges and seeks to subvert and displace the Jerusalem offered by acquisitive interests.

Isaiah 65:17–25

This prophetic oracle is at the extreme edge of Old Testament hope and is a remarkable act of imagination. We may suppose that, like the sequence suggested for the Micah oracle, this oracle is offered in response to loss and lament. The book of Isaiah works in much larger scope than the tradition of Micah. But there is no doubt that the oracles of judgment in the Isaiah tradition characterize, like Micah, an urban economy engaged in self-destruction through its limitless greed (see, for example, 3:1—4:1; 5:7, 8–10). Nor is there any doubt that at the center of the book of Isaiah, between chapters 39 and 40, we are to entertain the destruction of the city and the utterance of the book of Lamentations. (It is widely seen that the poetry of Isaiah 40–55, in some detail, can be heard as a response to the laments in the book of Lamentations.)[15] After chapter 40, the book of Isaiah moves to new possibility, imagining homecoming and restoration

15. See Willey, *Remember the Former Things.*

of the city.[16] But the Jerusalem to which there will be return is not the old city. It is a "new Jerusalem" that matches the anticipated "new heaven" and "new earth."

- The new city here imagined will no longer be a venue for "the sound of weeping and "the cry of distress," the kind of weeping and cries that arise in situations of suffering and pain imposed by greed (v. 19).[17]

- The new city here imagined will not be a venue for infant mortality, because the life of everyone, including newborn children, will be valued and protected by policy (v. 20).

- The new city here imagined will not be a place where folk die too soon, for even the old will be valued and protected (v. 20).

- The new city here imagined will be a place for neighborly economics in which there will not be foreclosure on one's home or the right of eminent domain in the interest of the elite (vv. 21–22).

- The new city here imagined will be a venue for healthy, joyous childbirth, for the old curse linked to childbirth will no longer pertain; all the newborn will be blessed (v. 23).

- The new city here imagined will be in the constant protective purview of YHWH, without the deep void produced by an "unclean people" (v. 24).

- The new city here imagined will be a place of reconciled "nature," because all creatures will be beyond the reach of hurt and destruction (v. 25).

It is clear that the city imagined by the traditions of Micah and Isaiah is one where human flourishing is attainable, because these poetic acts of imagination contradict the old, tired city of greed and the old, tired ideologies that continue to justify systemic greed. The listeners—the first listeners and many subsequent listeners—are invited into a contradiction where new choices are possible. As these poets know, and as the God who evokes the poets knows, it is possible to keep choosing the old, tired city of greed and to keep embracing the old, tired ideologies

16. Recovery and homecoming are given full, imaginative play in Isaiah 60–62 that conjure a wondrous, triumphant return.

17. On the cry, see Boyce, *Cry to God.*

that justify that greed. Such a choice, however, is not required. The work of the poem is to break the totalism of that ideology of greed—not to deliver the listener into a panacea, but into a context where alternatives are chooseable. "Flourishing" is not a given; but it is made chooseable.

VII

The work of such poetic imagination is to dislodge the "givenness" of the claims of acquisitive ideology. If that givenness is dislodged, then alternatives become thinkable and chooseable. My thesis is that the hard work of imagination (that claims divine rootage and divine propulsion) is a fundamental precondition for a society that can flourish. The sad reality of our contemporary society is that the possible venues for such imagination (that is rooted in and propelled by holiness out beyond the reach of human hubris)—perhaps the university, more likely the church or synagogue, or the mosque—have largely succumbed to the dictates of acquisitiveness that are disguised as virtues. The possibility of such imagination pivots on God-authorized contradiction that requires a kind of courageous intentionality that is not possible among those who deny or despair.

The hopeful reality is that Micah and Isaiah, in that ancient world, are not the last such voices of imagination that continue to echo. In the United States, there is no more dramatic instance of such imaginative public utterance that bespeaks flourishing than "I have a dream" by Martin Luther King Jr.[18] His use of "dream" seems to me to be a cagey, judicious way of claiming theological rootage in a society that is doubtful of such rootage, for "dream" is a world beyond managed memo, a world haunted by the spirit of truth beyond our weary categories.[19] Thus King speaks of "dream" and in fact lines out a particular, concrete alternative for society that the dream treats as possible.

It is clear in the cadences of his speech that he intends, point by point, to contradict the assumptions and practices of a racist society of greed and exploitation. Thus: "All men are created equal" defies racist hierarchy; "sons of former slaves and sons of former slave owners" refuses

18. King, "I Have a Dream," 404–6.

19. In Isa 2:1, the offer of an alternative Jerusalem is termed a "vision." It is suggestive that in the familiar "Holy City," the lyric begins: "Last night as I lay sleeping, / I had a dream so fair . . ." Perhaps the new Jerusalem, like the new America offered by King, is always a "dream."

racist distinctions; "sweltering with the heat of injustice and oppression" acknowledges the unbearable burden of old practices. And so on, point by point. King's speech is in close proximity to the promissory utterances of Micah and Isaiah. It is an act of hope. Clearly, however, it is also a summons to act toward possibility. That speech contributed—as intended and, as it turned out, in an effective way—to the passage of the crucial Civil Rights legislation of the decade. The speech named, exposed, and called out a society that vigorously refused self-criticism and self-awareness, and invited King's listeners into the heretofore unnamed contradiction between practice and creed. King ended his "oracle" with a riff on "Let freedom ring," a phrase from a beloved anthem, "My Country 'Tis of Thee." Without it being said, every listener knew that he meant not only *life in new freedom*, but also *freedom from old, killing assumptions*. The "ring of freedom" requires action; but it begins in the poetry of flourishing.

VIII

So now the United States (and the Western world with it) faces choices that are more difficult and demanding, even, than those of race, for economics is the toughest case. The possibility is that the old ideologies of acquisitiveness, birthed in coercive monologue and sustained by aggressive militarism, may be "dreamed" away. That will require emancipatory imagination, that is, poets who live and speak beyond the totalism of accepted truth. Poets of all sorts—artists, preachers, intellectuals, and ordinary folk who know better—have been in a long season of intimidation with failed nerve.[20] But pain may produce such poetry. And this may be such a time. Pain-produced poetry evokes communities that imagine alternatively and that initiate action that is both subversive and generative. Such flourishing is possible, granted God-given nerve. And when it is sounded among us, we will notice, yet again, how much Tim Gorringe has taught us so well.

Bibliography

Boyce, Richard Nelson. *The Cry to God in the Old Testament*. Atlanta: Scholars, 1988.

---

20. On such a condition, see Friedman, *Failure of Nerve*.

Brueggemann, Walter. "Psalms 9–10: A Counter to Conventional Social Reality." In *The Bible and the Politics of Exegesis: Essays in Honor of Norman K. Gottwald on His Sixty-Fifth Birthday*, edited by David Jobling et al., 3–15. Cleveland: Pilgrim, 1991.

———. *Solomon: Israel's Ironic Icon of Human Achievement*. Columbia: University of South Carolina Press, 2005.

Cavanaugh, William T. *Torture and Eucharist*. Oxford: Blackwell, 1998.

Friedman, Edwin H. *A Failure of Nerve: Leadership in the Age of the Quick Fix*. Bethesda, MD: Edwin Friedman Estate/Trust, 1999.

Gorringe, Timothy J. *Capital and the Kingdom: Theological Ethics and Economic Order*. Maryknoll, NY: Orbis, 1994.

———. *Harvest: Food, Farming and the Churches*. London: SPCK, 2006.

Gottwald, Norman K. *All the Kingdoms of the Earth: Israelite Prophecy and International Relations in the Ancient Near East*. New York: Harper & Row, 1964.

Jacques, Martin. *When China Rules the World: The End of the Western World and the Birth of a New Global Order*. New York: Penguin, 2009.

Johnson, Chalmers. *Blowback: The Costs and Consequences of American Empire*. New York: Holt, 2001.

———. *Nemesis: The Last Days of the American Republic*. New York: Metropolitan, 2006.

———. *The Sorrows of Empire: Militarism, Secrecy, and the End of the Republic*. New York: Holt, 2005.

King, Martin Luther, Jr. "I Have a Dream." In *Sociology of Religion: A Reader*, edited by Susanne C. Monahan et al., 404–6. Upper Saddle River, NJ: Prentice Hall, 2001.

Miller, Patrick D. *They Cried to the Lord: The Form and Theology of Biblical Prayer*. Minneapolis: Fortress, 1994.

Walzer, Michael. *Exodus and Revolution*. New York: Basic, 1985.

Wilder, Amos Niven. *Theopoetic: Theology and the Religious Imagination*. Philadelphia: Fortress, 1976.

Willey, Patricia Tull. *Remember the Former Things: The Recollection of Previous Texts in Second Isaiah*. Atlanta: Scholars, 1997.

Žižek, Slavoj. *The Universal Exception*. New York: Continuum, 2006.

3

Being Planted

Prophetic Visions of Human Sustainability

RACHEL MUERS

Tim Gorringe's concern for sustainable patterns of human interaction with the nonhuman environment is a very important aspect of the inclusive vision of *shalom* that inspires his theological work. His understanding of humanity's dependence on land, plants, and nonhuman animals is thoroughly practical as well as theoretical. Successive generations of students and colleagues have found themselves learning from him about the vicissitudes of farming life in Devon or the processes of honey extraction and cider production, alongside the more conventional subject matter of academic theology. With his experiences in India as well as in Britain to inform him, he was an environmentally aware theologian and activist long before environmentalism became fashionable in theological and political circles.

Clearly, Tim's interest in environmental sustainability owes nothing to a romanticized vision of untouched wild nature. He is well known, after all, as an incisive theological commentator on the *built* environment, and his environmental vision always encompasses the social and the political.[1] His interests are not in how humans can leave nature alone, but in how we can live rightly in our close relationships of dependence and

---

1. See his *Theology of the Built Environment*, chap. 9, 222–40.

interdependence with land, plants, and animals, in a way that enables and advances our flourishing. His work acknowledges that human creatures cannot flourish apart from, or over against, the rest of creation; we are, and remain, rooted deeply in the earth, part of a community of creation.

Throughout his oeuvre, Tim's theological voice is prophetic—exposing and critiquing the manifold structures of falsehood and violence that impede human flourishing in the world today, from the perspective of God's promise of liberation and fullness of life.[2] It might be suggested that a prophetic voice sits awkwardly with the kinds of perennial, everyday wisdom that are needed to maintain sustainable patterns of life in right relation to the nonhuman creation. The "Gaia" of some contemporary ecological theology and philosophy can be set in tension with the God of Christian Scriptures; the cyclical time of agricultural life can seem to fit awkwardly with the linear time of salvation history.[3] What do the prophets, whose voices move forward the narrative of God's action in history, have to say about farming practices, the maintenance of a city's infrastructure, or other ongoing tasks that sustain ordinary life?

In this essay, I offer a reading of one prophetic text, Hosea 13–14, in an attempt to display the theological reasoning that might inform a contemporary prophetic call for sustainable living, in line with that offered in Tim's work. A reflection on this text can help expose the theological dimensions of the growing environmental crisis—and move us, in responding to that crisis, beyond platitudes about the beauties of the unspoiled and untouched creation. The interconnected promise of *shalom*, encompassing as it does economic justice and well-being, nonviolent relations between creatures, and the flourishing of all life, is a possibility opened up by the prophetic voice that exposes and shatters the destructive illusions that hold people and societies captive.

FEAR, SECURITY, AND DELIVERANCE IN HOSEA

The penultimate chapter of Hosea presents a terrifying vision of destruction—not unparalleled in the Bible, but still shocking to the reader. The destruction both of human life and of the sources of human life is recounted in fearful detail, culminating in the deaths of infants and

2. Thus, for example, he chose, as the epigraph for *Built Environment*, Num 11:29: "Would that all the Lord's people were prophets."

3. See Ruether, *Gaia and God*.

unborn children in ferocious military conflict (Hos 13:16). The whole account, moreover, is suffused by divine anger; the destruction is not always presented as the *direct* work of God, but it is nonetheless closely linked to divine wrath. In stark contrast, the final chapter of Hosea presents an image of human flourishing, linked, in an extended comparison, with the flourishing of fruitful, cultivated plants, and secured by a promise of free and unconditionally generous divine love. At the hinge between the two visions comes the familiar prophetic call, the call to enacted repentance—"Return, O Israel" (Hos 14:1).

Coming after Hosea 13, the summons "Return" is spoken as if to people in desperate fear—people, moreover, who have no idea how to begin returning, and who have to be told, point by point, what to do in order to reconstruct their lives, to make flourishing, or even bare survival, possible. Now, the fear of an angry God looks, on the face of it, like a very bad place from which to start thinking about human flourishing. In recent years, as is well known, religion in general and Christianity in particular has repeatedly been accused of culpability for violence and for the exploitation of nonhuman nature[4]—besides untold psychological damage to those whose lives are dominated by fear of divine punishment. It might make sense, on many levels, for Christians to walk away from the prophetic text of violence and divine wrath. Christian supersessionism, which is alive and well in its popular forms even if theologians widely reject it, offers the tempting option of consigning the angry and violent God of Hosea 13 to the outdated Old Testament, while praising the loving God of Hosea 14 as foreshadowing the "God of the New Testament."

However difficult it is to read Hosea 13, it seems to me that some of the import of the prophetic voice is lost if the call to "return to God" is heard apart from a reminder of the horrifying consequences of pursuing certain courses of action and patterns of life. In interpreting Hosea 13 and similar texts of horror,[5] I would argue, firstly, that they are clear-sighted descriptions of some of the worst things that people do to each other, and some of the worst things that happen to people. It is, for example, simply a fact that small children often become victims of the multiple

4. For the latter, see most famously, or notoriously, White, "Historical Roots."

5. I use this term to distinguish them from the "texts of terror" (Trible, *Texts of Terror*) that legitimate or re-perform acts of oppressive violence. My reading of Hosea 13 and similar texts, despite the focus on the wrath of God, is that they acknowledge and cry out *against* the horrors they describe.

wrongdoings and failures of society; it is a fact (even more in the modern age than in most previous ages) that wars have large numbers of "civilian casualties"; and it is a fact, we are learning more and more in our own time, that even the victims of "natural" disasters are likely also to be the victims of human error, greed, or wickedness.[6]

The prophetic text voices—as, even more obviously, in Jeremiah[7]—not merely a detailed report of the facts, but also a lament. The prophet takes a stance of passionate concern towards those caught up in the horrors he describes, without on that account seeking a mitigating explanation of the horrors or a facile hope of resolution. This prophetic voice that directs the hearers' attention to the consequences of systemic wrongs—wrongs in which they themselves are, in a small way, participants, even if they lead ostensibly "good" lives—makes deep and uncomfortable sense in an age when we are rediscovering the implications of global ecological interconnectedness.[8] It might be echoed, in the contemporary age, by the voice of the committed researcher or investigative journalist, directing our collective attention to implications, which we would rather forget, of the global patterns of production and consumption in which we participate.

In my reading, then, the first point to remember about the prophetic horrors is that they are not a fantastic or remote threat, but an urgent reality check. Secondly, however, the prophetic voice that provokes and invokes fear exposes, in this context at least, the consequences of people's efforts to *free* themselves from fear—a quest that relies on acquiring and keeping the power to instill fear in others. Israel, as accused in Hosea, sought to make itself safe through acquiring "a king and rulers" (Hos 13:10), through forming a military alliance with the powerful state of Assyria, and through "riding upon horses" (Hos 14:3). It sought, in other words, to establish a military hierarchy and to secure the capacity to unleash lethal destructive force. Both the acquisition of a king and

---

6. A point I learned first from another prophetic theologian, Nicholas Lash, who was also speaking and writing about the magnitude of human-made environmental disaster before it became fashionable.

7. See for example Jer 4:19: "My anguish, my anguish! I writhe in pain! / Oh, the walls of my heart! / My heart is beating wildly; / I cannot keep silent; / for I hear the sound of the trumpet, / the alarm of war."

8. As has often been pointed out, the first and worst-affected victims of global climate change and of other forms of environmental degradation are, overwhelmingly, the poor in the Global South.

the taking away of a king—the establishment *and* the destruction of a center of military power—are associated, by this prophet, with the anger of God: "I gave you a king in my anger / and I took him away in my wrath" (Hos 13:11). In other words, the reliance on the "king"—or on "Assyria," or on warhorses, that is, military force—as the primary source of security is already an indication of fundamental estrangement from God. An economy of fear—of trying to escape fear by making oneself invulnerable, and acquiring the capacity to instill fear in others—is already present, even before the fear is directly felt by this society.

What does this have to do with contemporary questions about sustainability? We might think of the increasing incidence of, and the even more rapidly increasing fear of, wars over scarce resources, and of the response to global poverty and inequalities that calls for the greater fortification of the borders of wealthy countries. Economic injustice—the "trader in whose hands are false balances" (Hos 12:7)—is defended by violence, and the result is a continued degradation of the social and natural ecologies on which we depend.

The prophet's doom-laden voice, then, far from introducing fear where none existed, reveals the fear that lies at the heart of a certain way of constructing individual and communal life. It reveals the extent to which we have already constructed God and other people as objects of terror to be run away from, controlled, or destroyed. It also reveals the immense precariousness, indeed the unsustainability, of this system of competitive security-seeking that relies on acquiring the power to impose fear and insecurity on others.

The fact that this economy of fear is also represented as a system of *idolatry*, in which people "[make] a cast image for themselves" (Hos 13:2) and "say . . . 'Our God' to the work of [their] hands" (Hos 14:3), is neither accidental nor incidental. The security provided by the military or technological solution to a perceived threat is the work of *our hands*. The desire for we human beings to build or think ourselves out of trouble, and the unquestioning faith in the "work of our hands" to save us, often identified as the first sin of modernity, has a long history; the prophetic voice exposes it as both self-defeating and destructive. For a theology of human flourishing, it is important to realize that idolatry is not merely the misnaming of God, but rather the misdirection of ultimate trust—the misidentification of what, or who, can be relied on to produce security or to save from fear, and the misconstrual of what such reliance involves.

Thus, a key issue concerning idolatry in Hos 13–14 is, not merely the question of who should be called God, but the identity of the *savior* (13:4; 13:10; 14:3)—that is, of the one who provides deliverance from danger. The prophet says that the LORD declares "you know no God but me, and besides me there is no savior" (13:4); and then the prophet exposes the false claims of both the Israelite king (13:10) and the Assyrian alliance (14:3) to have the capacity to "save." The root *yasha'*, appearing in each of these contexts, carries military connotations—saving from the enemy through victory in battle—so it might be thought that God is being invoked here as the final guarantor of military power. Is the worship of God, rather than the idol, simply a matter of allying oneself with the strongest divine arm and the biggest divine army? That would be the suspicious reading of the prophetic voice, which allies it closely with nationalistic pride and the reinforcement of a closed national identity. If my reading of the "horrors" of Hosea 13 is at all plausible, however, there must be an alternative explanation of divine deliverance.

In fact, Hos 1:7 sets up a fundamental contrast around deliverance, *yasha'*, which provides the framework within which these later chapters can be read: "I will have pity on the house of Judah, and I will save (*yasha'*) them by the LORD their God; I will not save them by bow, or by sword, or by war, or by horses, or by horsemen." Here, military or technological superiority is acknowledged as a possible way to seek deliverance from everything that might assail or threaten human flourishing—and it is rejected. To reinforce this, in Hos 13:4 (in particular) there is a direct reference back to the context of the exodus—"I have been the LORD your God ever since the land of Egypt"—when the LORD saves the people at the Red Sea, from, rather than through, a formidable array of military hardware (Exod 15:30). The idea of military "deliverance" is kept in play, in a situation in which every nation including the prophet's own is concerned about its military status—but the effect of the prophet's words is to overturn this idea of deliverance from within. Attributing deliverance to God, rather than to one's command of lethal force or to some other aspect of the "work of one's hands," requires a rethinking of what deliverance might mean.

Read within the canon of Christian Scripture, Hosea's interrogation of *yasha'* points towards a similar interrogation in the New Testament of the deliverance offered in Jesus—whose name, of course, comes from this verbal root. Is Jesus providing "deliverance," salvation, on the world's existing terms, with all that that might imply in terms of the power and prestige of the saved and their competitive victory over the unsaved? Or does it demolish the entire pattern of thought within which my "deliverance" and security is associated with my power and superiority over others?

What alternative does the prophetic voice offer? Recall again the people's spoken act of repentance in Hos 14:3:

> Assyria shall not save us;
> we will not ride upon horses;
> we will say no more, "Our God,"
> to the work of our hands.

The underlying problem that this act of repentance identifies seems to be a fear of vulnerability, combined with strenuous efforts to deny that vulnerability. The people have, for reasons and in ways that the prophet does not fully trace, ceased to trust the one God and begun to trust the work of their hands. The appropriate response, the way back into a relationship of trust, is not *doing* something different, but a more fundamental reorientation of self—"Return, O Israel"—and the utterance of the words that express that reorientation (Hos 14:2: "Take words with you and return to the LORD"). The first move, the move of return, is emphatically not a new form of anxious self-creation, another attempt to find a way of making a community invulnerable to perceived threats. Nor does it, eventually, issue in invulnerability. Rather, as we shall now see, it issues in renewed *sustainability*.

FLOURISHING AFTER THE RETURN

The vision of human flourishing in Hos 14 contrasts most sharply with the earlier accounts of failed salvation. In an extended set of connected metaphors, Hosea compares the reconciled life of Israel to the life of plants—the lily (14:5), the forest (14:5), the olive tree (14:6), and the vine (14:7). The most obvious intrabiblical analogy is to Ps 1:3:

> [The righteous] are like trees
> planted by streams of water
> which yield their fruit in its season
> and their leaves do not wither.[9]

9. The NRSV's inclusive-language translation pluralizes the image that in Hebrew

It would be hard to envisage anything further from the anxious quest for constructed and defended security than the life of plants. The plant, in Hosea as in Psalm 1, flourishes and blossoms *through*, rather than *despite*, its reliance on sources of nourishment from outside itself. It "strike[s] root" and receives "dew" (14:5). It displays strength without defending itself, and "spreads out" (14:6) without jostling for space. It is recognized for its fruitfulness, beauty, and fragrance—that is, for the characteristics of its flourishing life that are intrinsically shareable.

The extended attention paid to the life of plants here makes sense in the context of the need to reimagine a community's place in the world. We are, the text suggests, more like plants than we are like gods. Our way of being in the world is more like "rootedness" in particular places and relationships than like perpetual motion ("riding upon horses") or omnipresence. Our flourishing is more like bearing fruit than like being creators. The horror of Hosea's earlier vision, of the deep unsustainability of projects of self-creation and security based on invulnerability, allows his hearers to see the extent to which "being planted" in and by God is good news. Note, also, that the plants to which people are compared at the end of Hosea (and also in Psalm 1) are *cultivated* plants—the fruit-bearing tree and the vine. The image conjured up is not of solitary and inscrutable splendor but of interdependence. Both the vine and the olive tree need to be tended, and need the right environment in which to exist.

Taking this a step further it is noteworthy in this text that God is also compared to a plant—an "evergreen cypress" (14:8)—beneath whose "shadow" people live (14:7). In other words, it is not merely that the human creature is more plantlike than godlike; it is that God's own life with creation, in delivering and protecting, is more like the life of plants than it is like the "life" attributed to idols. God's own life with creation is noncompetitive, nourishing, shareable rather than invulnerable, secured through rather than despite relationships.

The culmination of Hosea's renewed vision is a direct echo of the wisdom literature (and another echo of Psalm 1):

> Those who are wise understand these things;
>   those who are discerning know them.
> For the ways of the LORD are right,
>   and the upright walk in them,
>   but transgressors stumble in them. (Hos 14:9)

describes the "man [singular] who does not follow the advice of the wicked."

In another context, the reference to "right ways" and the stark contrast between the "upright" and "transgressors" might be misread as a threat that begins the cycle of fear and insecurity again. How are people supposed to know and to find the "ways of the LORD," and how can they be sure never to put a foot wrong? Indeed, Christians have often (mis) read "the Law" of the Old Testament and its injunctions as a collection of impossible demands, designed to provoke anxiety over one's imperfections, and to establish God as one who is to be feared.

The appearance of this text at the end of Hosea is a reminder that wisdom, in its close relationship to Torah, is the enacted acknowledgement of one's creatureliness—one's particular, limited, embodied existence in a community of creatures.[10] Walking in the ways of the LORD is not trying to be something one is *not* (perfectly knowledgeable, for example, or an invulnerable hero, or free from the multiple demands of other creatures); it is about accepting and being what one *is*. Nothing else, in the long or even the short term, is sustainable. The prophetic call to repentance is a summons away from the unsustainable effort to escape creaturely dependence and to establish a position of invulnerability. The alternative that the prophet offers is not an even more impossible dream but a call back to practical wisdom.

What might it mean to perform this kind of prophecy in the contemporary context, in which environmental and financial crises invite both doom-laden rhetoric and ambitious proposals for regaining security? A real concern about much contemporary environmental ethics—and environmental theology, in relation to environmental ethics—is that it risks becoming simply another set of anxiety-imposing demands, in a cultural context where people are already being urged to live up to multiple conflicting and equally impossible visions of human perfection. The central "turn" in Hosea, away from anxious self-creation and self-protection (and from the idolatries that this produces), is not always performed; grand-scale "solutions" to environmental and economic crises can produce equally unsustainable patterns of thought and behavior. At the same time, clear-sighted analyses of the unsustainability

10. Kelsey, *Eccentric Existence*, vol. 1, focuses his account of human creatureliness on the wisdom literature (rather than, as is more conventional, on Genesis 1–3). His plausible argument is that it is in the wisdom texts that the meaning and ramifications of creatureliness are most fully explored.

of existing ways of life have given rise to multiple, local, and small-scale responses that honor creaturely dependence and interdependence.[11]

Perhaps the truly prophetic response to the contemporary situation, then, is rather as Tim has repeatedly argued the church itself is—always local, "rooted," materially constituted by the particular context in which it emerges, constantly engaged both in attending to the call of God and seeking practical wisdom. Carefully chosen words, in this context, are essential—"Take words with you and return to the LORD"—but do not themselves effect sustainable human flourishing. Hosea ends, in fact, where words addressed to an *entire* people have to end, and where discerning and following the ways of the LORD, in particular localities and for particular lives, has to begin.

There is an urgent need, in our time, for such discernment inspired by prophecy, and Tim has done much over the years to inspire students, colleagues, and a wider public to engage in it. Theological and ecclesial communities can confidently expect many more words of both prophecy and wisdom from Tim, even after his retirement—but he will also have the well-earned opportunity to spend more time cultivating his own gardens.

Bibliography

Gorringe, Timothy J. *A Theology of the Built Environment: Justice, Empowerment, Redemption*. Cambridge: Cambridge University Press, 2002.

Kelsey, David. *Eccentric Existence: A Theocentric Anthropology*. Grand Rapids: Eerdmans, 2009.

Ruether, Rosemary Radford. *Gaia and God: An Ecofeminist Theology of Earth Healing*. San Francisco: Harper, 1992.

Trible, Phyllis. *Texts of Terror: Literary-Feminist Readings of Biblical Narratives*. Minneapolis: Augsburg Fortress, 1984.

White, Lynn, Jr. "The Historical Roots of our Ecologic Crisis." *Science* 155:3767 (10 March 1967) 1203–7.

---

11. An example, which is a current focus of Tim's research, is the Transition Towns movement, within which the churches—and non-Christian religious groups—play a varying, contested but often significant role.

4

Tree-Hogging in Eden

Divine Restriction and Royal Rejection in Genesis 2–3[1]

Francesca Stavrakopoulou

It is no overstatement to claim that the Eden story in Genesis 2–3 has had a profound impact on Western culture. As is well known, the story's twinned themes of disobedience and expulsion play a central role in Jewish and Christian constructions of identity—ancient and modern—and continue to undergird seemingly secular cultural assumptions and anxieties about "human nature." But though it is traditionally read as a tale designed to deal with the distancing of humanity from the divine, Eden's function as a cipher for human experience and destiny is primarily encouraged by its placement in the opening chapters of Torah, so that within the Jewish and Christian compilations of authoritative sacred texts, the Eden story was rendered the paradigmatic foundation myth of humanity. As Tim Gorringe has often shown us, however, we are never as far away as we might think, or as we might like, from the grit of politics and political ideologies—and the Eden story is certainly no exception.

Indeed, in common with many other mythic traditions indigenous to ancient West Asia, the Eden story was once just one among many

---

1. It is with great affection that I dedicate this essay to my colleague Tim Gorringe, Exeter's quintessential tree hugger.

41

myths dealing in specific, pointed ways with the changing proximity and distance between certain humans and their gods. The cultural and social specificity of ancient (and contemporary) myths is a characteristic often overlooked in favor of modernist, Western assumptions about the underlying universality of human experience and a preference for post-Enlightenment constructions of "religion" and its discourse.[2] But myths index precise social, political, ritual, and ideological contexts.[3] As such, the biblical Eden narrative harbors at its core not a sacred "truth" about the human condition, but an ideological, mythic response to a very specific socioreligious reality.

Given the carefully crafted context in which it now appears in Tanak, the mythic core of the Eden story is to a certain extent difficult to discern, for it is bound up in a complex intertextual relationship with other biblical narratives, sharing many of its themes with other traditions: like Abraham and Job, the man in the garden undergoes a divine test of obedience (Gen 22:1; Job 1:8–12; 2:3–6; cf. Gen 2:16–17; 3:11); like the nations of Israel and Judah, the man is exiled as a divine punishment for his disobedience (2 Kgs 17:7–19; 24:20; cf. Gen 3:17, 24); and like the wives of Solomon and like Queen Jezebel, the woman in Eden is responsible for her husband's disobedience (1 Kgs 11:1–4; 1 Kgs 21:25; cf. Gen 3:6, 12, 17). But a close reading of the narrative in Genesis 2–3 reveals that the story is essentially about the man, his eating from the tree, and his subsequent expulsion from the garden, rendering the roles of the woman and the serpent seemingly peripheral: it is the *man* who is forbidden to eat from the Tree of Knowledge of Good and Bad (2:16–17), and the *man's* disobedience that is discovered by Yahweh (3:9–11). So too it is specifically the *man* who is said to have become like one of the gods, and from whom the Tree of Life is to be kept (3:22); accordingly, it is the *man* who is expelled from the garden (3:23–24). Though they bear their own mythic trappings, the woman and the serpent appear not to be primary players in this particular plot.[4] Rather, and more specifically, it is the relationship between the man, the deity, and the tree(s) that seems to be the key concern of the story. And it is this relationship that points

---

2. Cf. Saler, *Conceptualizing Religion*; Dubuisson, *Western Construction of Religion*.

3. See further Patton and Doniger, eds., *Myth and Method*.

4. There is a great deal of scholarly literature on these figures, but see especially Wyatt, "Eve"; Charlesworth, *Good and Evil Serpent*.

to the mythic core of the biblical tradition, and the socioreligious reality embedded within it.

COSMIC CULTIVATION AND ITS ROYAL MANIFESTATION

The garden setting of the biblical story schematizes a complex of mytho-religious ideas about the relationship between life and death, order and disorder. Within ancient West Asian cultures, gardens were accorded a special mythic status not simply because they were manifestations of fertility, but because they were symbols of *cultivated* fertility: a rich, life-giving fecundity that could be carefully planned, constructed, and controlled. As such, gardens were particularly associated with the divine realm, for the gods were cosmic cultivators (cf. Gen 2:8–9; Isa 41:19).[5] Mesopotamian texts describe gardens as the dwelling places of the gods, watered by cosmic rivers and stocked with fruits, spices, and medicinal plants; these were sacred spaces in which the gods were believed to enjoy walking (cf. Gen 3:8), and in which certain rituals were performed.[6] This divine, controlling order manifested by the garden was perceived in op-positional relation to the mythic concept of the uncultivated wilderness, in which chaotic malice—and death—might reside.[7]

As a manifestation of controlled cultivation, a garden was thus a powerful ideological symbol of a distinctly urban, high-status socio-religious worldview, in which the built environment, in all its material-ity and monumentality, reflected the religio-political structuring of an imperialized cosmos, both in the earthly realm and in the divine world.[8] The construction of gardens thus played a vital role in the performance and promotion of human kingship and imperialism. In the tripartite view of the cosmos common to ancient West Asian cultures, in which the earthly world was caught fast between the heavenly realm and the underworld, a king was crucially and liminally positioned between the heavens and the earthly realm. He was the quasi-divine representative of

5. On the deity as cultivator, see Lang, *Hebrew God*, 139–69.

6. See further Wiseman, "Mesopotamian Gardens"; Oppenheim, "Royal Gardens"; Stordalen, *Echoes of Eden*, 111–38. It may be that trees and plants grown in these gardens were employed as offerings in temple gardens (so Wiseman, "Mesopotamian Gardens," 141–42).

7. Cf. Smith, *Origins of Biblical Monotheism*, 28–29; cf. Wyatt, "Significance of the Burning Bush."

8. Cf. Davies, "Urban Religion"; cf. Brett, *Decolonizing God*, 32–43.

his patron deity for his human subjects, and the embodiment of his nation in the eyes of the gods.[9] This was a world in which created order and destructive chaos were held together in a fragile balance, so that royal building programs at home and the conquest of "barbaric" wastelands abroad signaled the imposition of divine, cosmic order upon chaos. Ancient West Asian gardens were thus both visually impressive and horticulturally prestigious in their collections of trees and plants gathered from the furthest reaches of the empire, demonstrating the royal mastery of other peoples, their gods, and the produce of their lands.[10] In building, planting, and cultivating a garden, the king cast himself in a mythic and ritual sense as the "gardener" of the gods, undertaking his divinely endorsed duty to serve the deities.

Indeed, this is well reflected in the richly textured portrayal of Eden in Ezek 28:1–19, in which a royal figure is imaged in the divine garden, located at the center of the cosmos.[11] The placement of the primal man in the divine garden in Genesis 2–3 also reflects this prestigious and distinctly royal role, as illustrated in Gen 2:15, in which it is claimed that "Yahweh-Elohim took the man and placed him in the garden of Eden, to till it and tend it." This primal man is thus a paradigm of the king, carrying out his divinely ordained duty as the ritual gardener of God—cultic service of the highest order.[12] But what is so striking about this biblical presentation of a well-worn mythic trope is the *distancing* of the royal figure from the trees in the garden.

The King and the Tree

The so-called sacred tree motif was widespread throughout ancient West Asian cultures. As an (often schematized) iconographic motif, the

9. See further Wyatt, *Myths of Power*; Wyatt, "Royal Religion in Ancient Judah."

10. This is graphically illustrated by the well-known Neo-Assyrian banquet relief from King Ashurbanipal's palace in Nineveh, currently housed in the British Museum. It shows the king and queen feasting in the garden, attended by servants and musicians. In front of the attendant on the far left is a tree, and in its uppermost branches hangs a severed head: a trophy of imperial conquest. See further Bahrani, *Rituals of War*, 22–55.

11. Note that the divine garden also appears in Ezek 36:35; Gen 13:10; Joel 2:3; Isa 51:3.

12. As Nicolas Wyatt emphasizes, the common and loaded biblical designation "Yahweh's servant," frequently applied to kings and king-like figures, specifically means "Yahweh's gardener" (so Wyatt, "Garden for the Living"; see also Widengren, *King and Tree of Life*).

symbol of the sacred tree functioned as a cipher for a nexus of ideas about the perpetuation of life, the nature of the divine, and the structure of the cosmos. It was a divine symbol of remarkable adaptability and "translatability,"[13] embodying strong ideas about *perpetual* fertility and its divine promulgation—not only because a tree offers fruiting nourishment, protective shade, and healing seeds and balms, but also because it is a long-lived plant that can appear to regenerate itself.

But in a more specific sense, as a mythic and divine symbol, the tree was seen to intersect the whole cosmos: firmly rooted in the underworld, it stretched through the earthly realm, its uppermost branches reaching into the heavens. Given its special position in the cosmos, the tree could thus access and harness both the wisdom of the deified dead in the underworld, and that of the gods in the heavens—a specialized, divine wisdom often communicated in oracular form.[14] For this reason, in many ancient West Asian and Mediterranean traditions, the *axis mundi* is often imaged as a vast sacred tree that both manifests and represents cosmic order and divine wisdom. As such, it can also mark or manifest divine presence—whether on a local or cosmic scale.

Thus in some of its uses, the motif of the sacred tree might represent a particular deity, with whom the king was held to share a special relationship.[15] However, the sacred tree might also perform a more specialized function in the exhibition and promotion of divinely endorsed kingship. This is well attested in the iconography of Neo-Assyrian kingship. In the early ninth century BCE, when King Ashurnasirpal II built his famous Northwest Palace at Kalḫu (Nimrud), he commissioned a remarkable series of reliefs to cover almost every wall of the formal rooms of the palace. The repeated motif on each one is the sacred tree, a motif occurring over two hundred times.[16] Perhaps the most impos-

13. "Translatability" is the somewhat slippery term borrowed primarily from social anthropology and cultural studies that has come to be used by some scholars to describe how deities and divine symbols of different cultures might be identified, recognized, or assimilated across cultural boundaries. For a recent treatment, see Smith, *God in Translation*.

14. See further Wyatt, "Word of Tree."

15. Iconographic portrayals of this idea abound, but a particularly striking example is the repeated imaging of the Egyptian goddess Hathor (occasionally substituted by Isis or Nut) as a tree, suckling the king, often styled as Horus. See further Kempinski, *L'arbre stylisé*.

16. Richardson, "Assyrian Garden of Ancestors."

ing of representations is the central image, which is now housed in the British Museum, but in its original palace setting would have been located above the throne: here, the stylized, sacred tree is flanked by the king and the high god, who are in their turn flanked by winged divine beings. Above the sacred tree is the emblem of the imperial god. The whole scene functions as a divine endorsement of the king, his dynasty, his nation, and his politics, emphasizing by means of the sacred tree the king's prestigious, cosmic role as the gardener of the gods.[17]

Crucially, however, the symbol-system of Ashurnasirpal's palace also attests to a more specific aspect of this royal mythology. As was common within many ancient West Asian royal households, the ancestors of the monarchic line not only continued to exist in a postmortem state in the underworld, but they were also considered the deified dead, and thus played a part in the divine worlds the living sought to access by means of rituals, oracles, and other cultic actions.[18] The royal dead played an essential part in the accession, endorsement, and stability of the living king's position, bestowing blessings of fertility and protection on their descendant, his successors, and his kingdom.[19] In Ugarit and Judah, mortuary gardens—and all their mytho-symbolic and cosmic associations—were the setting for certain ancestor-cult rituals promoting the perpetuation of the royal dynasty and the well-being of the deified dead.[20]

Set within this context, the close association of the sacred tree with kingship functioned as a means of exhibiting the perpetual fertility, wisdom, and regeneration of the royal household. In Ashurnasirpal's palace, the number of sacred trees adorning its walls closely approximates the number of deceased kings listed in contemporary recensions of the Assyrian King List—a ritual catalogue of royal ancestors—suggesting that each sacred tree represented a dead king in a royal cult of ancestor veneration.[21] This "garden of ancestors," as Seth Richardson describes it,

17. See further Porter, *Trees, Kings, and Politics*.

18. See further Stavrakopoulou, *Land of Our Fathers*, esp. 18–25 and the literature cited there.

19. Wyatt, "Royal Religion," 73–75.

20. Stavrakopoulou, "Garden of Uzza."

21. As proposed by Richardson, "Garden of Ancestors." In his discussion, Richardson is quick to acknowledge and to address the apparent disparity between the numbers of sacred trees and dead kings, for which he offers several solutions based upon new reconstructions of Room I and the arrangement of its trees, the grouping of

would have been of crucial ideological importance to the living king, for his new palace was constructed in his newly relocated capital city, away from the royal tombs situated conventionally beneath the palace in the former capital: "A venerative royal cult to ancestors, situated on a grand scale in the new Kalḫu palace, would have supported Ashurnasirpal II's claims to legitimate and traditional kingship, and would have solved the peculiar problem and thorny issue of the relocation of the royal household without the relocation of the royal dead."[22] The marble reliefs adorning the walls of the Northwest Palace at Kalḫu would thus appear to present an iconographic mortuary garden, within which the dead ancestors of the royal line are imaged as sacred trees.

This ancestral casting of the sacred tree not only complements biblical evidence for the use of mortuary gardens in ancient Judahite cults of kingship,[23] but it casts new light upon the frequent biblical association of trees with kingship[24]—and more specifically, the dynastic dynamic of this imagery. In Ezek 17:3–10, for example, the monarchs of the Davidic dynasty are portrayed as parts of a great tree, while in Isa 11:1, the endurance of the royal line is imaged in the regenerative terms of a fertile tree: "A shoot shall come out from the stump of Jesse, and a sprout shall grow out of his roots" (cf. Isa 6:13; 11:10). Similarly, the perpetuation of the Davidic dynasty also underscores the imaging and designating of a future king as "branch," "sprout," or "offshoot," as found in several prophetic texts.[25] A further dimension to this powerful imagery is expressed in biblical texts employing the language of tree-felling and deforestation to describe dynastic destruction.[26]

The prominence of tree imagery in biblical portrayals of kingship is thus striking, not least in its occurrence in dynastic contexts, in which

---

dead kings into their dynasties, and comparative evidence concerning inconsistencies in Egyptian king lists.

22. Richardson, "Garden of Ancestors," 148–49.

23. See n. 21, above. Note that some biblical texts present trees within a context of death, burial, and the underworld. Thus the bones of Saul and his sons are buried beneath a sacred tree (1 Sam 31:13; 1 Chr 10:12), as is Rebekah's wet-nurse Deborah (Gen 35:8). See further Stavrakopoulou, *Land of Our Fathers*, esp. 96–99.

24. These texts include Num 24:6–7, in which the king appears to be likened to god-given gardens and trees, and 1 Sam 22:6, in which Saul sits as king beneath a tree. In Judg 9:8–15, a collection of trees seek to anoint one of their number as king.

25. E.g., Isa 4:2; Jer 23:5; 33,15; Ezek 17:22–24; Zech 3:8; 6:12; cf. 4:3.

26. E.g., Isa 10:33–34; Ezek 31:12–13; cf. Isa 10:18–19; Amos 2:9.

the Davidic line is imaged as a fertile, sacred tree, its roots symbolizing the royal generations past, and its branches and shoots symbolizing the kings to come. This is therefore a "family" tree, standing at the center of the cosmos and, like the king himself, traversing the boundaries between the divine and earthly realms. While Kirsten Nielsen has argued with reference to the book of Isaiah that this imagery is essentially poetic and metaphorical,[27] it is likely that it derives in part from a religious, cultic context in which the sacred tree played a role in a cult of kingship.[28] And this renders the distancing of the royal figure in Eden from the trees in the garden so significant.

ROYAL REJECTION IN EDEN

It is widely accepted that the story of the expulsion from Eden in Genesis 2–3 is closely related to—if not dependent upon—the tradition employed in Ezek 28:1–19, in which the royal figure in Eden is repeatedly said to possess great wisdom (28:2–7, 12, 17).[29] In this text, the king is cast out of the garden and into the place of mortality—the underworld (28:8, 17)[30]—for his abuse of what is to be understood as a divine wisdom (28:1–3). The interrelation of his crime and punishment is paralleled in the Genesis version of the myth, in which the primal king disobeys the command not to eat from the Tree of the Knowledge of Good and Bad, representing divine wisdom (Gen 2:16–17), and as a result is expelled from the garden in order to be kept from the Tree of Life, representing immortality (Gen 3:22).[31] Eating from these trees casts the royal figure "as a god" (Gen 3:5), and it would seem that this is what motivates Yahweh

---

27. Nielsen, *There Is Hope for a Tree*.

28. The ancestral dimensions of this cult may be reflected more specifically in Judg 9:6, in which Abimelech, whose name, notably, means "My father/ancestor is king," is made a king in the presence of a sacred tree. This might offer a new interpretation of Jer 2:26–27, in which the prophet mocks those "who say to a tree, 'You are my father/ancestor,' and to a stone, 'You gave me birth.'" See further Stavrakopoulou, *Land of Our Fathers*, 115.

29. See particularly Callender, *Adam in Myth and History*; Noort, "Gan-Eden."

30. Reading *'erets* in v. 17 as 'underworld' (cf. 26:19–20).

31. The expression "knowledge of good and bad" likely refers to a proficiency in discerning between the beneficial and the detrimental, as discussed by Rainer Albertz in his article "Ihr werdet sein wie Gott." In some biblical texts, "knowledge of good and bad" is explicitly portrayed as a divine wisdom (e.g., 2 Sam 14:17; 1 Kgs 3:9; cf. Gen. 3:5).

to expel the royal figure from the garden, just as the king in Ezekiel 28 is expelled from the garden for rendering himself "a god" (Ezek 28:2, 6, 9). A further variation of this myth occurs in the book of Isaiah, in which a king is cast down from his exalted position in the heavenly realm— where he claimed divine status (Isa 14:13–14)—to take up his humbled position among the dead of the underworld (Isa 14:12–20).[32] In all three texts, the royal figure is cast out of the divine realm and set instead in a place manifesting mortality.[33] Each tradition, though exhibiting its own distinctive variations, represents the same mythic nexus.

Given their apparent absence in Ezekiel and Isaiah, it is often assumed that the sacred trees of the Adamic version of the myth are particular to the book of Genesis. Indeed, there are notable problems concerning the trees in this text: at the outset of the story, the Tree of Knowledge of Good and Bad is forbidden, while the Tree of Life appears to be hidden, for only Yahweh and the narrator know of its presence in the garden.[34] And yet the two trees are inextricably interwoven, sug- gesting that they are perhaps best understood as distinct functions of one sacred tree,[35] for at the end of the story, eating from the Tree of Knowledge of Good and Bad leads to the possibility that the man will go on to discover the Tree of Life, eat from it, and thereby live forever.

But in view of the close correlation of the sacred tree with biblical and ancient West Asian ideologies of kingship, the trees of Eden are not so easily dismissed as a detail specific to the Genesis portrayal of the expulsion myth. Rather, they are best understood as a feature integral to the widespread myth of kingship on which the biblical traditions of heavenly expulsion draw. And support for this may be found in another closely related text in Ezekiel, in which the sacred tree and the king are identified.

Ezekiel 31 comprises an extended oracle in which a king is imaged as the cosmic tree at the center of the world and in whose shadow all the

32. So too Wyatt, "Garden for the Living," citing Barker, *Older Testament*, 234–35. On Isa 14, see Shipp, *Dead Kings and Dirges*.

33. Cf. Barr, *Garden of Eden*; cf. Levenson, *Resurrection and the Restoration of Israel*, 82–107.

34. Mettinger, *Eden Narrative*, 21–22, 60–63.

35. As Wyatt ("Garden for the Living") comments: "The Garden of Eden boasted two trees . . . Since they actually fused in later tradition, we may wonder whether their duality was not always problematic, or whether they really constituted one tree under two modes."

nations of the earth live. It is located "in the garden of God" (31:8–9) and hailed as "the envy of all the trees in Eden" (31:18). Evoking the mythic pattern described in Isa 14, the cosmic tree in the garden of Eden is proud of its height, reaching into the clouds; consequently, Yahweh allows the tree to be felled by the king's enemies (31:10–14). It is cast out of the divine garden, carved up, and consigned to Sheol, where it is left— limbless, low, and abandoned (31:14–18).[36] Though the royal figures in Ezekiel 31 and Genesis 2–3 share the same crime and the same fate, in the former text the sacred tree is not distinguished from the king, but aligned with him—just as a royal ideology would claim. The separation of the motif of the sacred tree from the figure of the king in Gen 2–3 thus likely performs a specific ideological function in the recasting of this pervasive biblical mythic trope.

Though the royal figures of Ezekiel 28, 31 and Isaiah 14 have been subsequently cast in their Masoretic form as foreign kings (of Tyre, Assyria, and Babylonia, respectively), the primal king of Gen 2–3 is pointedly Davidic. This is made apparent in the imaging of the Jerusalem temple (and Zion itself) as the garden of God: Isa 60:13 alludes to the presence of cultic trees in the temple of Yahweh (cf. Ps 92:12–14);[37] according to 1 Kings 6–7, sacred tree motifs cover the temple's walls; cherubim on the temple doors guard access to the sacred courtyard and similarly protect the throne of Yahweh inside the temple, just as they guard the boundaries of Eden (Gen 3:24; Ezek 28:16). The sacred river running out of the heart of Zion (Ezek 47:1–12) is called the Gihon, and plays a vital role in kingship rituals (1 Kgs 1:33–34, 38–40; Ps 110:7; cf. Ps 36:9–10); it is also to be found flowing out of Eden, the garden of God (Gen 2:13).[38] The Jerusalem temple thus appears to have been imaged as a divine garden, in which the Davidic king held a privileged and exclusive position as Yahweh's gardener. The myth in Genesis 2–3 of a primal man, created to tend the divine garden, is not so much a myth about creation, but a Jerusalem temple myth about the creation of kingship, endorsing and promoting the dynastic rule of the Davidic kings.

---

36. The same motif is found in Daniel 4, and this cosmic tree too is felled, mutilated, and debased by divine decree. See further Coxon, "Great Tree."

37. Steck, "Jesaja 60:13."

38. See further Stager, "Jerusalem and the Garden of Eden."

But in 597 BCE, the defeat and capture of Jerusalem by the Neo-Babylonians cast into doubt the divine and socioreligious potency of the Davidic line, for the king and his elites were exiled, and the temple was subsequently destroyed. In mythic terms, this marked the collapse of cosmic order, for which the king—as the personification of the great cosmic tree and the cipher of wisdom—was held partly responsible. As is well known, biblical writers responded to this catastrophe in different ways. For some, the hope for the restoration of the Davidic monarchy and the reconstruction of the Jerusalem temple was very real. In Ezekiel 17, for example, the exiled king is imaged as the topmost shoot of a great tree that is carried away by an eagle, but replaced by a seed from the same soil, and planted in the homeland.

But other biblical texts reflect the belief that the Davidic line had come to an end because its kings had repeatedly abused their privileged position in the cosmos by disobeying Yahweh and squandering their divine wisdom (cf. Deut 29:8; 30:11–14).[39] This is the probable context of the Eden story in Genesis 2–3.[40] The author of this narrative was writing in the aftermath of the exile of the king and the destruction of the Jerusalem temple in the sixth century BCE. For him, the Davidic monarchy had failed; the dynasty was now ritually impotent.

Therefore, in composing his narrative about Eden, the Genesis writer drew on the royal myth that cast the primal king as Yahweh's gardener. He imaged the eradication of the royal dynasty as the expulsion of the primal king from the divine garden—and, like the writer of Ezekiel 28 and 31 and Isaiah 14, saw this expulsion as the direct result of the king's disobedience and his arrogant abuse of divine wisdom. In doing so, the Genesis writer passes judgment on the failed Davidic monarchy. He asserts in his Eden narrative that the divine garden is no longer the setting for Davidic kingship. The Genesis writer thus not only displaces the primal king from the divine (temple) garden by expelling him, but separates the primal king from the sacred tree—the very symbol that simultaneously marks his divine wisdom, his dynastic perpetuation, and his role as the guarantor of cosmic order. In the Genesis narrative, the symbol of the sacred tree thus becomes the exclusive asset of Yahweh, and is transformed into twin symbols of the divine monopoly on wisdom (the Tree of Knowledge of Good and Bad) and immortality (the

39. Cf. Wyatt, *Myths of Power*, 280–82.
40. See too Brett, *Genesis*.

Tree of Life). These divine qualities were once shared with kings, but in the eyes of the Genesis writer, they are eternally separated from kingship. Accordingly, the Tree of Knowledge of Good and Bad is forbidden, while the Tree of Life is hidden and guarded. The story of disobedience and expulsion from the garden is thus an ideological assertion about the restriction of divine attributes from the king; it is a story about preventing the king from becoming like a god. The sacred trees become boundary markers, distinguishing the heavenly realm from the human, earthly realm. Yahweh's gardener, the primal king, is debased and dispatched to this place of mortality and humanity—the place where cult and cultivation no longer intersect.

Bibliography

Albertz, Rainer. "'Ihr werdet sein wie Gott . . .': Gen 3:1–7 auf dem Hintergrund des alttestamentlichen und des sumerisch–babylonischen Menschenbildes." *Welt des Orients* 24 (1993) 89–111.

Bahrani, Zainab. *Rituals of War: The Body and Violence in Mesopotamia.* New York: Zone Books, 2008.

Barker, Margaret. *The Older Testament: The Survival of Themes from the Ancient Royal Cult in Sectarian Judaism and Early Christianity.* London: SPCK, 1987.

Barr, James. *The Garden of Eden and the Hope of Immortality.* London: SCM, 1992.

Brett, Mark G. *Decolonizing God: The Bible in the Tides of Empire.* Sheffield: Sheffield Phoenix, 2008.

Brett, Mark G. *Genesis: Procreation and the Politics of Identity.* London: Routledge, 2000.

Callender, Dexter E. *Adam in Myth and History: Ancient Israelite Perspectives on the Primal Human.* Winona Lake, IN: Eisenbrauns, 2000.

Charlesworth, James H. *The Good and Evil Serpent: How a Universal Symbol became Christianized.* New Haven: Yale University Press, 2010.

Coxon, Peter W. "The Great Tree of Daniel 4." In *A Word in Season: Essays in Honour of William McKane,* edited by James D. Martin and Philip R. Davies, 91–111. Sheffield: JSOT Press, 1986.

Davies, Philip R. "Urban Religion and Rural Religion." In *Religious Diversity in Ancient Israel and Judah,* edited by Francesca Stavrakopoulou and John Barton, 104–17. London: T. & T. Clark, 2010.

Dubuisson, Daniel. *The Western Construction of Religion: Myths, Knowledge, and Ideology.* Baltimore: Johns Hopkins University Press, 2003.

Kempinski, Christine. *L'arbre stylisé en Asie occidentiale au 2e millénaire avant J.-C.* Paris: Éditions Recherche sur les civilizations, 1982.

Lang, Bernard. *The Hebrew God: Portrait of an Ancient Deity.* New Haven: Yale University Press, 2002.

Levenson, Jon D. *Resurrection and the Restoration of Israel: The Ultimate Victory of the God of Life.* New Haven: Yale University Press, 2006.

Mettinger, Tryggve N. D. *The Eden Narrative: A Literary and Religio-Historical Study of Genesis 2–3.* Winona Lake, IN: Eisenbrauns, 2007.

Nielsen, Kirsten. *There Is Hope for a Tree: The Tree as Metaphor in Isaiah*. Sheffield: JSOT Press, 1989.

Noort, Ed. "Gan-Eden in the Context of the Mythology of the Hebrew Bible." In *Paradise Reinterpreted: Representations of Biblical Paradise in Judaism and Christianity*, edited by Gerard P. Luttikhuizen, 21–36. Leiden: Brill, 1999.

Oppenheim, A. Leo. "On Royal Gardens in Mesopotamia." *Journal of Near Eastern Studies* 24 (1965) 328–33.

Patton, Laurie L., and Wendy Doniger, editors. *Myth and Method*. Charlottesville: University of Virginia Press, 1996.

Porter, Barbara Nevling. *Trees, Kings, and Politics: Studies in Assyrian Iconography*. Göttingen: Vandenhoeck & Ruprecht, 2003.

Richardson, Seth F. C. "An Assyrian Garden of Ancestors: Room I, Northwest Palace, Kalhu." *State Archives of Assyria Bulletin* 13 (1999–2001) 145–216.

Saler, Benson. *Conceptualizing Religion: Immanent Anthropologists, Transcendent Natives, and Unbounded Categories*. Leiden: Brill, 1993.

Shipp, R. Mark. *Of Dead Kings and Dirges: Myth and Meaning in Isaiah 14:4b–21*. Leiden: Brill, 2002.

Smith, Mark S. *God in Translation: Deities in Cross-Cultural Discourse in the Biblical World*. Tübingen: Mohr/Siebeck, 2008.

———. *The Origins of Biblical Monotheism: Israel's Polytheistic Background and the Ugaritic Texts*. Oxford: Oxford University Press, 2001.

Stager, Lawrence E. "Jerusalem and the Garden of Eden." *Eretz Israel* 26 (1999) 183–94.

Stavrakopoulou, Francesca. "Exploring the Garden of Uzza: Death, Burial, and Ideologies of Kingship." *Biblica* 87 (2006) 1–21.

———. *Land of Our Fathers: The Roles of Ancestor Veneration in Biblical Land Claims*. New York: T. & T. Clark, 2010.

Steck, Odil Hannes. "Jesaja 60:13—Bauholz oder Tempelgarten." *Biblische Notizen* 30 (1985) 29–34.

Stordalen, Terje. *Echoes of Eden: Genesis 2–3 and Symbolism of the Eden Garden in Biblical Hebrew Literature*. Leuven: Peeters, 2000.

Widengren, Geo. *The King and the Tree of Life in Ancient Near Eastern Religion*. Uppsala: A.-B. Lundequists, 1951.

Wiseman, Donald J. "Mesopotamian Gardens." *Anatolian Studies* 33 (1983) 137–44.

Wyatt, Nicolas. "Eve." In *Dictionary of Deities and Demons in the Bible*, edited by Karel van der Toorn, Bob Becking, and Pieter Willem van der Horst, 316–17. 2nd ed. Leiden: Brill, 1999.

———. "A Garden for the Living—Cultic and Ideological Aspects of Paradise." Forthcoming.

———. *Myths of Power: A Study of Royal Ideology in Ugaritic and Biblical Tradition*. Münster: Ugarit-Verlag, 1996.

———. "Royal Religion in Ancient Judah." In *Religious Diversity in Ancient Israel and Judah*, edited by Francesca Stavrakopoulou and John Barton, 61–81. London: T. & T. Clark, 2010.

———. "The Significance of the Burning Bush." *Vetus Testamentum* 36 (1986) 361–65.

———. "Word of Tree and Whisper of Stone: El's Oracle to King Keret (Kirta), and the Problem of the Mechanics of Its Utterance." *Vetus Testamentum* 57 (2007) 483–510.

5

Nonhuman Flourishing?

The Liberation of Creation and an Ecological Reading of Paul

David G. Horrell

In the time during which Tim Gorringe and I have been colleagues at Exeter, since Tim's arrival in 1998, one issue has risen inexo-
rably up the agenda in academic, political, and ethical discussion: the
environment. While the modern environmental movement has voiced
its concerns about the increasing impact of human activity upon the
planet since the 1960s, with Greenpeace and Friends of the Earth both
formed in 1971, it is only relatively recently that this issue has come to
be acknowledged as one of the most urgent and important matters of
global political and public concern. Climate change is of course the most
prominent environmental impact generating this level of concern, but
there are a host of other issues too, from deforestation and soil erosion to
loss of species and water pollution, and many others with both local and
global ramifications. Despite a certain amount of recent skepticism—and
one must suspect the influence of vested and powerful interests reluctant
to see any restriction on their wealth-creating activities[1]—the scientific
evidence for anthropogenic global warming seems robust. And there is

---

1. Cf. Gorringe, *Built Environment*, 231, with n. 44. See further Rowell, *Green
Backlash*, 140–50.

little room for doubt that a vast and expanding human population, using powerful technologies to achieve ever greater levels of production to meet human needs and wants, in an economic system that requires continual expansion, is demonstrably exerting destructive pressure on a finite planet.[2]

My own realization of the importance of this challenge, and of the corresponding need to live and to think differently, came, I confess, fairly late in the day, though it has occupied my attention to a considerable extent in recent years, through my work in a collaborative research project at Exeter on "Uses of the Bible in Environmental Ethics."[3] I mention this here because I am grateful for the opportunity not only to honor Tim's internationally important scholarly achievements but also to acknowledge publicly his influence on my own (all too limited) ecological awareness and commitments. And this influence has been exerted not through a holier-than-thou attitude—though Tim does not shrink from raising sharp questions about the frequency with which we fly to academic conferences, or encourage international students to fly to Exeter—but through the cheerful and resilient living of a life with integrity. His is a life that ties academic theological reflection seamlessly together with parish preaching and participation in local groups and communities, laboring to produce fruit, vegetables, honey, eggs, and so on, cycling to work, and a whole host of other things that embody a commitment to living sustainably and frugally, as well as joyfully and hospitably, in a locally focused way that is equally concerned for, and open to, the whole world.

AN ECOLOGICAL REFORMATION AND THE QUESTION OF NONHUMAN FLOURISHING

The environmental challenge is perhaps most quickly and easily associated with "ethics," and may thus too swiftly be reduced to a demand for certain actions: recycling, switching off lights, and so on. There is a

2. This very compact summary of the causes of environmental degradation draws on Martin-Schramm and Stivers, *Christian Environmental Ethics*, 10–23. See also the recent overview in Deane-Drummond, *Eco-Theology*, 1–11.

3. The project was funded by the Arts and Humanities Research Council of the UK. The major publications from the project are: Horrell, *Bible and the Environment*; Horrell, Hunt, and Southgate, *Greening Paul*; and Horrell, Hunt, Southgate, and Stavrakopoulou, eds., *Ecological Hermeneutics*.

danger that the focus thus becomes too individualized, too trivial, and fails to address the wider structural and macroeconomic issues. Ernst Conradie is surely right when he insists that the challenge must be taken much more broadly: "Ecological theology should not be reduced to environmental ethics as a sub-discipline of Christian ethics . . . There is also no need to add environmental concerns to an already over-crowded agenda of local churches and ecumenical bodies. Instead, the entire life and praxis of the church should include an ecological dimension and vision."[4] Indeed, Conradie argues that the task should entail, in words from a programmatic essay by James Nash, "an ecological reformation of Christianity" that is doctrinally as well as ethically comprehensive.[5]

Such a claim immediately raises questions about how radical such a reformation might be, and how far, for example, it might challenge the deeply entrenched anthropocentrism of the Christian tradition, with its sense of human uniqueness deriving from the declaration that humans (alone) are made in the image of God (Gen 1:26–27).[6] Some Christian environmental literature retains a strongly anthropocentric focus, stressing the need to confront issues like global warming because of its impact on the poorest and most vulnerable populations, who have done least to create the problems whose consequences they suffer.[7] Indeed, it is surely the case that the environmental challenge cannot properly be addressed without at the same time addressing issues of poverty and inequality, as Tim Gorringe has consistently made clear.[8] Without addressing the huge imbalance in the ecological impact of rich and poor countries, as well as the pressures on the poor to meet their own basic needs, the pressures on developing countries to exploit their natural resources, and the pressures exerted by global markets and transnational companies, one cannot expect to make headway on key aspects of environmental concern.

---

4. Conradie, *Ecological Christian Anthropology*, 1–2. Cf. Gorringe's insistence, "[l]earning from Barth . . . that for the theologian ethics and dogmatics cannot be separated" (Gorringe, *Built Environment*, 1).

5. Conradie, *Ecological Christian Anthropology*, 1. Cf. Nash, "Ecological Reformation."

6. Cf. Conradie's extended efforts to grapple with precisely this issue, in the context of elaborating an ecological Christian anthropology: Conradie, *Ecological Christian Anthropology*, 79–182.

7. E.g., Clifford, *All Creation Groaning*.

8. See, e.g., Gorringe, *Fair Shares*; Gorringe, *Built Environment*, 222–40; Gorringe, *Harvest*.

As such, issues concerning *human* flourishing remain at the center of the picture. Even in ecotheology and environmental ethics where this is not explicitly the case, one may suggest that this concern is inherently prominent. After all, it is clear that global warming, or other forms of anthropogenic effect, will not destroy the earth, though they will make it a significantly more challenging home for its human inhabitants.[9] Nevertheless, plenty of other species and ecosystems have been and will be affected, even extinguished, because of human action, so it is at least possible to cast our environmental concern in ways that express a sense of the *intrinsic* worth of other creatures and thereby embody a concern for *nonhuman* flourishing, too.

Without in any way minimizing the human and social justice concerns, I would want to argue for an ecological theology that does place intrinsic moral value on what we might broadly call the nonhuman creation, for its own sake. This can of course too easily become another manifestation of the luxury that is possible for wealthy (urban) Westerners, who can afford to care about nature for nature's sake and for whom the countryside is more a place of leisure and recreation than one of hard labor and fragile existence.[10] Moreover, any placing of ethical value on nonhuman creatures immediately raises difficult questions about how the relative (and sometimes competing) demands of humans and nonhumans might be weighed. Yet, such difficulties notwithstanding, there can I think be a less dubious form of ecotheological ethic, which finds grounds for a generous other-regard on the part of humans for other creatures, who may be regarded as kin in the earth community of which we are all part.

Famously expressed by Francis of Assisi, in his *Canticle of the Creatures*, this notion of an all-encompassing kinship may in a sense represent one of the most crucial contributions of an ecologically reformed theology that is both theologically and scientifically cogent. The urgent theological task may be to question the long-established emphasis on the uniqueness of humanity, which tends to undergird notions of our distinctness, our separation even, from "nature," and to

---

9. For an overview of the science of global warming, and an outline of the likely impacts of climate change, see Maslin, *Global Warming*, 39–55. For a perspective that stresses the threat to human existence, and also to other species and ecosystems, see Lovelock, *Revenge of Gaia*.

10. Cf. the comments in Gorringe, "Keeping the Commandments," 285–86.

rediscover and emphasize our embeddedness in what Jürgen Moltmann and Richard Bauckham call "the community of creation."[11] This is both theologically and, *mutatis mutandis*, scientifically cogent: if ecological science has taught us anything, it is that we are enmeshed in complex networks of dependence in which human flourishing is bound up with the flourishing and functioning of countless other creatures, from bees and earthworms to algae and oak trees.[12] Indeed, in describing reasons for our ecological crisis, Nash poetically and astutely refers to our "failure to respond benevolently and justly to the theological and biological fact of human kinship with all other creatures, from strawberries to dinosaurs." "This failure," he continues, "is especially evident in the increasing number of species becoming extinct, largely from economic overdevelopment."[13]

This notion of mutual interconnectedness is profoundly embedded in the assumptions of much of the Hebrew Bible: in the Prophets, in Leviticus, and elsewhere. For these ancient writers, there was an intrinsic connection between humanity, God, and "the land" (or, put in more modern terms, the whole ecosystem of which the ancient Israelites were a part). Human sin and violation of the covenant leads to degradation of the land, the manifestations of which are seen as expressions of the land mourning (cf. Lev 18:24–28; Isa 24:1–20; 33:9; Jer 4:28; 12:4, 11; 23:10; Hos 4:3; Joel 1:2–20; Amos 1:2).[14] Conversely, divine blessing and human obedience bring a flourishing and abundance from the land that are an essential basis for human flourishing (e.g., Lev 25:18–19; Isa 41:17–19; 43:19–20; Joel 2:21–32). There is much ecotheological potential in such a vision of holistic interconnectedness.[15] Indeed, more generally, there are good reasons why the Hebrew Bible has loomed larger than the New Testament in Christian ecological engagement with the Bible: with its focus on the patterns of conduct necessary for righteous living in the land, the Hebrew Bible is much concerned with what we might call the

11. Moltmann, *God in Creation*, xi, 5, and passim; Bauckham, *Bible and Ecology*, 64–102 and passim.

12. Cf. Gorringe, *Harvest*, 8–19.

13. Nash, "Ecological Reformation," 6.

14. See further Hayes, "*The Earth Mourns*"; Braaten, "Earth Community."

15. See further, e.g., Morgan, "Transgressing"; Horrell, *Bible and the Environment*, esp. 130–32; Bauckham, *Bible and Ecology*, esp. 64–102.

patterns of action and relationship necessary for sustainability and this-worldly flourishing.[16]

Nevertheless, if there is going to be an "ecological reformation of Christianity," it will have to include a fresh engagement with the New Testament and with the central figure of Jesus Christ. This means an engagement especially with the Gospels and the Pauline Letters, which together dominate the New Testament. Paul in particular presents a challenge. Positively, Paul's letters record the earliest theological reflection on the meaning of the Christ-event, one that decisively shapes all subsequent doctrinal discussion on topics such as Christology, eschatology, ecclesiology, and ethics. It is a crucial task for any ecological Christian theology to show how the Pauline tradition can be creatively and generatively engaged. But more negatively, that tradition would seem to offer scant resources for ecological theology and ethics: Paul does not share the Prophets' need to address the ethics of living in the land of Israel. His eschatological vision is centered upon a contrast between "the present evil age" and the already-inbreaking age to come, between life "in Adam," under the powers of sin and death, and life "in Christ," in the power of the Spirit. Moreover, Paul's main focus is on the salvation of human beings, traditionally interpreted as entailing a process of "justification by faith" in which the guilty sinner who comes to have faith is reckoned as righteous because of the atoning death of Christ. All this would seem to place the focus on the rescue of human beings *from* the material world, and on their *spiritual* transformation; certainly, there is a good deal in the Christian tradition that has taken Pauline theology in this direction.

AN ECOLOGICAL READING OF PAUL

Despite—or perhaps because of—the paucity of apparently eco-friendly material in Paul, there are a few texts in the Pauline corpus that are frequently appealed to in ecotheological discussion.[17] The most prominent of these is Rom 8:19–23, which is among the most frequently cited biblical texts in Christian literature on the environment. This is for good reason, since this text provides both a poignant expression of the

16. Cf. the engagement with mostly Old Testament texts in Gorringe, "Keeping the Commandments."

17. In the following discussion I draw broadly on material presented in more detail in Horrell, "New Perspective?" and Horrell, Hunt, and Southgate, *Greening Paul.*

negative situation ("creation groans") and a positive insistence that the whole creation is bound up in the process of salvation, sharing hope and expectation for a time of future liberation.[18] It is important to note that this is a text in which human beings—specifically, the children of God (that is, Christians, in Paul's view)—remain at the center of the story of salvation. It is the revealing of these "children" (*hoi huioi tou theou*) that the creation strains to see (v. 19), and their freedom it expects to share (v. 21). This certainly implies that human beings have a central role in the process by which God is bringing about the liberation of the whole creation, and, as such, implies something about their ethical responsibilities; but it does not necessarily imply that humans are of sole or unique value in the redeemed creation.[19] Recalling our observations about the vision of the interconnectedness of God, humans, and land in the Hebrew Bible, it is significant to note how this notion also appears here. With his characteristic use of the prefix *sun* ("with"), Paul depicts the whole creation as "co-groaning" and "co-suffering" (*sustenazei kai sunō dinei*)—not "among itself," as many commentators conclude, but rather as joined in this process with humans (*hēmeis . . . stenazomen*) and with the Spirit (vv. 22–23, 26).[20] Paul's main concern, of course, as the rest of the chapter makes clear, is to encourage and reassure the hard-pressed Christians at Rome that their hope is secure, but his placing of their suffering and hope within the context of the suffering and hope of the whole creation offers a fruitful vision of flourishing—expressed in theological terms as "freedom" and "glory" (v. 21)—in which both human and nonhuman are inextricably bound up.

The other Pauline text (though it may not be authentically Paul's) frequently cited in ecotheological discussion is Col 1:15–20, a Christ-hymn in which the all-encompassing scope of Christ's work in both creation and reconciliation is depicted.[21] Using language and imagery

18. For detailed discussion of this text and its ecotheological interpretation, see Hunt, Horrell, and Southgate, "Environmental Mantra?"; Horrell, Hunt, and Southgate, *Greening Paul*, 63–85.

19. An argument made by David Clough, who accepts a kind of instrumental anthropocentrism here, but rejects the idea that any "teleological anthropocentrism" is thus implied. See Clough, *On Animals*.

20. For the exegetical arguments in favour of this reading, see Horrell, Hunt, and Southgate, *Greening Paul*, 78–79.

21. For detailed discussion of this text and its ecotheological interpretation, see Horrell, Hunt, and Southgate, *Greening Paul*, 87–115.

different from that of Rom 8, and influenced by somewhat different philosophical and religious traditions, Col 1 stresses that "all things" (*ta panta*) were created in (*en*) and through (*dia*) Christ, and find their *telos* in him (*eis auton*, v. 16). Drawing on Stoic language and imagery, the hymn depicts all things as "holding together" in Christ (*en autō sunestēken*, v. 17). And the process of salvation is here depicted as one of reconciliation, which once again encompasses *ta panta* (v. 20). All this conveys what is aptly called a cosmic Christology, which, despite the ecclesiological editing of the hymn (v. 18), may reflect the Platonic and Stoic notion of the universe as a living organism, a body, here specifically the body of Christ.[22]

As long ago as 1961, in an ecumenical address to the World Council of Churches, Joseph Sittler argued for the ecological significance of the cosmic Christology of Col 1: "the sweep of God's restorative action in Christ is no smaller than the six-times repeated *ta panta* . . . and all things are permeable to his cosmic redemption because all things subsist in him."[23] Sittler argued that it was time to explore the untapped potential in this cosmic Christology, a potential that could lead from doctrine to ethical engagement, and described care of the earth as a "christological obedience": "The way forward is from Christology expanded to its cosmic dimensions, made passionate by the pathos of this threatened earth, and made ethical by the love and the wrath of God."[24]

To highlight these two texts, however, is only to identify two short passages in the Pauline Letters, both of which have already been frequently cited in ecotheological discussion. If we are to contribute to the comprehensive ecological reformation of Christianity for which Nash and Conradie call, we must ask whether there is scope for a broader ecological rereading of Paul, or whether a few proof texts is as much as we can manage.

Without losing sight of the significance of these important passages, and without denying the diversity and ambivalence of the Pauline Letters, there is nonetheless the potential, I would argue, for an ecological reconfiguration of Pauline theology that is both exegetically cogent and

22. See further van Kooten, *Cosmic Christology*, 110–46, 204–13; Balabanski, "Critiquing Anthropocentric Cosmology"; Balabanski, "Hellenistic Cosmology."

23. Sittler, "Called to Unity," 39. The phrase *ta panta* appears as such four times in Col 1:15–20, plus the plural forms *pro pantōn* and *en pasin*.

24. Sittler, "Called to Unity," 48.

ethically fruitful. We may begin by noting that the cosmic Christology of the Colossian hymn finds resonances elsewhere in the Pauline corpus, although in the undisputed letters it tends to be expressed in theocentric rather than Christocentric terms.[25] With respect to creation, 1 Cor 8:6 declares that "all things" come from God (*ex hou ta panta*) through Christ (*di' hou ta panta*), a Christian reinterpretation of the creation narrative (cf. John 1:1–3; Heb 1:2) that for Paul, like the writer(s) of Genesis 1, implies the essential goodness of all created things. This conviction evidently shapes Paul's rather convoluted instruction about eating food offered to idols (1 Cor 10:25–26; cf. 1 Tim 4:4). While the creedal confession of 1 Cor 8:6 does not express a cosmic teleology (*hēmeis eis auton*), unlike Col 1:16, the doxology of Rom 11:33–36 concludes with a declaration that locates both the origins and the telos of all things in God: "for from him and through him and to him are all things (*eis auton ta panta*)" (v. 36).

The vision of the incorporation of all things into Christ, as it is depicted in the Christocentric letters to the Colossians and the Ephesians (cf. Col 3:11; Eph 1:10), is also found in a more theocentric form in 1 Cor 15, where the culmination of the events leading up to "the end" (*to telos*, v. 24) is the subjection of Christ to God, "so that God may be all in all" (*panta en pasin*, v. 28).[26] This kind of panentheistic or panenchristic vision would seem to offer a significant resource to an ecological theology, as Leonardo Boff suggests in recommending a "Christian Pan-entheism" as part of the kind of spirituality that is needed for "a new ethical order" that "is not more anthropocentric but ecocentric, striving as it does to bring about the equilibrium of the entire cosmic community."[27]

From this perspective, Pauline soteriology is focused on the incorporation of all things into God/Christ. This vision of incorporation is central to the ways in which Paul depicts the two key Christian rituals of baptism and Lord's Supper. Baptism enacts the process by which many diverse peoples become one in Christ (1 Cor 12:12–13; Gal 3:27–28), while the Lord's Supper celebrates this social and soteriological

25. On this cosmic perspective in Pauline theology, see Gibbs, "Pauline Cosmic Christology."

26. There is no neat distinction, however, between the generally theocentric vision of the undisputed Paulines and the Christocentric vision of Colossians and Ephesians, as a comparison of 1 Cor 15:27 and Phil 3:21 makes clear.

27. See Boff, *Ecology and Liberation*, 50–51 (on Christian panentheism), and 137 (for the quotation above).

achievement: "we many are one body" (1 Cor 10:17), which is precisely why the divisions among the congregation at Corinth are to Paul such a scandal (1 Cor 11:17–34). While Paul's focus is clearly and indisputably on the incorporation of human beings, both Jews and Gentiles, into the ecclesial community that he describes as the body of Christ (1 Cor 12:12–27; cf. Rom 12.4–6), we have seen that there are grounds for setting this primary focus in the context of a wider vision, in which the body of Christ encompasses *ta panta*, created, sustained, and reconciled in him. To be sure, there is no explicit statement to this effect about the (cosmic) *body* of Christ itself—though it may have been expressed in an earlier version of the Colossian hymn, and may remain implicit in Col 1:17 (cf. 2:19). But given that the Pauline Letters speak not only of human beings but also of all things being "in Christ,"[28] then with or without the specific notion of the body of Christ, the conviction that the incorporation "in him" encompasses not just the church but the whole universe seems well grounded.

To place at the center of an ecological engagement with Pauline theology the motif of the incorporation of all things into Christ also implies that the most ecologically pertinent construal of Pauline soteriology will be one focused on the idea of participation in Christ, rather than justification by faith, with its more anthropocentric and judicial connotations. Correspondingly, it also seems that the language of reconciliation, rather than justification, is likely to be more fruitful for an ecological reading of Paul. Both motifs convey in their different ways the process by which the restoration of relationship to God takes place, and both can be juxtaposed by Paul in close parallel—implying, of course, that he found both to be appropriate ways to describe what this soteriological process entails (Rom 5:9–11). The juxtaposition in Rom 5 indicates that justification has to do with atonement, blood, and wrath, while reconciliation has to do with bringing enmity to an end. In 2 Cor 5:18–20, in a context shaped by Paul's desire to confirm his own recent reconciliation with the Corinthians, he also describes the saving act of God in terms of reconciliation: "in Christ God was reconciling the world (*kosmos*) to himself" (v. 19).[29] As we have already seen, the theme of

28. The frequent and distinctively Pauline use of such "in" language—in phrases such as "in Christ," "in the Lord," "in him," and so on, has long been noted, at least since Adolf Deissmann. See Deissmann, *Paul*, 140.

29. On the exegetical details of this verse, see Bieringer, "Die Versöhnung der Welt."

reconciliation then becomes a prominent motif with which to depict the salvation God has wrought in Christ, in both Colossians and Ephesians (Col 1:20, 22; Eph 2:16).

We can, then, make an exegetically cogent case that at the center of Pauline theology stands a vision of incorporation into Christ, a soteriological process accomplished (by God) through reconciliation. These theological and soteriological motifs already and intrinsically contain ethical implications: the imperative to work out in community the transcending of distinctions and enmity in Christ, the creation of a oneness that does not mean uniformity or sameness but allows diversity and difference to remain. If this "corporate solidarity" is thereby one of the central metamoral norms of Pauline ethics, the other such norm, I have argued elsewhere, is what we may term "other-regard," a "looking to the interests of others" that is fundamentally an imitation of the paradigmatic self-giving of Christ (cf. Rom 15:1–3; 1 Cor 10:24—11:1; 2 Cor 8:9; Phil 2:1–8).[30]

It is, of course, beyond dispute that for Paul the predominant focus for this corporate solidarity and other-regard is interhuman relationships in the various Christian communities to which he writes. To this extent, his theology and ethics remain anthropocentric, indeed ecclesiocentric. Nonetheless, as we have seen, the scope of reconciliation, of incorporation into Christ (or into God), is literally all encompassing (*ta panta*). So while Paul's focus, for obvious reasons, is ecclesial, the community that is incorporated into Christ is universal, encompassing nonhuman and human; and this means, crucially, that the other-regard that is owed to fellow members of the community is rightly extended not only beyond the church, but beyond the human species, too. In a final section, I explore briefly what all this might mean for a contemporary ecological appropriation of Pauline ethics.

PAULINE CONTRIBUTIONS TO AN ECOTHEOLOGICAL ETHIC

To read Paul from an ecological perspective is clearly to read him from a modern context that lies beyond the horizon of Paul's own assumptions and concerns. Such is the nature of biblical studies, however, even at its

---

For further comments on its ecological potential, see Horrell, "Ecojustice in the Bible?"

30. See Horrell, *Solidarity and Difference*.

most ostensibly historical, since the concerns and perspectives of the discipline are shaped by its contemporary location.[31] This calls for historically and exegetically disciplined research, in order to keep us from simply making the texts say what we want them to say, but it is also the key to an engagement between biblical studies and theological ethics that is both critical and fruitful. We must remain alert to the differences between Paul's priorities and worldview and those of the twenty-first century: even at the points where Paul seems most amenable to an ecological reading, it would be anachronistic to identify his concerns too closely with our own. When the Pauline Letters depict cosmic reconciliation, for example, their focus is on "principalities and powers" (Col 1:16; 2:15), not on polar bears and rainforests. Yet at the same time, such themes and motifs in Pauline theology are open to a creative and contemporary rereading in a new and challenging situation.

At the center of an ecologically reconfigured Pauline ethic I would place the two central norms of that ethic: corporate solidarity and other-regard. As we have seen, given the universal, cosmic scope of incorporation into Christ, the "community" to which this solidarity relates, and the others to whom regard is owed, encompasses all things. It is indeed "the community of creation." Thus, just as those humans who find themselves in positions of relative power and strength are called to self-giving for the sake of those humans who are weaker (cf. 2 Cor 8:9–14), so too humans may be challenged to a generous and kenotic other-regard for nonhuman creatures. It is common—and important!—to hear of the need for restraint and moderation on the part of the relatively rich, out of concern for the impact of environmental degradation on the human poor, an environmentalism driven fundamentally by concerns for social justice. But an ecological ethic inspired and informed by a Pauline vision of cosmic community would also call for humans to restrain their self-interest and acquisitive desires out of a generous regard for other creatures, all of whom in some sense constitute the weak—in terms of their limited ability, relative to humans, to affect and transform the conditions of their existence. In this vein, Christopher Southgate has called for an "ethical kenosis" as central to an ecological ethic, a self-emptying with regard to our aspirations, appetites, and acquisitiveness.[32] Such a

---

31. For a demonstration of this point in relation to the so-called new perspective on Paul, see Horrell, "New Perspective?" 4–7.

32. Southgate, *Groaning of Creation*, 101–3; cf. Horrell, Hunt, and Southgate,

call rapidly raises difficult questions about the extent to which humans should be expected to suffer deprivation for the sake of other species, or about the evaluation of competing demands (e.g., for living space). It does not offer any easy or obvious solutions to concrete ethical dilemmas. But the call for humans to demonstrate an other-regard that goes beyond the human species seems to me one of the most significant and specifically Pauline contributions to a contemporary ecological ethic.

In considering the shape that such an other-regard might take, Paul's instructions to the Corinthians are significant: appealing to the example of Christ, Paul urges the Corinthians to generous giving to his collection for the poor in Jerusalem.[33] But he also insists that his aim is not that they end up suffering deprivation themselves. It is rather a matter of equality, a redistribution that achieves an equity expressed in the citation from Exod 16:18: "The one who had much did not have too much, and the one who had little did not have too little" (2 Cor 8:15; NRSV). The other prominent motif that expresses the pattern of relationships among the all-inclusive community in Christ is of course reconciliation. Once again, this motif is less than straightforward to apply to the realm of ecology. The vision of universal reconciliation is inspiring, just as is the oft-cited Isaianic vision of a peaceable, reconciled future in which lions and oxen, sheep and wolves lie contentedly together, munching straw (Isa 11:6–9). But while one can fairly easily move from the prophets' vision of the nations at peace to a contemporary call for peacemaking and disarmament (cf. Isa 2:2–4; Mic 4:1–3), it is less obvious to see what "peace" might mean in the animal world, or in human interaction with other animals. For some, the most pertinent challenge is to become vegetarian, thus anticipating the peaceable kingdom by renouncing the violence of humans against animals.[34] But such a renouncing of violence clearly cannot be expected of lions and wolves: the removal of enmity cannot mean an end to predation. Nor is a commitment to vegetarianism necessarily the best way to envisage patterns of ecologically sustainable agriculture that embody generous and compassionate forms of human-nonhuman relationship.[35] Perhaps

---

Greening Paul, 195–200.

33. On the collection and its significance, see Horrell, *Solidarity and Difference*, 231–41.

34. See, e.g., Linzey, *Animal Theology*; Webb, *Good Eating*.

35. See Pollan, *Omnivore's Dilemma*, 304–33; Southgate, "Protological and

we might make better sense of the vision of universal reconciliation in terms of a peaceable coexistence that allows (ecologically) balanced and nonoppressive relationships—what in modern terms could be labeled "sustainable" communities. This vision of reconciliation would be one that is concerned to enable "space," in all senses of the word, for the diverse community of countless other creatures to flourish. Once again, though, it is immediately clear that this provides no easy resolution to specific eco-ethical dilemmas: How far should humans interfere in order to ensure the sustainability of fragile and complex ecosystems? How can we manage the brute pressures exerted by a massive and still expanding human population? To what extent should we intervene to prevent species extinction?[36]

Unsurprisingly, then, a Pauline ecological ethic does not immediately or easily provide answers to specific challenges and ethical dilemmas. Yet it does provide a theological and ethical framework that offers resources for reshaping our sense of human relationship with, and responsibility towards, the nonhuman creation. From a Pauline perspective, the "freedom" or liberation of the Christian can never signify an individual's freedom to meet her own needs, or to act without discipline or restraint. And this applies equally to the human species as a whole. The liberation of humans cannot be separated from the liberation of creation, which is to say, in other words, that human and nonhuman flourishing are inextricably bound up. As we have already noted, this is one of the most obvious lessons of ecological science, but it also finds theological resonance in the Pauline vision of mutual interconnectedness and responsibility within the cosmic body of Christ. One of the problems with the post-Enlightenment, Baconian vision of science is not only its hubristic vision of the human vocation but also its sense that nature is there—can be understood, subdued, manipulated—to meet human needs.[37] This is also one of the problems with a certain kind of evangelical response to environmentalism, one that not only questions

---

Eschatological Vegetarianism"; Gorringe, *Harvest*, 64–66.

36. Southgate argues that reducing both anthropogenic and natural extinctions should be part of the eschatological human calling, and reflects on some of the ways in which this might conceivably be done in an era of rapid climate change. See Southgate, *Groaning*, 124–32; Southgate, "New Days of Noah?"

37. On the development of this particular interpretation of human "dominion" (Gen 1:26–28) in the Renaissance and Enlightenment, see Bauckham, *God and the Crisis*, 128–77; Harrison, "Subduing the Earth."

the scientific evidence for environmental degradation but also displays an optimism that, in its transformation from "wilderness" to "garden," nature will continue to supply ample resources to meet the needs of ongoing human expansion.[38] What is missing from such perspectives is the Pauline theme of other-regarding humility, which calls for a generous and costly regard on the part of humans for all other creatures, all part of *ta panta* encompassed and incorporated into Christ. Just as a host of other creatures by their unconscious and involuntary giving make our living possible, so humans are called to a gracious concern for the welfare of these others, on whose sustaining provision we so demonstrably depend. Creation, Paul declares, strains to glimpse the redeemed children of God, in the hope that—put in modern terms—their "altered lifestyle and revised ethics [will] begin to restore the ecological system that had been thrown out of balance by wrongdoing . . . and sin."[39] It remains to be seen whether that hope will prove to have been in vain.

Bibliography

Balabanski, Vicky. "Critiquing Anthropocentric Cosmology: Retrieving a Stoic 'Permeation Cosmology' in Colossians 1:15–20." In *Exploring Ecological Hermeneutics*, edited by Norman C. Habel and Peter Trudinger, 151–59. SBL Symposium Series 46. Atlanta: SBL, 2008.

———. "Hellenistic Cosmology and the Letter to the Colossians: Towards an Ecological Hermeneutic." In *Ecological Hermeneutics*, edited by David G. Horrel, Cherryl Hunt, Christopher Southgate, and Francesca Stavrakopoulou, 94–107. London: T. & T. Clark, 2010.

Bauckham, Richard J. *Bible and Ecology: Rediscovering the Community of Creation*. London: DLT, 2010.

———. *God and the Crisis of Freedom: Biblical and Contemporary Perspectives*. Louisville: Westminster John Knox, 2002.

Beisner, E. Calvin. *Where Garden Meets Wilderness: Evangelical Entry into the Environmental Debate*. Grand Rapids: Acton Institute for the Study of Religion and Liberty, 1997.

Bieringer, Reimund. "2 Kor 5,19a und die Versöhnung der Welt." *Ephemerides Theologicae Lovanienses* 63 (1987) 295–326.

Boff, Leonardo. *Ecology and Liberation: A New Paradigm*. Maryknoll, NY: Orbis Books, 1995.

Braaten, Laurie J. "Earth Community in Joel 1–2: A Call to Identify with the Rest of Creation." *Horizons in Biblical Theology* 28 (2006) 113–29.

38. Beisner, *Garden Meets Wilderness*. A fine survey of the competing perspectives within contemporary US evangelicalism and fundamentalism is provided by Maier, "Green Millennialism."

39. Jewett, "Corruption and Redemption," 35.

Clifford, Paula. *"All Creation Groaning": A Theological Approach to Climate Change and Development*. London: Christian Aid, 2007.

Clough, David. *On Animals: Theology*. London: T. & T. Clark, forthcoming.

Conradie, Ernst M. *An Ecological Christian Anthropology: At Home On Earth?* Aldershot: Ashgate, 2005.

Deane-Drummond, Celia. *Eco-Theology*. London: DLT, 2008.

Deissmann, Adolf. *Paul: A Study in Social and Religious History*. Translated by William E. Wilson. London: Hodder & Stoughton, 1926.

Gibbs, John G. "Pauline Cosmic Christology and Ecological Crisis." *Journal of Biblical Literature* 90 (1971) 466–79.

Gorringe, Timothy J. *Fair Shares: Ethics and the Global Economy*. London: Thames & Hudson, 1999.

———. *Harvest: Food, Farming and the Churches*. London: SPCK, 2006.

———. "Keeping the Commandments: The Meaning of Sustainable Countryside." In *Ecological Hermeneutics*, edited by David Horrel, Cherryl Hunt, Christopher Southgate, and Francesca Stavrakopoulou, 283–94. London: T. & T. Clark, 2010.

———. *A Theology of the Built Environment: Justice, Empowerment, Redemption*. Cambridge: Cambridge University Press, 2002.

Harrison, Peter. "Subduing the Earth: Genesis 1, Early Modern Science, and the Exploitation of Nature." *Journal of Religion* 79 (1999) 86–109.

Hayes, Katherine M. *"The Earth Mourns": Prophetic Metaphor and Oral Aesthetic*. SBL Academia Biblica 8. Atlanta: SBL, 2002.

Horrell, David G. *The Bible and the Environment: Towards a Critical Ecological Biblical Theology*. Biblical Challenges in the Contemporary World. London: Equinox, 2010.

———. "Ecojustice in the Bible? Pauline Contributions to an Ecological Theology." In *Bible and Justice: Ancient Texts, Modern Challenges*, edited by Matthew J. M. Coomber, 158–77. London: Equinox, 2011.

———. "A New Perspective on Paul? Rereading Paul in a Time of Ecological Crisis." *Journal for the Study of the New Testament* 33 (2010) 3–30.

———. *Solidarity and Difference: A Contemporary Reading of Paul's Ethics*. London: T. & T. Clark, 2005.

Horrell, David G., Cherryl Hunt, and Christopher Southgate, editors. *Greening Paul: Rereading the Apostle in a Time of Ecological Crisis*. Waco: Baylor University Press, 2010.

Horrell, David G., Cherryl Hunt, Christopher Southgate, and Francesca Stavrakopoulou, editors. *Ecological Hermeneutics: Biblical, Historical and Theological Perspectives*. London: T. & T. Clark, 2010.

Hunt, Cherryl, David G. Horrell, and Christopher Southgate. "An Environmental Mantra? Ecological Interest in Romans 8.19–23 and a Modest Proposal for its Narrative Interpretation." *Journal of Theological Studies* 59 (2008) 546–79.

Jewett, Robert. "The Corruption and Redemption of Creation: Reading Rom 8:18–23 within the Imperial Context." In *Paul and the Roman Imperial Order*, edited by Richard A. Horsley, 25–46. Harrisburg, PA: Trinity, 2004.

Kooten, George H. van. *Cosmic Christology in Paul and the Pauline School: Colossians and Ephesians in the Context of Graeco-Roman Cosmology, with a New Synopsis of the Greek Texts*. WUNT 2.171. Tübingen: Mohr/Siebeck, 2003.

Linzey, Andrew. *Animal Theology*. London: SCM, 1994.

Lovelock, James. *The Revenge of Gaia: Earth's Climate Crisis and the Fate of Humanity.* New York: Basic, 2006.

Maier, Harry O. "Green Millennialism: American Evangelicals, Environmentalism, and the Book of Revelation." In *Ecological Hermeneutics*, edited by David G. Horrell, Cherryl Hunt, Christopher Southgate, and Francesca Stavrakopoulou, 246–65. London: T. & T. Clark, 2010.

Martin-Schramm, James B., and Robert L. Stivers. *Christian Environmental Ethics: A Case Study Approach.* Maryknoll, NY: Orbis, 2003.

Maslin, Mark. *Global Warming.* Rev. ed. WorldLife Library. Grantown-on-Spey: Colin Baxter Photography, 2007.

Moltmann, Jürgen. *God in Creation: An Ecological Doctrine of Creation.* London: SCM, 1985.

Morgan, Jonathan. "Transgressing, Puking, Covenanting: The Character of Land in Leviticus." *Theology* 112 (2009) 172–80.

Nash, James A. "Toward the Ecological Reformation of Christianity." *Interpretation* 50 (1996) 5–15.

Pollan, Michael. *The Omnivore's Dilemma.* London: Bloomsbury, 2006.

Rowell, Andrew. *Green Backlash: Global Subversion of the Environmental Movement.* London: Routledge, 1996.

Sittler, Joseph. "Called to Unity." In *Evocations of Grace: The Writings of Joseph Sittler on Ecology, Theology, and Ethics*, edited by Steven Bouma-Prediger and Peter Bakken, 38–50. 1962. Reprint, Grand Rapids: Eerdmans, 2000.

Southgate, Christopher. *The Groaning of Creation: God, Evolution, and the Problem of Evil.* Louisville: Westminster John Knox, 2008.

———. "The New Days of Noah? Assisted Migration as an Ethical Imperative in an Era of Climate Change." In *Creaturely Theology*, edited by Celia Deane-Drummond and David Clough, 249–65. London: SCM, 2009.

———. "Protological and Eschatological Vegetarianism." In *Eating and Believing: Interdisciplinary Perspectives on Vegetarianism and Theology*, edited by Rachel Muers and David Grumett, 247–65. London: T. & T. Clark, 2008.

Webb, Stephen H. *Good Eating.* Grand Rapids: Brazos, 2001.

6

Reading Matthew's Gospel with Deaf Culture

LOUISE J. LAWRENCE

> [I]t is a non-deaf world which has created deafness as a
> subject of discourse.

Tim Gorringe has always had an eye for the real alternatives that have been submerged and ignored by mainstream views, and a feel for the practices of attentiveness that can allow those alternatives to resurface. Contextual biblical interpretation is one such practice: it seeks to redress the marginalization sustained by "dominant" readings by voicing "alternative" views—and in this essay, in honor of Tim, I want to explore one example of such redress, in relation to a long-overlooked marginal perspective: Deaf culture.[1]

Sally Sainsbury maintains that "the historical neglect of deaf people is as disgraceful as it is perplexing" and demands urgent remedy.[2] This

---

1. On language: "Deaf with capital D refers to culturally deaf people" (see Lewis, *Deaf Liberation Theology*, x). Hereafter I will capitalize Deaf to denote the cultural model of deafness, namely a community united by their use of sign language and social identity through Deaf clubs, etc. Where I cite other authors, however, I have retained their original capitalization.

2. Sainsbury, *Deaf Worlds*, vii.

71

essay constitutes one small response to her challenge. First, labels of "ability" and "disability" with regard to the Deaf will be exposed as social constructions promoted by the (dominant) hearing world. As a result, the Deaf will be defined, not through their sensory impairment but rather as a (sign-) language minority culture. In light of these insights, and utilizing perspectives from postcolonial theory, I will then approach Matthew's Gospel to see whether it is a hearing-dominated text that associates sense-impairment with stigma. Following this largely "resistant" reading, I will then move on to the more positive task of exploring aspects of Deaf culture, including emphasis on the significance of vision, sight, and light, the use of sign language and minority cultural status, the collective ethos of communities, and the use of storytelling to consider how, if at all, these Deaf cultural aspects could in fact be recovered in readings of the Gospel of Matthew.

DEFINING DEAF: "[SENSE-]ABILITY" NOT "DISABILITY"

Imagine the experience of a hearing man who accidentally falls into a valley populated by the congenitally deaf. He falsely believes that in a non-hearing world, the hearing man is king; however, he soon finds out that if a culture is specifically designed around deafness, then the hearing person is in effect disabled from social interaction within it. Inept and incompetent within his new context, the deaf valley-dwellers decide the only solution is to gouge out the hearing man's "diseased" ear canal so that he can fully participate within their society.[3]

Cultures that challenge dominant ideas of the "abled" and "disabled" make us aware of the social construction of our categories. Martha's Vineyard, an island situated off the coast of Cape Cod, Massachusetts, is frequently mentioned in discussions of deafness, given that there is an inordinately high instance of genetically inherited deafness within the community.[4] Hearing and non-hearing alike were socialized into a world where sign language was the norm for communication. As a result, the deaf were not excluded or underprivileged in that context at all. Indeed, often when anthropologists asked hearing members of the community to identify d/Deaf members, they could only name a couple,

3. This is a creative adaptation of H. G. Wells' short story "The Country of the Blind" (1904), but here made to reference d/Deaf experience. Wells is cited and discussed in McDermott and Varenne, "Culture as Disability."

4. McDermott and Varenne, "Culture as Disability."

despite knowing many more. This illustrates that for this community deafness was "so integral a part of life on the Vineyard that it attract[ed] neither attention nor moral evaluation."[5] Robert Johnson similarly describes the universal use of sign language (for hearing and deaf) in a Yucatec-Mayan village and reveals how the d/Deaf had full access to both the social and political life of the community in that context.[6]

What all these examples serve to show us is that "being able or unable to hear does not emerge as significant in itself; instead it takes on significance in the context of other sets of meaning to which . . . [one is] exposed."[7] In short, while in both Martha's Vineyard and the Yucatan-Mayan village it was "normal" to be deaf, these sorts of environments are very rare exceptions. For the most part, dominant hearing discourses constitute what is "normal" and deafness constitutes a deviation from that norm, a "dis-ability." Lennard Davis goes further in underlining the binary nature of labels of "normalcy" and "disability" when he states:

> Disability is not an object—a woman with a cane—but a social process that intimately involves everyone who has a body and lives in the world of the senses. Just as the conceptualisation of race, class and gender shapes the lives of those who are not black, poor or female, so the conception of disability regulates the bodies of those who are "normal." In fact, the very concept of normalcy by which most people (by definition) shape their existence is in fact tied inexorably to the concept of disability, or rather the concept of disability is a function of a concept of normalcy. Normalcy and disability are part of the same system.[8]

Often the hearing world seeks to "normalize" the deaf within a hearing framework through oralism (oral methods of education in which lip-reading is central, though this has been identified as a contributory factor in poor language acquisition among deaf children) or the insertion of cochlear implants. In Tony Booth's terms, "the purpose of normalization is seen not only as giving deaf and partially deaf young people access to the hearing world but also as *making them more acceptable to it*."[9]

5. Gregory and Hartley, *Constructing Deafness*, 5.
6. Johnson, "Sign Language."
7. Padden and Humphries, *Deaf in America*, 22.
8. Davis, *Enforcing Normalcy*, 2.
9. Booth, "Challenging Conceptions," 157, my emphasis.

In contrast to the medical model of disability that defines deafness as a biological hearing impairment, or the social-situation model that sees disability less as an essential categorization and instead views different environments as abling or dis-abling for individuals, the cultural model of Deafness (with a capital *D*) sees the Deaf community as an ethnic group, with their own cultural mores and language. J. G. Kyle and B. Woll's definition of the Deaf community in their study of sign language illustrates these traits: "It involves a shared language . . . it involves social interaction and politics . . . but all of these interrelate and interact with attitudes towards other Deaf people. The choice to communicate and share information with other people must be seen as a primary feature, and because of the language used by members of the community this communication will generally be restricted to other Deaf people."[10]

Harlan Lane, from a Deaf-advocacy perspective, believes that the Deaf community should be understood as an ethnic group, for then "they would have the protections offered to such groups" including the fostering of "linguistic minorities" and ensuring "that children and adults have adequate opportunities to learn the minority language." For, in Lane's opinion, "like all members of other ethnic minorities, Deaf people are generally not disturbed by their identity, despite the need to struggle for their rights. Culturally Deaf people have always thought and think today that being Deaf is a perfectly good way to be, as good as hearing, perhaps better."[11] Conceiving of the Deaf as a cultural minority, akin to an ethnic group, has also allowed interpreters to utilize insights from postcolonial theory to reflect on oppression suffered under the imperialistic hearing world. Hannah Lewis reveals that historical instances of the disempowerment of the Deaf (particularly in reference to their own language) are analogous to political colonization defined as "a process of physical subjugation, imprisonment of an alien language . . . and the regulation of education on behalf of colonial goals."[12] The "colonization" of the Deaf community by the hearing in educational, religious, and academic contexts in many ways parallels ethnic colonization, for "if an *ethnos* is defined as a culturally similar group sharing a common language, then the Deaf conceivably fit that category."[13] Davis has like-

10. Kyle and Woll, *Sign Language*, 5.
11. Lane, "Ethnicity."
12. Lewis, *Deaf Liberation Theology*, 32.
13. Davis, *Enforcing Normalcy*, 77.

wise drawn comparisons between racial stigmatization and Deaf stig-matization as "outsiders."[14] The accessibility (or rather inaccessibility) of texts in sign language has undoubtedly perpetuated this "outsider" status. With these thoughts in mind, we approach Matthew to see what definition of "normal" is operative within the Gospel and whether the Deaf are stigmatized as a result.

SENSE AND STIGMA: MATTHEW AS A HEARING-DOMINATED TEXT

For Erving Goffman, "stigma" is emblematic of how certain individuals are discredited and dis-identified from dominant maps of the "normal" held within societies. As such "stigma" involves "perception of a nega-tive attribute" and "devaluation of a person with such an attribute";[15] it is a concept manifested in social exchanges, rather than a static condi-tion dependent on "biomedical" factors. As Thomas Reynolds explains, "stigma is not the property of an individual body but rather the result of complex social projections that represent bodies, lumping them into general stereotypes insofar as they display undesired qualities."[16]

Reading strategies of resistance that expose "stigmatization" op-erative within texts are suspicious of the oppressive power structures sustained by particular authors. The central concern here is to gauge whether Matthew's conception of the "normal" is audio-centric and as a result whether d/Deaf experience is stigmatized. At the outset is it important to note that the faculty of hearing is of course fundamen-tal in oral cultures, and Matthew reflects this assumption. Moreover, he has produced a written text, a medium that belies a certain "word-centricity." Wayne Morris has recently challenged the utility of "texts" such as the Gospel of Matthew from a Deaf perspective given that "for Deaf people, words—spoken or written—are thought to be a peculiarly hearing phenomenon."[17] Because sign languages' primary mediums are visual and spatial, sounds and texts are not part of their communicative repertoire. Morris also claims that metaphors, as understood by hearing cultures, literally "fall on d/Deaf ears" within the Deaf community. In

14. Ibid., 78.

15. Yong, *Theology*, 84.

16. Reynolds, *Vulnerable Communion*, 63.

17. Morris, *Theology Without Words*, xiii.

Morris's words, they are "linguistic characteristics . . . peculiar to hearing people."[18] In this respect, many of Jesus' parables within Matthew's Gospel, which convey two levels of meaning, would be hard for Deaf communities to comprehend. In Morris's study it was revealed that the parable of the Sower, for example, was viewed in Deaf reception to have "more to do with farming techniques than the eschatological significance which Jesus attaches to it."[19]

If the form of the Gospel itself seems to marginalize Deaf encounters with it, what of its actual substance? Even a cursory look at the Gospel in reference to "sonic" themes reveals a cacophony of "aural" imagery and thus a suspicion that the text "disables" the full participation of the Deaf community within its discourses. The term *akouō* occurs nineteen times within the Gospel. God's revelations are heard, as at the baptism (3:17) and transfiguration (17:5). Moreover, testimonies regarding Jesus' activities are heard (11:4), and Jesus' primary mode of communication is speaking to others in parables and extended discourses (15:10; 21:33, etc.). The faculty of hearing and the organ of the ear also becomes a synecdoche for cognition and discernment: "He who has ears to hear let him hear" (11:15; see also 13:9). For Matthew, "true hearing involves listening and understanding," thus "to have deaf, heavy, or uncircumcised ears is to reject what is heard."[20] As Matthew's Jesus declares, "This is why I speak to them in parables, because . . . hearing they do not hear, nor do they understand" (13:13).

When encountering Matthew from a Deaf perspective, one is immediately struck by the general disinterest in the agency of deaf characters (they are portrayed as passive sites of divine healing). Often Matthew lists the deaf and mute among other "defective" individuals including lepers, the blind, the lame, and the maimed (11:5; 15:30–31), indicating a specific conception of "deficiencies" that will be rectified in the kingdom. Worse still, however, deaf characters are themselves made largely "invisible" within Matthew's Gospel, its translations and its receptions. We encounter *kophos*, a term that can encompass muteness or deafness, only twice within Matthew's account, in 9:32–34 and 12:22. In redacting Mark, Matthew has deliberately downplayed deaf references: in a parallel account in Mark 7:32–37, the mute is defined as deaf, and

18. Ibid., 98.
19. Ibid., 92.
20. Ryken, Wilhoit, and Longman, *Dictionary*, 223.

Jesus inserts his fingers into the man's ears to illustrate this graphically. However, modern translations and commentators of Matthew's account (9:32–34) view the characters as "mute" rather than "deaf" (NRSV, NIV, etc.). Daniel Harrington, for example, notes in reference to 9:32 that "*kophos* can have several meanings: unable to speak, unable to hear or both. Since the sign of the healing is the fact that the man could speak the translation 'mute' seems most appropriate."[21] Similarly, in reference to the 12:22 account, Harrington submits that the supplicant was "blind and mute" (not deaf): "the result of Jesus' healing him is that he both speaks and sees, that is, both conditions are healed."[22] Even those exceptions among commentators who offer the possibility of these respective characters being deaf, still understand them as functioning within the plot to illustrate Matthew's more central interests in prophetic fulfillment and the kingdom of God, rather than the social agency of the deaf character. Warren Carter, for example, notes in reference to 9:32–34 that "deaf mutes are promised to hear and speak (Is 29:18–20)" in messianic hopes;[23] similarly, Donald Hagner confirms that "the direct, unmediated healing of the man's inability to speak symbolizes the fulfillment and joy of the kingdom announced by Jesus."[24] The "bit parts" of the sensory impaired characters within these two stories are illustrated further by the way in which the narrative stereotypes their respective identities (the demon possession featured in the 9:32–34 account is a typical deviance label and stigmatizing strategy) and, accordingly, swiftly narrates their healings. Harrington notes in reference to 9:32–34 that "the healing of the mute demoniac is told so quickly that one gets the impression that Matthew's real interest lay in contrasting the reactions of the crowd and the Pharisees."[25] Likewise, given the startling brevity of the 12:22 account, in which the complaint and healing are accomplished in just one verse, one is forced to admit that the account serves to highlight the "focus on the accusation of the Pharisees and Jesus' response" rather than any sustained reflection on the transformed position of the healed individual.[26] Matthew seems to assume the social marginality of the characters within

21. Harrington, *Gospel of Matthew*, 132.

22. Ibid., 182.

23. Carter, *Matthew*, 229.

24. Hagner, *Matthew 1–13*, 258.

25. Harrington, *Gospel of Matthew*, 133.

26. Ibid., 341.

these stories. They are silent and exhibit no social agency within the narrative whatsoever. In common with many caricatures of disability within literature, here these individuals are "not real people who happen to be deaf, but deaf characters that on the whole appear not be real people."[27] Rather they stand as static props in the plot to exhibit the restoration of wholeness and illustrations of the nature of the kingdom of God.

One aspect of Matthew's account that could, however, possibly be used to disrupt the hegemony of hearing is silence. Jesus, for example, maintains silence in the trial narrative in his resistant response to the questioning of the high priest (26:63). It is also stated that "he will not wrangle or cry aloud, nor will any one hear his voice in the streets" (12:19), which links silence to his servanthood and flies in the face of a culture that values prestige and honor-precedence. Developing this trajectory, one could also consider how silent characters within the Gospel could, in effect, be conceived as "resistant" characters that challenge what Stanley Hauerwas has termed the "tyranny of normality."[28] To take just one example, the Canaanite woman in chapter 15 pleads on behalf of her daughter, who Matthew tells us is "tormented by a demon" (15:22). The daughter is "off stage," inactive, and silent throughout the whole account. Donald Senior has recognized exorcisms as specific instances where the clash between the "cult of normality" and deviations from this are most explicit.[29] Deaf, resistant readers could protest that the woman and her daughter are "normalized" within the exchange—the daughter is cured of her possession; the mother starts to speak like a (proselytized?) Jew: "Have mercy on me, Lord, Son of David" (15:23). Developing such resistant lines, Laura Donaldson names the daughter as a silent figure who is characterized as overcome by the demonic possession that has seized her. Donaldson, however, deconstructs this reading and pictures the daughter's plight quite differently from transgression of cultural rules about what bodies should be like. Donaldson warns that the passivity of the daughter's silent witness "insistently calls the able to investigate rigorously their own complicity in oppressively naturalized ideologies of health."[30] Donaldson chastises the history of interpretation for "robbing" this daughter of her indigenous power. Rather creatively, she probes the

27. Gregory, "Deafness in Fiction," 294.

28. Hauerwas, "Community and Diversity," 37.

29. Senior, "Beware," 12–13.

30. Donaldson, "Gospel Hauntings," 101.

idea that "rather than evoking the illness pejoratively identified in the Christian text as demon possession, the daughter might instead signify a trace of the indigenous [spirituality] . . . and rather than manifesting a deviance subject to the regimes of coercive (Christian) curing, she might be experiencing the initial stages of a vocation known to indigenous people for millennia as shamanism."[31] One could also creatively probe the daughter's status from a Deaf perspective; she is silent and absent from public communication, but that which is labeled as "demonic" by the power structures operative in the text could instead be her use of sign language as a major channel of communication. Such musings produce counter-memories, or hidden transcripts, and "interrupt the hegemonic through hallucinatory confrontations with other histories."[32] Likewise, Davis, from a Deaf perspective, has noted the violations through silence that can be effected within narratives. In his words, "deafness in effect is a reminder of the 'hearingness' of narrative. It is the aporetic black hole that leads to a new kind of deconstruction of narrativity."[33]

If multiple features of Matthew's Gospel do sustain the stigmatization of d/Deaf perspectives and promote the "cult of the hearing" as normal, then any method of "recovery" will need to access "the social-symbolic world of persons with disabilities, such that the disabling framework of the normal becomes questionable."[34] My next task therefore is to sketch some general features of Deaf culture and then see if the Gospel text itself can be "sensitized" along those lines.

DEAF CULTURE AND MATTHEW'S GOSPEL

If the Deaf are not to be understood primarily through their hearing impairment, but rather, as suggested previously, as a specific cultural group akin to an ethnic minority with its own language and values, then attention in recovery readings must also move beyond a sole focus on physical deafness to what Carol Padden and Tom Humphries have termed the "far more interesting facets of Deaf people's lives."[35] Within studies and ethnographies of Deaf culture, particular characteristics and models are

31. Ibid., 105.

32. Ibid., 98.

33. Davis, *Enforcing Normalcy*, 115.

34. Reynolds, *Vulnerable Communion*, 15.

35. Padden and Humphries, *Deaf in America*, 1.

repeatedly identified. This is not to essentialize Deaf culture as static or monolithic—there are of course different national Deaf cultures and also variations within cultures according to differentials of race, gender, age, and geography—but rather only to define general contours that unite Deaf experience and are frequently represented within the literature. Paddy Ladd has identified the "culture concept" as central in movements of resistance and change. In his opinion "culture is the key held in common with other colonized peoples and linguistic minorities. Political and economic power may or may not be the driving forces behind language oppression. But both the key and the lock in which it turns is culture."[36]

Deaf cultural traits and values that will be explored here are as follows: (a) the significance of vision, sight, and light; (b) the use of sign language and minority cultural status; (c) the collective ethos of communities; and (d) the use of storytelling. Each one of these Deaf cultural features will be explored and then read alongside selected features of the Gospel of Matthew. Hannah Lewis, in her construction of Deaf liberation theology, recognizes that for the Bible to have relevance to the Deaf community, it must be "read in a way that affirms the distinctive language and culture of Deaf people."[37] The imaginative and creative connections offered here between Matthew's text and Deaf culture will, I hope, be a step in the right direction toward producing the sorts of interpretations Lewis campaigns for.

Significance of Vision, Sight, and Light

Those cultures that communicate without sound often put far greater emphasis on visual perception. Illustrating this, George Veditz speaks of the Deaf as "first, last and for all time a people of the eye."[38] Knowing the world through sight and communicating through visual performances also demands appropriate use of light. My previous work with Deaf communities taught me that a room needs to be brightly lit, without shadows, in order for sign communication to ensue. Others speak of the special resonance that images of light and darkness have within visual cultures.[39] Many witness that the image of "darkness to light" is

36. Ladd, *Understanding Deaf Culture*, 8.
37. Lewis, *Deaf Liberation Theology*, 112.
38. Veditz, cited in Padden and Humphries, *Deaf in America*, 2.
39. Lawrence, *Word in Place*, 91–104.

frequently used to denote "lostness in the [dark] world" and subsequent enlightenment in "finding one's people and one's home in the Deaf community." Deaf cultural stories likewise often include references to a so-called lamppost trope where stories involving the imagery of a light, under which people are able to communicate in sign, are told.[40]

Reading Matthew with "sensitivities" attuned to sight and vision, one encounters a text in which forms of *orao* occur over forty times. Statistically, therefore, it would seem that Matthew is a visiocentric text and thus, at least in part, open to Deaf perception. Moreover if d/Deaf experience is largely filtered out by Matthew, stories of the healing of the blind occur quite frequently and are even exaggerated by redacting Mark's account so that two blind characters as opposed to one feature in Matthew's narrative (9:27; 20:30). Blindness is reserved as a synecdoche for the hypocrisy and misconceptions of Jesus' bitterest enemies, the scribes and Pharisees. In chapter 23, Matthew's great diatribe against the religious establishment, Jesus' opponents are over and again character-ized as "blind guides" (23:16–17, 19, 24, 26) despite their supposed com-mand of the written Scriptures. These features would seem to indicate that blindness is conceived both physically and spiritually as a far graver sense-impairment than deafness within Matthew's world.

Continuing to trace ocular themes, and in line with Peter Hitching's estimation of Deaf theology, Matthew seems to "move away from a pure-ly wordy God to one [conceived] in terms of vision and touch."[41] The wise men from the east are led by heavenly portents (2:10) and warned in a dream to not go back via Herod's palace (2:12); Joseph, in vision-ary dreams, is given reassurance about the source of Mary's pregnancy (1:20) and about the family's flight to Egypt (2:19–20). Pilate's wife is the only voice of truth in the passion narrative when she narrates her troubling dream and urges her husband to "have nothing to do with that innocent man" (27:19). It seems that for Matthew, God communicates through visions and, as a result, often usurps those whose authority is based on hearing or written words alone. It is no accident that Herod, while quizzing scribal authorities about written prophecy (2:3–5), still remains, unlike the magi, "unenlightened" regarding Jesus' true identity and role. Visions also play a central role in Jesus' career: a public vi-sion of "the Spirit of God descending like a dove" (3:16) accompanies

40. See Ladd, *Understanding Deaf Culture*, 257.

41. Hitching, *Church*, 21.

the baptism; the transfiguration likewise features Jesus' face "shining like the sun" (17:2); extraordinary cosmic signs accompany Jesus' death (27:51–53), and the close of the Gospel features the disciples witnessing a vision of the resurrected Christ on a mountain (28:17).

The imagery of darkness and light, featured within studies of Deaf culture, is likewise attested in Matthew's Gospel. Darkness is used to symbolize religious, social, and political realities, and Jesus' coming is pictured as part of God's prophetic enlightenment project: "the people who sat in darkness have seen a great light, and for those who sat in the region and shadow of death light has dawned" (4:16). Akin to the lamppost trope so prevalent in Deaf culture, Jesus and the community he founds are shown to be a "light of the world" (5:14), a "lamp" giving light to the whole house (5:15), and a moral example to be shone before others so that they also may also "see your good works and give glory to your Father in heaven" (5:16). In some ancient conceptions of sight, the eye was believed to emit the light by which an object was seen.[42] Such ideas may stand behind the graphic visual image of the "eye" as a "lamp of the body" (6:22) regulating moral disposition. In reference to mission, likewise, Matthew's Jesus states that what is told in the dark, his disciples are to "utter in the light" and "proclaim on the housetops"— significantly, one of the most visible places from which to deliver a message. Lewis notes that "so much communication in the Deaf world starts with 'LOOK-AT-ME' . . . that it seems the Deaf Preachers [likewise frequently] perceived Jesus as beginning his teaching in the same way."[43]

In short, Matthew's Gospel is vision-orientated and, in this respect, is open to access by Deaf culture. Indeed, the God of visions and dreams in Matthew's Gospel often subverts the power of those scribal classes who are masters of the written word and exercise hegemony over knowledge. Light and vision is positively featured and evocative for sign language users for whom face-to-face performance is central and cannot be "seen in the dark."

Use of Sign Language and Minority Cultural Status

One of the most significant factors uniting Deaf culture is of course the use of sign language. Harlan Lane speaks of "the mother tongue"

---

42. Lindberg, *Theories of Vision*, 3–6.

43. Lewis, *Deaf Liberation Theology*, 141.

as an "aspect of the soul of a people" and a visible mark of ethnicity within a specific culture.[44] Accordingly, "a language not based on sound is the primary element that sharply demarcates the Deaf-World from the engulfing hearing society."[45] The respective media by which spoken and signed languages are communicated are very different. The former is based on sounds and words, the latter on three-dimensional uses of hand and body movements and facial expressions. Of course, the visible presence of God witnessed in Matthew's "Emmanuel" (1:23–24) is itself one that fits more neatly with Deaf culture than a physically absent deity who can only be heard. Morris talks of the "idea of God being seen in human form, present among us" as having weighty significance within Deaf culture.[46] For, in sign language, one must be able to see face-to-face the person one is communicating with. Accordingly, Morris cites Mary Weir's description of "Christ as a sign" allowing Deaf people's communication with God. Likewise, unlike Mark's absent Christ at the close of his Gospel (Mark 16:1–8), Matthew's Jesus appears on a mountaintop and assures his followers that he will be with them always "to the end of the age" (28:20).

Matthew's Gospel of course does not feature sign language as such, but it does feature nonlinguistic gestures. Although these gestures are significantly different and lacking linguistic traits such as grammatical agreement inherent in sign communication,[47] nevertheless these too can be viewed positively within Deaf culture. Morris cites the example of a Deaf interpretation of healing narratives that use "physical and visual" gestures to illustrate some degree of understanding, on the part of Jesus, of communicating in ways beyond speech and words.[48] For example, touch is "seen" within Matthew's Gospel and forms of *haptō* occur eight times. Jesus "stretches out his hand" to heal a leper (8:3) and through touch cures Peter's mother-in-law (8:15), blind men (9:29; 20:34), and an epileptic (17:7). A bleeding woman famously touches the hem of Jesus' garment to be healed (9:21) and is accordingly, without words, made whole. Likewise, hands and body parts within the Gospel are not only instruments of movement but also tools of communication. Frequently,

44. Lane, "Ethnicity," 293.
45. Ibid.
46. Morris, *Theology without Words*, 101.
47. Senghas and Monaghan, "Signs," 75.
48. Morris, *Theology without Words*, 103.

Matthew speaks of the right hand as a place of honor (20:21–23; 22:44; 25:33; 26:64). The gestures central to the passion narrative in Matthew are also hugely evocative signs readily received by Deaf receivers of the Gospel. The dipping of the bread in the dish symbolizes the one who will hand Jesus over (26:63), and the subsequent kiss of betrayal (26:49) visually enacts deception; the actions of institution at the Last Supper operate as a sign of Jesus' material presence in the ritual life of the community (26:26); Pilate's symbolic washing of hands in the trial narrative denotes disassociation from the capital punishment sentence he delivers (27:24); the crown of thorns and the reed placed in the right hand of Jesus (27:29) are visible illustrations of the ironic mocking of his kingly power. The crucifixion itself has also been interpreted, in relation to Deaf culture, as the graphic pinning of Jesus' hands to the cross so he cannot sign or communicate; this acts as the most arresting and iconic sign of the total "disability" that torturous powers have inflicted on him. While there can be no simple or naive equivalence drawn between sign and gesture, nevertheless from a Deaf cultural perspective the exhibition of bodily means of communication beyond speech can function as impor-tant re-"membered" practices in Deaf recovery readings. As Paddy Ladd likewise submits, Deaf culture "embrace[s] the planet by communicat-ing through those very parts of our own bodies which we ourselves are afraid to utilize. Through the unique plasticity of sign languages, they move in and out of each other's very different cultures like shoals of fish, eagerly seeking out new information about different ways of living in this world of ours."[49]

Another defining feature of those who use sign language is of course their minority status within a hearing culture. Ladd states, "sign language users know that they cannot find 'home' within a majority so-ciety until the day when that society is able to use their language." They must endure the daily struggle of coexisting "alongside majority culture members who do not understand them."[50] Deaf clubs and schools are accordingly often pictured as "safe houses" in which sign language is the norm and in which there is a "general disassociation from speech."[51] One of the most explicit ideological clashes between signed and spoken languages has occurred in the promotion of oralism within educational

49. Ladd, *Understanding Deaf Culture*, 25.
50. Ibid., 16.
51. Padden, "Deaf Community," 43–43.

practice, with oralism defined as "an ideology that privileges spoken (and written) languages over signed ones, often denying the validity or linguistic nature of signing altogether."[52]

While Matthew is undoubtedly a speech-dominated text (forms of *legō* occur over two hundred times in the Gospel), and citations of spoken and written prophecies (1:22; 2:5, 15, 17, 23; 3:3; 8:17; 12:17; 13:35; 27:9) and law codes (5:27, 31, 33, 38, 43; 12:2–3; 15:3–5; 19:4–5) occur throughout, as outlined earlier, there is a certain ambivalence surrounding the authority of those who presume to be professional readers of Scripture. Likewise, one of the traits Matthew often uses to show Jesus' subversion of his opponents' authority is that he is able to understand what they are thinking (12:25). Morris understands such interceptions as a signer's adaptation to an oral culture (through lip and gesture comprehension) that actually subverts that word-centric culture. In his words, "Jesus knows what the scribes are saying about him without being able to hear them . . . [for he has] been watching their lip patterns and demeanor in order to get this information."[53]

While Matthew's textual world may not be one in which the battle between sign and speech is extensively played out, Deaf marginal perspectives can no doubt find resonance with the depiction of Matthew's marginal community. Warren Carter has posited Matthew's Gospel as a counter narrative, representative of a "minority community of disciples" who "resist the dominant Roman imperial and synagogal control."[54] It is no accident that Matthew celebrates the revelation of God to vulnerable "infants," people without speech or words, in contrast to the "wise and understanding" literate class (11:25). Likewise, the marginal child, unvalued and disposable, becomes the icon of true discipleship (18:3; 19:14; 21:16). Children demonstrate the "social location of powerlessness"[55] and thus function as powerful signifiers for all those who struggle at the margins of society, including minority sign language users. In Carter's terms: "All disciples are called children. Parents have no place in the alternative households. Their absence indicates a basic rejection of a hierarchical and patriarchal structure in which power is

---

52. Senghas and Monaghan, "Signs," 83.

53. Morris, *Theology without Words*, 149.

54. Carter, *Matthew*, xvii.

55. Ibid., 362.

exercised over others and the creation of a different social order . . . in which all are equal."[56]

For Matthew, marginality is at the heart of the Christian community's identity, ritual, and practice. And as such, as Sathianathan Clarke reminds us, it stands at one with those cultures whose social location demands that reflection and practice be unified: "It is pertinent to register the point that communities that work with their hands and are intimately related to the products they create do not have a need to separate reflective activity from the material activity they are involved with. Thus production, reflection and communication are connected and integrated into a human way of living. Praxis is a way of life."[57] While Matthew's Gospel may display hegemonic "textual" discourses that have kept the Deaf and their language on the margins, nevertheless, through its subtle critiques of authority based on words and mastery of written traditions, it does also indirectly acknowledge the great contribution that cultures that speak with their hands, rather than words, can offer. Matthew's ethos also resonates firmly with a context that is on the margins, for following Matthew's Christ inevitably leads to experiencing paralyzing rejection outside a city's walls.

The Collective Ethos of Communities

Ladd voices a consensus when he states that "Deaf cultures are not cultures of individualism, but of collectivism, a trait which they share with 70 percent of the global population."[58] One of the most significant features of collective communities is of course the explicit demonstration and performance of communal identity. Lane likewise considers that "self-recognition and recognition by others is a central feature of ethnicity."[59] It is not incidental that Deaf advocates have accordingly adopted labels like "Deaf-World" and "Deaf-Way" to illustrate their communal identity and belonging. Richard Senghas and Leila Monaghan see the spatial elements of "Deaf-World" as being particularly evocative in relation to Deaf identity. They submit that the "DEAF-WORLD is seen as transcending national borders and invokes the experiences of d/Deaf

56. Ibid., 386.
57. Clarke, "Viewing the Bible," 264.
58. Ladd, *Understanding Deaf Culture*, 16.
59. Lane, "Ethnicity."

individuals and groups as unifying events."[60] Both Lane and Ladd have plotted the "global" and "universal" potential of Deaf-World. Lane reveals how Deaf people from two cultures can nonetheless still communicate at least in part with one another and as such function like other "Diaspora ethnic minorities worldwide," who are subject to "prejudice in the host society."[61] Ladd also points to the adaptability of sign language, which he defines as a mode of "global communication" that cultivates "citizens of the entire planet." In Ladd's opinion, "such a powerful experience cannot continue to be constrained by the feeble diminutive of 'deafness'; hence the concept of Deaf seeks to encompass those larger dimensions."[62]

In picturing Deaf culture as akin to ethnic minority cultures united by experience across geographical limits, many commentators focus on the strong emphasis on social and family ties operative within them.[63] Ladd concurs that "tropes such as family and home are widely used and might well be drawn into a coherent symbol system" within Deaf cultural experience.[64] Similarly, the protection of the in-group through endogamous marriage, consensual decision-making, and positive identification with the language and values of the culture also serve to protect and propagate the interests of the minority collective.[65]

While the substance of the collective identity in Matthew's Gospel may be substantially different from Deaf culture, nevertheless the broad structure of communal identity featured there does find resonance with Deaf experience. (Indeed, sign language as a mode of communication in a collective culture may be far nearer the earliest Palestinian "oral" modes of transmission of "gospel" traditions than our texts would imply). Matthew offers a number of communal identity labels by which his community can understand themselves. These include "ekklēsia," "infants," and "little ones." Such labels, as Carter recognizes, serve, like Deaf-World, to "secure separation from other communities [and] reinforce group identity."[66] Likewise, fictive kin and households are dominant tropes within Matthew's world. Jesus provocatively asks, "Who is

---

60. Senghas and Monaghan, "Signs," 80.

61. Lane, "Ethnicity."

62. Ladd, *Understanding Deaf Culture*, 14.

63. Padden, "Deaf Community," 42–43.

64. Ladd, *Understanding Deaf Culture*, 257.

65. See Lane, "Ethnicity."

66. Carter, *Matthew*, 9.

my mother and my brothers?" (12:48) only to conclude it is those with whom he shares faith and experience (12:49). Claims of exclusive revelation—"To you it has been given to know the secrets of the kingdom of heaven, but to them it has not been given" (13:11)—also serve to underline the different bases of authority operative within the new collective identity of the ekklesia. Particular "signs" of that community identity are also materially and visually performed: baptism (28:19), worship (5:23–24), governance (18:15–20), Eucharistic meals (26:26–29) and prayer (6:9–13), to name just a few. Such rituals serve to "create order, sustain a community in an alternative way of living and effect transformation."[67]

The global potential of Deaf world and communication is also discerned in the way in which Matthew's Gospel plots a mission that at first is limited to "the lost sheep of the house of Israel" (10:6) but careers towards a universal mission (ethnically and racially diverse), articulated in the great commission at the climax of the account: "Go therefore and make disciples of all nations, baptizing them in the name of the Father, Son and Holy Spirit" (28:19). Like Deaf world, Matthew exhibits a strong collective identity that he wishes to promote and through which he hopes to transcend barriers of race, class, nationality, and geography.

Use of Storytelling

A frequently cited feature of Deaf culture is "storytelling." Roger Hitching shows how the Deaf not only convey information through stories but also use them as a coping strategy: "In their stories, they include self-mocking elements and make fun of interactions with hearing people. Storytelling also influences how they conceptualize reality and create their worldview. In Deaf culture the storytelling mode, the dialectical nature of encounter and the greater experience of immediacy create differences in the backdrop against which reality is interpreted."[68] Paddy Ladd has hypothesized that this feature may find its genesis in the fact that "thirst for information is a major theme in a culture not only denied access to broadcast media and public communication . . . [and] because of the additional oralist restrictions and exclusions from parental and educational information."[69] Of course, Matthew's gospel was itself de-

---

67. Ibid.

68. Hitching, *Church*, 69.

69. Ladd, *Understanding Deaf Culture*, 309.

livered in a culture where estimated literacy rates were only 10 percent, and so has some resonance with this situation. Matthew likewise needs to adopt vivid storytelling elements for a nonliterate audience. From the comic-strip jibe of taking a speck from a neighbor's eye while a log sits in one's own (7:5) to the figurative storytelling marking episodes like the cursing of the fig tree (21:18–22), Matthew draws his audience imaginatively into his narrative world.

Making texts relevant to particular contemporary situations is of course the hallmark of midrashic modes of interpretation.[70] Matthew has, in various ways, been understood to contain midrashic elements. To give just one example, the birth narrative is often read as midrashic haggadah: midrashic, because scriptural prophecies are woven into the entire complex and haggadah, because "the story is not told for the sake of facts alone, but in order to illustrate their deeper meaning, that is, the theological significance of Jesus as the fulfilment of OT prophecies."[71] Likewise, in Deaf culture, "storytelling is a form of oral transmission of text . . . and in the hands of a skilled practitioner accurately transmits what is seen as the essence of the narrative."[72]

Moreover, the characterizations and attitudes operative within the Gospel (for example of the Pharisees and scribes as opposed to Jesus) likewise form an important part of the telling. In stories told in sign language, often the performer will physically change position, posture, and facial expression to denote a change of character and illustrate the outlooks of respective individuals. In such telling, aspects, manner, and mood become central parts of the storytelling endeavor. In Hitching's terms such interpretations are not merely giving the meaning "but also the speaker's attitude to his listeners and to what he is saying" within the performance.[73]

MATTHEW AND DEAF WORLD: IDENTIFYING COMMON TOUCHSTONES

Notions of "ability," "disability," "normality," and "abnormality" are socially constructed and often largely dependent on the environment in

---

70. Lawrence, *Word in Place*, 91–104.

71. Hagner, *Matthew 1–13*, 16.

72. Ladd, discussed in Lewis, *Deaf Liberation Theology*, 118.

73. Hitching, *Church*, 70.

which they are used, and by whom they are advanced. In contrast to a medical model of deafness, the cultural model that conceives of the Deaf as a linguistic or ethnic minority group challenges us to disrupt our classifications surrounding what is "normal" and interpret d/Deafness as "difference not defect."[74] For, as Deborah Creamer reminds us, every individual is limited in some respect, and as such binary categories of "us" and "them" in reference to disability are very hard to sustain.[75] Encountering Matthew with Deaf sensitivities, on first sight it seemed a predominantly audiocentric document that stigmatized, even stifled, d/Deaf presence within it. While the exposure of and resistance to oppression by a hearing "cult of normalcy" is an important part of Deaf readings, so is finding positive touchstones that allow the "meaning of the text [to] shift" in view of contemporary liberation agendas.[76] By elucidating key features of Deaf culture and allowing them to reverberate and echo within Matthew's world, a dynamic exchange with the text in light of contemporary experience was initiated, albeit by a hearing academic. Harlan Lane, Robert Hoffmeister, and Ben Bahan warn of the "inevitable collision with the values of DEAF-WORLD, whose goal is to promote the unique heritage of Deaf language and culture" that will occur when a hearing person undertakes a journey such as the one attempted here, for "the disparity in decision-making power between the hearing world and DEAF-WORLD renders this collision frightening for Deaf people."[77] Heeding this warning, this essay does not claim to be the last "sign" on this topic, but rather poses an open invitation for Deaf people themselves to partake in creative interactions with texts such as the Gospel of Matthew and as such curb the perpetuation of Deaf absence from biblical texts and interpretation.

Bibliography

Booth, Tony. "Challenging Conceptions of Integration." In *Constructing Deafness*, edited by Susan Gregory and Gillian M. Hartley, 157–64. London: Pinter in association with The Open University, 1991.

Carter, Warren. *Matthew and the Margins: A Sociopolitical and Religious Reading.* Maryknoll, NY: Orbis, 2000.

74. Creamer, *Disability*, 109.

75. Ibid.

76. Lewis, *Deaf Liberation Theology*, 107.

77. Lane, Hoffmeister, and Bahan, *Journey*, 371.

Clarke, Sathianathan. "Viewing the Bible Through the Eyes and Ears of the Subalterns in India." *Biblical Interpretation* 10 (2002) 245–66.

Creamer, Deborah Beth. *Disability and Christian Theology*. Oxford: Oxford University Press, 2009.

Davis, Lennard J. *Enforcing Normalcy: Disability, Deafness, and the Body*. London: Verso, 1995.

Donaldson, Laura. "Gospel Hauntings: The Postcolonial Demons of New Testament Criticism." In *Postcolonial Biblical Criticism*, edited by Stephen D. Moore and Fernando F. Segovia, 97–113. London: T. & T. Clark, 2005.

Gregory, Susan. "Deafness in Fiction." In *Constructing Deafness*, edited by Susan Gregory and Gillian M. Hartley, 294–300. London: Pinter in association with The Open University, 1991.

Gregory, Susan, and Gillian Hartley, editors. *Constructing Deafness*. London: Pinter in association with The Open University, 1991.

Hagner, Donald A. *Matthew 1–13*. Word Biblical Commentary. Dallas: Word, 1993.

Harrington, Daniel J. *The Gospel of Matthew*. Sacra Pagina Series. Collegeville, MN: Liturgical, 1991.

Hauerwas, Stanley. "Community and Diversity: The Tyranny of Normality." In *Critical Reflections on Stanley Hauerwas' Theology of Disability*, edited by John Swinton, 37–43. Binghamton, NY: Haworth Pastoral, 2004.

Hitching, Roger. *The Church and Deaf People*. Carlisle: Paternoster, 2003.

Johnson, Robert E. "Sign Language, Culture and Community in a Traditional Yucatec Maya Village." *Sign Language Studies* 73 (1991) 461–74.

Kyle, Jim G., and Bencie Woll. *Sign Language: The Study of Deaf People and Their Language*. Cambridge: Cambridge University Press, 1988.

Ladd, Paddy. *Understanding Deaf Culture: In Search of Deafhood*. Clevedon: Multilingual Matters, 2003.

Lane, Harlan. "Ethnicity, Ethics, and the Deaf-World." *Journal of Deaf Studies and Deaf Education* 10 (2005) 291–310. Online: http://jdsde.oxfordjournals.org/content/10/3/291.full.

Lane, Harlan, Robert Hoffmeister, and Benjamin J. Bahan. *A Journey into the Deaf-World*. San Diego: DawnSign, 1996.

Lawrence, Louise J. *The Word in Place: Reading the New Testament in Contemporary Contexts*. London: SPCK, 2009.

Lewis, Hannah. *Deaf Liberation Theology*. Aldershot: Ashgate, 2007.

Lindberg, David C. *Theories of Vision from Al-Kindi to Kepler*. Chicago: University of Chicago Press, 1976.

McDermott, Ray, and Hervé Varenne. "Culture as Disability." *Anthropology & Education Quarterly* 26 (1995) 324–48.

Morris, Wayne. *Theology without Words: Theology in the Deaf Community*. Aldershot: Ashgate, 2008.

Padden, Carol A. "The Deaf Community and the Culture of Deaf People." In *Constructing Deafness*, edited by Susan Gregory and Gillian M. Hartley, 40–45. London: Pinter in association with The Open University, 1991.

Padden, Carol A., and Tom Humphries. *Deaf in America: Voices from a Culture*. Cambridge: Harvard University Press, 1988.

Reynolds, Thomas E. *Vulnerable Communion: A Theology of Disability and Hospitality*. Grand Rapids: Brazos, 2008.

Ryken, Leland, Jim Wilhoit, and Tremper Longman, editors. *Dictionary of Biblical Imagery*. Downers Grove, IL: InterVarsity, 1998.

Sainsbury, Sally. *Deaf Worlds: A Study of Integration, Segregation, and Disability*. London: Hutchinson, 1986.

Senghas, Richard J., and Leila Monaghan. "Signs of Their Times: Deaf Communities and the Culture of Language." *Annual Review of Anthropology* 31 (2002) 69–97.

Senior, Donald. "Beware of the Canaanite Woman: Disability and the Bible." In *Religion and Disability*, edited by Marilyn Bishop, 1–26. Kansas City: Sheed & Ward, 1995.

Yong, Amos. *Theology and Down Syndrome: Reimagining Disability in Late Modernity*. Waco, TX: Baylor University Press, 2007.

7

Gerrard Winstanley

Radical Interpreter of the Bible

CHRISTOPHER ROWLAND

Tim Gorringe has been a friend and companion for over twenty years. We learned how to survive Oxford together, and Tim introduced me to aspects of radicalism that have become a staple part of my life. One was the annual commemoration of the Levellers, shot in May 1649, at Cromwell's behest, for refusing to serve in Ireland. The commemoration takes place in the churchyard of Burford Church, and I have been privileged enough to read the dedication several times over the last few years. Taking part in that wonderful event, I get as close as I ever do to understanding the importance of a religious procession, as the motley crew of Leveller sympathizers process round this Cotswold beauty spot on a Saturday in May. I have often thought of Gerrard Winstanley (1609–1676) on such occasions. Indeed, he described himself as a "True Leveller." Tim's commitment to peace and justice comes from Scripture, but also from the tradition informed by it, especially the Levellers and Diggers, and so it is appropriate that one of their major spokespersons is included in this tribute to him.

THE CHARACTERISTICS OF WINSTANLEY'S
BIBLICAL INTERPRETATION

Qu: What use is to be made of the Scriptures?

Ans: First, they are, or may be kept as a record of such truths as
were writ not from imagination of flesh, but from pure experience, and teachings of the Father. Secondly, we are taught thereby
to waite upon the Father with a meek and obedient spirit, till he
teach us, and feed us with sincere milk, as he taught them, that
wrote these Scriptures.[1]

These words exemplify the heart of Winstanley's hermeneutic. They are
typical of a way of reading the Bible that one may find paralleled among
the Quakers, as well as in some forms of spiritual anabaptism such as
that we find in the writings of Hans Denck.[2] It is based on the premise
that there is a subtle interplay between text and reader, with the experience of the latter being in some sense a criterion, and at least a source for
the understanding of and engagement with texts that are deemed to have
affinities with the experiences of the interpreter. The distance between
the text and the reader is overcome, and knowledge of God is appreciated primarily through experience, though informed through what one
finds in the Bible. It is this kind of hermeneutic that is then linked with
a commitment to political change. Indeed, the commitment to political
change is the central context of scriptural interpretation in Winstanley's
work, and in that respect he is very much a precursor of Latin American
liberation theology.[3]

We know little of Winstanley's background, except that he origi-
nated in Wigan, and even less of what became of him. The burst of writing on which we are dependent is confined to a period of less than five
years, during which time he was involved in claiming the right to the
common land and enacting the original biblical vision of the whole creation belonging to all of humanity, not the favored few. In his tract "The

---

1. "Truth Lifting up his Head," Sabine, 128; CHL, 1:435. All references are to the
editions of Winstanley's works by Sabine, *Works*, and Corns, Hughes, and Loewenstein,
Complete Works (CHL).

2. Baumann, *Denck*; Rowland, *Blake*, 157–80.

3. So rightly Holstun, *Ehud's Dagger*, 41–111, and Hill, *Bible*, 447–52, and further
Bradstock and Rowland, *Radical Christian Writings*; Rowland, *Radical Christianity*; and
Rowland and Corner, *Liberating Exegesis*.

New Law of Righteousness," he writes of the present as a moment when the reordering of society in line with God's purpose is now imminent.[4] The sense of his age as a special moment in history led Winstanley and his companions to action. From April 1649 (Charles I was executed in January of that year) to March 1650, Winstanley's career and writing were intimately bound up with the Digger commune. He was prompted by a revelation that he and his companions should dig the common land, thus claiming what they regarded as their rightful inheritance.[5] The action of the Diggers provoked hostility from local landowners and complaints to the Council of State, and they were finally driven off the land in the spring of 1650.

Spiritual regeneration and structural change are intimately linked, therefore, if the earth is to become a common treasury as it was in the beginning, and if the new heaven and earth are something to be seen here and now. Royal power is the old heaven and earth that must pass away. The New Jerusalem is not some vague hope for the future, "to be seen only hereafter," but rather lies *within* creation. Christ's second coming is the establishment of a state of community in the present, for now is "the fulnesse of time."[6] God is not located far above the heavens, therefore, but is to be found in the lives and experiences of ordinary men and women. The second coming of Christ will be the perfect society, when there takes place "the rising up of Christ in sons and daughters, which is his second coming."

There are several key hermeneutical characteristics that are central to Winstanley's work even in the early material: the use of the dualistic contrasts in the Bible; the importance of "experiment," and with it the protest against the view that visions and revelations are over;[7] the presentation of the human person as a site of a struggle between flesh and spirit;[8] and the view that "original" sin is an acquisitive attention on the outward (i.e., covetousness), as a consequence of which attention to the promptings of the spirit within is blocked. Winstanley holds that such covetousness leads to possession and to the maintenance of possessions

4. "New Law," Sabine, 170, 184; CHL, 1:493, 506.

5. "True Levellers' Standard" or "Declaration to the Powers of England," Sabine, 260–2; CHL, 2:13–15.

6. "New Law," Sabine, 184; CHL, 1:506; Hill, *Law of Freedom*, 86–87.

7. "Truth Lifting up his Head," Sabine, 100; CHL, 1:410.

8. "Truth Lifting up his Head," Sabine, 99; CHL, 1:409.

to the exclusion of others, and this conviction then becomes the corner-stone on which his political theology is built.

He sometimes proof-texts in order to make a point, or as a way of buttressing an argument, but this is less evident in the writings of the Digger period. Indeed, the amassing of references sits uncomfortably with Winstanley's assertion that what counts is the Spirit within teaching the humble, the meek, and the poor. One may assume that this is part of the apologetic aim to convince his readers of the rectitude of his theological position and also of the Digger cause. He often makes reference to passages such as Acts 4:32, for example, to underline the scriptural basis of his view that the earth is a common treasury,[9] though it is clear that this passage resonates with Winstanley's visionary experience. Thus, in "True Levellers Standard," this work to make the earth a common treasury is said to have been "shewed us by Voice in Trance, and out of Trance, which words were these, 'Work together, Eat Bread together, Declare this all abroad.'"[10]

Indeed, Winstanley describes his own vocation in words from Gal 1 and Revelation. In the former, Paul describes the moment when he was confronted with "the apocalypse of Jesus Christ" (Gal 1:12 and 16). Winstanley writes of the way in which he was a good Christian man, but "since it pleased the Father to reveal his Son in me (cf. Gal 1:16), and cause me to speak what I know from an inward light and power of life within,"[11] then he entered onto a new phase of religious life. The words of Scripture offered him a language with which to articulate his own experience, just as Paul had used the prophetic words in his Scriptures to describe what had happened to him (cf. Gal 1:15). Words have ceased to be merely objects of study, therefore, but have become existentially transformative.

Throughout, we see the Bible is functioning at a much-developed level affecting the structure of his thought and belief. Thus, passages like Romamns 7–8, with their contrasts between two spirits at work in the human person, and 1 Cor 2:9–16, are important. In the latter, we have the *locus classicus* for the way in which a law written on the heart might actually work itself out, without any resort to an external authority—for example: "This second man is the spirituall man, that judges all things

---

9. "New Law," Sabine, 184, 198, 201; CHL, 1:506, 520, 523.

10. "True Levellers' Standard," Sabine, 261; CHL, 2:14–15.

11. "New Law," Sabine, 243; CHL, 1:567.

according to the law of equity and reason, in moderation and love to all, he is not a talker, but an actour of Righteousnesse. 1 Cor 2:15" (the reference is explicitly cited by Winstanley).[12] The spirit that anointed Jesus will indwell all people, so that the King of Righteousness and peace will rule in all. This Winstanley links with the fulfillment of Jer 31: 34 (KJV): "And they shall teach no more every man his neighbor, and every man his brother, saying, Know the Lord: for they shall all know me, from the least of them unto the greatest of them, saith the Lord: for I will forgive their iniquity, and I will remember their sin no more."[13]

BIBLICAL INTERPRETATION IN "THE NEW LAW OF RIGHTEOUSNESS"

In many ways, "The New Law of Righteousness" epitomizes Winstanley's theology and biblical hermeneutics better than any other of his works. It was written in the heady days at the beginning of 1649 shortly before his Digger period and the end of monarchy in England, when hopes for a different kind of society were at their zenith. In it Winstanley begins by addressing the twelve tribes of Israel that are circumcised in heart and scattered through the earth. They are true Abrahamites (here he alludes to Romans, especially 2:14[14]). They are seen as a hidden remnant from whom Christ will declare himself, despite the fact that they are now persecuted. Winstanley then resorts to a trope that is a familiar feature of his (and much mainstream Christian) writing: the dualistic contrast, based on that between the oppressive elder son and the younger son, referring either to Jacob and Esau, or to Cain and Abel.[15]

Winstanley criticizes a preoccupation with history and gets readers to identify their own experience with what is found in the biblical text taken as a description of the spiritual struggle within—an example of contemporary, "actualizing" exegesis.[16] Thus, Adam and Eve are in every man and woman, and the longing for "creature objects" and the exercise of power that tyrannizes over others to maintain this hold, is a universal human experience: That which a man seeks for, whereby

12. Ibid., Sabine, 179; CHL, 1:502.

13. Ibid., Sabine, 161; CHL 1:484.

14. Ibid., Sabine, 150; CHL 1:474.

15. Ibid., Sabine, 176–77; CHL, 1:474; Hill, *Bible*, 208–12.

16. "Actualization" means reading the Bible in the light of new circumstances: Houlden, *Interpretation*.

he might have peace, is within the heart, not without.[17] Righteousness comes to rule in everyone's heart, when a person kills the first Adam.[18] Adam was not just a past representative, therefore, for he dwells in every one: "we may see *Adam* every day before our eyes walking up and down the street."[19]

Two opposing powers are at work in humankind but, significantly, in Winstanley's biblical interpretation, they have existed in humanity from the beginning rather than only subsequent to the Fall, as in Rom 5:12–14. There is no period of innocence, therefore, at the beginning of creation, though there is a fall in the sense that one power gets the upper hand in the behavior of the human person. Oppression comes about when this is acted out, and only ceases with the universal spreading of divine power, not by the pulling of tyrannical power out of others' hands. It is only by ensuring that the universal power of righteous laws is written in hearts that the power of Mine and Thine can be swallowed up in the law of righteous actions one to one another.[20]

Winstanley refused to allow a simple reversal of fortunes in which the first will become last and the last first, for the end could never justify the means. Thus, the redemption does not take place by force, nor does it resort to the stratagems that had been typical of the old age. Christ in himself, in his humility and death, destroys the powers of the Beast, and thereby offers a model for all who respond in a similar way to the spirit within to do the same. In the "prison of Jesus Christ, the Lamb, the Father fought against the Beast: and killed him; for the Dragon was cast out of that Heaven or Creation, in whom the Father dwelt bodily; for that flesh was wholly made subject to the Spirit."[21] That paradigmatic overcoming of the Beast in the flesh of Christ is what is about to happen everywhere with the overcoming of "covetous unrighteous flesh in every son and daughter" and the "bruising of that Serpent's head."

Winstanley challenges the scholarly attempts to create distance between text and reader and instead stresses the centrality of "experimental knowledge" in contrast to an abstract reflection on the Bible

---

17. "New Law," Sabine, 158; CHL, 1:480–1.

18. "Fire in the Bush," Sabine, 468–70; CHL 2:196.

19. "Truth Lifting up his Head," Sabine, 120, cf. 203, 258; CHL, 1:427; cf. 525–26, 2:11; Hill, *Bible*, 201.

20. "New Law," Sabine, 161; CHL, 1:484.

21. Ibid., Sabine, 229; CHL 1:553.

followed by secondary application. "While a man is busying his head in studying what hath been done in *Moses* time, in the Prophets time, in the Apostles, and in the Son of mans time, called Jesus Anointed, [he] doth not wait to find light and power of righteousnesse to arise up within his heart."[22]

Winstanley instead stresses the centrality of "experimental knowledge" in contrast to an abstract reflection on the Bible and secondary application of it: "This man is a piteous, barren creature, though he have all the learning of Arts and Sciences under the Sun; for the knowledge of Arts is but to speak methodically of what hath been; and conjecture what shal be; both which are uncertain to the Speaker: But he that speaks from the original light within, can truly say, I know what I say and I know whom I worship."[23] Like William Blake after him, he challenges the resort to memory and invokes the power of inspiration through the King of Righteousness within:

> The sight of the King of Glory within, lies not in the strength of memory, calling to mind what a man hath read and heard, being able by a humane capacity to joyn things together into a method; & through the power of free utterance, to hold it forth before others, as the fashion of Students is in their Sermon work; which a plough man that was never bread in their Universities may do as much; nay, they do more in this kind (as experience shews us) than they that take Tythes to tell a story.
>
> But the sight of the King within, lies in the beholding of light arising up from an inward power of feeling experience, filling the soul with the glory of the Law of Righteousnesse, which doth not vanish like the taking in of words and comfort from the mouth of a hearsay Preacher, or strength of memory.[24]

The Bible is a confirmation of the witness of the indwelling Christ within. Scripture is none other but "Christ in the letter, lying under the experimentall words of those Pen-men, setting forth the one Almighty, in his severall actings." That is, the hermeneutical dynamic is a witness to the experience of the apostles, with which the reader's contemporary experience resonates, and there is a mutual confirmation of the authenticity of both as the divine spirit works within.

---

22. Ibid., Sabine, 224; CHL, 1:547.
23. Ibid., Sabine, 224; CHL, 1:547–8.
24. Ibid., Sabine, 233; CHL, 1:557; Rowland, *Blake*, 5–14.

It is not, therefore, book learning that counts, but what one has received, whether by experience or revelation.[25] Winstanley believes that men and women ought to speak no more than they know from experience. All people everywhere equally have access to the divine spirit within, and those who assert their authority to tell others the meaning of the Scripture miss the fact that the divine spirit within each enables all understanding of God. The Bible is an ancient testimony to the experiences of the apostles and prophets, and is not the word of Christ itself, which rather indwells all people. In writing thus, Winstanley sides with Quaker positions over against those of the emerging Baptist position on the Bible.[26]

The "plough man" is in as good a position as the university scholar to understand God. The poor and outcast will be the instruments of change, as was the case with the first coming of Christ (cf. Matt 11:25):

> The Father now is rising up a people to himself out of the dust, that is, out of the lowest and despised sort of people, that are counted the dust of the earth, man-kind, that are trod under foot. In these, and from these shall the Law of Righteousnesse break forth first, for the poor they begin to receive the Gospel, and plentifull discoveries of the Fathers love flows from them, and the waters of the learned and great men of the world, begins to dry up like the brooks in Summer. Matt 11:25; 1 Cor 1:27.[27]

This is then combined with the image of the apocalyptic struggle between Christ and the dragon, understood as the preoccupation with the "letters, words and histories" at the expense of the attention to the promptings of the divine Spirit:

> Nay let me tel you, That the poorest man, that sees his maker, and lives in the light, though he could never read a letter in the book, dares throw the glove to al the humane learning in the world, and declare the deceit of it, how it doth bewitch & delude man-kinde in spiritual things, yet it is that great Dragon, that hath deceived all the world, for it draws men from knowing the Spirit, to own bare letters, words and histories for spirit: The light and life of

---

25. Hill, *Bible*, 223–24.

26. Underwood, *Primitivism*, 20–33.

27. "New Law," Sabine, 186; CHL, 1:508, text citations in original.

christ within the heart, discovers all darknesse, and delivers mankind from bondage; *And besides him there is no Saviour.* [28]

BIBLICAL INTERPRETATION IN THE LATER WORKS

Little more than a year after the writing of "The New Law of Righteousness," we see these themes reemerge in the context of the life of the Digger commune. In "True Levellers' Standard," when the Diggers had started to plant and manure the waste land (possibly on 20 April 1649), many of the same themes emerge, but here Winstanley spells out the consequences of serving the human flesh, or the king of beasts, by delighting in the objects of creation.[29]

Winstanley's particular form of allegorical exegesis is evident in the way in which the commandments are related to the political challenge of the present: "And hereby thou wilt *Honour thy Father, and thy Mother*: Thy Father, which is the Spirit of Community, that made all, and that dwells in all. Thy Mother, which is the Earth, that brought us all forth: That as a true Mother, loves all her Children. Therefore do not hinder the Mother Earth, from giving all her Children suck, by thy inclosing it into particular hands, and holding up that cursed Bondage of Inclosure by thy Power."[30]

In "New-Yeer's Gift," there is an echo of Fifth Monarchist sentiments that the reign of King Jesus has begun after the end of the reign of the succession of beasts (Daniel 2 and 7). Winstanley calls his contemporaries to match their words with actions. He points out that they have begun setting Christ upon the throne of England by their commitments (and acts of Parliament) to cast out kingly power, and to make England a free commonwealth. Winstanley pleads with his readers to make words and promises a reality: "Put all these into sincere Action, and you shall see the work is done, and you with others shall sing *Halelujah* to him that sits upon the Throne, and to the Lamb for evermore."[31] Here political action and worship are equated, and the worship around the heavenly throne in Rev 4–5 is not seen as something separate from political life.

28. Ibid., Sabine, 214; CHL, 1:537.
29. "True Levellers' Standard," Sabine, 251; CHL 2:4–5.
30. Ibid., Sabine, 265; CHL, 2:18.
31. "New-Yeer's Gift," Sabine, 386; CHL, 2:141.

Winstanley criticizes clerics who interpret the inheriting of the earth by the poor and meek as a matter of "inward satisfaction." Instead, Christ, "this great Leveller," shall cause men to beat their swords to ploughshares and spears into pruning hooks (Isa 2:4).[32] But, as in "The New Law," there is to be no vindictiveness. [33] Indeed, Winstanley even enjoins people to make "peace with the cavaliers" on the basis of love of enemies and the Golden Rule: "*Love your enemies, and doe as you would be done by*" (cf. Matt 7:12).[34]

The Scriptures were written by the hand of ordinary people. In contrast, Winstanley alleges, "the Universitie public Ministrie runs before he be sent; they take up another mans message, and carries abroad other mens words, or studies or imagines a meaning; and this is their ministrie."[35] What is required of ministers is to preach the truth, "purely and experimentally." Thereby one reflects the Scriptures that were written "by the experimentall hand of Shepherds, Husbandmen, Fishermen and such inferiour men of the world."[36] The biblical writings have been subject to dark interpretation and glosses of the university-learned ones. Consequently, "the true Penmen in whom the Spirit dwells," are told not to meddle with spiritual things.[37] Thus, "by covetous policy," in opposition to the righteous spirit, the university-learned ones "engrosse other mens experimentall spirituall teachings to themselves; as if it were their owne by University or Schoole learning succession. Pope like."[38]

APOCALYPTIC AND ESCHATOLOGICAL THEMES

Throughout Winstanley's work there is a sense of the propitious time in which he writes and acts. This echoes the important sense within the New Testament that the writers and readers are living in a special moment in the divine economy. This may be exemplified by the opening words of Jesus in the Gospel of Mark: "The time [*kairos*] is fulfilled, and the kingdom of God is at hand: repent ye, and believe in the gospel

32. Ibid., Sabine, 391; CHL, 2:145.
33. Ibid., Sabine, 390; CHL, 2:144.
34. Ibid., Sabine, 389; CHL, 2:143–44.
35. "Fire in the Bush," Sabine, 474; CHL, 2:200.
36. Ibid., Sabine, 474; CHL, 2:200.
37. Ibid., Sabine, 475; CHL, 2:200.
38. Ibid., Sabine, 475; CHL, 2:200–1.

(Mark 1:15)."[39] The *kairos* is both promise and threat, however, and in a clever use of Rev 5–6, Winstanley employs the Lion/Lamb contrast found there to indicate the judgment on those who do not respond to the King of Righteousness within: "if you do not, the Lamb shall shew himself a Lion (cf. Rev 5:5), and tear you in pieces for your most abominable dissembling Hypocrisie."[40]

"Heaven within himself" means that the human person is a site of an apocalyptic struggle. Human imagination is a negative power for Winstanley. It is the god that everyone worships [41] and that leads to envy, censure, and destruction of the weak by the powerful. Redemption is the gradual overcoming of the exercise of this power. Winstanley describes the struggle, utilizing to the full the dualistic language of apocalypticism:

> These two powers are *Michaell* and the Dragon, and this battaile is fought in Heaven [cf. Rev 12:7] (that is, in mankinde, in the garden of *Eden*) where God principally resolves to set up his throne of righteous government, it is not fought in the spirit of Beasts; but in Heaven in the spirit of Mankind, who is the Lord [cf. 2 Cor 3:16]. And this battaile in our age of the world, growes hotter and sharper than formerly; for we are under the dividing of time, which is the last period of the Beasts raigne; And he will strive hardest now.[42]

The other, competing side of the human person is the word of life: Christ the restoring spirit, which is to be found within a person—"The Kingdom of heaven [which is] Christ is within you." It is only with the restoration and the deliverance from the curse of preoccupation with external objects that other creatures and the earth will be restored. It is a time when everyone will know the Law; and everyone shall obey the Law, for it shall be written in everyone's heart (cf. Jer 31:31–3).[43]

Winstanley expresses the conviction that the New Jerusalem might be built "in this green and pleasant land," like his great fellow radical, William Blake.[44] He had a firm belief in the coming of a this-worldly kingdom, a belief that was only strengthened by his conviction in 1649–

---

39. Rowland, *Blake*, 88.

40. "New-Yeer's Gift," Sabine, 386; CHL, 2:141.

41. "Fire in the Bush," Sabine, 455–56; CHL, 2:180–81.

42. Ibid., Sabine, 457; CHL, 2:182.

43. "New Law," Sabine, 162; CHL, 1:484.

44. Rowland, *Blake*, 120–21.

so that he was living in the Last Days. He worked with a three-stage salvation history that is reminiscent of a Joachite view of history but has echoes in Pauline theology, too.[45]

The implications of the mystery of the coming of age of righteousness are, therefore, not just for life after death, for that age has already begun to appear.[46] Universal freedom has never filled the earth, but it has been foretold by prophets.[47] When it happens, it will be a new heaven and earth.[48] The great day of judgment is the Righteous Judge sitting upon the throne in every man and woman.[49] Winstanley is working with an inaugurated eschatology, therefore, but one that is capable of being interpreted of the inner life, much as had happened in Familist texts of the sixteenth century.[50] Such sentiments are echoed in Winstanley's words: "Some there are, nay almost every one, wonders after the Beast . . . they seek for new *Jerusalem*, the City of *Sion*, or Heaven, to be above the skies, in a locall place, wherein there is all glory . . . But when the second *Adam* rises up in the heart, he makes a man to see Heaven within himself."[51]

Winstanley's view of individual transformation runs in tandem with his conviction about the demise of oppression in society. Winstanley takes up the imagery of Dan 7 (as also in Rev 13 and 17) to interpret the oppressive behavior of the wielders of political and economic power of his day. According to Winstanley, the first of the four beasts in Daniel was royal power, which by force makes a way for the economically powerful to rule over others, "making the conquered a slave; giving the Earth to some, denying the Earth to others";[52] the second Beast he saw as the power of laws, which maintain power and privilege in the hands of the few, by the threat of imprisonment and punishment; the third Beast is what Winstanley calls "the thieving Art of

45. "New Law," Sabine, 163, 1813, 194, 205; CHL 1:486, 504–6, 517, 527; cf. "True Levellers' Standard," Sabine, 261; CHL, 2:14.

46. "New Law," Sabine, 170; CHL, 1:493.

47. Ibid., Sabine, 184; CHL, 1:506–7.

48. Ibid., Sabine, 226; CHL, 1:550.

49. Ibid., Sabine, 183; CHL, 1:506.

50. Hendrik Niklaes, "Glass of Righteousness," 27, in Bradstock and Rowland, *Radical Christian Writings*, 100–101; Hayes, *Winstanley*; Smith, *Perfection*, 144–84.

51. "New Law," Sabine, 226–27; CHL, 1:550.

52. "Fire in the Bush," Sabine, 465; CHL, 2:190.

buying and selling, the Earth with her fruits one to another";[53] the fourth Beast is the power of the clergy, which is used to give a religious or (in something like Marx's sense) an ideological gloss to the privileges of the few. According to Winstanley, the Creation will never be at peace, until these four beasts are overthrown, and only then will there be the coming of Christ's kingdom.[54]

In two ways Winstanley's biblical interpretation is typical of radical biblical interpretation down the centuries. First of all, the biblical images are related to both personal and social transformation. Second, the biblical texts offered him a language for life, a response to the divine call that demanded change politically and economically as well as personally. He captured this in some memorable words:

> Not a full yeere since, being quiet at my work, my heart was filled with sweet thoughts, and many things were revealed to me which I never read in books, nor heard from the mouth of any flesh, and when I began to speak of them, some people could not bear my words, and amongst those revelations this was one, *That the earth shall be made a common Treasury of livelihood to whole mankind, without respect of persons*; and I had a voice within me bad me declare it all abroad, which I did obey, for I declared it by word of mouth wheresoever I came, then I was made to write a little book called, *The new Law of righteousnesse*, and therein I declared it; yet my mind was not at rest, because nothing was acted, and thoughts run in me, that words and writings were all nothing, and must die, for action is the life of all, and if thou dost not act, thou dost nothing. Within a little time I was made obedient to the word in that particular likewise; for I tooke my spade and went and broke the ground upon *George-hill* in Surrey, thereby declaring freedome to the Creation, and that the earth must be set free from intanglements of Lords and Landlords, and that it shall become a common Treasury to all, as it was first made and given to the sonnes of men.[55]

These last are the first words we hear from Gerrard Winstanley in Kevin Brownlow and Andrew Mollo's wonderful film *Winstanley* (1975). The film ends with the moving words from Winstanley's "A New Yeer's Gift," which are a fitting testimony to the witness he and many

---

53. Ibid., Sabine, 465; CHL, 2:191.

54. Ibid., Sabine, 464–71; CHL, 2:190–6.

55. "A Watch-Word to the City of London," Sabine, 315–16; CHL, 2:80.

other have borne to the radical gospel of Jesus of Nazareth down the centuries. This is a vision which has been understood and acted out by Christian radicals and which Tim Gorringe understands so well: "And here I end, having put my Arm as far as my strength will go to advance Righteousness: I have Writ, I have Acted, I have Peace: and now I must wait to see the Spirit do his own work in the hearts of others, and whether *England* shall be the first Land, or some other, wherein Truth shall sit down in triumph."[56]

Bibliography

Bauman, Clarence. *The Spiritual Legacy of Hans Denck: Interpretation and Translation of Key Texts*. Leiden: Brill, 1991.

Bradstock, Andrew. *Faith in the Revolution: The Political Theologies of Müntzer and Winstanley*. London: SPCK, 1997.

———. *Radical Religion in Cromwell's England: A Concise History from the English Civil War to the End of the Commonwealth*. London: Tauris, 2010.

———. *Winstanley and the Diggers, 1649–1999*. London: Routledge, 2000.

Bradstock, Andrew, and C. Rowland. *Radical Christian Writings: A Reader*. Oxford: Blackwell 2002.

Corns, Thomas N., Ann Hughes, and David Loewenstein. *The Complete Works of Gerrard Winstanley*. 2 vols. Oxford: Oxford University Press, 2009.

Hayes, T. Wilson. "The Peaceful Apocalypse: Familism and Literacy in Sixteenth-Century England." *Sixteenth Century Journal* 17 (1986) 131–43.

———. *Winstanley the Digger*. Cambridge: Harvard University Press, 1979.

Hill, Christopher. *The English Bible and the Seventeenth-Century Revolution*. Harmondsworth: Penguin, 1993.

———. *The Religion of Gerrard Winstanley*. Past and Present Supplement 5. Oxford: Past and Present Society, 1978.

———. *Winstanley: The Law of Freedom and Other Writings*. Cambridge: Cambridge University Press, 1973.

———. *The World Turned Upside Down*. London: Penguin, 1972.

Holstun, James. *Ehud's Dagger: Class Struggle in the English Revolution*. London: Verso, 2002.

Houlden, J. Leslie, editor. *The Interpretation of the Bible in the Church*. London: SPCK, 1994.

Rowland, Christopher. *Blake and the Bible*. New Haven: Yale University Press, 2011.

———. *Radical Christianity: A Reading of Recovery*. Cambridge: Polity, 1988.

Rowland, Christopher, and Mark Corner. *Liberating Exegesis: The Challenge of Liberation Theology to Biblical Studies*. London: SPCK, 1990.

Sabine, George H., editor. *The Works of Gerrard Winstanley*. Ithaca, NY: Cornell University Press, 1941.

Smith, Nigel. *Perfection Proclaimed: Language and Literature in English Radical Religion, 1640–1660*. Oxford: Clarendon, 1989.

56. "A New-Yeer's Gift," Sabine, 395; CHL, 2:149.

Underwood, Ted LeRoy. *Primitivism, Radicalism, and the Lamb's War: The Baptist-Quaker Conflict in Seventeenth-Century England.* Oxford: Clarendon, 1997.

8

The Emergence of Schleiermacher's Theology and the City of Berlin

GRAHAM WARD

INTRODUCTION

Back in 1993, when Tim was the Chaplain of St. John's College, Oxford and I was the Chaplain of Exeter College, we began discussions about a new approach to Christian theology. Most of the accounts of major Christian theologians were theological—that is, expositions of their teachings on various aspects of dogmatics. Many such accounts might add an historical and biographical introduction, but the far richer sense that our thinking, imagining, and interpreting are embedded within the times and the cultures within which we live was lacking, on the whole. Furthermore, more recent approaches to social and cultural theory had drawn attention to the archaeologies and genealogies (Foucault), the fields of cultural productivity and habituses (Bourdieu), the circulations of social energy (Greenblatt's new historicism), and the cultural politics (de Certeau) that related any intellectual endeavor, its public success or failure, to the specific contexts within which they were undertaken. And so, in a seminar we shared on the theology of Schleiermacher, we undertook to show how his theology, while doing something startlingly original, had to be understood as a development and modification of the changing debates, issues, and

values, the political and economic developments, and the shifting social mores of Prussia between the end of the eighteenth century (in the
aftermath of the French Revolution) and the third decade of the nineteenth. We then took this approach one step further: we opened talks
with Oxford University Press about a very ambitious project—nothing
less than a large collection of monographs, each devoted to either a major theologian or a major theological movement, specifically orientated
to showing the intimate relationship between the social, historical, and
intellectual context and the theology produced. Tim's own volume, the
first in the series, was *Karl Barth: Against Hegemony* (1999), and recently
the series (now also coedited with Serene Jones) published its eighth
volume: *Origen: Scholarship in the Service of the Church* by Ronald E.
Heine (2010). Unfortunately, the volume that I proposed to offer has
never appeared. It was to be on Schleiermacher. I was, at the time, becoming fascinated with the city, a fascination that led to the volume,
written when I had left Oxford, titled *Cities of God*. And the volume I
proposed to Oxford University Press was focused on relating the changes in Schleiermacher's theology to the urban developments that took
place in Berlin between the time of Friedrich the Great (who created
the cityscape Schleiermacher experienced when he arrived in Berlin in
1796) and his grandson, Friedrich Wilhelm IV. I wanted to demonstrate
the way in which the city informed Schleiermacher's somatic, emotional,
and intellectual development as both a theologian and a philosopher. As
I said, though the project was conceived in some detail, it was never
executed. And so, in this Festschift for Tim, honoring his work, I want
to offer some fulfillment of a promise I made to him almost twenty years
ago: I want to write about the relationship between the rise of the modern metropolis and the rise of modern theology (since Schleiermacher
is often viewed as the first modern theologian). Given the limitations of
space, I can only treat Schleiermacher's first extended stay in the city—
the years 1796–1802.

BERLIN AND FRIEDRICH SCHLEIERMACHER

As the urban and historical geographers inform us, between 1800 and
1910, the population of Berlin grew from 172,000 to over two million
inhabitants, to become one of the leading cities in Germany. It is important to understand, however, that the development of the city to which
the urban and historical geographers mainly refer is a phenomenon of

the industrial revolution.[1] Because of this, most of the analysis of the development of German cities and urban planning concentrates on post-1850s Berlin; yet the Berlin experienced either by Schleiermacher or Hegel was only beginning to emerge as an industrial city. So what we are treating at the end of the eighteenth century and the beginning of the nineteenth is a cityscape developed by an absolute monarchy, and inspired by that peerless example of absolute monarchy, Louis XIV, in his conception of Versailles. If Louis XIV was to be equated quite physically with his state ("*L'état c'est moi*"), then the urban planning of absolute monarchy was to embody this idea. So, at Versailles, the center of his palace was his own bedchamber, and all roads from Paris and a number of other places converged on that spot.[2] We will begin to see what this means for Berlin, and for Schleiermacher, as we proceed.

In Germany, until 1808 and the passing of the municipal ordinance (the *Städteordnung*), any urban planning and development was a ruler's initiative and prerogative.[3] So, prior to this, Schleiermacher arrives at Prussia's *Kaiserstadt*. "Before his move to Berlin, Schleiermacher's intellectual productivity was analytic and isolated. After his 1796 entry into the Berlin circle of early romanticism, his first publications were the rhetorical fruition of his suddenly blossoming social life."[4] My attention here is on how the imperial city both creates and expresses the material conditions either conducive to or constraining social life. Schleiermacher had arrived in Berlin in fact in 1794, for a six-month stay as an instructor at a gymnasium. He was engaged at the time in a long treatise that was never published—*Über die Freiheit*—which spoke of the need to appropriate and respond to the world in what is a phenomenology of human choosing and the formation of subjective consciousness issuing from such choosing. He was intellectually prepared then to take on the city—but he left after six months. The old city walls were still intact—a sort of star-shaped defensive fortification crossing two tributaries of the river Spree. Within the walls were approximately 170,000 people, drawn there by the court of Friedrich Wilhelm II. In 1794, Schleiermacher kept to himself. He did not take possession of the city: he didn't engage in citizenship despite having friends like Alexander von Dohna who lived

1. As overall guides, see Lees and Lees, *Cities*, and Dennis, *Cities in Modernity*.

2. Bloomer and Moore, *Body, Memory, Architecture*, 12.

3. Sutcliffe, *Planned City*, 11.

4. Blackwell, *Schleiermacher's Early Philosophy*, 3.

there. Most of his time until this point had been lived in either the country, for his pietist schooling, the university township of Halle, or the country estate of the von Dohna family (where he was a tutor). When he returned to Berlin in 1796, his post was as Royal Chaplain to the Charité Hospital, and we are fortunate in having a map of Berlin composed just three years prior to his arrival. We can find Charité, which later formed the basis for the medical school and teaching hospital that still dominates the northern quarter of Berlin's inner city today, outside the city wall to the north; once more surrounded by countryside, a location due in part to the fact that the hospital was founded following an outbreak of plague in the early eighteenth century. In Schleiermacher's time, it was a military hospital. The barracks for the formidable Prussian army dominated a district to the east of the old city: König Stadt. Berlin, at this point, had grown beyond its fortified walls, and although new walls and gates into the city had been created, they were to come down early in the nineteenth century.

In the 1870s, a historian of the city, Robert Springer, in his *Berlin: Die deutsche Kaiserstadt*, described the growth of the city in this way: "There thus emerges from a fishing village an imperial city—from insignificant and scattered fishermen's cottages the capital of an internally strong, extensive, populous, politically important state, glittering with masterpieces of architecture and sculpture, distinguished for artistic zeal and intellectual culture, for academic learning, for the flowering of commerce and industry, for the higher progress of social life."[5] Most of this was to come when Schleiermacher arrived, though we can see from the map the various outlying areas of the old fortified town: König Stadt where Friedrich Wilhelm I moved his court from Königsberg and built his palace on being crowned King of Prussia in 1701; Spandaur Vierthel and Köpnicker Viethel—two of the oldest settlements beyond the walls; then Friedrich Stadt and Neustadt to the west; and Stradauer Viethel to the east. Further south was the separate town of Potsdam, where Schleiermarcher spent time as a court preacher since Friedrich the Great had built a palace there. What was most impressive was the new expansion under Friedrich the Great toward the Thiergarten, and the formation of promenades in the Thiergarten itself.

From the old castle, Friedrich had created what still today is a stunning architectural panorama: the great ceremonial boulevard known as

5. Springer, *Berlin*, 6.

Unter den Linden, lined on either side, beyond the lime trees, by palaces, but importantly housing the Berlin Opera House and the Royal Library. This was the cultural focus of the city when Schleiermacher arrived in 1796. It was crowned by the erection of the Brandenburg Gate, finished in 1791, which led out to the Thiergarten. Commissioned by Friedrich Wilhelm II, the gate was consecrated to peace. But the *Quadriga* that surmounts the gate is the goddess of victory driving her chariot before her. Nevertheless, with its Doric columns, this was not an *Arc de Triomphe* like the French recapitulation of Titus's victory arch in Rome, this was a gateway to the new Athens on the river Spree. This whole concourse architecturally is designed to dwarf the human body, to immerse it in a new beauty that was both imperial and imperious.

We can see from the map that the old city of Berlin was a warren of close mediaeval streets, except for Spandaustrasse where the wealthy tended to be housed. The old city was very much the city as fortress. But the Brandenburg Gate announced a different kind of city—one that was open, fearlessly so, proud and self-confident of its power, despite the French Revolution, which had toppled one of the major absolutist powers in Europe. Although Unter den Linden was constructed to allow for military parades and a demonstration of Prussian regal might, it was also constructed in terms of monumental architecture, both graceful and rational. It was an early example (the planning and architectural execution of Washington would be another) of the city as an artwork; the city as itself a new aesthetic form. Neustadt was the construction of a public space—a space in which to be seen, to meet and congregate. So we have, in the closing years of the Prussian *ancien régime* when, due to economic pressures with respect to the rise in land and grain prices, the feudalism of the nobility was becoming increasingly unsustainable, the beginnings of a public sphere and the rise of the *Bürgertum*. "Berlin is certainly one of the handsomest cities in Europe," George Forster declared after visiting the city in 1779.[6]

In part the expansion came with the Prussian state's administrative expansion and its choice of Berlin for its military headquarters. *Mitte*, old Berlin, housed the wealthy (bankers, jewelers, and important merchants), those who held key offices within the royal bureaucracy, the diplomats, the homes of foreign ambassadors and landowning

---

6. Hertz, *Jewish High Society*, 24.

noblemen. Friedrich Stadt was laid out in 1688 and then extended in 1721.[7] Neustadt was developed by Friedrich the Great, and as it expanded, the very wealthy began to leave the old city and move as close to the Unter den Linden as possible.

What was more, Berlin was a central European melting pot for languages and cultures. French Huguenots settled here near the Brandenburg Gate in the early eighteenth century, accounting for around 20 percent of the city's population; Friedrich the Great himself loved all things French. Here also were wealthy Jews who fled from Vienna when Austria expelled them, Jews whose historical backgrounds lay in Amsterdam and Portugal. Then, as the Kingdom of Poland ceased to exist, large chunks of that land were taken by the Prussians. So the city was inhabited by various peoples from Bohemia, Silesia, and even Austria. It was a place where religions met each other under Enlightenment auspices of toleration; where Jews (though they were not given the full rights of citizenship until 1871), Protestants, and Catholics (Friedrich built them a magnificent cathedral) came together and lived together.

The city did not have a university, but it did have the Royal Academy of Science, whose first president was Gottlieb Leibniz, and it had several learned societies—like the Wednesday club—where lectures were given and academic papers discussed. It had commercial as well as court theatres, two important and competing newspapers, lending libraries, and a private art collection open to the public.

It was, then, a city that buzzed with commercial, bureaucratic, and intellectual business; a city that looked to the future, saw progress as imperative, and believed in the power of ideas. Within the confines of a traditional social hierarchy or *Stände* (nobility, *Bürgertum*, peasantry) bubbled a cultured and creative energy that pushed at the boundaries of the traditional. It was the land of the *arrivistes*: "men who shared nothing but their aspiration to official positions and to intellectual prominence chose Berlin as the city in which to realise their dreams."[8]

Often, the originality of Schleiermacher's approach to religion and Christian theology, as expressed in his 1799 *On Religion: Speeches to Its Cultured Despisers*, is put down to sheer individual genius. No doubt there was genius or a sharp, quick-thinking intelligence. No doubt also living with Friedrich Schlegel, and founding with him, his

7. Sutcliffe, *Planned City*, 10.

8. Hertz, *Jewish High Society*, 50.

brother Augustus, and their common friend (soon to be Schlegel's wife) Dorothea Mendelssohn Viet, the journal *Athenaeum*, were contributory factors. But they were factors made possible by living in the same city, meeting every day for lunch at Dorothea's house. Even intelligence needs stimulating and nurturing. The city was now a new vibrant experience for Schleiermacher. It presented opportunities and encouragements he had not had before, most particularly an environment where dialogue and social interaction were paramount. His description of Plato's work, written just after his stay in the city, says much both about what he valued in Plato (as one of his major translators) and in civic life: Plato's medium of dialogue was "fashioned like a living being, with parts in proportion and body appropriate to mind."[9] Berlin provided him with the material, cultural, and social conditions necessary to take his concept of freedom—as both bounded and yet infinite—and embody it. More so, because when Friedrich Wilhelm III came to power in 1797, he swept away some of the oppressive censorship of the old regime and "raised hopes for greater freedom and constitutionalism" in the German state.[10]

Space is different in a city: there are modes of distance and proximity, shades of intimacy and estrangement, as buildings and streets close in upon or dwarf the urbanite. And so relations between citizens are different: encountering a friend becomes easier and more regular than in the country; one also continually encounters the stranger, the foreigner. In its turn this generates different senses of community and modifies what it is to be human, to be a social animal. The old mediaeval city emphasized familiarity (with all the paternal connotations of that term), intrigue, and insularity. Neustadt spoke of a freedom to move and so to think. Its architecture exposed the citizen to light, grand vistas, and the broad expanses of the Thiergarten. It awoke new levels of sensation, experience, and imagination; a different sense of being alive; life's boundless potential. "Life" plays an important philosophical role in the work of Schleiermacher, as it did with Hegel and Hölderlin in their Frankfurt days.

The city created a new hunger for experience that *Bildung* disciplined and gave direction, narratives, and a teleology. The aspirations of *Bildung*, the ideal subjectivity it fashioned and promulgated, are inseparable from the growth in urban culture and modern citizenship. As

9. Blackwell, *Schleiermacher's Early Philosophy*, 135.

10. Crouter, "Introduction," xv.

we will see, the experiences of a new spatiality (modeled in terms of the finite and the infinite), a new appreciation of relations and reciprocity, and a new sense of community become fundamental to understanding Schleiermarcher's early writing and later theological and philosophical development.

In the city, time is different: there are appointments to make and to keep, there are invitations to events, times at which shops and libraries close and open, performances begin and end, and concerts take place. The modern city is orientated toward the future; it is this that solicits the dreams of utopians.[11] It is also preoccupied with the intensity of the present; *carpe diem* is the watermark inscribed in the very walls and pavements of its banking, commercial, governmental, juridical, and entertainment districts. Neustadt was an expression of the French Enlightenment view of progress and the intellectual development of European civilization, whereas Mitte and the fortified walls of the older city remained locked into a defensive past. The new city had to plan for the future of its expansion. It had to think of civic amenities (and the buildings that housed and institutionalized them). It had to think of flows of traffic, pedestrians, water, sewage, and energy supplies.[12] European tourism was becoming fashionable: cities like Berlin had to prepare themselves to welcome future visitors able to spread the gospel of its magnificence. There is an urgency about Schleiermacher's writings between 1796 and 1802—the urgency of a man who has to make his mark and his future; time had become intensified.

One scholar has emphasized what the letters exchanged between Friedrich, Dorothea, and her childhood friend, Henrietta Herz, all remarked upon: Schleiermarcher "was a connoisseur of the art of friendship."[13] It was the city of Berlin that provided him with the intimate friendships from which his writing and its originality sprung. In fact, it was the very *avant-garde* sense that Berliners living in the wake of enlightened monarchs had that made possible new kinds of relationship and new freedoms in relationship. As many have noted, both Schlegel and Schleiermacher enjoyed very close relationships with women who, in the early days, were not their wives. In fact, both Dorothea and Henrietta were married women. Although Schleiermacher had met

11. See Pinder, *Visions of the City*.

12. See Masur, *Imperial Berlin*, and Ribbe, *Geschichte Berlins*.

13. Richardson, "Berlin Circle," 828.

Henrietta earlier, when he was a teacher at the Gedike Gymnasium, they belonged to two quite different classes. She a Jew, married to a wealthy banker and with close associations with princes, the nobility, important officials and writers like the Humboldt brothers and Ludwig Tieck, diplomats, financiers, musicians and artists; he a young, unknown son of a Lutheran pastor, albeit with a noble patron (the Count von Dohna), a royal civil servant. But no one can overlook the inner connections of this crowd. Count Alexander von Dohna was the son of a very important nobleman from an old and celebrated family; he was also an influential and upwardly mobile public servant—particularly so under Friedrich Wilhelm III; Schleiermacher had worked for Alexander's father; Alexander von Dohna knew the Herzes very well indeed—in fact, when Marcus Herz died in 1803, Dohna, who was infatuated with Henrietta, proposed to her; Dohna was an important patron for Schleiermacher. It is likely that Schleiermacher first met influential people in his career like the Humboldts at Henrietta's *salon*; Dohna was a close friend of the Humboldt brothers, whose father had been a gentleman of the bedroom under Friedrich Wilhelm II.

Only the city, and the important mediatorial role *salons* played not only in the cultural and intellectual life of the city, but also in mediating across traditional social barriers, made possible not only Schleiermacher's career advancement but his self-cultivation (*Bildung* through an aestheticization of one's experience). The *salon* that met at Henrietta's house (she was, with her husband—the doctor and professor, Markus—the first to establish *salonière* culture in Berlin) was a focus for both *Kultur* and *Bildung*, and even though in that city Jewish people were socially differentiated, the drawing room provided a space that crossed strongly traditional barriers with respect to gender, class, religion, and ethnicity. "The salon, as a temporary compromise between private aspirations and public realities, was an aesthetic form since it was a means of adapting the public realm to conform to the ideal sphere of personal privacy."[14] As Schleiermacher described it in his *Monologen*, using, note, a theological term, "where there is such a society, there is my paradise."[15] It is important to remember that remark, for redemption

---

14. Davies, "Sociability in Practice and Theory," 29.

15. Schleiermacher, *Monologen*, 32.

for Schleiermacher, as developed in his much later *Glaubenslehre*, issues from "reciprocal relations."[16]

THE CITY'S IMPACT UPON
SCHLEIERMACHER'S THOUGHT

The city articulated and materialized three concerns: humanity in all its heterogeneity, the freedom to make one's way, and the condition for *Bildung* or what the French called *l'education sentimental*—an education in the cultured ways of the world. Before then commenting more particularly on the way civic living impacts upon one's ideas in his groundbreaking *On Religion*, Schleiermacher's contribution to the first volume of *Athenaeum* was a fragment titled "*Idee zu einem Katechismus der Vernuft für edle Frauen*" in which he daringly announced his own creed: "I believe in infinite humanity [*unendliche Menschheit*], whoever they are, prior to their adopting the garments [*die Hülle*] of masculinity or femininity . . . I believe in the power of the will and education to bring me close again to the infinite and to release me from the chains of cultural ignorance [*Bildung, mich dem Unendlichen wieder zu nähern, mich aus den Fesseln der Mißbildung zu erlösen*]."[17] We can observe that the verb *erlösen* does mean "to release," but it is also a theologically inflected word meaning "to deliver," and it was used in the German rendition of the Lord's Prayer: "deliver us from evil." The language of the infinite bears all the traces of early Romanticism, but not when it is associated with the object "humanity"; it is the sheer wealth of the human condition Schleiermacher is bearing witness to. Furthermore, this is not a dissolving of the finite into the infinite (as Friedrich Schlegel or Novalis described it) but a "bring[ing] close to it." I emphasize this because time and again Schleiermacher returns us to the material and the social; and if there is a suggestion of Romanticism's flirtation with androgyny, in other early work he is much more clear that one of the most important forms of reciprocal relationality was that between man and woman.

He takes up the question of sexual difference in his next published work, which was explicitly on what he termed "free sociality" [*freie*

16. Schleiermacher, *Christian Faith*, 21 (where it describes relations between the individual and God that determines the spirituality and morality of all) and 727 (where it describes Trinitarian relations). For a more detailed analysis of this reciprocity, see Shults, "Reciprocal Relationality."

17. Schleiermacher, *Idee zu einem Katechismus*, 153–54.

Geselligkeit], published in 1798: *Versuch einer Theorie des geselligen Bretragens*. The essay is a sociological and anthropological reflection upon *salon* life or the functioning of free associations more generally, which because they are constituted between the private and public domains (in what will increasingly become established as civil society), are, Schleiermacher believes, best organized around women. In a manner that, while giving prominence to women, articulates a male Romantic take that only reinforces the conventional view of women at the time, Schleiermacher views women as ideal facilitators of free sociality because their public role is also their private role. "[P]recisely because women have no class in common with me besides being cultured persons, it is they who would become the founders of a better society."[18] The essay is, then, a reflection upon the role of Henrietta Herz (and those other prominent, mainly Jewish women who organized Berlin *salon* life) in the fashioning of a free society. And Schleiermacher here is already using a distinction that will be made far more famous by the German sociologist Ferdinand Tönnies in 1887: the distinction between *Gesellschaft* and *Gemeinschaft*.[19] Interestingly, in an explanatory footnote in the text on *"freien Geselligkeit der Gesellschaft,"* Schleiermacher understands *Gemeinschaft* as the equivalent of the Greek term *koinonia*, but *Gesellschaft* (which he associates with free sociality) is the equivalent of the Greek term *sunousiai*.[20] He employs a distinctly theological vocabulary, but the Church for Schleiermacher is, like the state, an institution for public life (as a chaplain, he was in fact a civil servant). This is how, ecclesiologically, he understands *koinonia*. Salon life, his avowed paradise, is a *sunousiai*. This a coined term, not found either in ancient or New Testament Greek—*sun* as the prefix "in the company of," "together," and *ousia* as the highly metaphysical noun meaning "being" or "essence." It is a coining reminiscent of several Pauline inventions to describe our condition in Christ, where he also prefixes *sun* to more familiar verbs and nouns to articulate the nature of our participation in Christ. Paul becomes particularly inventive with the prefix *sun* when

---

18. Schleiermacher, *Versuch einer Theorie*, 178. See here also the role that Ernestine plays as the *Hausfrau* preparing for the Christmas festivities in Schleiermacher's 1804 essay *Die Weihnachtsfeier*. This essay is one of the earliest explorations I know of a theology of sexual difference.

19. Tönnies, *Gemeinschaft und Gesellschaft*.

20. Schleiermacher, *Versuch einer Theorie*, 169.

describing the nature of the church as the body of Christ. Witness *syn-ekerasen*, "has composed together with," in 1 Cor 12, and the deutero-Pauline terms *synēgeiren* (raised together with) and *synekathisen* (sit together with) in Eph 2:6. The Pauline association would have come easily to Schleiermacher with his profound knowledge of both Greek and the Scriptures.

The essay sets out three "laws" governing and defining "free sociality." These are not rules of conduct, for such would compromise any notion of "free." In an early adoption of a Kantian transcendental argument (which Schleiermacher will use to great effect in the introduction to the second edition of his *Glaubenslehre*), the "laws" are more the conditions for the possibility of free society. These are: first, everything is to be governed by reciprocal action (a formal law, in his terminology); second, all are "to be stimulated to a free play of thoughts through the communication of what is [distinctively] mine"[21] (a material law); and third, "social activity should always remain with the boundaries within which a particular society can exist as a whole,"[22] and so each person must be governed by an overall propriety toward the others in the group (a quantitative law). This concern for the other person is echoed throughout the writings of these early years: in a sketch titled "*Versuch über die Schamhaftigkeit*," he calls for respect for the other person.[23] The other person always qualifies one's understanding and practice of my own freedom.[24] The primary axiom behind these three laws is that human beings are social animals; that free sociality is "an unavoidable natural tendency";[25] being human is being in relation and becoming fully human is participating in such relations. What is uppermost in the operations of these laws (besides the evident bourgeois intellectual elitism of it all) is the self-fashioning that issues from the social phenomenon of cultural exchange. And so both the self and the society become works of art in the manifestation of the operation of *Bildung*. Social life is construed as a work of art[26] wrought by the ongoing dialectics of the individual and society, the private and the public, receptivity and activity, feeling

21. Ibid., 170.

22. Ibid., 171.

23. Schleiermacher, "Versuch über die Schamhaftigkeit."

24. See also *Monologen; Soliloquies*, 79.

25. Schleiermacher, *Versuch einer Theorie*, 168.

26. Ibid., 167.

and doing, expressing and knowing, the personal style [*Manier*] and the communal tone [*Ton*]. It is a work of art because it has no other object or telos than itself; it transcends Enlightenment instrumental reasoning. One becomes humanized by participation in such dialectics; and to be human is to be cultured. Life is an ongoing education; *Bildung* is a means both of self-transcendence and self-fulfillment. As Schleiermacher wrote to his sister Charlotte on 23 March 1799, receiving such an education within such a forum is a moral responsibility: *"Jeder Mensch muß schlechterdings in einem Zustande moralischer Geselligkeit stehn."*[27]

Now, although there are intimations of a theology here—in terms of a theological anthropology, a soteriology ("emancipation through self-cultivation"[28] in and through other people), and an ecclesiology— Schleiermacher does not develop them here. All the work that follows, from *On Religion* onwards, is a theological development, and modification, of what is stated here in what we might term a transcendental sociology or even an early piece of phenomenology (a phenomenology of believing). The point I wish to make is how the newly emerging city of Berlin exists like a palimpsest beneath the structure of this discourse. The city as a work of architectural art and the social body that occupies, maps, walks, and orchestrates its urban planning in the creation of its social and cultural life, is the very watermark within the paper on which this reflection is written. The city, as architecturally designed buildings and urban layout, is experienced, and this experience is translated in various ways into the lives of the city's inhabitants. To use Schleiermacher's categories: it affects their feelings—where feelings [*Gefühl*] are not simply corporeal sensations and emotional affects, but also intuitions of right order or, as he puts it, "the immediate presence of whole undivided being."[29] These feelings, always qualified by the word *intuition*, which I want to gather collectively into what, existentially, after Heidegger, we might call "the feeling of dwelling," are articulated (verbally, gesturally, in any number of *Gestalten*) and so become doings—and doings facilitate understanding or knowledge of the built environment and the social and cultural praxes it fosters. This is not, *pace* Hegel, a subjectivist

27. Schleiermacher, Briefe an die Schwester, 49.

28. Davies, "Sociability in Practice and Theory," 30.

29. *Christian Faith*, 7. Schleiermacher is here approving of a definition of feeling found in Steffen's *Falsche Theologie*, but it is a definition that accords with his own extended analysis on pp. 6–8.

account of religion,[30] and it is not, *pace* Tillich, an emotivist account of religion.[31] As Schleiermacher recognized, this internalization of the aesthetics of the city provoke an aestheticization of experience more generally. Following the lead of German philosopher Alexander Baumgarten, who relates aesthetics with the Greek *aistēsis*—"sensation"[32]—minds and bodies are thus inseparable. Thus the city as a work of art, and the moral and spiritual life of its citizens as a work of art, each impacts upon, and makes possible, the other. This dialectical activity is made possible by an anthropological *a priori* that Schleiermacher states quite explicitly in his *Brouillon zur Ethik*: *"alle Menschen sind Künstler."*[33]

I am aware I have said very little explicitly about theology as such. Two premises are important for the steps that follow and the interpretation of Schleiermacher's theology and philosophy that they afford. First, the "feeling of dwelling," which is the basis for our experience, means that feelings are not private, inner reflexes; they are social both in terms of source and orientation. Religion then is not a private matter either; it is not only a communal activity but issues from and maintains that community. Two words distinctively mark Schleiermacher's approach to religion in *On Religion*: "experience" (*Erlebnis*) and immediate "feeling" (*Gefühl*). Both words lead directly to his understanding of religion as the "*Sinn und Geschmack fürs Unendliche.*"[34] Second, there is no direct knowledge of God. As Schleiermacher puts it in his *Glaubenslehre*: "we have no formula for the being of God in Himself as distinct from the being of God in the world,"[35] and so "we must declare the description of human states of mind to be the fundamental form, while propositions of the second and third forms [statements about God or the world as they appear in self-consciousness] are permissible only in so

---

30. For excellent analyses of the debate here between Hegel and Schleiermacher, see Nowak, *Schleiermacher und die Frühromantik,* 288–95, and his more recent and highly readable biography *Schleiermacher,* 409–19. For the role played by Hegel's student, Hermann Hinrichs, in the debate, see von der Luft, *Hegel, Hinrichs, and Schleiermacher.* The introductions to the texts are exemplary, and Luft translates (for the first time into English) important sections of the first edition of 1821–22 *Der christliche Glaube.*

31. See Tillich, *Perspectives,* 95–102.

32. His two volumes of *Aesthetika* appeared between 1750 and 1759. See also *Christian Faith,* 7.

33. Schleiermacher, *Brouillon zur Ethik,* 108.

34. Schleiermacher, *On Religion,* 103.

35. Schleiermacher, *Christian Faith,* 748.

far as they can be developed out of the propositions of the first form, for only on this condition can they be authenticated as expressions of religious emotions."[36] Now I am not agreeing or disagreeing with either of these two premises, or the implications of Schleiermacher's theological method for various aspects of his dogmatics. What I am pointing to is the profound relationship between his experience as a Berliner and his theology. What becomes clear from the move Schleiermacher makes in his early life in Berlin for defining a "*freie Geselligkeit*," and defining religion with respect to experiencing such a sociality, and the move he makes toward understanding the basis of dogmatics as the feeling of absolute dependence, the consciousness of such a feeling and "reciprocal relationality" in the *Glaubenslehre*, written following Schleiermarcher's return to Berlin in 1807, is that religion and morality are never epiphenomena of feeling and experience. That is, they are not secondary descriptive effects of a foundational and ineffable experience. The nature of religion as a taste for the infinite, and morality as a social reciprocity in pursuit of the good on the basis of understanding that all is gift in that all is absolutely dependent, are both given in experience and feeling itself. This is important to grasp for understanding Schleiermacher, and especially for understanding why he is not a liberal. For the liberal theologian (and we can take Rudolph Otto as an example) the religious feeling or intuition is primary and ineffable and its subsequent expression in a cultural-linguistic system is secondary. Hence, then, there is no real problem for such liberal thinking with religious pluralism because at base all religions are expressions of the same fundamental experience. This is absolutely not so for Schleiermacher. Certainly, cognition and consciousness, which is only possible on the condition of the reception of what is experienced and felt, give expression to what is given *in* the experience and feeling. But the content of that feeling and intuition is its unfolding; there is no arbitrary division between the two. The feeling or intuition is the soul or form that governs the body or matter that is shaped. We move from the abstract to the more concrete accounts of experience and feeling in and through language inseparable from cognition; but the one is the direct outworking of the other. That such outworking is necessarily determined also by historical, social, and cultural conditions is accepted; but the "also" is fundamental here—for there is

36. Ibid., 125–26.

that in the feeling or intuition that is universal.[37] And experience and feeling, as I am presenting them here, related to living in urban Berlin at the turn of the nineteenth century, when cities were becoming the grandiloquent stage-sets for modern life as we know it.

That there is no major difference between the early Schleiermacher of the *freie Geselligkeit* and the later Schleiermacher of "reciprocal relationality" can be recognized from a statement that demonstrates the dependency of his theology upon the newly emerging urban sociality. In *On Religion*, he writes: "Once there is religion, it must necessarily also be social. That not only lies in human nature but also is preeminently in the nature of religion . . . In the continuous reciprocity, which is not only practical but also intellectual, in which he stands with the rest of his species, he is supposed to express and communicate all that is in him."[38]

As I said above, there are two sides to the Brandenburg Gate. On the one hand, it is the ceremonial entrance to Berlin as the new Athens—an Athens that prided itself on its civic freedoms—and dedicated to peace. On the other, it is crowned by the goddess of victory and so emblematic of Prussian dominance. Only diplomats of royalty and royalty itself could use the central arch; all other ranks had to use the side arches. The space that it opens on to, and exits from, is an urban space expressing the dialectic between lordship and bondage, already articulated by Hegel in his early essay in 1798–99 "The Spirit of Christianity"—years before its famous articulation in the *Phenomenology of Spirit*. It was a space in which the drama of self-consciousness, subjectivity, and mutual recognition, was played out; with the potential for community and reciprocal relations. Schleiermacher, as a citizen of no mean city, embodied the tension at its very entry. He was the enjoyer of civic freedoms in his attendance at *salons* and learned societies like the Wednesday club; he was also a civil servant paid by the crown as Chaplain of Charité. In a letter written in 1798, he acknowledged the tension: "if it were to become too well known that I live so entirely among these people [his *salon* intimates], an unfavorable opinion would inevitably be produced

37. It is for this reason that Schleiermacher differs from certain early Romantics like Friedrich Schlegel: because for Schlegel the ethical (and the religious) is the aesthetic, whereas for Schleiermacher the aesthetic is the creative activity whereby the unfolding of what is intrinsically there in the givenness of experience and feeling (which is moral and religious) becomes conscious in cognition (the language of thought).

38. Schleiermacher, *On Religion*, 163.

by many."[39] The two sides of the tension became evident when his career mentor and old family friend, the Cathedral Preacher, Friedrich Samuel Gottfried Sack, worried about Schleiermacher's socializing, arranged for him to spend some time away from the city at Potsdam, where he had to preach before Friedrich Wilhelm III. The two sides collided on Schleiermacher's return, with the publication, even though anonymous, of his *On Religion*. Berlin gossip easily uncovered the true identity of the author. The same Friedrich Samuel Gottfried Sack was also the Censor for the Prussian government. He sent a letter written five months earlier to Schleiermacher at the opening of 1801, castigating his friends and their "stream of sophistry"[40]: "I know also that in the circle in which you live, men like me are held to be feeble-minded," he wrote. In his reply, Schleiermacher acknowledged that the friends to which reference was made "would be uncommonly glad to see me no longer a preacher,"[41] but nevertheless he expressed the need to avoid preachers being "outlawed in the realm of society." [42] But outlawed he was. In 1802 Sack arranged for Schleiermacher's departure to an obscure town on the Baltic Sea, as court chaplain. As Wilhelm Dilthey comments, in his monumental biography of Schleiermacher, this was "a kind of exile."[43] And in this way Schleiermacher left Berlin . . . at least for a time.

Bibliography

Blackwell, Albert L. "The Antagonistic Correspondence of 1801 between Chaplain Sack and His Protégé Schleiermacher." *Harvard Theological Review* 74 (1981) 106.

———. *Schleiermacher's Early Philosophy of Life: Determinism, Freedom, and Phantasy.* Chico, CA: Scholars, 1982.

Bloomer, Kent C., and Charles W. Moore. *Body, Memory, and Architecture.* New Haven: Yale University Press, 1977.

Crouter, Richard. "Introduction" to Schleiermacher, *On Religion*, xi–xl.

Davies, Martin. "Sociability in Practice and Theory: Henriette Herz and Friedrich Schleiermacher." *New Athenaeum/Neues Athenaeum* 2 (1991) 29.

Dennis, Richard. *Cities in Modernity: Representations and Productions of Metropolitan Space, 1840–1930.* Cambridge: Cambridge University Press, 2008.

39. Blackwell, "Antagonistic Correspondence," 106.

40. Ibid., 115.

41. Ibid., 119.

42. Ibid., 117.

43. Dilthey, *Leben Schleiermachers* I/1, 541. Nowak also speaks of "exile," without attributing it to Dilthey. See Nowak, *Leben, Werk und Wirkung*, 124.

Dilthey, Wilhelm. *Leben Schleiermachers* I/1. Edited by Martin Redeker. Göttingen: Vandenhoeck & Ruprecht, 1970.

Hegel, Georg Wilhelm Friedrich. *The Spirit of Christianity and Its Fate*. In *Friedrich Hegel on Christianity: Early Theological Writings*, translated by T. M. Knox, edited by Richard Kroner, 182–301. New York: Harper, 1948.

Hertz, Deborah. *Jewish High Society in Old Regime Berlin*. New York: Syracuse University Press, 2005.

Lees, Andrew, and Lynn Hollen Lees. *Cities and the Making of Modern Europe, 1750–1914*. Cambridge: Cambridge University Press, 2007.

Luft, Eric von der. *Hegel, Hinrichs, and Schleiermacher on Feeling and Reason in Religion: The Texts of Their 1821–22 Debate*. Lewiston, NY: Edwin Mellen, 1987.

Masur, Gerhard. *Imperial Berlin*. New York: Basic, 1970.

Nowak, Kurt. *Schleiermacher: Leben, Werk und Wirkung*. Göttingen: Vandenhoeck & Ruprecht, 2001.

———. *Schleiermacher und die Frühromantik: Eine literaturgeschichtliche Studie zum romantischen Religionsverständnis und Menschenbild am Ende des 18. Jahrhunderts in Deutschland*. Göttingen: Vandenhoeck & Ruprecht, 1986.

Pinder, David. *Visions of the City: Utopianism, Power and Politics in Twentieth-Century Urbanism*. Edinburgh: Edinburgh University Press, 2005.

Ribbe, Wolfgang, editor. *Geschichte Berlins*. Berlin: Berliner Wissenschafts-Verlag, 2002.

Richardson, Ruth Drucilla. "The Berlin Circle of Contributors to 'Athenaeum': Friedrich Schlegel, Dorthorthea Mendelssohn Viet, and Friedrich Schleiermacher." In *200 Jahre "Reden über die Religion,"* edited by Ulrich Barth and Claus-Dieter Osthoevener, 816–58. Berlin: de Gruyter, 2000.

Schleiermacher, Friedrich D. E. "Briefe an die Schwester [Charlotte] 23.3.1799." In *Kritsche Gesamtausgabe*, edited by Hermann Fischer et al. Band 5.3: *Briefwechsel 1799–1800*, edited by Andreas Arndt and Wolfgang Virmond. Berlin: de Gruyter, 1992.

———. *Brouillon zur Ethik (1805/06)*. Edited by Hans-Joachim Birkner. Hamburg: Meiner Felix, 1998.

———. *The Christian Faith*. Translated by H. R. Mackintosh and J. S. Stewart. Edinburgh: T. & T. Clark, 1989.

———. *Idee zu einem Katechismus der Vernuft für edle Frauen*. In *Kritsche Gesamtausgabe*, edited by Hermann Fischer et al. Band 1.2: *Schriften aus der Berliner Zeit 1796–1799*, edited by Günter Meckenstock, 153–54. Berlin: de Gruyter, 1984.

———. *Monologen*. In *Kritsche Gesamtausgabe*, edited by Hermann Fischer et al. Band 1.3: *Schriften aus der Berliner Zeit 1800–1802*, edited by Günter Meckenstock, 6–61. Berlin: de Gruyter, 1988.

———. *On Religion: Speeches to Its Cultured Despisers*. 2nd ed. Cambridge: Cambridge University Press, 1996.

———. *Schleiermacher's Soliloquies: An English Translation of the Monologen*. Translated by Horace Leland Friess. Westport, NY: Hyperion, 1926.

———. *Über die Freiheit*. In *Kritsche Gesamtausgabe*, edited by Hermann Fischer et al. Band 1.1: *Jugendschriften 1787–1796*, edited by Günter Meckenstock, 217–356. Berlin: de Gruyter, 1983.

———. *Versuch einer Theorie des geselligen Bretragens*. In *Kritsche Gesamtausgabe*, edited by Hermann Fischer et al. Band 1.2: *Schriften aus der Berliner Zeit 1796–1799*, edited by Günter Meckenstock, 163–84. Berlin: de Gruyter, 1984.

————. "Versuch über die Schamhaftigkeit." In *Vertraute Briefe über Friedrich Schlegels Lucinde*. In *Kritsche Gesamtausgabe*, edited by Hermann Fischer et al. Band 1.3: *Schriften aus der Berliner Zeit 1800–1802*, edited by Günter Meckenstock, 168–78. Berlin: de Gruyter, 1988.

————. *Die Weihnachtsfeier: Ein Grespräch*, in *Kleine Schriften und Predigten 1800–1829* 1, edited by Hayo Gerdes and Emanuel Hirsch, 226–27. Berlin: de Gruyter, 1970.

Shults, F. LeRon. "Schleiermacher's 'Reciprocal Relationality': The Underlying Regulative Principle of His Theological Method." In *Schleiermacher on the Workings of the Knowing Mind*, edited by Ruth Drucilla Richardson, 177–96. Lewiston, NY: Edwin Mellen, 1998.

Springer, Robert. *Berlin: Die deutsche Kaiserstadt*. Damstadt: Haude & Spenersche, 1878.

Sutcliffe, Anthony. *Towards the Planned City: Germany, Britain, the United States, and France*. Oxford: Oxford University Press, 1981.

Tönnies, Ferdinand. *Gemeinschaft und Gesellschaft: Abhandlung des Communismus und des Socialismus als empirischer Culturformen*. Leipzig: Fues, 1887.

9

"There Is No Wealth but Life"

John Ruskin and Public Theology

ZOË BENNETT

THE BEATING OF ONE'S HEART IN A NIGHTMARE

"**Y**our *Fors*," wrote Archbishop, later Cardinal, Manning to John Ruskin on 21 October 1873, "is a vigorous and human protest against this degradation of man and of Society." "*It is like the beating of one's heart in a nightmare.*"[1]

The imagining and pursuit of human flourishing, and the exposure of its betrayal, are central to the life's work of John Ruskin (1819–1900)— aesthetic and social critic, and Victorian sage. *Fors Clavigera*, to which Manning refers, is a series of, initially monthly, public letters written between 1871 and 1884 to "the workmen and laborers of Great Britain," encapsulating and driving home the living nightmare that was the downside of industrialized Victorian Britain, awakening the conscience and daring to risk critique of public policy and practice.

Ruskin's "turn to the human" had, however, come earlier than this, with the publication in 1860 of four essays on political economy in the

---

1. Ruskin, *Works*, 36:lxxxvii and lxxxvi, my italics. Quotations from Ruskin's published works are taken from Cook and Wedderburn, *Works of John Ruskin*, referred to by volume and page number.

Cornhill Magazine, later published in 1862 in book form as *Unto this Last.* The year 1860 had seen the publication of the fifth and final volume of the magisterial *Modern Painters,* which had established Ruskin as the foremost art critic of his generation. For several reasons, not the least of which has to do with his "unconversion" from a narrow evangelical faith in the late 1850s, Ruskin moved in that year from the great tomes of *Modern Painters* to the quasi-sermonic form of the short essays that comprise *Unto this Last*; from concentration on landscape to fixation with human social life; and from "eyesight" to "heart-sight."[2]

"A heavenly book, written by our largely forgotten national arch-angel," is how Jonathan Glancey characterized *Unto this Last* in *The Guardian* recently; it "deserves to be read anew, by all of us, but mostly by expense-sullied politicians in search of a moral compass with practical, humane and honest bearings."[3] Or hear Andrew Hill, Associate Editor and City Editor of the *Financial Times*: "Ruskin's savage attack on the complacency and sterility of market economics, seems overdue for rehabilitation."[4] Such contemporary commentators echo in today's circumstances the admiration for *Unto this Last* held by the first twenty-nine elected Labour MPs who in 1906 declared it was the book that had most affected them, by Mahatma Gandhi who claimed it had changed his life, and by Martin Luther King Jr., whose case of personal effects on display at the King Center in Atlanta, Georgia, includes an Indian copy of the book.

RUSKIN THE "PRACTICAL THEOLOGIAN"

It will not have escaped the reader's attention that there are certain qualities of John Ruskin's work that make him an appropriate subject for inclusion in a book of essays in honor of Tim Gorringe. Ruskin's intention, through his public writing and lecturing, was to make an intelligent and passionate critique of social, cultural, and economic practices, and in so doing to change the way things were done in his time. More than that, Ruskin was a man of faith—albeit a changing, not-easily-pinned-down faith. His deep and lifelong private and public engagement with the Bible informs his work. Theological reflection is turned by Ruskin,

---

2. As he says of J. M. W. Turner, *Works,* 7:377.

3. *The Guardian,* 19 June 2009.

4. From his introduction to a new edition of *Unto this Last.*

exquisitely, courageously, and at times eccentrically, into an active force in the public world.

There are three factors that substantially characterize the nature and quality of Ruskin's theological reflection. The first is his commitment to good "seeing," reiterated throughout *Modern Painters*: "the greatest thing a human soul ever does in this world is to *see* something, and tell what it saw in a plain way. Hundreds of people can talk for one who can think, but thousands can think for one who can see. To see clearly is poetry, prophecy, and religion,—all in one."[5]

On 29 October 1858, Ruskin gave an inaugural address at the opening of the Cambridge School of Art, later named after him as part of Anglia Ruskin University, in which he said: "To be taught to read—what is the use of that, if you know not whether what you read is false or true? To be taught to write or to speak—but what is the use of speaking, if you have nothing to say? To be taught to think—nay, what is the use of being able to think, if you have nothing to think of? But to be taught to see is to gain word and thought at once, and both true."[6]

Seeing is the primary act, although thinking and telling importantly follow. This is a manifesto for practical theology. Ruskin is an omnivorous "seer," a voracious reader of "texts." He is a reader of multiple texts, and he brings them into dialogue with one another. This is the second characteristic of his theological reflection.[7] These "texts" include paintings, drawings, and architecture, that is, aesthetic texts; the human and social world, that is, the "living human documents" of practical theology; and the text of the Bible—that text that was embedded in him and ever springs out of him like living water, from the days when he learned it painstakingly, daily, chapter by chapter, at his mother's knee.

A third characteristic is Ruskin's refusal to compartmentalize and dissect, to distance the objects of his gaze from himself and to reduce them to lifelessness. He writes: "All true science begins in the love, not the dissection, of your fellow creatures; and it ends in the love, not the analysis, of God."[8] Critical subjectivity that seeks to integrate rather than divide up is of the essence of practical theology.

5. *Works*, 5:333.
6. Ibid., 16:180.
7. For Ruskin as a practical theologian, see Bennett, "To See Fearlessly."
8. *Works*, 26:265–66.

As he draws near to the end of the five volumes of *Modern Painters* and to that turn to the human that *Unto this Last* signals, Ruskin talks about the courage that true seeing requires. He refers still to color in painting, but the moral and the human are just around the corner.

> Now, as far as I have watched the main powers of human mind, they have risen first from the resolution to see fearlessly, pitifully, and to its very worst, what these deep colours mean, wheresoever they fall; not by any means to pass on the other side, looking pleasantly up to the sky, but to stoop to the horror, and let the sky, for the present, take care of its own clouds. However this may be in moral matters, with which I have nothing here to do, in my own field of inquiry the fact is so; and all great and beautiful work has come of first gazing without shrinking into the darkness.[9]

Gazing without shrinking into the darkness, without fear and with deep pity: that is the move in human affairs that Ruskin is about to make, and before his life is over he will have gazed into more darkness than most—not only the horrors of unbridled capitalism, human injustice, and environmental disaster, but also public opprobrium, personal loss, and debilitating bouts of insanity.

RUSKIN AS BIBLICAL INTERPRETER

Ruskin read the Bible daily throughout his life. This began when his mother gifted him with "the most precious, and, on the whole, the one *essential* part of all my education," and by this process "established my soul in life," and "gave me secure *ground* for all future life, practical or spiritual."[10] It continued through his childhood and adolescent reading and writing of sermons, detailed notes of wrestling with the Bible in personal diaries, and annotations on medieval biblical manuscripts that he used (in Greek) for his daily reading. It finds public voice in lectures, letters, books, and essays. It persists through all phases of faith: the evangelical until about 1858, followed by the troubled "religion of humanity" until about 1875, and finally through the open and ecumenical, if somewhat unorthodox, faith of Ruskin's old age. In 1898, on the basis of what had then been published of his work, Mary and Ellen Gibbs were able to produce a three hundred-page volume of Ruskin's biblical

9. *Works*, 7:271.

10. *Works*, 35:42–43.

quotations, and H. J. Brunhes's *Ruskin et la Bible* was in 1901 one of the first books published after his death.[11] Speaking of "un vrai prophète," Brunhes divides this work into the two halves of Ruskin's lifework: "La Bible et la nature" and "La Bible et les idées sociales."

Robert Hewison has given in *John Ruskin: The Argument of the Eye,* a sophisticated account of how an evangelical typological understanding underpins the aesthetic criticism of the early Ruskin—corresponding to Brunhes's "la Bible et la nature."[12] The later Ruskin, however, the Ruskin of "les idées sociales," uses the Bible in a very different way. To understand this, it is necessary to look closely at what happens to Ruskin's biblical interpretation when he ceases to embrace an evangelical perspective. The Bible does not disappear; it serves a different function. While some of that function is literary-formal—as Dinah Birch points out, his style in his morally crusading essays and letters is highly sermonic[13]—the Bible itself is used in a substantively different way with a new strategy for interpretation, which will be described as a "hermeneutic of immediacy."[14]

There is a pivotal point in time around which the typological interpretation, based in evangelical biblical strategies and applied to aesthetic criticism, turns into the hermeneutic of immediacy, based in a more free and confident attitude, deeply colored by a commitment to justice. That point is 1858–59. Ruskin gives three different accounts of his "unconversion" in Turin in the summer of 1858.[15] There seems to have been a moment when Paul Veronese and the "gorgeousness of life" symbolically won out over a "squeaking little idiot" in a Waldensian Chapel, but that moment was surrounded by years of struggle during which he was able to internalize belief.[16] One area of struggle appears in a fascinating set of notes, as yet unpublished, from Ruskin's diaries of 1858–59, titled "The Content of Faith." For example, in 1859, beginning on Sunday, August 7, in Baden while on a tour of Germany with his parents, he wrestles daily with the text of the first five chapters of St. Paul's Letter to the Romans.[17] He is using the Greek text, and is working

11. Gibbs and Gibbs, *Bible References*; Brunhes, *Ruskin et la Bible.*

12. Hewison, *Argument.*

13. Birch, "John Ruskin."

14. See Bennett, "Fact Full of Power," and "Ruskin, the Bible."

15. Hilton, *Ruskin*, 253–56.

16. Hewison, *Ruskin on Venice*, 248–49.

17. Ruskin Foundation (Ruskin Library, Lancaster), RF MS 11, fos. 284–301.

out a detailed exegesis for himself. This is characteristic of his engagement with the Scriptures, although the theological content is unusually intensified, and what is crucial for our understanding of his turn to the human at this stage in his life is the repeated and firm commitment to justice as the key to these chapters. Here we have passages of Paul that are the cornerstone of an evangelical conception of justification by faith. Ruskin repeatedly insists on translating *dikaiosune*—justice or justification or righteousness—as *justice*; on opposing not faith and works but fear and works; and on emphasizing the quality of practical obedience as integral to faith. "Injustice," he writes, is here declared to be "the great comprehensive Crime of crimes."[18] In this lively, internal diary dialogue we see emerging that commitment to human justice that all through his later life he would back up with reference to the Christian Scriptures, as it had been nurtured in him through those same Scriptures.

Unto this Last saw the light of day the next year.[19] In its four essays, and its title—taken from the parable of the laborers who are all paid the same though they have worked for different hours (Matt 20:1–14)—Ruskin shows continually how formed he is in his views of justice by the text of the Bible. His interpretation of the parable inserts into the discussion of political economy the key notion that the way human beings behave towards one another, and form a community based on values other than the monetary, is what characterizes the nation's life, and makes it more or less just. To quote the socialist motto with its origin in Karl Marx (though Ruskin was no socialist or communist), it is a matter of "from each according to his ability and to each according to his needs." Interestingly, this very expression has its roots in the New Testament.

Ruskin works with the Bible at three levels. At the most general, and perhaps the most significant level, the biblical text fuels and shapes his vision of humanity and human community. It is burned into his soul, not least through the very parable from which he takes his title, that, "THERE IS NO WEALTH BUT LIFE. Life, including all its powers of love, of joy, and of admiration. That country is the richest which nourishes the greatest number of noble and happy human beings; that man is richest who, having perfected the functions of his own life to the utmost,

18. Ibid., fo. Folio 287. Note also in *Unto this Last* how in "Qui Judicatis Terram" Mal 4:2 is translated "Sun of Justice"; Ruskin argues in a footnote that "righteousness" is too weak a word in common parlance to carry the meaning clearly (*Works*, 17:59).

19. For a modern critical edition, see Wilmer, *Unto this Last*.

has also the widest helpful influence, both personal, and by means of his possessions, over the lives of others,"[20] because this is the vision he has come to read in the Bible. There is no biblical quotation here, but the source of his thinking is in the injunctions of the Psalms, the life and teachings of Jesus, and the stories of the wisdom of Solomon.[21]

It is important to note that at no point does Ruskin use the Bible *purely* strategically. He does have a certain strategic interest, as he himself points out. In Letter VIII of *Time and Tide: Twenty-Five Letters to a Working Man of Sunderland on the Laws of Work* (1867), Ruskin gives a brilliant summary of Victorian public attitudes to the Bible, which would still hold much truth today. His fourfold typology moves from literalism (inerrancy), to infallibility in matters of faith and doctrine, to the opinion that the Bible is not free from error but does bear true witness to God's dealings with human beings, to the view that the Bible represents "the best efforts which we hitherto know" in discovering the spiritual world, but has no more authority than other religious texts.[22] While clearly allying himself with the fourth view, he indicates that he is always aware that his readers will be likely to hold one of these, and if he strategically addresses those holding the fourth he will pick up, *a fortiori*, the others. He is quite adamant, however, that it is not religion that makes a person honest but the other way round—"Your honesty must be based as the sun is, in vacant heaven, poised, as the lights of the firmament . . . If you ask why you are to be honest . . . 'because you are a man,' is the only answer . . . a knave's religion is always the rottenest thing about him."[23]

Underlying this attitude, in which Ruskin eschews biblical proof-texting but holds a profound biblical vision of what it means to be human, is a strong and deeply personal belief in Providence and the Fatherly care of God for his children. He repeatedly uses the beautiful image of children playing in the Father's garden, as birds do, learning above all things to get on well with each other in obedience to the good Father's

---

20. *Works*, 17:105.

21. He alludes specifically to this at the beginning of "Qui Judicatis Terram" (*Works*, 17:57–59), and Michael Wheeler has made a persuasive case that Ruskin saw himself as a Victorian Solomon (Wheeler, *Ruskin's God*).

22. *Works*, 17:348–50.

23. *Works*, 17:348.

ways.[24] With Barth he might have said that (Christian) ethics was about "the quiet and gentle and intimate awakening of children in the Father's house to life in that house."[25] Privately in the same year, 1867, he wrote to his cousin, Joan Severn:

> I notice in one of your late letters some notion that I am coming to think the Bible "the word of God"—because I use it—out of Rosie's book—for daily teaching . . . —But I never was farther from thinking—and never can be nearer to, thinking, any thing of the sort. Nothing could ever persuade me that God writes vulgar Greek . . . If there is any divine truth at all in the mixed collection of books which we call a Bible, that truth is, that the Word of God comes *directly* to different people in different ways . . . [t]hat cross in the sky . . . in the clouds . . . and the calm sky . . . by and through the words of *any* book . . . the Word of God may come to us: and because I love Rosie so, I *think* God does teach me, every morning, by her lips, through her book.[26]

This crucial and very moving passage demonstrates one of the most endearing and admirable things about Ruskin and the Bible, that is, his capacity to enjoy it and continue to engage with it, critically and playfully, trusting it to be one of the many ways in which God speaks with his children and invites them to cocreate and to share a world in which there is no wealth but life itself.

At the next level Ruskin draws on the Bible in *Unto this Last* and in his other social and political work, by making direct reference to it.[27] Along with such reference he often allows himself a sideways comment on how little it is heeded by so-called Christian England. For example, "The writings which we (verbally) esteem as divine, not only denounce the love of money as the sources of all evil, and as an idolatry abhorred of the Deity, but declare Mammon service to be the accurate and irreconcilable opposite of God's service."[28]

---

24. *Works*, 27:206–7; Burd, *Winnington Letters*, 132–35: Ruskin Foundation (Ruskin Library, Lancaster), RF MS 11, fo. 171.

25. Barth, *Church Dogmatics* 4/1:100.

26. Dickinson, *Correspondence*, 88–89. Ruskin's love for "Rosie" and its relationship to his reading of the Bible is further expanded in Bennett, "By Fors," and "A Fact Full of Power."

27. The clearest example in this text is his sustained exposition of the sayings of the "Jew Merchant," Solomon (see note 20).

28. *Works*, 17:75–76.

His wicked appeal, as Slade Professor of Fine Art at the University of Oxford, to the good people of Tunbridge Wells as those who know the Psalms well, being regular members of the Church of England, and his innocent assumption that the Psalms with their condemnation of oppression were not written for the Jews only, is an object lesson in what can be done by those of us with a mission who are invited, courtesy of our academic status, to lecture in dilettante society.[29] But Ruskin never proof-texts: "It is not, therefore, because I am endeavouring to lay down a foundation of religious concrete, on which to build piers of policy, that you so often find me quoting Bible texts in defence of this or that principle or assertion."[30] He is rather appealing to the sensibilities and the imaginations of a whole society, himself included, who have been brought up with the biblical vision of human flourishing.

And so to his characteristic hermeneutical move—the hermeneutic of immediacy. At its most glorious, he weaves the biblical text into his rhetoric allusively and imaginatively, sometimes alongside classical and mythological references, so as to, in William Blake's words, "rouze the faculties to act" in the reader, and engage the public imagination and crucially also the public will, in "better seeing and better acting."[31] This strategy is everywhere in Ruskin's later work. From the marginalia in his private Bible reading—the chief priests say of the money Judas returns that it is not lawful to put blood money into the treasury (Matthew 27); "Our priests don't even warn our Chancellor of the Exchequer of such unlawfulness," writes Ruskin[32]—to the high octane rhetoric of *Fors Clavigera*, this move is inescapable. It is like a verbal equivalent of what Stanley Spencer does in his paintings of Cookham, superimposing Christ's entry into Jerusalem on Cookham High Street or the Resurrection on Cookham churchyard.[33] The laying of the two side by side, the biblical and the contemporary, invites us to see both in a new light, but most of all to reevaluate our actions and practices in the present.

Consider this passage from *Unto this Last*: "Ye sheep without shepherd, it is not the pasture that has been shut from you, but the Presence.

29. *Works*, 16:396–99.

30. *Works*, 17:348.

31. Ruskin Foundation (Ruskin Library, Lancaster), RF MS 11, fo. 147.

32. Ruskin's annotation to Greek Gospel Lectionary, Egerton 3046, 65R, in the British Library.

33. Bennett, "'Fact Full of Power,'" 45.

Meat! Perhaps your right to that may be pleadable; but other rights have to be pleaded first. Claim your crumbs from the table if you will; but claim them as children not as dogs; claim your right to be fed, but claim more loudly your right to be holy, perfect, and pure!"[34] Here Ruskin evokes all the passages in the Scriptures about sheep and shepherds from Isaiah and Ezekiel to John 11 and 1 Peter, the Shechinah and the Holy of Holies, the feeding of the children of Israel in the desert, the gospel story of the Syrophoenician woman, Dives and Lazarus, and the myriad biblical injunctions to holiness, perfection, and purity along with the eschatological promises that one day these will be ours. He weaves them into a rhetoric of exhortation that is at the same time a rhetoric of promise. Thus he captures here, as so often, that sense of both gift and task with which Christianity has always, at its best, juggled.

RUSKIN AS PASSIONATE PROPHET

To see clearly is prophecy, Ruskin says. The greatest thing a human soul can do is "to *see* something, and tell what it saw in a plain way." It is no good seeing if we do not tell what we see. To do so may require courage. Ruskin paid dearly for his "turn to the human." His father, ever his would-be mentor, and indeed throughout his life the source of his income, opposed his move from aesthetic to social critique. *Unto this Last* was not initially well received; Thackeray at the *Cornhill* called a premature halt to the series of essays, and the *Saturday Review* called the essays "eruptions of windy hysterics," "intolerable twaddle," "whines and snivels" and said the world was not going to be "preached to death by a mad governess."[35]

The references to "preaching" and to a "governess" reveal the tenor of the underlying insults. Ruskin should stick to the "feminine world" of art criticism and not meddle in the "man's" world of political economy, about which he knew little. Furthermore, he should not try to insert values, and even worse religious convictions and fervent zeal, into this man's world. Ruskin had been rumbled; he was dealing in human values and feelings with the zeal and the generalizations of a preacher, and this was not wanted in the real, hard, public, masculine, Victorian world. Budding public theologians might blanch—but then might take courage

34. *Works*, 17:107.
35. *Works*, 17:xxviii.

that this "preaching governess" deeply influenced Mahatma Gandhi, Martin Luther King Jr., and the origins of the British Labour Party. Most of us would settle for that.

The art of "theological reflection" is much debated amongst practical theologians these days. While the issues of what it is and how it is to be done occupy most of the discussion, I have become interested in a further question: how are the fruits of that theological reflection to be made to do the work we want them to do in the public world? Ruskin can help us here.

It is instructive for the art of theological reflection to summarize the features of Ruskin's "telling" of what he sees. First, it is *penetratingly and thoughtfully rooted in his contemporary world.* While he may not be an expert in political economy, he knows how to read "the signs of the times . . . in the light of the Gospel."[36] He knows what people do; he knows how people live together; he knows what is manufactured, and under what conditions; he knows that art and architecture themselves have a political economy; he knows what the weather is like; he address economics, social relationships, creativity, crime, consumption, the built environment, ecological disaster, and religion.

Second, it *draws on his Christian heritage and resources.* This essay has shown how *Unto this Last* and other work of Ruskin's in social critique draw from the deep well of his continually refreshed biblical knowledge. But for Ruskin there was more than a *written* text. His late work *The Bible of Amiens* is an example of what he did all his life, reading the Christian story in stone, here the architecture and the sculptures of Amiens Cathedral—as he did with Venice and as he did with the Gothic, or with the "wall-picture" of the Campo Santo in Pisa on which was depicted for him "the entire doctrine of Christianity, painted so that a child could understand it."[37]

Third, it is not only the material content of what Ruskin has to tell that is important—his attention to the world in which he lives and his ability to engage this with the Christian heritage he knows so well—it is also *the style and form of how Ruskin tells it.* "In a plain way" is both disingenuously simple and utterly true. Ruskin always taught his drawing pupils to copy, and he spent hours in the discipline himself—painstakingly

---

36. The Pastoral Constitution on the Church in the Modern World, *Gaudium et Spes*, promulgated by His Holiness Pope Paul VI on 7 December 1965.

37. *Works*, 35:351.

accurate representation of what was there before his eyes. He also has
a verbal equivalent of this—either a "word painting" of something in
nature, or the *ekphrasis,* in which he renders what is before his eyes as a
literal painting in a "word picture" so his reader can "see" the painting.[38]
But literal representation of what is before the eyes is just the beginning;
great art requires the "penetrative imagination," that which sees, understands, and represents "heart-sight" as well as eyesight. This is what he
believed Turner could do so well, and why Turner is the prophet telling
the truth of God as revealed in Creation. One might ask whether the
penetrative imagination must tell the truth not only of Creation but also
of eschatology; as Tim Gorringe writes of Turner, "he was an eschatological painter. He is the painter of the book of Revelation. He always
paints *into* the sun, not with his back to it," as Constable does.[39]

The point is made most strikingly by observing an example of how
Ruskin represents to us that which he sees in nature; he will use analogous skills of eyesight, heart-sight, and rhetoric to present to his public
the darkness of contemporary human society into which he does not
shrink from looking. The following passage from *Praeterita,* Ruskin's
autobiography, evokes the Rhone at Geneva.

> But here was one mighty wave that was always itself, and every
> fluted swirl of it, constant as the wreathing of a shell. No wasting
> away of the fallen foam, no pause for gathering of power, no help-
> less ebb of discouraged recoil; but alike through bright day and
> lulling night the never-pausing plunge, and never-fading flash,
> and never-hushing whisper, and, while the sun was up, the ever-
> answering glow of unearthly aquamarine, ultramarine, violet-
> blue, gentian-blue, peacock-blue, river-of-paradise blue, glass of
> a painted window melted in the sun, and the witch of the Alps
> flinging the spun tresses of it for ever from her snow.[40]

It is a heady mix of observation (aquamarine, ultramarine, violet-blue,
gentian-blue) and penetrative imagination (the witch of the Alps), which
invites the reader to attend to the precise details of what Ruskin saw, but
also flings wide the gates of the mind to delight and to the discovery of
meaning.

38. Bennett, "Creation Made Image."

39. Gorringe, *Education,* 2, and see also 36.

40. *Works,* 35:327.

So the presentation of what is seen is *carefully and creatively crafted*. It is also *performative*. The performative function in the passage about the Rhone is to evoke the scene, to allow the reader to stand there and to experience it for herself, perhaps to know something about nature that she didn't know before, but Ruskin's longer-term purposes go beyond this. While the purpose of *Modern Painters* was initially to vindicate Turner in the eyes of the British public, the purpose of *Unto this Last* and the other social and political writings is to galvanize that same public into shame and into taking action to remedy the ravages, aesthetic but above all human, of industrialization. To this end all his powers of rhetoric are bent.

CONCLUSION: *FURTHERING HUMANITY?*

I have told a little bit of the story in this essay of a great Christian man who witnessed in his own way to what he saw, in the service of the good God and Father of us all. I have told it because his life and his work inspire me, because some parts have not been told or seen in this theological light before, and because much of what he stood for and how he stood for it put me in mind of Tim Gorringe's work. This sentence, from the concluding paragraphs of Tim's *Furthering Humanity*, beautifully sums up John Ruskin: "They need to tell the story, trust in God, pray in the darkness, act for justice as the prophets commanded, and cheerfully wait to see what happens."[41]

Bibliography

Barth, Karl. *Church Dogmatics 4, The Doctrine of Reconciliation*. Translated by G. W. Bromiley. Edinburgh: T. & T. Clark, 1956.

Bennett, Zoë. "'By Fors, Thus Blotted with a Double Cross': Some Notes upon the Death of Rose La Touche." *Ruskin Review and Bulletin* 5:2 (2009) 27–34.

———. "Creation Made Image and Image Made Word: John Ruskin on J. M. W. Turner's 'Snow Storm.'" In *Approaches to Visuality in Religion*, edited by D. Pezzoli-Olgiati and C. Rowland. Göttingen: Vandenhoeck & Ruprecht, forthcoming.

———. "'A Fact Full of Power or a Dream Full of Meaning': The Influence of Religion and the Bible on Ruskin's Social, Political and Economic Critique." *Ruskin Review and Bulletin* 6:2 (2010) 35–47.

———. "Ruskin, the Bible and the Death of Rose La Touche: A 'Torn Manuscript of the Human Soul.'" In *The Oxford Handbook of Reception History of the Bible*, edited by Michael Lieb et al. Oxford: Oxford University Press, 2011.

41. Gorringe, *Furthering Humanity*, 266.

————. "'To See Fearlessly, Pitifully': What Does John Ruskin Have to Offer to Practical Theology?" *International Journal of Practical Theology* 14:2 (2011) 189–203.

Birch, Dinah. "John Ruskin." In *The Blackwell Companion to the Bible in English Literature*, edited by Rebecca Lemon et al., 525–35. Oxford: Blackwell, 2009.

Brunhes, H. J. *Ruskin et la Bible.* Paris: Perrin et Cie, 1901.

Burd, Van Akin, editor. *The Winnington Letters: John Ruskin's Correspondence with Margaret Alexis Bell and the Children at Winnington Hall.* Cambridge, MA: The Belknap Press of Harvard University Press, 1969.

Cook, E. T., and A. Wedderburn, editors. *The Works of John Ruskin.* 39 vols. London: Allen, 1903–1912.

Dickinson, Rachel, editor. *John Ruskin's Correspondence with Joan Severn: Sense and Nonsense Letters.* London: Modern Humanities Research Association and Maney Publishing, 2009.

Gibbs, Mary, and Ellen Gibbs, arr. *The Bible References in the Works of John Ruskin.* London: Allen, 1898.

Glancey, Jonathan. "Of Skeletons and Souls." *The Guardian*, 19 June 2009.

Gorringe, Timothy J. *The Education of Desire: Towards a Theology of the Senses.* London: SCM, 2001.

————. *Furthering Humanity: A Theology of Culture.* Aldershot: Ashgate, 2004.

Hewison, Robert. *John Ruskin: The Argument of the Eye.* London: Thames & Hudson, 1976.

————. *Ruskin on Venice.* New Haven: Yale University Press, 2009.

Hill, Andrew. Introduction to *Unto this Last*, 9. London: Pallas Athene, 2010.

Hilton, Tim. *John Ruskin.* New Haven: Yale University Press, 2002.

Wheeler, Michael. *Ruskin's God.* Cambridge: Cambridge University Press, 1999.

Wilmer, Clive. *Unto this Last and other Writings by John Ruskin.* London: Penguin, 1985; reprinted with revised further reading, 1997.

10

Not Anarchy but Covenant

*A Nonconformist Response to Matthew Arnold's View of
Religion and Culture*

PAUL S. FIDDES

THE CRISIS OF FAITH AND THE NONCONFORMISTS

In his poem "Dover Beach," Matthew Arnold stands by the shore at night, watching and listening to the tide going out in the darkness. So, it seems to him, the Sea of Faith "was once, too, at the full," but now he can only hear:

> Its melancholy, long, withdrawing roar,
> Retreating, to the breath
> Of the night-wind, down the vast edges drear
> And naked shingles of the world.

In Arnold's reflection the Christian faith is retreating before the onset of secularization, whose tide he sees as coming in. Written in 1851, the poem detects the growing secular mood, not just among intellectuals but among the mass of people in western Europe. In particular Arnold discerned a widespread rejection of the Bible that he treasured as the highest poetic expression of the moral and spiritual aspirations of the human race.

It may seem extraordinary that in the face of this crisis he turns in his prose works to launch an attack on the Nonconformist churches of his time, condemning them as cultural Philistines. Surely, one might think, given the situation, he would have better targets than the Congregationalists, Baptists, Presbyterians, Quakers, and Methodists in England. But, while he subjects them to a devastating critique, he is paying them the compliment of believing that they *matter* in the great conflict between faith and unbelief that is coming. As the backbone of the middle class that was the powerful player in the industrial and commercial world of the time, they had great influence on the situation. If only, thought Arnold, they could be changed and renewed—if above all they could become more *cultured*—then something might be done to stop the tide of the Sea of Faith running out.

This is a fascinating social commentary on Christian faith, at a time when it seemed to many observers that religion was going to be shortly swept away by the tide of secularism, stemming largely from the new scientific revolution. We might of course be inclined to dismiss Matthew Arnold's attack on Nonconformity as coming from a prejudiced quarter. He was not only a member of the Church of England, but son of Thomas Arnold, Headmaster of the quintessentially Anglican Rugby School, and himself Professor of Poetry at Oxford for ten years, in a University where students were required to conform to the Thirty-Nine Articles of the Church of England. But Matthew Arnold was for the whole of his professional life a Government Inspector of Schools, and those he inspected were all supported and sometimes run by Nonconformists. So, traveling up and down the country, he came to know English Nonconformity well—or at least he thought he knew it well. "Look," he exclaims, "at the life imaged in such a newspaper as *The Nonconformist*—a life of jealousy of the establishment, disputes, tea-meetings, openings of chapels, sermons . . ."[1]

With this narrow cultural life he compares his great love, Oxford, writing: "steeped in sentiment as she lies, spreading her gardens to the moonlight, and whispering from her towers the last enchantments of the Middle Age, who will deny that Oxford, by her ineffable charm, keeps ever calling us nearer to the true goal of all of us, to the ideal, to perfection?"[2] Oxford for Arnold is the symbol and focus of culture,

1. Arnold, *Culture and Anarchy*, 58.

2. Arnold, Preface to *Essays in Criticism*; cf. Arnold, *Culture and Anarchy*, 61.

and stands over against the grey life of those whom he condemns as cultural Philistines, the newly enriched middle classes of his day. Among these, the Nonconformists or members of the Free Churches are his chief target. The Nonconformist tea-meeting or even the functional structure of a Nonconformist tabernacle is certainly bound to come off badly when compared to the spires of Oxford, but we should not forget that all Nonconformists had been excluded from taking degrees at the Universities of Oxford and Cambridge since 1662, and were still excluded when Arnold was writing.

Arnold is using the word *culture* in the sense of what we now call "high culture," the arts and learning; he defines it as "the best that has been thought and said in the world,"[3] and Oxford is its marker. Culture is the study of perfection. It concerns the pursuit of "sweetness and light," or beauty and intellect, understanding the life of the mind to be a scientific passion to "see things as they really are." All this Arnold summarizes under the label of "Hellenism," as distinct from "Hebraism," to which we will come in a moment. In *modern* usage, the term *culture* may now carry the anthropological sense of "the whole way of life of a people,"[4] such as when we talk of "British culture" or "American culture": "culture" can cover football, McDonald's fast food, TV "soaps," and even going to church—a whole lifestyle, everything people typically do. More precisely, "culture" may be used to focus on the "meaning-dimension" of these social practices, referring to the beliefs, norms, worldviews, and values held by a particular people.[5] But, as Raymond Williams rightly pointed out in his formative studies of culture,[6] a conjunction is always needed between the older and newer senses, and in this essay I shall myself be keeping both in mind.

Tim Gorringe, however, alerts us to the danger of simply *conflating* the two senses of culture—"way of life" and high creative achievement ("the best that has been thought or said"). The result may be that we think of culture as uniformly positive, whereas all cultures are in fact deeply marked by imbalances of power, on gender, racial, and class lines. Arnold himself, Tim judges, tended to miss seeing the abuses of power. While appreciative of Arnold's insistence on the integration between

---

3. Arnold, *Culture and Anarchy*, 6.

4. See, e.g., Kroeber and Kluckhohn, *Culture*, 5off.

5. See Benedict, *Patterns of Culture*, 16.

6. Williams, *Long Revolution*, 57; Williams, "Culture Is Ordinary," 4.

religion and culture,[7] and of his egalitarian desire to extend culture and its spiritual ethos to the masses, Tim suggests (with Karl Barth) that we should not *totally* identify religion with culture; if we do, we will fail to notice that there is a "remainder" in religion that cannot be reduced into culture, and that is critical of its deficiencies and injustices. This is why, he suggests, culture should always stand under the sign of hope, which is bound up with the life, death, and resurrection of Christ: "there is a 'strange new world' towards which culture is directed, the theological symbol for which is the kingdom."[8] Tim's work on developing this kind of theology of culture has often been in dialogue with Matthew Arnold, and so I am delighted to offer this chapter in admiration of his achievement as an innovative theologian of society. Through considering the way that Arnold dealt with the Nonconformists of his time, I aim to come in due course to what Tim might call a "remainder" in religion that Arnold seems to have overlooked, and that may enable us to grapple with secular challenges to faith in our day.

For the moment, we notice that, with his passion for finding "the best" in culture, Arnold launches an attack on Nonconformists for at least two reasons.

MORAL AND VOLUNTARY RELIGION

First, he finds Nonconformist religion to excel in its single-minded pursuit of *moral* perfection, while ignoring the other perfections that are to be found in culture. In his view, this makes Dissenters narrow, parochial, and mean-spirited. They are experts in what he calls "Hebraism," but woefully ignorant of Hellenism.[9]

Here we need to get to grips with Arnold's distinction between the "Hebraic" and the "Hellenic," between religion and culture. For Arnold, religion is the practice of right conduct, but suffused and motivated by emotion. Religion is morality touched by emotion.[10] It is an expression of the Hebrew mind, which is concerned to walk the path of righteousness before God. Arnold is not being negative about this: he is using the word *Hebraic* in a thoroughly *appreciative* sense. Right conduct, and so

---

7. Gorringe, *Furthering Humanity*, 26–31.

8. Ibid., 45.

9. Arnold, *Culture and Anarchy*, 37–38.

10. Arnold, *Literature and Dogma*, 20–21.

religion, is "three-fourths of human life." Under "conduct," he includes "eating, drinking, ease, pleasure, money, the intercourse of the sexes, the giving free swing to one's temper and instincts."[11] Religion, as the pursuit of righteousness, concerns such huge areas of life. But this is only three-quarters of life. There is another quarter, which is culture, or Hellenism: the pursuit of beauty and intellect, sweetness and light. Arnold sees this as drawing on all the voices of human experience—on art, science, poetry, and philosophy—where Hebraism specializes in one kind of experience only, that of righteousness.[12] Culture is a pursuit of total human perfection. Men of culture have indeed often failed in morality, but perfection cannot be reached without an appreciation of sweetness and light, beauty, harmony, and intellect.

Now, Arnold admits that it was necessary in the early years of the Christian era for Hebraism to triumph. It was right for human development that Hebraism should come to rule the world. Christianity conquered as an attractive development of Hebraism, replacing obedience to the letter of a law of righteousness by conformity to the image of someone—Christ—who *lived out* righteousness in a self-sacrificing way. It replaced a law that had become impersonal and mechanical by a dying and rising with Christ. But it is not so obvious to Arnold that Hebraism should have overcome Hellenism at the time of the Renaissance, which is what happened in the Reformation. The Reformation suppressed the central idea of the Renaissance—a return to seeing and exploring things "as they really are," which means seeing them in their beauty and harmony. Especially in England, according to Arnold, Puritanism checked the movement of the Renaissance, and the Nonconformists are the successors of the Puritans.[13] Arnold believes that the Reformation began a wrong move, and that in his own day the balance needs to be righted: there needs to be a flowering of Hellenism and culture.

He finds the confusion of the present time to result from a suppression of a cultural movement in which human beings can explore themselves and their world with a playfulness of thought. The time has come for a new spontaneity of consciousness, but in the face of this, the Nonconformists are insisting on mere strictness of *conscience*. The result is muddle. The Hebraic must open itself up to the Hellenic, to

11. Ibid., 16.

12. Arnold, *Culture and Anarchy*, 47–48.

13. Ibid., 136–42.

enlarge its whole view of the world[14] (an idea Arnold derives from the poet Heinrich Heine). Room must be given for new discoveries in science, new forms of expression in the arts. Arnold's poem "Dover Beach" presents a gloomy picture of the crisis of the present time, when it seems that armies are fighting by night, blind in the darkness, not being able to identify who their friends or their enemies are. His prose writing, in his book *Culture and Anarchy* (1869), is more hopeful. If Christianity is to survive in the modern world, it must count culture as its friend. To treat it as an enemy is to prevent a necessary renewal of Hebraism by Hellenism, and the result will be that Christian faith will simply be overwhelmed by the incoming tide.

Nonconformists, though Hebraic, are ironically also Philistine,[15] despising culture. The main point Arnold is making is that the life of Christian discipleship needs to be in contact with a wider culture than itself for its own health. Otherwise it becomes self-absorbed and self-defensive. We shall need to take account of this point, even though we may feel that Arnold gives an unfair and unsympathetic account of chapel life.[16]

There is a second reason that Arnold discerns for the unsettled mood of the time, and this also is a critique of Nonconformity. It is what he perceives to be a spirit of "doing as one likes" that is pervading society. Freedom is worshipped as an end in itself, and the policy of free trade has become an idol without its devotees noticing that one in nineteen of the population still lives in total poverty. Modern life has unleashed a spirit of mere self-will, a passion for giving in to the worst in oneself just because one can. In short, Arnold detects a mood of anarchy, which was symbolized by riots in Hyde Park in 1866 when the park railings were pulled down by protestors. Arnold, perhaps surprisingly, saw the Nonconformist chapel as a seedbed of anarchy; of course, he did not regard it as a hotbed of political agitation, but he did see it as a place where the voluntary principle, the stressing of individual choice and self-will, were placed at the center of religion as much as in politics and industry.[17] Referring to the "voluntaryism" of the well-known Baptist

---

14. Ibid., 143–48.

15. Ibid., 258, cf. 52–53.

16. David Bebbington draws a much more rounded picture, in "Gospel and Culture."

17. Arnold, *Culture and Anarchy*, 88–89.

preacher C. H. Spurgeon,[18] he believed that Dissenters made a fetish of free choice in regard to separating from the establishment and deciding which church they wanted to join. They were "doing as one likes," and so the middle classes should not be surprised if the masses decide to join in. In a piece of savage irony, Arnold refers to the masses' insistence on "the Englishman's right to do what he likes . . . march where he likes, meet where he likes, enter where he likes, hoot as he likes, threaten as he likes, smash as he likes."[19] As far as middle classes doing what they like: "the graver self of one kind of Philistine likes fanaticism, business and money-making; his more relaxed self, comfort and tea-meetings."[20]

Many of the new owners of industry were, indeed, Nonconformists. Like Blake, Arnold inveighs against the "dark Satanic mills" of the mind and the cityscape, but quite unlike Blake, he associated these with Nonconformist Christianity. The antidote was culture, as a unified expression of humanity. "Our best self," writes Arnold—that is, the self perfected and disciplined through reading and thinking—"is not manifold and vulgar and unstable, and contentious, and ever-varying, but one, and noble, and secure, and peaceful, and the same for all mankind."[21] We have reason to be suspicious of this emphasis on one, unified culture, and the modern sense of culture rightly recognizes plurality and diversity; yet Arnold has a valid concern that society should not be a place of conflict of the will, a mere game of power play. Though he has no clear view of how it might be achieved, Arnold thinks that the state can be the expression of our best self and the organ of culture

THE MEANING OF COVENANT

I want now to respond to the second of Arnold's critiques, that the Free Churches are based on an exercise of self-will, on a choice by individuals of faith and of the form of church they personally prefer (that is, what Arnold sees as the roots of "anarchy"). Thus we will work back to the first critique. Arnold here shows himself totally unaware of the theology of covenant that underlies much of Nonconformist ecclesiology. In sociological terms, the local congregation is indeed envisaged as an

18. Ibid., 157.
19. Ibid., 76.
20. Ibid., 107.
21. Ibid., 204.

"intentional community";[22] there is a voluntary element to it, since faith cannot be coerced. But understood as a *covenant* grouping, this is not just a "voluntary" society that people choose to join or not. In Baptist and Congregational ecclesiology in particular, Christ as covenant-maker has taken the initiative and called disciples into community.[23] Church is not based on the will of the believer but the will of Christ. This is not anarchy but the rule of Christ as king, alongside his other "offices" as prophet and priest. When Christian disciples make covenant with each other to live together in fellowship and mission, they are not just *drawing* together, but *being drawn* together.

At the roots of early English Dissent was an understanding of covenant as having two dimensions, vertical and horizontal. At the time of the Reformation, stress was laid upon the church as the new covenant community, brought into being through the blood of the new covenant in the cross of Christ. That is, the vector line of the covenant was vertical, as a "covenant of grace" between God and humanity. But in the wake of the Reformation, radical Separatists in early-seventeenth-century England were beginning to use the word *covenant* in another sense, as well, to denote the agreement that members of a congregation made between themselves. Often under the pressure of persecution, they made a church covenant in which they promised to "walk together and watch over each other." It was an early Baptist, John Smyth, who made the creative theological step of linking this "horizontal" covenant and the "vertical" covenant together; so in 1607 he defined the church as a visible community of saints where "two, three or more saints join together by covenant with God and with themselves."[24]

These two dimensions of covenant, vertical and horizontal, are, moreover, held within a third dimension. Though this idea is less clearly defined in early Dissenting thought, we may think of the covenant of grace with humanity as being based in an eternal covenant within the life of the triune God.[25] The eternal sending forth of the Son from the Father ("eternal generation") is inseparable from the sending of the Son into the world in a mission of redemptive love: "procession"

22. See Farley, *Ecclesial Man*, chs. 4–5; also Gadamer, *Truth and Method*, 215–30.

23. For this theme, see at length Fiddes, "'Walking Together.'"

24. Whitley, *Works of John Smyth*, 1:252. See also White, *English Separatist Tradition*, 129.

25. Further, see Fiddes, "'Walking Together,'" 35–37.

is the basis for mission.[26] So we may say that our covenant with God, freely given in grace, is bound up with the covenant in God's own communion of life in which God freely determines to be God. God makes covenant with God's self—as Father, Son, and Spirit—and with us in the same movement of self-determination. As created beings share life with each other, they are participating in an eternal movement of relational love, drawn into the ebb and flow of self-giving and self-receiving within the divine life.

This vision of the covenant community should mean living in a spirit of creative tension and negotiation, sharing in the movement of God's life that is like a dance, weaving a pattern and finding what fits in new circumstances. In the Nonconformist tradition, the local church lives in such tensions, holding together the authority of Christ, Scripture, and the church meeting—in that order, but with a need for discernment which gives rise to healthy disagreements. Oversight (*episkope*) flows freely between personal and communal forms.[27] All members of the church are encouraged to do a kind of "everyday theology" (to use a term of Kathryn Tanner)[28] in which they meet new challenges to established practices with a feel for the possibilities of Christian living, trying to see how new activities fit in with the rest of what they do, say, believe, and value as disciples of Christ. An appropriate response is to be found to the needs of a particular situation, to make the best of the opportunities it affords for Christian witness and service.

There is a search for consistency here, especially with Scripture, but there is also an element of playing the game as it happens, without a rigid set of rules that will sort out problems in advance. This is the difference between a contract where the conditions are set out before entering it, and a covenant that (in the words of an early Separatist tradition) is a "walking together in ways known *and to be known*."[29] Negotiations and maneuvers over finding authority for belief and action within the covenant community call for a very large element of trust—in Christ and each other.

26. Moltmann, *Church*, 53–56.

27. See, e.g., *London Confession*, 168, Art. XLIV.

28. Tanner, *Theories of Culture*, 69–71.

29. A phrase, often repeated, from the covenant made by the congregation at Gainsborough in 1906–1907: see Bradford, *History of Plymouth Plantation*, 1:20–22.

This concept of covenant, at the heart of the Nonconformist tradition, is very different from mere voluntarism, or "doing as one likes." Arnold was no doubt correct to find the debasement of the covenant principle in his time into mere self-will in religious life and in business life. But I suggest that there is a foundation for the openness of the church to wider culture in the idea of covenant itself. The kind of negotiation, and the living within productive tensions that Christians practice *within* the covenant, can also be turned outward to other cultural contexts, since the Christian community cannot be a self-contained social group; its own particular culture is bound to be influenced by the cultures among which it resides.[30]

Postmodern critique of modern cultural theory rightly points out that there are no absolute breaks in social interaction between groups. Correspondingly, a radical separation of cultures is difficult to maintain. A culture cannot be a unified and sealed package of beliefs and values, discontinuous with other cultures around it, such as was envisaged by earlier modern cultural theorists; diverse cultures *share* cultural elements, with open boundaries between them.[31] For the Christian church, this is not just an unfortunate situation to be resisted. There is a theological basis for this relation in a vision of a covenant-making God. Scripture assures us that God makes covenant with created beings beyond the confines of the chosen people. In the Old Testament, the covenant after the Great Flood stands as one symbol of this, where God makes an "everlasting covenant . . . with every living creature that is upon the earth" (Gen 9:9-10, 16-17). Karl Barth affirms that, in the face of the revelation of God's redemptive work in Christ, we must understand the eternal covenant of grace to be made with all humankind. When God elects the eternal son, this is a covenant of love with all human sons and daughters.[32]

This does not mean that there is no difference between the church and the cultures surrounding it. The Hebrew Bible shows us not one homogeneous covenant, but many forms of covenant made between God and human beings—some made with the whole people, some with a small group, some with individuals; some covenants are made in the royal court, some on journeys and while wandering in the wilderness.

---

30. Tanner, *Theories of Culture*, 97-109.

31. See, e.g., Cottom, *Text and Culture*, 18ff.

32. Barth, *Church Dogmatics*, 2/2, *123-25, 161-65, cf. 6-9, 26; 4/1, 45-6.*

To say that all human persons participate in the triune movements of God's life that have the patterns of a covenant, is not to say that they all participate in the same way. A covenant way of life will take on a particular shape when people consciously enter the covenant relationship, and when it is sealed and continually nourished by the practices of baptism, the Lord's Supper, and preaching.

MECHANICAL RELIGION AND
THE WAY OF RIGHTEOUSNESS

I have been rooting covenant, and openness to culture, in the Christian idea of the Trinity, whereas Matthew Arnold rejects this doctrine as a mechanical dogma. Arnold finds Nonconformist religion to be fixated on formulas and contracts, with a theology that is akin to the machinery of business and commerce.[33] A key example here for Arnold is the very idea of "righteousness" on which he finds Nonconformity, as a form of Hebraism, to focus as the "one thing needful."[34] In his book *Literature and Dogma* (1873), he expands on his view that, unfortunately, Christians of his time misunderstand the meaning of righteousness in the bible. The great insight of Hebrew religion, he thinks, is that "righteousness tendeth to life" (Prov 11:19, cf. 12:28)[35] and that righteousness brings happiness. This he takes to mean that there is an underlying moral law of life, that right conduct, when it is touched and suffused by emotion, will lead to a life full of satisfaction and joy.

There is a dimension of righteousness, he observes, that is not under our control or our calculation, and so the word *God* refers to an eternal power, not ourselves, by which we get a sense for righteousness, and from which we find help to do right. God is the eternal power "that makes for righteousness";[36] when we set out along the path of right conduct we find that we are supported and carried by a "stream of tendency by which all things fulfil the law of their being."[37] Arnold dismisses talk of God as Trinity as a "pseudo-science," as an abstract deduction absent from the Bible, which simply bears witness to the power that makes for

33. Arnold, *Culture and Anarchy*, 59, 74, 101, 151, 157.

34. Ibid., 150–52.

35. Arnold, *Literature and Dogma*, 26–27.

36. Ibid., 32.

37. Ibid., 41.

righteousness. This truth of experience has been turned into dogmas and formulas that have to be believed—what Arnold calls *Aberglaube* or "extra beliefs."

Arnold proposes that the faith and conduct of Israel gradually became external and mechanical, fixed on laws rather than the dynamic experience of righteousness, and Jesus renews and revives the true sense that "righteousness tends to life." For Arnold, Jesus discloses the "secret" that the way of righteousness is the path of the cross, a self-renunciation in which we can die to our worst self and find the true life of our best self.[38] This is the righteousness that leads to happiness and fulfillment, and nothing could be further from "doing as one likes."

For this experimental truth that "righteousness leads to life" Arnold significantly uses the biblical language of covenant.[39] He thinks that people enter a kind of covenant with the eternal power that makes for righteousness: if they pursue right conduct, they will find themselves supported and helped and will finally fulfill the inner law of their own being. This covenant has degenerated, Arnold suggests, into a mere contract. The language of the Reformers, the Puritans, and now the Nonconformists about a "covenant of grace" made in the Council of the Trinity is a myth. It is a "fairy-tale" of three supernatural persons,[40] one of whom (the Son) makes a contract with another (the Father) to satisfy his legal demands and to redeem the world by dying, while the third (the Spirit) applies the effects of this contract in human lives.[41]

St Paul's words about "Christ our righteousness" have also therefore been misunderstood, as Arnold sets out to show in his book *St. Paul and Protestantism* (1870). Righteousness has been turned into a *mechanism* of justification, a kind of contract or bargain in which we receive the righteousness of Christ as something imputed or reckoned to us in a legal agreement with God. In fact, Paul is talking about our passionate identification with the person of Jesus, our sharing in his dying to self and so our participation in his resurrection to life. We identify in our whole being with the righteousness of Christ and so find the motivation and power to walk the path of righteousness ourselves. As

38. Ibid., 86–91.

39. Ibid., 66–68, 299–300.

40. In the early editions of *Literature and Dogma*, Arnold writes satirically of "the story of three Lord Shaftesburys": ibid., 310.

41. Ibid., 200, 204, 306–7, 309, 310; cf. Arnold, *St. Paul*, 15–17.

Arnold puts it, when Paul found Christ, "the struggling stream of duty ... was suddenly reinforced by the immense tidal wave of sympathy and emotion,"[42] and to this new and potent influence Paul gave the name of faith. But, writes Arnold, the scheme as set forth in Puritan thinking with its "covenants, conditions, bargains, and parties-contractors could have proceeded from no one but the born Anglo-Saxon man of business, British or American."[43] Puritans, and their Nonconformist successors, had turned feeling into formula. Philistines in culture, they were also Philistines in religion, converting everything into the machinery of commerce and industry.

Arnold's diagnosis of the secular movement of his day was that the mass of people was calling for what can be proved, and dogmas about what was going on inside the Trinity were unverifiable. His fear was that in rejecting dogma, the masses were also rejecting the bible, with its poetic expression of the way of righteousness. Arnold's claim was that his version of religion was *in fact* scientific and verifiable. For him, religion rests on the solid foundation of our experience of the inner moral law as moral beings: salvation through righteousness, finding the path of right conduct that leads to life, was in his view a natural truth. It could be tested out experimentally.[44] Such a religion was open to perfection through the many voices of culture.

RIGHTEOUSNESS AND RIGHT RELATIONS

Now, was Arnold right in his diagnosis and remedy? Could the tide of scientific secularism be held back by replacing the old metaphysics with conformity to a moral law? From the perspective of our time, we see things a little differently. In our present culture we no longer hold Arnold's assumption that an inner moral law is something verifiable by science. We can see that his own concept of a "power that makes for righteousness" is unverifiable and metaphysical, no less than the Christian story of the Trinity. Anyway the mood today is not a search for verification; there is no unqualified confidence in a scientific view of the world any longer. The desire is rather for stories that make sense of the world, and that convince by their power of explanation.

42. Arnold, *St. Paul*, 70.

43. Ibid., 19.

44. Arnold, *Literature and Dogma*, 41–43; *St. Paul*, 90–91.

On the other hand, Arnold is surely right to withstand any reduction of the biblical concept of covenant to a business or legal model of a contract. Where this was happening among Nonconformists, he was right to identify it as Philistinism and to oppose it. But the Trinitarian story of covenant is precisely not a contract. It is not a story of a bargain concluded between three supernatural beings, but expresses a giving and receiving of love in eternal relationships. It is about three relations of love and justice, which are like a Father sending out a son in mission into the world, a Son responding in love and gratitude to a Father, and a Spirit of hope always opening up new depths in this relationship. We may, of course, also find other dimensions of gender in these three personal relations, and use at times the metaphor of a relation between a mother and a daughter. Such language is not observational, as if we could see God as an object, even in our mind's eye: it only makes sense as participatory, as a language about sharing in these relationships. We do not receive a bargain concluded by the Trinity, but participate in movements of self-sacrificing love. Here again Arnold is right about Paul's theology, at least insofar as righteousness is sharing in the dying and rising with Christ. But Arnold fails to read the Bible properly on the great theme of righteousness. At heart this is not right conduct, an inner moral law, but a matter of right relationships—with each other and with God. Right conduct flows from this rightness of relationship.

The pervasive worldview today, even in the domain of science, is not one of a set of laws, but an organic relatedness at every level of nature. We are increasingly aware of connections between human beings and all other living things in our ecosystem. A concept of righteousness that is about proper relationships, expressed in covenant and the Christian image of Trinity, fits our sense of the way that the world is. We recall Arnold's great theme: there is an eternal power that makes for righteousness. We can rewrite the theme like this: there is an eternal power that makes for *relationship*, because it is supremely relational. Arnold's insight is right that there is a *tendency* or "immense wave" carrying us towards life in which we can be caught up: but this is what Trinity is actually all about—being immersed into movements of life and love.

As Arnold makes a link between religion and culture, both seeking for perfection, each necessary to the other, so we might make the link between culture and a triune God. The Christian believer lives *consciously* within the covenant, and this means living *deliberately* within the story of Jesus, in the context of the story of Israel, and further still in the context of the story of the Trinity. The Trinity is the supreme metanarrative: the story that God goes out from God's self on mission, in the openness to the future that is the power of the Spirit. If culture is the "meaning-dimension" of a people, then a central part is the stories that people tell to understand themselves and their place in the world. The distinctiveness of the Christian community, living in constant negotiations with other cultures, will be the story by which it lives. Christians will tell the story in different ways; they will be identified less by an authorized and strictly defined version of the story than by a concern to tell, explore, and live the story.

Moreover, hints and recollections of the story will be found in all cultures, since they have some kind of covenant relation with the triune God. Wherever in the world people give themselves to others or sacrifice themselves for others, these actions will match the movement in God which is like a Son going forth on mission in response to the purpose of a Father; their acts will share in the patterns of love in God, and so in them we can discern the body of Christ. Wherever there is the movement of a measure of music, or of a stroke of a brush, or of a blow of a chisel, or of a sequence of thought in the arts or sciences that reflect God's truth and beauty, these too share in the dynamic flow of the life of God.

Let the last word be with the poem "Dover Beach." Having faced the oncoming tide, and the retreat of organized religion, Arnold does not in fact turn to the certainty of moral law as in his prose works. What matters finally is relationship, as he turns to his new wife Lucy and exclaims:

> "Ah, love, let us be true
> To one another! . . ."

Bibliography

Arnold, Matthew. *Culture and Anarchy*. Edited by J. Dover Wilson. Cambridge: Cambridge University Press, 1969.

———. *Essays in Criticism*. Oxford: Clarendon, 1918.

———. *Literature and Dogma*. 2nd ed. London: Smith, Elder, 1873.

———. *St. Paul and Protestantism*. 3rd ed. New York: Macmillan, 1875.

Barth, Karl. *Church Dogmatics*. *Translated and edited by* G. W. Bromiley and T. F. Torrance. Edinburgh: T. & T. Clark, 1936–1977.

Bebbington, David. "Gospel and Culture in Victorian Nonconformity." In *Culture and the Nonconformist Tradition*, edited by Jane Shaw and Alan Kreider, 43–62. Cardiff: University of Wales Press, 1999.

Benedict, Ruth. *Patterns of Culture*. New York: Houghton Mifflin, 1934.

Bradford, William. *History of Plymouth Plantation, 1620–1647*. Edited by W. C. Ford. Boston: Massachusetts Historical Society, 1912.

Cottom, Daniel. *Text and Culture: The Politics of Interpretation*. Minneapolis: University of Minnesota Press, 1988.

Farley, Edward. *Ecclesial Man: A Social Phenomenology of Faith and Reality*. Philadelphia: Fortress, 1975.

Fiddes, Paul S. "'Walking Together': The Place of Covenant Theology in Baptist Life Yesterday and Today." In *Tracks and Traces: Baptist Identity in Church and Theology*, 21–47. Milton Keynes: Paternoster, 2003.

Gadamer, Hans-Georg. *Truth and Method*. London: Sheed & Ward, 1975.

Gorringe, T. J. *Furthering Humanity: A Theology of Culture*. Aldershot: Ashgate, 2004.

Kroeber, Alfred L., and Klyde Kluckhohn. *Culture: A Critical Review of Concepts and Definitions*. Cambridge: Harvard University Press, 1952.

The London Confession (1644). In W. L. Lumpkin, *Baptist Confessions of Faith*, 144–70. Philadelphia: Judson, 1959.

Moltmann, Jürgen. *The Church in the Power of the Spirit*. Translated by M. Kohl. London: SCM, 1977.

Tanner, Kathryn. *Theories of Culture: A New Agenda for Theology*. Guides to Theological Enquiry. Minneapolis: Fortress, 1997.

White, Barrington R. *The English Separatist Tradition: From the Marian Martyrs to the Pilgrim Fathers*. Oxford: Oxford University Press, 1971.

Whitley, William T., editor. *The Works of John Smyth*. Cambridge: Cambridge University Press, 1915.

Williams, Raymond. "Culture Is Ordinary." In *Resources of Hope*, 3–18. London: Verso, 1989.

———. *The Long Revolution*. Harmondsworth: Penguin, 1965.

11

Redefining Sainthood and Martyrdom
The Case of Dietrich Bonhoeffer

JOHN W. DE GRUCHY

In *Redeeming Time*, Tim Gorringe speaks of God's action in history as a form of divine pedagogy, working so that "human beings should have life and have it more abundantly, that through the educational process persons may be more fulfilled and therefore more creative, more free and therefore more loving, more loving and therefore more free. The ultimate aim . . . is the becoming of human being."[1] In so writing, he echoes Dietrich Bonhoeffer's evocation of the "mature worldliness" to which Christ calls us:[2] a life of responsibility, creativity, playfulness, freedom, and friendship in the world. Such fullness of life stands at the heart of all Tim's work; and it is as witness to such life that Bonhoeffer might properly be called a saint and martyr.

SAINTS AND MARTYRS

The cult of the saints developed as a result of the martyrdom of many Christians during the early centuries of the Church. A martyr literally means being a "witness" and, specifically within a Christian context, a

1. Gorringe, *Redeeming Time*, 7.
2. Bonhoeffer, *Letters and Papers*, 369.

witness to Jesus Christ. But those who were put to death because of their faithful witness were accorded a special place. The shedding of their blood was a baptism patterned on the death of Jesus, and they became models of what it meant to follow in his steps as disciples. They were the true saints, examples of what it means to be a Christian. And since their martyrdom was a precious gift to the Church, their earthly remains (or relics) were preserved, often buried beneath the altars of churches, and venerated. In due course, these relics became more than a reminder of the witness of the saints; they also were regarded as having special power, especially the power to heal the sick.

Although there were those saints, such as Mary and the Apostles, who were regarded as having a special status by Christians in every part of the Church, many saints were local Christian heroes, most probably unknown beyond their own region. Much depended on whether or not they were accepted as saints by the local church, and recognized as such by virtue of both what they achieved in the course of their lives and by the miracles performed both then and after their death. It seemed perfectly natural to ask them to pray for those who were still struggling with the problems of life and the challenges of faith. So the intercession of the saints became central to the cult of the saints.

To begin with, the cult of the saints simply grew without any control and was subject to abuse. However, in the tenth century, the Roman Catholic Church began to institute a process of canonization to regulate the phenomenon. In the Orthodox Church, the process was far less regulated, and there are many more local saints, some of them distinguished bishops and theologians, but some very simple, uneducated people who are deemed to be "holy fools" for the sake of Christ. But the basic premise is the same. Saints are those who through their lives and their deaths have reached a state of perfection ("theosis"), and as such they have become models for the rest of us. They can be venerated, depicted in icons, and asked to intercede for us.

In rejecting the cult of the saints, Protestants may have done away with the veneration of relics and dependence on the intercession of the saints, but they did not do away with the notion of or need for people who are regarded as exemplary Christians. The Reformers may not be designated formally as saints, but they do have a special place as witnesses to Christ, and some of their portraits have taken on a quasi-iconic status. The same is true of many other "Protestant saints"—John Wesley, for example—who have had a profound influence on shaping the lives of Christians even if they may be known to few, or to many—like Bonhoeffer, who has become something of a cult figure, a Protestant martyr and saint.

Hanging above my desk is a large portrait of Bonhoeffer painted by a friend. It resembles an icon, though it lacks a halo, and appropriately so. For while we may well think of Bonhoeffer as a martyr, it is difficult to imagine him being portrayed in the way that saints are normally portrayed. Nor would he have relished the idea. As he tells us in his letters from prison, he gave up on aspiring to be a saint or "trying to live a holy life."[3] So his status as a saint, at least in the Catholic and Orthodox sense of the word, is problematic, and his status as a martyr has been hotly contested. Both these issues will concern us as we proceed. Before going further, however, I want to address three dangers that face us in trying to interpret Bonhoeffer's legacy today that derive from his cult status, and that are inevitably present among those for whom he is a saint and martyr.

The first danger has to do with co-opting Bonhoeffer for our own purposes and projects in ways that misuse his legacy and sanitize his challenge. This does not mean that we should not engage his legacy in ways that relate to our own context and the issues we now face. But we need to take care that we do not end up with a Bonhoeffer made in our preferred image, giving legitimacy to our ideological interests and pet causes rather than challenging us by his own witness.

The second danger stems precisely from the recognition of Bonhoeffer's status as a martyr and, for many, a saint. To *sanctify* Bonhoeffer's legacy as though his witness precludes critical judgment or the need to go beyond him when necessary, is to do him a grave injustice. Our task of understanding Bonhoeffer cannot be confined to archival retrieval or a parrot-like repetition of what he said. That would be a travesty of all that Bonhoeffer stood for and did. The problem of regarding Bonhoeffer as a saint and martyr is that it could put his life and thought beyond critical judgment.

The third danger is reducing Bonhoeffer's legacy to a one solely of academic interest and intellectual curiosity—what we might call *sanitizing* his legacy. This is, in fact, the danger of not taking seriously the claim that he is a saint and martyr and not just a challenging theologian who

3. Ibid., 369.

has raised important questions and provided some radical answers. It is the danger of separating Bonhoeffer's theology from his life and witness as a Christian.

For both saints and martyrs are, above all else, witnesses to Jesus Christ in their lives and in their dying. So our quest to understand Bonhoeffer as saint and martyr must begin with the question he frequently asked himself: "Who is Jesus Christ really for us, today?"—and, of course, with the answers he gave to his own question not just in his theological writings, but more especially in his life and death.

THE CHRIST AT THE CENTER

Bonhoeffer's question first became explicit in his seminal lectures on "Christology," which he gave in Berlin in 1933 on the eve of Hitler's triumph as Führer of the Third Reich.[4] In giving them, Bonhoeffer first of all called us to a reverent silence before the Word rather than rushing in with our own ideas and agenda. He then spoke of the form of Christ who is present for us both individually and corporately as Word, Sacrament, and church-community (*Gemeinde*), and the place of Christ within the world, a subject to which we will shortly turn. Then he affirmed the kernel of Christian tradition, carefully avoiding ancient heresies and their modern equivalents that distort the meaning of Jesus as the Christ. Having thus set the parameters for Christology, he began to explore the contemporary and contextual questions concerning the meaning of Christ for us, here and now. In doing so, he lifted Christological reflection out of purely academic discourse and placed it in the trenches of the emerging struggle against Nazism.

In seeking to answer the question of Christ's contemporary significance, Bonhoeffer appropriated Martin Luther's "theology of the cross" (*theologia crucis*), insisting that the primary question in Christology is "about the concealment of the God-Man in his humiliation."[5] In Jesus Christ, God freely places himself at the service of humanity and the world "for me" and "for us" (*pro me* and *pro nobis*), whether in the cradle or on the cross, whether on the eucharistic altar or in the proclamation of the gospel. It is in and through God's humiliation in Christ that the world is redeemed and the new humanity born. As with Luther, so with

4. Bonhoeffer, *Christology*.

5. Ibid., 54.

Bonhoeffer, affirming the "theology of the cross" meant a categorical rejection of all "theologies of glory," that is, theologies that sanction a triumphalist Christianity, church, or nation, where the cross, even in portraying the suffering of Christ as graphically as in the movie *The Passion of Christ*, becomes a symbol of triumph and domination rather than God's hiddenness, foolishness, and weakness.

This "theology of the cross" is fundamental to all else that follows in Bonhoeffer's life and theology. For it was from this basis that Bonhoeffer interpreted reality from the perspective of the victims of the state and society, and eventually, in prison, began to develop his nonreligious interpretation of Christianity. As Larry Rasmussen has put it: "Bonhoeffer trekked to what were for him the margins in order to see the center from the edges and, if need be, to relocate his viewpoint."[6] Or as Bonhoeffer himself wrote in his reflections titled "After Ten Years" shortly before his arrest: "We have learnt to see the great events of world history from below, from the perspective of the outcast, the suspects, the maltreated, the powerless, the oppressed, the reviled—in short, from the perspective of those who suffer."[7]

For Bonhoeffer, the question, "*Who* is Jesus Christ?" led directly to the question, "*Where* is Jesus Christ?" Where is the hidden God present in the world? Bonhoeffer's answer is that Christ is present as the center of human existence, the center of history and the state, the center between God and nature. But Christ is the center in a radically different way to what is normally understood by those in the corridors of power, whether in state or church. Christology does not have to do with a Christ controlled by religion, the church, or domesticated by the nation, for their own purposes, but with the crucified and humiliated one who, in speaking and embodying truth, becomes a new center of power. As such he challenges the abuse of power and acts vicariously in solidarity with its victims.

Bonhoeffer's lectures on "Christology" had a passion and an urgency that were absent from his earlier academic theology, as anyone reading them in relation to *Sanctorum Communio* and *Act and Being* will immediately recognize. One reason for this was the dramatic change in the historical situation that was taking place in the birth of the Third Reich as he gave his Christology lectures. But there was an equally

6. Rasmussen, *Dietrich Bonhoeffer*, 35.

7. Bonhoeffer, *Letters and Papers*, 17.

important reason, namely, the transformation in Bonhoeffer's life that occurred just prior to these lectures, and that led, in his own words, to the theologian becoming "a Christian." The crucified Christ had not only become the center of Bonhoeffer's theology, but also the center of his life leading to costly discipleship and eventually to martyrdom.

MARTYRDOM REDEFINED

Bonhoeffer did not learn much theology at Union Theological Seminary during his sojourn there in 1931–32, but he did discover the existential significance of the Sermon on the Mount and underwent a remarkable personal transformation, which he later described in these words:

> For the first time I discovered the Bible . . . I had often preached, I had seen a great deal of the church . . . but I had not yet become a Christian . . . I know that at that time I turned the doctrine of Jesus Christ into something of personal advantage for myself . . . Then the Bible, and the Sermon on the Mount, freed me from that. Since then everything has changed . . . It was a great liberation. It became clear to me that the life of a servant of Jesus Christ must belong to the church, and step by step it became plainer to me how far that must go. Then came the crisis of 1933 . . . The revival of the church and of the ministry became my supreme concern.[8]

Bonhoeffer's words read like an account of a traditional evangelical conversion. Through an encounter with Christ, as he later put it, "He lost his life to Christ, (and) Christ became his life."[9] This awoke in him a new desire to search the Scriptures in a way that combined academic rigor and existential commitment, something evident in the many sermons, exegetical studies, and lectures that he now prepared and delivered. But Bonhoeffer's conversion was no pious "born-again" experience that led him away from social reality and struggle. On the contrary, his liberation was, as he described it later in prison, a move from "phraseology to reality."[10] This forced him to relinquish any armchair approach to theology, launched him into the ecumenical struggle for peace in Europe at a time of rising nationalism and rearmament, and plunged him into the church struggle against German Christianity with vigor and resolution.

8. Quoted in Bethge, *Dietrich Bonhoeffer*, 205.
9. Bonhoeffer, *Ethics*, 149.
10. Bonhoeffer, *Letters and Papers*, 275.

At the time that he wrote about his personal transformation, Bonhoeffer was the director of the Confessing Church seminary at Finkenwalde, busily engaged in theological formation, writing essays, tracts and sermons, and completing his book on *Discipleship*. The question he was addressing as he taught his students was how they could become a community of disciples of Jesus and thus be equipped as pastors in the Confessing Church in a way that engaged the rampant racism, nationalism, and warmongering of Nazi Germany. He wanted to demonstrate that following Jesus the suffering Messiah as described in the Synoptic Gospels was directly related to what it meant to live by faith in Jesus Christ as Lord within the "body of Christ."

In this way, Bonhoeffer was intent on countering the psuedo-Lutheran tendency to separate "justification by faith alone" from costly discipleship. This, he argued, was at the heart of the problem of the Evangelical (Protestant) church in Germany. Such a separation inevitably resulted in the cheapening of grace and the undermining of true evangelical faith and witness. By contrast, he wrote, "whenever Christ calls us, his call leads us to death."[11] So, Bonhoeffer insisted, "only those who believe obey, and only those who obey believe."[12] Bonhoeffer's obedience eventually led to his martyrdom, a status now carved in stone on the façade of Westminster Abbey.

There have been many, however, who have been perplexed and bothered by what, in the end, led to his death. Was not his martyrdom the outcome of his political involvement in the plot on Hitler's life, and therefore an action that compromised his Christian witness based on the Sermon of the Mount? But as Bethge observed years ago, Bonhoeffer—and others in the twentieth century who followed a similar path in their discipleship—redefined our understanding of martyrdom. They have done so by demonstrating how their confession of Christ involved political resistance in solidarity with the victims of the state.[13] The principalities and powers of this world today are not particularly worried by Christian confession *per se*, for saying "Jesus is Lord" no longer carries the political implications that it did in times past. But the powers that be are threatened and concerned when such a

---

11. Bonhoeffer, *Discipleship*, 87.

12. As translated in Bonhoeffer, *Creation and Fall*, 54.

13. As translated in *Cost of Discipleship* (Fuller translation), 54.

confession leads to protest against the abuse of power, as we discovered in the struggle against apartheid.

Bonhoeffer's martyrdom is, in fact, a key to interpreting his life and his significance for us today, a trajectory in his theology and witness that finally binds it together as a whole. As Craig Slane rightly reminds us, what Bonhoeffer "became by his death was something greater than what he was at any stage along the way."[14] In his martyrdom, his life and theology finally converge in an inseparable unity that, above all else, accounts for his ongoing relevance, challenge, and attraction. The theologian of martyrdom becomes a martyred theologian, the supreme act of witness to Christ. But between his confession of Christ and that moment of martyrdom, Bonhoeffer had begun to ponder who Christ was for him in a way that radically challenges us to rethink what it means to be a saint.

A SAINT OR A *MENSCH*?

On 5 April 1943, Bonhoeffer was arrested by the Gestapo and incarcerated in Tegel prison charged with "subversion of the armed forces." During that period, he wrote what eventually became his *Letters and Papers from Prison,* posthumously edited and published by Bethge in the early 1950s. Many of us who read Bonhoeffer's *Discipleship* prior to reading the *Letters and Papers from Prison* wondered whether this could possibly be the same person. This was because his proposals for a "non-religious" interpretation of Christianity clearly indicated something of a shift away from what he had written in *Discipleship.*

In a letter to Bethge from prison on 21 July 1944, he wrote:

> I remember a conversation that I had in America thirteen years ago with a young French pastor [Lasserre]. We were asking ourselves quite simply what we wanted to do with our lives. He said he would like to become a saint . . . At the time I was very impressed, but I disagreed with him, and said, in effect, that I should like to learn to have faith. For a long time I didn't realize the depth of the contrast. I thought I could acquire faith by trying to live a holy life, or something like it. I suppose I wrote *Discipleship* at the end of that path.[15]

14. Slane, *Bonhoeffer as Martyr,* 97.
15. Bonhoeffer, *Letters and Papers,* 369.

In *Discipleship*, there is a lengthy chapter titled "The Saints" in which Bonhoeffer deals with the doctrine of sanctification. It is a very powerful exposition of the classic approach to the subject from the perspective of Reformation theology and the writings of St. Paul. At no point, however, does Bonhoeffer get into a discussion of the history of the problem as it has developed by way of comparison between the Catholic and Orthodox traditions on the one hand, and the Protestant on the other. For Bonhoeffer, "saints" refers to all the members of the body of Christ, for all are called to be saints, all are called to live as disciples, and therefore all are under the discipline of the Church in pursuing their calling. The final paragraph of the chapter begins: "*Those who have faith are being justified; those who are justified are being sanctified; those who are sanctified are being saved on judgment day.*" [16] And the reason Bonhoeffer gives for this is not that some Christians are holier than others, or engaged in special spiritual disciplines to become so, but, quoting St. Paul, because Christ "himself is our sanctification" (1 Cor 1:30).

In prison, Bonhoeffer, in continuing the quotation I gave earlier, commented that he began to see the dangers of his book *Discipleship*, even though he stood by what he had written.[17] The danger was clearly not costly discipleship or engagement in the struggle for justice and peace, but that *Discipleship* would be read in a pietistic way, lifting Christian discipleship out of the world in a search for holiness ("making something of oneself")[18] and thus confining it to an ecclesiastical or religious ghetto. Holiness is rather about our sanctification in Christ, as he wrote in *Discipleship*, even though discipleship implies the discipline of following Jesus. So to be a Christian, Bonhoeffer now insists in his prison letters, "does not mean to be religious in a particular way, to make something of oneself (a sinner, a penitent, or a saint) on the basis of some method or other." Rather it means being "a human being (*Menschsein*)—not a type of human, but the human being Christ creates in us."[19]

"It is not the religious act that makes the Christian," he writes, but participation in the sufferings of God in the secular life. That is *metanoia*:

16. Bonhoeffer, *Ethics*, 280.

17. Bonhoeffer, *Letters and Papers*, 369.

18. Bonhoeffer, *Christology*, 369.

19. Bonhoeffer, *Letters and Papers*, 361.

not in the first place thinking about one's own needs, problems, sins, and fears, but allowing oneself to be caught up into the way of Jesus Christ.[20]

Rather than trying to be religious, Christ demands of us a "mature worldliness," not "the shallow and banal this-worldliness of the enlightened, the busy, the comfortable, or lascivious, but the profound this-worldliness, characterized by discipline and the constant knowledge of death and resurrection."[21] "Mature worldliness" is a way of being *Christian* in the world that is *fully human, truly of the earth*; one that involves not only living responsibly in the world but also living what Bonhoeffer described as a genuinely "aesthetic existence" of creativity, playfulness, freedom, and friendship, something that he felt should characterize the life of the church.[22] It is an affirmation of life and humanity, of confidence and hope, amidst struggle, suffering, and death.[23] Paradoxically, at this moment when his own death seemed inevitable, he does not write, as in *Discipleship*, that "when Jesus calls us, he bids us come and die," but Jesus calls us "not to a new religion, but to life."[24]

From the early 1930s, Bonhoeffer had been engaged in an ongoing debate with Nietzsche's critique of Christianity as hostile to life.[25] This now leads him to embrace what he described as the "polyphony of life," of which Christ is the *cantus firmus*. In this regard he makes two significant Christological observations. The first is a reference to the Song of Songs with its portrayal of "ardent, passionate, and sensual love" which, he says, "is probably the best 'Christological' exposition."[26] The second observation concerns the two natures of Christ that, according to the Chalcedonian Definition, are "undivided and yet distinct." So, for Bonhoeffer the Christian life is a blending of the bodily and the spiritual without their confusion, or, put differently, the blending of eros and agape. "Christianity," he writes, "puts us into many different dimensions of life at the same time; we make room in ourselves, to some extent, for

20. Ibid., 361.

21. Ibid., 369.

22. See the discussion in de Gruchy, *Christianity, Art, and Transformation*, 147–58.

23. See de Gruchy, "Dietrich Bonhoeffer as Christian Humanist."

24. Bonhoeffer, *Letters and Papers*, 362.

25. Already in his reflections on ethics while a vicar in Barcelona (1928) Bonhoeffer engaged Nietzsche. Bonhoeffer, *Barcelona, Berlin, New York*, 363, 366.

26. Bonhoeffer, *Letters and Papers*, 315.

God and the whole world."[27] Where "the *cantus firmus* is clear and plain," Bonhoeffer writes, "the counterpoint can be developed to its limits."[28] This is very different from the kind of asceticism normally associated with saints—and it resembles, to an extent, the body-friendly and world-friendly asceticism described by Tim Gorringe.

And yet, for this to happen, for "nonreligious Christianity" and "mature worldliness" to become a reality in which Christ remained central to life and faith, it was necessary to develop a spirituality adequate to the task. This is what Bonhoeffer meant by the "secret discipline," something that he derived in fact from the Desert Fathers. The spirituality that had formed and informed Bonhoeffer's own life from the time he had, in his words, become a Christian, continues to shape his life in prison until the end. "All Christian thinking, speaking, and organizing," Bonhoeffer insisted from prison, "must be born anew out of [this] prayer and action."[29] This, I suggest, is the language of a true saint, but one who has, by his life and witness, helped us redefine what sainthood means.

Bibliography

Bethge, Eberhard. *Dietrich Bonhoeffer: A Biography*. Revised and edited by Victoria J. Barnett. Minneapolis: Fortress, 2000.

Bonhoeffer, Dietrich. *Barcelona, Berlin, New York 1928–1931*. Edited by Clifford J. Green. Dietrich Bonhoeffer Works 10. Minneapolis: Fortress, 2008.

———. *Christology*. Translated by John Bowden. London: Fontana, 1971.

———. *The Cost of Discipleship*. Translated by R. H. Fuller. London: SCM, 1959.

———. *Creation and Fall: A Theological Interpretation of Genesis 1–3*. Translated by John C. Fletcher. New York: Macmillan, 1959.

———. *Discipleship*. Edited by Geffrey B. Kelly and John D. Godsey. Translated by Barbara Green and Reinhard Krauss. Dietrich Bonhoeffer Works 4. Minneapolis: Fortress, 2001.

———. *Ethics*. Edited by Clifford J. Green. Translated by Reinhard Krauss et al. Dietrich Bonhoeffer Works 6. Minneapolis: Fortress, 2005.

———. *Letters and Papers from Prison*. Translated by Reginald H. Fuller et al. London: SCM, 1971.

———. *No Rusty Swords: Letters, Lectures, and Notes, 1928–1936*. Edited by Edwin H. Robertson. Translated by Edwin H. Robertson and John Bowden. Collected Works of Dietrich Bonhoeffer 1. London: Collins, 1965.

27. Ibid., 310.

28. Ibid., 303.

29. "Thoughts on the Day of the Baptism of Dietrich Wilhelm Rüdiger Bethge," in Bonhoeffer, *Letters and Papers*, 300.

De Gruchy, John W. *Christianity, Art, and Transformation.* Cambridge: Cambridge University Press, 2001.

———. "Dietrich Bonhoeffer as Christian Humanist." In *Being Human, Becoming Human: Dietrich Bonhoeffer and Social Thought*, edited by Jens Zimmerman and Brian Gregor, 3–24. Eugene, OR: Pickwick, 2010.

Gorringe, Timothy J. *Redeeming Time: Atonement through Education.* London: DLT, 1986.

Rasmussen, Larry. *Dietrich Bonhoeffer—His Significance for North Americans.* Minneapolis: Fortress, 1990.

Slane, Craig J. *Bonhoeffer as Martyr: Social Responsibility and Modern Christian Commitment.* Grand Rapids: Brazos, 2004.

12

Reformation, Renaissance, and Enlightenment
Christian Ideas of Nationalism and Equality in India[1]

DUNCAN B. FORRESTER

Two very different periods of Tim Gorringe's career as a radical theologian are the concern of this essay—his years on the staff of the radical Tamil Nadu Theological Seminary in Madurai, South India, and his years at the oldest Scottish University, St Andrews. He made a challenging contribution to the work of each institution, and learned much from encountering radical theological and religious notions and practices in the very different settings of Scotland and Tamil Nadu, yesterday and today. Tim is the very epitome of the contextual theologian who relates constructively and challengingly to the various contexts in which he has been called to work and to witness. And Tim's teaching and his practice have had a profound influence on multitudes of students in Britain and in India, and on his colleagues as well.

Contexts, of course, change and develop over time, and the wise contextual theologian relates not only to the contexts of the day, but also to the past development of these contexts, from which much can be learned that is challengingly relevant to the theological issues of today.

---

1. Some of the material in this essay has also appeared in chap. 7 of *Forrester on Christian Ethics*. It is used here with permission.

Insights, successes, and failures in one context may have much to offer in a very different context. Accordingly in this paper I intend to explore some aspects of the relationship between the Scottish Enlightenment and the Bengal Renaissance, in particular, debates about the relationships of religion, equality, and nationalism.

CHRISTIANITY AND THE SCOTTISH ENLIGHTENMENT

The Scottish Enlightenment, like the Enlightenment in general, was far less hostile to religion and to Christianity in particular than has commonly been assumed. Most of the great Enlightenment thinkers professed Christian belief in some form or other. The French *philosophes*, and able but slightly maverick figures elsewhere, were avowedly religious skeptics. In the Scottish Enlightenment, David Hume was by far the most notable of those who criticized religion. For the most part, however, the leaders of the Scottish Enlightenment found it possible to develop a constructive accommodation with religion and with theology. Scottish theology emerged from the Enlightenment debates as a confident form of rational Calvinism that believed that it had been vindicated and strengthened by the rigorous testing of the Enlightenment. Natural theology, it was believed, could demonstrate its truthfulness to any intelligent rational being, and was a prolegomenon to revealed theology, which in its turn could be commended successfully to any fair-minded, educated, and honest person. The theologians were, in short, not only convinced of the truth of Christianity but also convinced that it could and must be communicated to others. The spread of Christianity and the diffusion of Enlightenment were seen as one great mission, a responsibility that could not be avoided or shirked.

David Hume's critique of religion took a more skeptical line in relation to the "truths of religion." Hume's thought continues to be vigorously debated today, but at the time most Scots intellectuals, and certainly the theologians and the Presbyterian *literati* at the time, felt that he had been successfully refuted. The refutation of Hume was regarded not only as a vindication of truth against falsehood, but as a safeguarding of morality and the civic virtues, which were generally believed to be incompatible with atheism or religious skepticism. But, despite the confidence of his opponents that they had fatally worsted Hume in the intellectual arena, his ideas continued to be compellingly attractive to many in the younger generation.

Virtually all the leaders of the Scottish Enlightenment subscribed in some way or other to what George Davie has called "the democratic intellect."[2] Among many other things, the democratic intellect involved a passion about the importance of education, so that even Christian mission was often seen as simply a process of education, and a kind of egalitarianism that was skeptical of traditional hierarchies and believed—even though this was sometimes combined with educational elitism of a sort—that there should be open access for anyone of ability to educational opportunity. The broader influence of Scots in education in Bengal in the late eighteenth and early nineteenth centuries was immense. Laird comments that "it is probably only Scottish teachers who in the late eighteenth century could reasonably be criticized for trying to teach their pupils too much"![3]

HUMEAN SKEPTICISM IN THE BENGAL RENAISSANCE

David Hare (1775–1842) and David Drummond (1787–1843), Scots who came to Bengal around the turn of the nineteenth century, were in many ways typical Scots of their time. Neither came from an aristocratic background. They were representatives of the "democratic intellect": passionately intellectual, missionaries of Enlightenment and of egalitarianism, proponents of a radical critique of religion, society, and culture, but cautious about any direct challenge to the political order. Hare's roots were in Aberdeen, and he came to Bengal in 1800 as a watchmaker. Very soon he was found running schools at his own expense, with a stress on secularism and a sympathy for vernacular education. He became a leading figure in the Calcutta Schools Society and the Hindu College. He was sometimes regarded with some suspicion as a "freethinker," and on his death, the chaplain of St Andrew's Church, Calcutta was criticized by some for giving him a Christian burial.[4]

David Drummond, who arrived in Bengal in 1813, was the son of a Scottish Presbyterian minister. He administered and taught in the Dharmatala Academy, where he introduced the study of English grammar and literature, Latin, bookkeeping, and "the use of the globes." He

2. Davie, *Democratic Intellect*.

3. Laird, *Missionaries and Education*, 192. Part 2 of Laird's book gives a good survey of the Scots' contribution to education in Bengal.

4. Mitra, *David Hare*. I have so far been unable to find out anything of significance about Hare's education or background in Scotland.

was regarded as a considerable scholar in his own right, and he published "Objections to the Philosophy of Emmanuel Kant," and "Objections to Phrenology." He had the reputation of being an admirer of Hume, and he led his students through the writings of Dugald Stewart, Reid, and other luminaries of the Scottish Enlightenment. For Drummond "the right of private judgement, claimed by the fathers of the Reformation . . . was a very precious thing. He would believe nothing and accept nothing, unless it could be made as evident as a mathematical axiom."[5]

The most important disciple of Hare and Drummond was the dazzling charismatic teacher Henry Derozio, who took "Young Bengal," already questioning the tradition, by storm. Accused of teaching his students to cut their way through beef and pork and drink beer, to disrespect their elders, and to become infidels, Derozio defended himself by saying that he not only taught Hume's skepticism, but the refutation of it by Reid and by Dugald Stewart.[6] "I am neither afraid nor ashamed to confess," he wrote, "having stated the doubts of philosophers upon the existence of God, because I have also stated the solution of these doubts."[7] His method included public lectures on philosophy, and drawing his disciples into vigorous debating societies. Derozio, like Drummond and Hare, reflected the radical and religiously skeptical wing of the Scottish Enlightenment. Derozio taught his students to think for themselves, and in doing so aroused great excitement among Young Bengal, and considerable alarm among their traditionalist elders.

ALEXANDER DUFF

The direct Christian appeal to young intellectuals, already in revolt against much in the tradition, was left to Alexander Duff, and it was the contacts that he fostered and the highly distinctive content of his teaching that made possible a direct Christian contribution to the shaping of

5. Laird, *Missionaries and Education*, 50 and 222. Laird quotes from Edwards, *Henry Derozio*, 19. Cf. Madge and Dhar, "Old Calcutta." Once again, I am short on Drummond's background and education.

6. "I therefore thought it my duty to acquaint several of the College students with the substance of Hume's celebrated dialogue between Cleanthes and Philo, in which the most subtle and refined arguments against theism are adduced. But I have also furnished them with Dr Reid's and Dugald Stewart's more acute replies to Hume—replies which to this day continue unrefuted." Letter to H. H. Wilson, in Madge, *Henry Derozio*, 44.

7. Ibid., 8.

early nationalist ideas. Duff had been educated at St Andrews University in the confident rational Calvinism that had emerged out of the Scottish Enlightenment.[8] He arrived in Calcutta in 1830 as a missionary, with instructions to found a school in a country town some safe distance from the supposedly corrupting influences of metropolitan Calcutta. Typical of Scotland at the time was an emphasis on education, enlightenment, and civilization as necessary preliminaries to direct evangelism. Dr. John Inglis, a leader of the Moderate party in the Church of Scotland and for many years Convener of the Church's India Mission, believed that "little could be expected from mere preaching to an uneducated and barbarous people," for "till the human mind be, to a certain extent, cultivated and enlightened, it may be fairly regarded as, in one respect, incapable of entertaining the faith of the Gospels."[9] Before revealed religion could be preached, it was necessary that the mind and manners be prepared by teaching *natural religion*: "the testimony furnished by the light of nature, to the existence, attributes, and moral government of God, and the duty and destiny of man."[10] Maxwell speaks of "Duff's *absolute* confidence in the natural, self-evident rationality of his own philosophical, theological and linguistic tradition."[11]

Duff and his colleagues and supporters at home emphatically rejected the view of Sydney Smith that "in comparison to many other nations who are equally ignorant of the truths of Christianity, the Hindus are a civilized and moral people."[12] And they found their view confirmed by discovering young educated Hindus who had already vehemently rejected their own tradition as inadequate, and by their alliance with the Anglicists, such as C. E. Trevelyan.

Duff's initial survey of Calcutta and its environs persuaded him that there was already a considerable demand for English education in the city, and that his institution should be established close to the Hindu College where, under the prodigious influence of the brilliant young teacher Henry Derozio, a generation was being entranced by

8. On Duff, see Laird, *Missionaries and Education*; on his intellectual formation, see Maxwell, "Alexander Duff."

9. Mackichan, *Missionary Ideal*, 113; Smith, *Alexander Duff*, 1:34.

10. *Missionary Record* 1:61, cited in White, "Highly Preposterous," 124. Although some Hindus referred to their faith as "natural religion," Duff would have none of it.

11. Maxwell, "Alexander Duff," 162.

12. Sydney Smith, "Indian Missions," 179.

the very debates of the Scottish Enlightenment out of which Duff's own theology and strategy of mission had emerged.[13] Duff's attitude to the Hindu College and Derozio's influence was ambivalent. "The more advanced of the young men," he claimed in 1830, "have in reality, though not openly and avowedly, shaken off Hindooism, and plunged into the opposite extreme of unbounded scepticism."[14] The situation was pregnant with possibilities for good or ill: he saw his task as that of reclaiming "these wanderers, whose education and worldly circumstances invest them with such mighty influence among their fellow countrymen," an effort that must "in some degree affect and modify the future destinies of India."[15] This would be done largely by educating a new breed of "rational leaders" who would occupy a leading role in the India of the future.[16] Derozio had opened up an area of debate and of influence in which the Scots felt thoroughly at home; his work was not to be undone, but corrected and built upon. Duff was convinced of the importance of the Derozians. They were likely, he believed, to be "the leaders of those who may be instrumental in introducing a new era into the history of Hindoostan."[17]

From 1830 onwards, in addition to the work of the school, Duff and his colleagues gave great attention to series of "lectures . . . in the English language, on the Evidences of Natural and Revealed Religion to a number of Heathen youth, whose minds were previously opened by an acquaintance with European literature and science."[18] Duff had frequently attended the debating and literary society meetings that had been set up by the students of the Hindu College following the dismissal of Derozio, and that met in defiance of the college authorities. He now organized his own lectures according to a pattern with which he had been familiar since his own student days at St Andrews. The content of the lectures followed closely the themes of Scottish theology at the time. Each lecture was followed by discussion, during which any objections to the teaching

---

13. The remarkable report on Duff's survey of mission possibilities in Bengal, compiled a mere six weeks after his arrival in Calcutta, is now housed in the National Library of Scotland.

14. National Library of Scotland, MS 7530, Letter of 15 October 1830.

15. Ibid.

16. Maxwell, "Alexander Duff," 145.

17. National Library of Scotland, MS 7530, cited in ibid., 159.

18. Ibid.

of the lecture would be responded to. The impact of these lectures was cumulatively important, and resulted in significant conversions. The lectures, and the College that Duff quickly established, represented, as he declared in Scotland in 1837, with characteristically Scottish modesty, "a design which simply consists in transporting to the plains of Hindustan, and vigorously applying for its reformation, that very system of 'teaching and preaching combined,' which, in the hands of our own Knoxes and Melvilles, once rendered Scotland an intellectual, moral and religious garden, among the nations of the earth."[19]

CHRISTIANITY AS THE MIDWIFE OF THE NATION

Derozio had inculcated patriotism into his disciples; the Scots missionaries felt no need to question this aspect of his teaching, for they too felt they were assisting at the birth of a great nation.[20] But the missionaries were convinced that only Christianity, not Derozio's skepticism, could provide a secure foundation for true patriotism.

Duff and his colleagues believed that Christianity offered the only basis for sound and healthy social life, and that without Christianity, India had no future as a nation. If India were to remain Hindu, no national consciousness could develop, they believed, for Hinduism (which Duff regarded as one, closely integrated, "gigantic system") was a prison-house of the mind. In the short term, a Hindu India would always resist the "beneficent effects" of British rule; and in the long term it was incompatible with the development of nationhood because its genius was to divide people from each other rather than binding them together by shared purposes and common aspirations. The secularism and skepticism of the Derozians provided no firmer basis for nationhood. Duff regarded the Derozians as rootless, egoistic sophists with no ultimate care save for their own interests. From their ranks, however, he hoped would come the leaders of the new India. But first they must replace their volatile skepticism with a more securely based commitment that, in Duff's view, could only be adherence to Christianity. Secular Western education such as had been given in the Hindu College, and which many influential government officials wished to spread throughout India in preference to education based on Christianity, would, Duff believed,

19. Duff, *Vindication*, 44, cited in Maxwell, "Alexander Duff," 194.
20. Mackay, *Missionary's Warrant*, 15.

produce infidels and rebels. The Revolt of 1857 was later presented as a demonstration of the dangers that flowed from government sponsorship of purely secular education. Separation between India and Britain might be inevitable and even desirable in the long run, but the inculcation of Christianity among the leaders of India would delay that separation and ensure that, when the day came, independent India would be based on sound foundations.[21]

Duff's strategy involved the direct confrontation and refutation of basic Derozian ideas, the conversion of key individuals, and the gradual percolation of Christian ideas through these converts to society as a whole. Christianity would not triumph suddenly, and individual conversions were on the whole less important in his scheme than the gradual undermining of Hinduism through the reception of Christian ideas. The real need, to Duff's mind, was for a "decided permanent change in the *national intellect*."[22] W. S. Mackay, one of Duff's leading colleagues, put the appeal of the Scottish missionaries very clearly in his lecture on Deism to an audience of young men in Calcutta:

> And, if we long, and pray and glow with desire for the moral and spiritual enlightenment of India; if we would give our right hands or our right eyes, to see this nation rescued from superstition and misery and redeemed unto God can it be that there is no corresponding feeling among you? In the generous warmth and flush of youth, with floods of novel light and novel truth pouring into your minds, with fame to win, and blessings awaiting you, and opportunity and high and glorious enterprise beckoning you on—and the end the regeneration of your own beloved country it surely cannot be that the blight of Hinduism is upon you and that you will leave the work to strangers.[23]

Such appeals to share with the missionaries in the work of national enlightenment and regeneration led to the baptism of a number of leading Derozians and other young intellectuals in Calcutta, and also in connection with the Scottish missions in Bombay and Madras. The most notable names among the Calcutta converts were Lal Behari Day, K. M. Banerjea, Michael Madhusudhan Dutt, Kali Charan Chatterjee, Gopinath Nandi, Mohesh Chunder Ghose, and Ananda Chand Mozumdar. The

21. Duff, *Vindication*, 408ff., 456. Cf. his *Missionary Addresses*, 40.
22. Duff, *India*, 317.
23. Mackay, *Lecture*, 4.

converts were seen by Duff and his colleagues as destined to be the real leaders of the renaissance and reformation upon which the future of India depended. They were to be the Pauls, the Luthers, the Knoxes of their own native land. Reformation and renaissance were regarded as virtually a single process that was the presupposition of progress, enlightenment, and national maturity.

The emphasis placed upon religious reformation reflected how closely for the Scots missionaries the Reformation of the sixteenth century and their own national consciousness were bound together. Nor was it in any way absurd to see a connection between the European Reformation and the genesis of European nationalism, or to posit a similar religious reformation as a necessary precondition for Indian nationalism. In the context of the time, there was nothing strange in seeing the *replacement* of Hinduism with Christianity as in no significant way different from the sixteenth century reformation of the church in Europe. Ram Mohan Roy and others who sought to reform Hinduism while remaining Hindus were characteristically dismissed as pusillanimous Erasmian equivocators. A reformation, the Scots missionaries believed, was always sparked off by outside influences, but it could only be carried through by indigenous reformers. Western learning understood as a coherent corpus of Christian truth was to be the outside stimulus for the Indian Reformation/Renaissance; the converts, having drunk deeply at this well, were to be the Indian Reformers:[24] "Some Indian Luther may be roused to give expression to the sentiments that have long been secretly, though it may be vaguely, indefinitely, waveringly, cherished in the bosoms of thousands. Whole districts may awaken from their slumbers. Whole cities may proclaim their independence. Whole provinces may catch the flame of liberty—all India may be born in a day."[25]

THE OUTWORKING OF THE VISION

Here was a heady vision indeed. But in practice, of course, things did not work out as the missionaries had hoped. They recruited a small cadre of truly remarkable men who were very deeply influenced by the missionaries' teaching. But although Duff and his colleagues professed that their own role was modest and temporary, in practice they contradicted their

24. Duff, *India*, 355–410.

25. Ibid., 377.

own theories by refusing equality of status to the converts, who gradually in consequence either scattered as ministers in other denominations and parts of India, or entered secular employment. When the converts produced proposals for a national church, or claimed a share in control of the mission, they were met with uncomprehending and paternalist rebukes at the hands of the missionaries. Practice belied theory, and the missionaries showed themselves highly suspicious of their converts' attempts to relate their Christian faith to Indian culture and aspirations. It was quite acceptable for a convert to attack Hindu Reform movements such as the Brahmo Samaj, as Lal Behari Day and K. M. Banerjea in particular did, arguing that the "new Vedantism" has never produced any practical change for the better in the institutions of the country, "so that it will never regenerate India."[26] But endeavors to demonstrate that becoming Christian did not alienate one from Indian culture, and indeed that Christian faith was the true fulfillment of the Vedic tradition, more truly Indian than the Hinduism of the day, were frowned upon.[27] K. M. Banerjea's emphasis on religious continuity and Christian patriotism was not what the missionaries expected or approved. "I have heard it said," he wrote, "that we Christians have no feeling for our country or our race, and that our adoption of the Christian religion is an act of treachery to India and her institutions, both ancient and modern . . . I think I could prove to any jury of educated Hindus that the charge is utterly unfounded; that we Christians have never, in a religious point of view, renounced any of India's institutions, which they themselves do not denounce as idolatrous." Indeed, he concludes, "we are better patriots than the Brahmos."[28]

The missionaries' belief that their converts were to be new Luthers was shown, among other things, in their encouragement of the converts to write. These writings, in English and the vernacular, are of considerable quantity and form a corpus of extremely interesting material, documenting in detail a fascinating phase of cultural and religious interchange. They range from essays directly sponsored by the missionaries and published in newspapers such as the *Madras Native Herald* and the *Calcutta Christian Observer*, to substantial and independent works

---

26. Banerjea, *Lectures*, 28–30.

27. See Kopf, "Missionary Challenge," esp. 17–18.

28. Banerjea, *Peculiar Responsibility*, 14–16.

of literature such as Lal Behari Day's *Bengal Peasant Life* or Michael Madhusudhan Dutt's poetry.

Our specific interest in these writings is, however, the nationalist ideas that they contain. On the whole, they reflect fairly precisely the theology of the missionaries and suggest a willing acceptance of the reforming role for which the converts had been cast. But to this general acceptance of their mentors' views the converts add a far more detailed knowledge and a more sensitive appreciation of Indian things, and they not infrequently notice and underline implications of the missionaries' positions that were not recognized by the missionaries themselves. Two instances of this arise in relation to the understanding of providence and the assessment of caste.

PROVIDENCE AND NATIONALISM

The notion of a divine providential ordering of history was a dominant theme in the Scottish missionaries' thought.[29] This decisively shaped their understanding of their own task, and that of their converts. Sometimes the missionaries suggest, in almost Hegelian or Marxist style, that prior to the western and Christian impact, India had been an ahistorical society, which had only in recent times been brought within history. But certainly the missionaries generally understood British rule as a providential ordering, a sign of God's care for India rather than simply an opportunity for the making of individual converts. The British in India are, consciously or unconsciously, agents of divine providence, but fallible agents, as the failures that contributed to causing the Mutiny demonstrated.

Almost, but not quite invariably, the missionaries stop with the veiled suggestion that British rule is in some sense the ultimate dispensation of providence for India. The converts, on the other hand, while accepting the missionaries' general understanding of history and agreeing that the British rule by divine ordering, are far clearer and more unanimous in seeing and affirming that the Scottish missionaries' views logically lead to regarding British rule as a *stage* to national independence.

29. On the relation of understandings of providence and the missionary movement, see Studdert-Kennedy, *Providence* and *British Christians*; Greenlee and Johnston, *Good Citizens*; and Stanley, "Commerce and Christianity."

EQUALITY, CASTE, AND NATIONAL UNITY

It was similar with the missionary attack on caste. Protestant missionaries as a whole were peculiarly vehement and consistent in their onslaught on caste.[30] The converts accepted and repeated all the main counts in the missionary indictment. Caste, they said, was an integral part of Hinduism, and also its Achilles' heel. It was quite different from European concepts of class and rank, and fundamentally incompatible with Christian ideas of social order. Caste impeded evangelism, and forbade humane relationships and even acts of ordinary morality between those of different castes. It narrowly circumscribed the diffusion of knowledge, and was responsible for the intellectual and social stagnation of India. But other charges are given pride of place in many of the converts' writings on caste. Narayan Sheshadri, one of John Wilson's converts in Bombay, argues that caste is responsible for the paucity of Indians who are "like the patriots of Greece and Rome. This monster-system of caste, by extinguishing patriotism and other social feelings, has, in many ways, done much to lower the national character of the Hindus."[31] K. M. Banerjea agreed that national character had degenerated as a result of caste, which was "the principal cause of India's humiliation." Caste not only discourages patriotism and weakens character, but it puts "an end to unity and strength in the nation by setting caste against caste and fragmenting society." Thus, he continues, "a people divided and sub-divided like the Hindus, can never make head against any power that deserves the name. The Muhammadan conquest was the natural result of such national weakness." By implication it was caste also that had laid India prostrate before the British. Then comes the exhortation that is the key to much of the thinking of Banerjea and other converts: "If India is destined in the counsels of Providence to look up once more among the nations of the earth, it will only be by unlearning the institution of caste, and by adopting the religion of her present rulers with all its temporal and spiritual blessings."[32]

30. See my *Caste and Christianity*, and Cederlöf, "Politics of Caste."

31. Sheshadri and Wilson, *Darkness and Dawn*, 34. The same point is developed in Irving, *Theory and Practice*, 38–40.

32. Banerjea, "Hindu Caste," 70. A detailed discussion on caste in which four young converts took part in Madras in 1845 is fully reported in the *Madras Native Herald*, and reprinted in Roberts, *Caste*, 63–131. In later life, Banerjea modified his opposition to caste. It remains an evil, but he fears that any attempt to eradicate it "may produce a far

Furthermore, converts were quick to draw out implications of the missionaries' position on caste that were often uncongenial to their mentors. They inquired, for instance, what was the difference between the caste distinctions that were rejected with such vehemence and the denominational rivalries among Christians, and they suggested that the refusal of communion between the various churches was no different in principle from the prohibition of commensalism between Brahmin and Pariah. They realized that the egalitarianism on which the attack on caste was based also condemned attitudes of racial superiority, shown even by some missionaries. The church that they saw as central to a new Indian nationhood was both more Indian and more united than the denominations imported by the missionaries.

CONCLUSION

Christianity, for Banerjea and the other converts, was seen as providing the only adequate answer to India's problems, and the only possible basis for true nationhood. They agreed with the Hindu reformers, as against the Derozians, that patriotism must have a religious basis, but denied that contemporary Hinduism was capable of sustaining healthy national feeling. Only Christianity, they believed, could provide the proper foundation for progress and nationhood. And they went on to argue that Christianity, so far from being an imported and alienating system, was more truly the heir of the ancient Indian tradition than was the decadence of contemporary Hinduism.[33]

Some of the ideas of the Scottish mission converts were peculiarly interesting and in the long run increasingly significant, particularly their insistence on concepts of providence and equality and on the need for religious change to undergird national revival. Yet most of the converts did not become significant public figures, and Christian ideas did not for long continue to feed as directly and impressively into the national awakening. The dialogue out of which the converts arose, and to which they contributed, did not last long. Many of the converts held leading positions within some branch of the church, but became rather isolated from the broader society. The Calcutta converts in particular were widely

---

greater evil than its own most malignant form, and the remedy may prove worse than the disease" (Banerjea, "Origin").

33. See Banerjea, *Moonduck Oopunishad*; various comments in *The Enquirer* magazine, of which he was editor, in 1834 and 1835; *Lectures*; and "Hindu Caste."

scattered, and within the churches the disturbance of their questioning was gradually effectively neutralized. Their central belief that without Christianity national renewal would be impossible was unrealized in the sense that few national leaders were to be Christians, and the Christian community, which remained small and uninfluential, played little part in the development of the national movement. Yet through the early converts and through leading figures such as Keshub Chunder Sen and P. C. Mozoomdar, who were sympathetic to Christianity but not technically members of the church, specifically Christian ideas continued to have their impact on the early development of nationalist thought.[34] But that is another story.

The contribution of the Derozians as sowing "a seed of secular and radical nationalism" has often been recognized. But it is not enough to suggest, as do Premen Addy and Ibne Azad, that "isolation and harassment" eventually drove some of the leading Derozians to embrace Christianity.[35] Many of these converts adopted out of intellectual conviction a coherent position that was at the same time specifically Christian and at least potentially nationalist, which added a new dimension to the debate and which should be regarded as itself one of the seeds of Indian nationalist thought.

M. K. Hardar is in a sense right that the Bengal Renaissance was not followed by great historic movements like the Reformation and the European Enlightenment.[36] But a case can also be made that there was a continuous undercurrent of egalitarian thought that drew both on the Derozian and the Duff traditions, surfacing from time to time in expressions such as Bankim Chandra Chatterji's 1879 essay *Samya*: "All of you are equal. All are sinners, everyone can get salvation through good deeds. Caste differences are false. Sacrifices and worship are false. The Vedas are false, the Sutras are false, earthly happiness is false, who the king is, who the subject is, are all false. Only Dharma is true. Give up the pursuit of falsehood, follow the true Dharma."[37]

Is it fanciful to suggest that out of this vigorous exchange of ideas in Bengal in the early decades of the nineteenth century emerged

34. See Thomas, *Acknowledged Christ*.

35. Addy and Azad, "Politics and Society," 98.

36. Haldar, *Foundations of Nationalism*, 178.

37. See ibid.; Chatterji, *Renaissance and Reaction* (an English translation, with an introduction by Haldar, of *Samya*), 154–55. Cf. Mohanty, "Towards a Political Theory."

impulses that much later found their embodiment in the egalitarian emphases of the Indian Constitution? No, and the fact that most Indian Christians today are Dalits—formerly known as Harijans or Untouchables—has led to Christian thinkers and Christian ideas on equality playing a major role in struggles for social justice in India in more recent times. And the development of Dalit theology is of the greatest importance, not only in India.

But that is another story, with which Tim Gorringe was much in volved during his time in Madurai.

Bibliography

Addy, Premen, and Ibne Azad. "Politics and Society in Bengal." In *Explosion in a Subcontinent*, edited by Robin Blackburn, 79–150. Harmondsworth: Penguin, 1975.

Banerjea, K. M. "Hindu Caste." *Calcutta Review* 15 (1851).

———. *Lectures to Educated Native Young Men: Lecture IV on Vedantism*. Calcutta, 1851.

———. "Origin and Development of Caste." *Transactions of Bengal Social Science Association* 7 (1878).

———. *The Peculiar Responsibility of Educated Natives and their Duty Thoughtfully to Enquire into the Christian Scheme of Salvation*. Calcutta, 1865.

———. *A Review of the Moonduck Oopunishad, translated into English*. Calcutta, 1833.

Cederlöf, Gunnel. "The Politics of Caste and Conversion: Conflicts among Protestant Missions in Mid-Nineteenth Century India." *Swedish Missiological Themes* 88:1 (2000) 131–57.

Chatterji, Bankim Chandra. *Renaissance and Reaction in Nineteenth Century Bengal: Bankim Chandra Chattopadhyay: An English Translation of the Bengali Essay "Samya"*. Columbia, MO: South Asia Books, 1977.

Davie, George E. *The Democratic Intellect: Scotland and Her Universities in the Nineteenth Century*. Edinburgh: Edinburgh University Press, 1961.

Duff, Alexander. *India and Indian Missions*. Edinburgh, 1839.

———. *Missionary Addresses*. Edinburgh, 1850.

———. *A Vindication of the Church of Scotland's India Missions*. Edinburgh, 1837.

Edwards, T. *Henry Derozio: The Eurasian Poet, Teacher and Journalist*. Calcutta, 1884.

Forrester, Duncan B. *Caste and Christianity: Attitudes and Policies on Caste of Anglo-Saxon Protestant Missions in India*. London: Curzon, 1980.

———. *Forrester on Christian Ethics and Practical Theology: Collected Writing on Christianity, India, and the Social Order*. Aldershot: Ashgate, 2010.

Greenlee, J. G., and C. M. Johnston. *Good Citizens: British Missionaries and Imperial States, 1870 to 1918*. Montreal: McGill-Queen's University Press, 1999.

Haldar, M. K. *Foundations of Nationalism in India: A Study of Bankimchandra Chatterjee*. Delhi: Ajanta, 1989.

Irving, B. A. *Home and Foreign Missionary Record of the Church of Scotland*, Old Series 1 (1838).

———. *The Theory and Practice of Caste*. London, 1853.

Kopf, David. "The Missionary Challenge and Brahmo Response: Rajnarain Bose and the Emerging Ideology of Cultural Nationalism." *Contributions to Indian Sociology*, New Series 8 (1974) 11–24.

Laird, Michael. *Missionaries and Education in Bengal, 1793–1837*. Oxford: Clarendon, 1972.

Mackay, W. S. *Lecture V on Deism*. Calcutta, n.d.

———. *The Missionary's Warrant and the Church's Duty: A Sermon*. Calcutta, 1850.

Mackichan, D. *The Missionary Ideal in the Scottish Churches*. London: Hodder & Stoughton, 1927.

Madge, E. W. *Henry Derozio: The Eurasian Poet and Reformer*. Calcutta: Naya Prokash, 1982.

Madge, E. W., and K. N. Dhar. "Old Calcutta: Its Schoolmasters." *Calcutta Review*, New Series 1 (1913) 338–50.

Maxwell, Ian Douglas. "Alexander Duff and the Theological and Philosophical Background to the General Assembly's Mission in Calcutta to 1840." PhD diss., Edinburgh University, 1995.

Mitra, P. C. *A Biographical Sketch of David Hare*. Calcutta, 1877. New ed., Calcutta: Jijnasa, 1979.

Mohanty, Manoranjan. "Towards a Political Theory of Inequality." In *Equality and Inequality: Theory and Practice*, edited by André Béteille, 243–91. Delhi: Oxford University Press, 1983.

Roberts, Joseph, editor. *Caste, in Its Religious and Civil Character, Opposed to Christianity*. London, 1847.

Sheshadri, Narayan, and John Wilson. *The Darkness and the Dawn in India: Two Missionary Discourses*. Edinburgh, 1853.

Smith, George. *The Life of Alexander Duff, D.D., LL.D.* London: Hodder & Stoughton, 1879.

Smith, Sydney. "Publications respecting Indian Missions." *The Edinburgh Review* 23 (1808) 151–81.

Stanley, Brian. "'Commerce and Christianity': Providence Theory, the Missionary Movement and the Imperialism of Free Trade, 1842–1860." *Historical Journal* 26:1 (1983) 71–94.

Studdert-Kennedy, Gerald. *British Christians, Indian Nationalists, and the Raj*. Delhi: Oxford University Press, 1991.

———. *Providence and the Raj: Imperial Mission and Missionary Imperialism*. Walnut Creek, CA: AltaMira, 1998.

Thomas, M. M. *The Acknowledged Christ of the Indian Renaissance*. London: SCM, 1970.

White, Gavin. "'Highly Preposterous': Origins of Scottish Missions." *Scottish Church History Society Records* 19 (1976) 111–24.

13

Does God Care?

DHYANCHAND CARR

It is indeed a great privilege to have been asked to produce a chapter for this Festschrift for Tim Gorringe, a close friend and one-time colleague. Though he is younger than I, I regard Tim a mentor, for in terms of scholarship and wisdom he is by far my senior. However, despite this indebtedness and unreserved acknowledgement of his superior theological ability, I have decided in this article to take issue with him on his understanding of providence, in the light of the devastating events of 2009 in Sri Lanka. I feel that to pursue this conversation with Tim is particularly appropriate given that he pays not altogether deserved praise to the Tamil Nadu Theological Seminary as his teacher, where we were colleagues, and also because he has raised the question as to how to pray for situations such as the one in Sri Lanka in the chapter "For What Can We Pray?" in his book *God's Theatre*, subtitled *A Theology of Providence*.

I shall narrate the not-so-well-known background to the story of the tragedy that befell the Tamils of Sri Lanka in early 2009, because, to my mind, I cannot accommodate what happened as falling within God's attractive providence. I do want to argue, however, for an alternative view of God's providence. I want to argue that the story falls within God's plan to redeem the descendants of Cain (that is, all those of us who in spite of our unworthiness enjoy God's providential protection and care), through the forgiveness offered by the suffering Community of Abel, participants in the Cross of Christ. God's action is to be located in his drawing alongside the communities of Abel, suffering together with them, and paradoxically also enabling them both to struggle against the oppressors and to offer forgiveness to them if they repent.

Martin Luther King Jr., Jürgen Moltmann, and James Cone have all said that undeserved suffering can be redemptive. To my knowledge, the question of how this can be so has not been effectively answered. Even Tim, toward the end of *God's Theatre*, makes only an allusive reference, so it seems to me, when he says, "In the same way God's providence is the account of the story of the crucified Jew Jesus bears on human history. It is, in other words, the *history* of the atonement. The 'atonement' is not something which happened only on Calvary; it is Calvary made real in human history through the Holy Spirit."[1] Why then did he not spell this point out more clearly, and apply it to situations such as those that prevailed in Northern Ireland, Lebanon, and Sri Lanka, where he was only too aware of the devastation and ravages? I will return to this question at the end, after I have narrated the story of the Sri Lankan Tamils.

THE STORY

The Emergence of the Sinhala Consciousness

The population of Sri Lanka is roughly 74 percent Sinhalese and 26 percent Tamil. Three different groups comprise this 26 percent: Native Tamils (13 percent), Muslims (5 percent),[2] and the Plantation Tamils (7 percent).[3] The Native Tamil minority people have been living in Sri Lanka for many centuries in a contiguous territory (Homeland) encompassing the northwest region of Sri Lanka (the Mannar region); the Vanni area, which is the region north of Vavuniya and south of the Gulf of Jaffna; and the eastern region comprising the Trincomale District, Batticoloa District, and Ampara District down the East Coast.

---

1. Gorringe, *God's Theatre*, 101.

2. The Tamil speaking Muslims of Sri Lanka call themselves Moors—i.e., people of Arab trader descent—and maintain that they came to be Tamil-speaking because they were taught Islam by *Maulvis* (teachers) who came from south India.

3. 1981 figures, Department of Census and Statistics, "Population by Ethnic Group." The Plantation Tamils come from the indentured labor brought to Sri Lanka from India by the British in 1833 with promise of good earnings and citizenship rights to work in the upcountry plantations. They have never been part of the Elam struggle.

Many of the Sinhalese of Sri Lanka have always adamantly maintained that the entire island of Sri Lanka belongs to the Sinhala Buddhists only. All other ethnic/religious and linguistic minorities are in their view like creepers that have wound themselves around a huge tree, totally dependent on the tree for their support. Among the Sinhala population, more than ninety percent embrace Theravada Buddhism, while nine percent belong to the Christian Church (Catholic, Anglican, Methodist, Baptist, Presbyterian, and Dutch Reformed in that order of relative strength) and one percent to Islam. The Christian Church in Sri Lanka also has a considerable

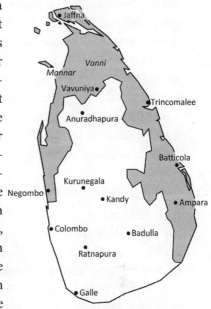

number of Tamils in it; in fact, Christianity is the only religion that has both Tamil and Sinhalese adherents, and in many ways has therefore maintained a unique witness to the possibility of interethnic harmony.

Sinhala nationalism was heightened during the period of British rule in the island. For while the two earlier colonial powers (the Portuguese and the Dutch) had treated the Tamil territory and the southern Sinhala territory as distinct administrative units, the British who succeeded them in 1833 merged the two into one administrative unit.

The Buddhists on the island, all of whom are Sinhalese, hold to the *Māhavaṃsa* (Great Tradition). According to the *Māhavaṃsa* story, Buddha himself visited Sri Lanka and converted the natives to Buddhism, and declared that the entire island of Sri Lanka belonged to the Buddhists.[4] However, this is not the only story among the community, who also believe that Buddhism came to Sri Lanka through a great king who in fact was born to a lion and an Indian Princess.[5] The national symbol of the lion and the "Sinhalese" name are derived from this story. The king Dutta Gamini, considered a descendant of this dynasty, is supposed to have achieved the unity of Sri Lanka by conquering and chasing away the Tamils. All this is supposed to have happened at the beginning

4. *Māhavaṃsa*, chap.1.

5. Ibid., chap. 6.

of the Christian Era. Sinhalese politicians have exploited these mythical stories and played on the religious sentiments of the people in their genocidal war against the Tamils of the island.

History, though, provides little basis for the belief that Sri Lanka belongs only to the Sinhalese Buddhists. In 1799, Sir Hugh Cleghorn, the British Colonial Secretary, made the following remark: "Two different nations from a very ancient period, have divided between them the possession of the island . . . These two nations differ entirely in their religion, language and manners."[6]

The Emergence of the Demand for Tamil Elam

Now we turn to how the Tamils of Sri Lanka, particularly those we might call the "native" Tamils, came to claim the right for self-determination, leading to a demand for Tamil Elam, a separate sovereign state with the traditional homeland of the north and east as the base. The native Tamil people of Sri Lanka speak Tamil with certain significant differences from the way Tamil is spoken in Tamil Nadu (India). This is not just in terms of accent and pronunciation but also in terms of diction and idiom. A vast majority are adherents of Saivism but they assert that they are not Hindus. For them their religion is simply Saivism.

Consciously and deliberately thus asserting their difference from the Tamils of India, they did not in the first instance register a protest when in 1833 the British rulers brought about a merger of the Tamil and the Sinhala regions into a single administrative unit. Rather, they grabbed the opportunity for education and jobs. Nearly 25 percent of the Homeland dwellers migrated southwards to Colombo. The Tamils were reputed to be more ambitious, hardworking, and venturesome, and their students higher achieving, than many of the easygoing Sinhalese. Certainly, the Tamils became prosperous over the years—though the so-called Kandy elite[7] among the Sinhalese were equally ambitious.

---

6. See Pieris, "Administration of Justice and Revenue." Historic maps, such as that provided by Robert Knox in his seventeenth-century description of travels in Ceylon, show "Coylot Wanees Country" as a separate kingdom spanning the northern and northeastern parts of the country. A clear 1692 Dutch engraving of the map is available online at http://commons.wikimedia.org/wiki/File:MapofEelamTamilcountryeng raving1692.jpg; the 1681 English original, from Knox, *Historical Relation*, is available online at http://commons.wikimedia.org/wiki/File:RobertKnox1681mapCeylonTamilc ountrynortheast.jpeg.

7. Kandy is known as the cultural capital of Sri Lanka. Many elite Buddhists origi-

Resentment of the development and progress of the Colombo Tamils began to take root among the Sinhalese.

No sooner had Sri Lanka become independent from the British than the rulers, who were mostly the Kandy elite group, began a systematic program to contain the progress and development of the Tamil people. Within months of independence (1948), the Citizenship Act was passed disenfranchising nearly one million Tamils of Indian origin (that is, those who had come as indentured labor under the British rule in 1834). Beginning with the Citizenship Act, the cleavage between the Tamils and the Sinhalese widened exponentially with each decade.

In the year 1956, the Government passed the "Sinhala Only" law making Sinhala the sole language of administration and instruction. The most important outcome of the promulgation of this Act was that many Tamils who knew English well but had not studied Sinhala at school were thrown out of their jobs. Only one small section of socialist parliamentarians protested from within the Sinhala community. Later, under pressure from Buddhist leaders, even they withdrew their protest. For the first time, the native Tamils woke up to protest nonviolently against this Act. However, this protest was crushed with brute force.

Then began the demands for devolution of power. The Federal Party of the Tamils indicated that they would be happy for a federal form of government within a united Sri Lanka. But they were pushed further and further by repeated betrayals. First, a pact was made (1958) to form regional councils with relative autonomy and the use of Tamil within the Tamil region. This was unilaterally dropped by the Bandaranaike government almost as soon as it was signed. Nonviolent, Gandhian-style protests continued. In 1961, when the Federal Party organized a peaceful demonstration in Jaffna, it was brutally crushed using the army. Then there was the agreement to form District Councils comprising smaller administrative units with devolved power. Once again it was scrapped. An irate Buddhist monk, feeling that Bandaranaike would one day give in to Tamil demands for devolution, shot him dead. This was the first of a series of infamous political assassinations in Sri Lanka.

When the government declared in 1972 that Sri Lanka was a Sinhala Buddhist Republic, it precipitated the demand for a sovereign Tamil state known as Tamil Elam. Along with this Act came also the policy of Standardization. This policy allowed the marks of all Tamil

---

nated from this area. Almost all of them had their education in Britain.

students passing their O and A Level exams to be reduced by a certain percentage, while simultaneously the marks of Sinhalese students were increased. This was supposed to be an act of positive discrimination for the Sinhalese.

The Federal Party of the Tamils would have been happy with a federal form of governance. Words such as *federal, devolution,* and *homeland* had, however, become anathema to the leaders of Buddhism. They believed strongly that it would undermine the rights bestowed on them by Buddha himself, bequeathing the whole of Sri Lanka to the Buddhists. Successive governments of Sri Lanka also indulged in several other ways of marginalizing the Tamil people of Sri Lanka. The Sri Lankan army and the police force were gradually made "Sinhalese Only" forces. The armed forces, more than the police, were deployed to disperse and disrupt any protests by the Tamils. Extrajudicial killings and disappearances became commonplace. In addition, a Special Task Force was formed under the direct command of the President. The STF was very ruthless. The STF were allowed to use violence not only against the "deemed rioters" but also against all and sundry civilians deemed as backing the protesters, indulging in rape and murder of women and in looting of the property.

Politically, the Government also adopted a policy to control and distort the demographic composition of parliamentary constituencies. Therefore quite a few constituencies that once had a Tamil majority and returned a Tamil member to the Parliament were turned into Sinhalese majority constituencies by cleverly redrawing the boundaries or by the colonization of a Tamil majority area with Sinhalese settlers by means of offers of free land and financial support for resettlement. A special contingent of the STF provided security for the new settlers.

None of this is exaggerated. For instance, if we look at the census statistics, in 1946 the population distribution in the Trincomalee district in the east was: Sinhalese, 11,606 (15.3 percent); Tamils, 33,795 (44.5 percent); and Muslims, 23,219 (30.6 percent). In 1981 it was: Sinhalese, 86,341 (33.6 percent); Tamils, 93,510 (36.4 percent); and Muslims, 74,403 (29 percent). Though the Muslims were Tamil-speaking, politically they threw in their lot with the Sinhalese. In 1946 the combined strength was less than that of the Tamils. But this was changed due to the policy of settling a large number of Sinhalese from the south under the patronage of a Buddhist monk. The settlement was made in the lands to be irrigated by building a dam across the river Manal Aru (its Tamil Name, meaning Sand River; it was renamed in Sinhala: Weli Oya).

Since the Tamils from Jaffna could move down to Colombo and settle there, it could of course be contended that other communities were also free to move and settle anywhere. But here was a government-aided settlement program aimed at only one section of the population, without the same privilege being extended to the poor among the Tamils. Not only did the move reduce Tamil representation in the parliament, it also broke the contiguity between the Jaffna Peninsula, Vanni, and the East.

It is not surprising, therefore, that the Federal Party of the Tamils in 1977 decided that peaceful coexistence with the Sinhalese was not possible and enunciated the demand for Tamil Elam. The party then metamorphosed into the Tamil United Liberation Front. It is important to remember that the demand for Tamil Elam was not made originally by an armed militant group, but by the elder Selvanayagam. He is fondly remembered as Thanthai Selva (that is, Father Selva). The demand for Tamil Elam, however, resulted in mobs rioting against Tamils all over the country. The government abetted the riots, and incited young people to resort to violence especially against vulnerable Tamil people caught in pockets surrounded by the Sinhalese.

The riots of 1978 and the burning down by the armed forces of the Jaffna Library (home to some ninety thousand volumes and many unpublished research papers and ancient manuscripts) in 1981 jointly gave rise to armed militancy. Guerilla warfare was resorted to and the militants attacked army camps, killed many soldiers who resisted, and, when most of the soldiers ran away, looted their arms and ammunition. The bodies of slain soldiers sent down south and the presence of many defectors in their midst incited one of the most gruesome mob riots in history in Colombo, starting on the 26 July 1983 and lasting for well over a week. This happened right under the supervision of armed person-nel with the connivance of the political bosses. Only a few thousand were reported as killed, but more than sixty thousand "disappeared." Women who fled the Wellawatta Tamil ghetto in Colombo took refuge in temples, but they were hunted down by the STF men and were subject to indescribable acts of sexual humiliation.

The armed insurgency, however, lacked unity. Many groups emerged with differing shades of ideological opinion, each claiming they were the true representatives of the Tamil people and that they alone would be able to provide a proper democratic socialist government of Tamil Elam. There were also regional differences in culture among the Native Tamils, which played a part in the emergence of such rivalries. In time, the Liberation Tigers of Tamil Elam (LTTE) emerged as the most powerful and well-organized group. While they carried on a struggle against the Government of Sri Lanka (GOSL) forces, they also began (it must be admitted) to gain military supremacy over the other groups by means of a program of assassinations. This mutual animosity among the groups resulted in nearly all the groups except the Tigers laying down arms and siding with the government. They did not disband themselves nor did they unite with LTTE, but they became allies of the very government that had refused to grant even limited devolution of power in district councils. The government allowed them to maintain their offices of propaganda while they in turn provided espionage services against the Tigers.

Nearly eighteen thousand of the soldiers of the LTTE lost their lives in different engagements against GOSL forces. However, in spite of the commitment of the Tiger cadres, the GOSL was successful in crushing and annihilating the LTTE in 2009. This victory for the GOSL was a long time coming. Although far more powerful, and with a larger and more sophisticated military force, for many years GOSL could not contain the Tamil militants. Even by cutting off food and medical supplies to the civilian Tamil population, the government was unable to quell the rebellion. Their victory in 2009 was possible only because of the support of India. Since the start of the armed conflict, more than 150,000 civilians have lost their lives, nearly four hundred thousand have been internally displaced, and an equal number are refugees in various countries around the world. This is nearly one third of the Tamil people as per the records of the Tamils in the 1981 census. Thus the tragic end to the legitimate struggle for freedom of the Tamils of Sri Lanka came in March 2009.

The question that does not easily go away is why God, who, as some of us strongly believe, inspired oppressed Tamils to struggle against terrible oppression, watched the annihilation of that struggle. Is it enough to claim that, as the Cross is at the center of providence, we should expect such tragedies? Does this help the people who have suffered? Does it really help in bringing about repentance among those who resorted to killing and annihilation without any stirring of the conscience?

DOES GOD CARE?

I would like to engage Tim in a dialogue. I quote from his book (to each quote I assign my own title):

1. *God is one who acts and is not a deist deity.*

   In the blurb on the back cover, Tim writes: "The image used of God here, after much discussion of the problems of providence when thought of in connection with either God or human beings, is that of the theatre director . . . In this perspective God can be present as one whose job it is to evoke talents, skills and capabilities people did not know they had. God is given a supremely active and creative role, and one which does not destroy, or manipulate human autonomy. And in this perspective, men and women are given hope, that *they will not find love's labours lost.*"[8] In the same blurb Tim also asserts that, because of this understanding, it is possible for individuals and groups to bring their concerns to God in prayer hoping that God will act in response to such prayers.

2. *The presence of evil is real, but God can turn evil back on itself.*

   "Freedom and love, which together constitute 'grace,' are at the heart both of the possibility of pain, sin and evil, and of the response to this. The question of inequality is bound up with this in a world where purpose works through chance, and chance is embraced by purpose. It is the reality of chance which makes it seem that we exist as flies to the wanton gods. But in the first place, it is precisely this chance which is the instrument of the Creator who gives and seeks love, and secondly, God is not at the mercy of 'the law of large numbers.' In and through the free reign of chance he accomplishes his purpose. How this can be affirmed is what the doctrine of providence seeks to discern."[9]

3. *We should not be limited by rationality or by science, for Jesus simply said, "Ask and it shall be given."*

   "Assumptions about what it is we think God can or does do clearly lie behind them [i.e., hesitations to pray for rain, healing, etc.], assumptions which touch the deepest nerve of Christian faith. Belief in providence, we have said, is not just the belief that God guides

---

8. Gorringe, *God's Theatre*, back cover; my emphasis.

9. Ibid., 46.

events and achieves his purpose through them but that we can bring all things to him in prayer . . . Should we pray only for inner strength, power to love and to forgive? . . . Why is it that God could not have stopped the murder of six million Jews? . . . When I pray that my children may be kept safe, what do I expect God to do?"[10]

Let me start by saying that personally, I resonate with Tim. My lines have fallen in pleasant places, and looking back I could attribute my turning to God as due to the fervent prayers of my grandmother as also my father's intent to equip me for a professional career that took me to Britain, which led me to come under the influence of John Stott—a great pastor as much as theologian and preacher. I became a pastor, I have been an activist theologian, and it has been exciting and I have suffered little. I am thankful to God. But do I have the right, therefore, to read other people's tragic histories as also falling within the same kind of divine providence, accepting that in these cases God could do no more than be a fellow sufferer because the Cross is the most important aspect of God's providence?

Yes, indeed we need to learn to pray, putting ourselves in the direction and discerned purpose of God, if God is to act in response to our prayers. In the case of the Tamils, I know of many Christian Tamils who prayed fervently and believed that the struggle for freedom was something God had invoked in the consciousness of all the Tamils. The Tamil Nadu Theological Seminary was part of an ecumenical initiative to draw alongside the Tamil cause. There were some with a commitment to justice from among the Sinhalese Christians, some secularists and some among the Muslims who also rallied around the initiative. Ours was only a very small initiative, but there was the much larger international initiative led by the Netherlands with support from Finland. But in spite of all this, all efforts at bringing about a just solution failed. We could only watch helplessly when the freedom fighters and a large number of unarmed civilians were being routed ruthlessly. If it was God who initiated and encouraged us in these attempts, why did God also simply join the ranks of those who watched helplessly, without being able to do anything? There were fervent prayers from many quarters.

I find it extremely difficult simply to be satisfied with the sure knowledge of God's involvement in and along with these people. People's

10. Ibid., 88–89.

hopes for a just future were completely crushed. Their pain and losses in the war are immeasurable. Neither our suggestion that one should learn to experience God's presence with one, nor our proclamation that ultimately God will prevail, will help these people.

Is God in control of history? If not, how do we come to believe in God? In 1994 I was part of a consultation with representatives drawn from different oppressed and marginalized people of Asia under the auspices of the Christian Conference of Asia. During the consultation, when someone suggested that we needed to revise our idea of God Almighty and begin to think of the vulnerability of God, one of the participants asked straightway, "What use is there to people like us of such a God?" This question clearly put me on the spot. All of us activist theologians and the resource people at the consultation were forced to ask ourselves if we had a right to speak about God to people who had suffered a great tragedy.

So it is not enough simply to speak about God's love, and about God becoming a fellow sufferer: we need to be able to see God from the point of view of the suffering and struggling people. It is with this background that I would like to explain my thoughts. However, I want to be clear in saying that I am not indulging in theological articulation on behalf of the people who have suffered. What I say, I say to fellow members of the Cain Community.

I have come to understand God as self-giving. God has instilled this ability to give oneself to others in, for example, all mothers who give of themselves so much for their children. For us Christians, the self-giving of God was made supremely tangible in the giving of Jesus the Son of God to the sinful and ungrateful world. This understanding of God as self-giving means that there is nothing I can hold on to as mine. The self-giving God is also self-abdicating: that is, God refuses to be a sovereign monarch, in that God resolutely respects human freedom and the autonomy granted to nature, which means we cannot blame God for any accident, any natural disaster, any political tyranny, or any war. The self-giving, self-abdicating God is also self-implicating. God is no deist God. God takes full responsibility for our abuse of God-given freedom and therefore is implicated as co-sufferer in the lives of the victims of the abuse of the freedom by the members of the Community of Cain. This is the meaning of the Cross. The cry of dereliction is indeed the cry of faith from the oppressed, as it is from a lament psalm that concludes with an affirmation of faith. This means clearly that all the victims of abuse of human freedom are incorporated in Jesus' prayer, "Father forgive them." In other words, Jesus, through the so-called cry of dereliction which is in fact the affirmation of faith of a member of the Abel Community, identifies himself totally with them—and, conversely, enabled by the Holy Spirit to overcome the demand for vengeance, members of the Abel Community join themselves in that prayer of forgiveness for all the oppressors. This means all undeserved suffering is vicarious, as much as the suffering of Jesus is, but not in the traditional sense of bearing the punishment legitimately due to the sinners. Rather, in the sense that it is we as members of the Cain Community who inflict the pain and who are forgiven by those whom we hurt. Therefore God also is ready to forgive.

Though Tim does not spell this out, I believe the way I have explained would be acceptable to him, because he says, "The atonement did not happen only in Calvary, it is Calvary made real in history."[11]

There are indeed signs of this forgiving spirit being made manifest within this strife-torn community of Sri Lanka. The Christian Church, through its solidarity with the war-ravaged people, has made it possible for many to forgive their tormentors and start a new chapter of reconciled relationships even as the fallout of the tragedy continues. Rehabilitation efforts on the part of the government are mere eyewash. There is no intent that land and houses taken over by the forces should be restored to their real owners. But there are the grassroots Sinhala activists and other human rights groups who are carrying on a courageous advocacy work. Those of us who have been converted from among the Cain Community need to work hard to bring about an overall repentance among the rest of the Cain Community, so that they are willing to seek forgiveness from the people who suffer as a result of our neglect and wantonness. This indeed is not a vain hope. The Sri Lankan story also has some signs of hope.

SIGNS OF HOPE

Having highlighted the tragic nature of such situations as the Tamil struggle for freedom in Sri Lanka, I do want to point out some hopeful signs that will contribute towards human flourishing.

---

11. Ibid., 101.

1. During the Black July riots of 1983, quite a few Sinhala Christian leaders stood up to the rioters. Significant among them was Rev. Soma Perera, the President of the Methodist Church, who opened the gates of the Church compound and gave refuge to the fleeing Tamils and himself stood guard at the gate day and night for three days, challenging the Sinhala rioters.

2. The Church also gave a significant lead in getting the tsunami relief work done in consultation with Tamil Saivite leaders, Buddhist monks, and leaders of the Muslim community, and this created a good rapport among many youth drawn from the different communities. During a meeting, participants from different communities said that serious steps should be taken to erase wounds of memory and to encourage the building up of a community without borders.

3. The most hopeful sign was that many of the war-ravaged people of Vanni said that their faith in God had been revived, and that they felt it was time that they worked for a reconciled human community in Sri Lanka.

All these indeed are signs of hope. They are only dimly burning wicks, however, and if they are to be kindled into a big flame there must be serious heart-searching among the entire Cain Community in the whole world, and a mass turning to God as in the time of John the Baptist. This turning to God should bring with it real humility to seek forgiveness and reconciliation from the hurt and ravaged peoples of the world.

Let there be human flourishing, let there emerge the new humanity.

Bibliography

Department of Census and Statistics, Sri Lanka. "Population by Ethnic Group and District, Census 1981, 2001." Online: http://www.statistics.gov.lk/abstract2010/chapters/Chap2/AB2-11.pdf.

Gorringe, Timothy J. *God's Theatre: A Theology of Providence.* London: SCM, 1991.

Knox, Robert. *An Historical Relation of the Island of Ceylon, in the East-Indies.* London: Richard Chiswell, 1681.

The Mahavaṃsa. Translated by Wilhelm Geiger. London: H. Frowde, 1912. Online: http://ia600100.us.archive.org/15/items/mahavamsagreatchoogeigrich/mahavamsagreatchoogeigrich_bw.pdf.

Pieris, Ralph. "Administration of Justice and Revenue on the Island of Ceylon under the Dutch Government (The Cleghorn Minutes)." *The Journal of the Royal Asiatic Society (Ceylon Branch)* 3 (1953) 131.

14

More, Or, A Taxonomy of Greed

Stanley Hauerwas

Avarice is an even more timely topic now than when Tim Gorringe wrote *Capital and the Kingdom*. Our current economic downturn is often attributed to greed grown out of control. For many of us it is unclear how greed is causally related to our economic troubles, but we are usually ready to believe those who tell us that there is a correlation between the unbridled pursuit of profits in the financial sector of our economy and the current recession. We are suffering because some became too greedy. We continue to be troubled, moreover, that some make millions in bonuses without any reason to assume that there is a connection between the bonus and the work they have done. Greed seems to have no limits or shame.

That we are able to make such judgments presumes that we know what we are talking about when we talk about greed. I think, however, that presumption may be just that, that is, presumptive. The desire for money may be an indication of greed, but I hope to show that greed is a much more subtle vice than simply the desire to be rich. It is interesting, however, that even if avarice is understood primarily as the desire for wealth, we seldom hear sermons about greed. That we do not seems strange because at least as far as the New Testament is concerned greed is considered to be a greater threat to the ability to follow Christ than lust.[1]

---

1. Aviad Kleinberg observes that though Jesus was neither a glutton nor a libertine he seems to have viewed gluttony and lust with a compassion that was distinctively

In the Sermon on the Mount, Jesus says quite clearly, "you cannot serve God and wealth" (Matt 6:24). Paul confesses in Romans 7 that he would not have known sin, he would not have known the many forms of covetousness that possessed his life, if the law had not said, "You shall not covet." In 1 Tim 6:10 Paul even suggests that the love of money is the root of all kinds of evil leading some to wander away from the faith because of the self-inflicted pains they have suffered due to their desire for money. At least one of those pains that greed produces is identified with idolatry in Col 3:5.[2]

In the book of James, Christians are unrelentingly chastised for thinking they can delay doing God's will in order that they can go to this town or that town to do business and make money. Such people simply fail to realize that their wealth will not save them from miseries or death (Jas 4:13—5:5). James is very blunt: "You want something and you do not have it; so you commit murder. And you covet something and cannot obtain it; so you engage in disputes and conflicts" (Jas 4:2).

Scripture is clear. If you are a Christian who is wealthy or desire to have wealth, you have a problem. Yet in our day greed is seldom identified as a major problem for Christians. Lust, which is usually associated with sexual misconduct, seems to have become the sin that Christians worry about. I confess it is not clear to me why that is the case, but it may be that we think we know what it looks like when we are under the power of lust. For all the changes alleged to be characteristic of our sexual ethics, it is still assumed that we can spot promiscuity or adultery. We assume, moreover, that such behavior can be attributed to lust understood as out of control sexual desire.

Yet I suspect that greed grips our lives more than lust. But we fail to focus on greed because we are not sure that we know how to identify what greed looks like. Indeed I am of the opinion that what is often identified as lust may actually be a form of greed. The very fact that the lust

---

different from his condemnation of greed. Kleinberg, in particular, calls attention to the rich man and Lazarus as an indication that Jesus regarded wealth itself as an obstacle to salvation. *Seven Deadly Sins*, 101.

2. Brian Rosner provides a very useful background that helps us understand the connection between greed and idolatry in his *Greed and Idolatry*. He concludes that the claim that greed is idolatry presumes that "to have a strong desire to acquire and keep for yourself more and more money and material things is an attack on God's exclusive rights to human love and devotion, trust and confidence, and service and obedience" (173).

that grips so many lives is never satiated suggests that lust has become a form of greed. For if any one characteristic is to be associated with greed, it is the presumption that no matter how much we may have, we need more. We need more because we cannot be sure that what we have is secure. So the more we have the more we must have in order to secure what we have.

Bill May observes that the vices in traditional catalogues of sins were often associated with various body parts—lying with the tongue, lust with the genitals, gluttony with the throat, pride with the chest, conceit with the turned head, and avarice with the arms and legs. The person possessed by avarice reaches for and grasps the goods of another. Things come into the possession of the greedy by reaching for and holding. Mastery and possession are the marks of a person who is determined by avarice.[3]

That greed names the felt necessity to have more may help explain the seeming paradox that greed seems to become a particularly prominent challenge in economies of plenty. It is quite interesting, for example, that with the rise of money economies in western Europe in the eleventh and twelfth centuries, there is a distinct increase in references to the sin of greed by theologians and bishops.[4] Money, it seems, allowed more people to manifest signs of wealth, which meant the more wealth they had the more wealth they needed to sustain the wealth they had. For the rich there is never enough.

I do not mean to suggest that avarice only became a named vice with the development of moneyed economies. The rise of monasticism clearly was the crucial development necessary for the articulation of the seven deadly sins.[5] Augustine would identify pride as the cardinal or original sin, but the monks who inhabited the Egyptian desert thought greed to be the sin that birthed the other sins. "They observed a deep human fear of dependence on God that manifested itself in a

---

3. May, *Catalogue of Sins*, 51–52.

4. Newhauser, "*Avaritia and Paupertas*," 330–31.

5. Newhauser, *Early History of Greed*. According to Newhauser, Basil the Great drew on the developing monastic tradition to identify avarice as the failure to care for the needs of one's neighbors because of a concern for one's own material well-being. Basil applied this to monk and laity alike demanding that both "purify themselves from avarice and the desire for excessive ornamentation. By concentrating their attention on God alone, they would avoid giving serious thought to a superfluous amount of life's necessities or possessions meant only for themselves" (25–26).

perennial desire to accumulate some small margin of protective, sustaining property."[6]

That monasticism preceded the identification of avarice as the primal sin is a nice confirmation that our very ability to name our sins is a theological achievement. In other words, the very presumption that we can name our sins and declare that we are sinners prior to God's grace is an indication that we are possessed by sin. For we are only able to confess that we are possessed by sin on our way out of sin. Accordingly a community must exist that makes possible the identification of the subtlety of sin. That is particularly true when you are dealing with a sin as subtle as greed.

I think, for example, that it is not accidental that you needed a Saint Francis for the discovery by Christians that we had lost the ability to recognize how greed possessed our lives. The subsequent development of the Franciscan order was crucial for the acknowledgment by the church that the church itself was possessed by possessions. Yet the very order that had at its center the discipline of begging was soon able to make holiness a commodity subject to greed.[7] William Langland in *Piers Plowman* depicts the friars' ability to turn their alleged sanctity into a means to acquire money. Langland characterized the friars, in the words of Kelly Johnson, as "hawkers of holiness," who are "all the more prone to simony because of their practices of poverty and begging."[8] Thus in the "Prologue" to *Piers Plowman* the dreamer says,

> I found there friars from all four orders,
> Preaching to people to profit their gut,
> And glossing the gospel to their own good liking;
> Coveting fine copes, some of these doctors contradicted authorities.
> Many of these masterful mendicant friars
> Bind their love of money to their proper business.

6. Reno, *Genesis*, 87. I have never been able to decide if it is helpful to identify one sin as *the* primal sin. Augustine, and much of Christian tradition, identified pride as the primal sin. The monks, however, often focused on avarice as even more basic than pride. Given the complexity of our lives, I suspect that our sins are interrelated in a manner that defies easy identification of one sin as the source of all other sins.

7. Kleinberg argues that the failure of the Franciscan order was more than an episode in internal ecclesiastical politics, but rather that in the struggle between God and mammon it was clear that mammon had won. That mammon had won, moreover, was an indication that the attempt to reinvigorate the Christian world had failed. *Seven Deadly Sins*, 108.

8. Johnson, *Fear of Beggars*, 64.

> And since charity's become a broker and chief agent for lords' confessions
> Many strange things have happened these last years;
> Unless Holy church and charity clear away such confessors
> The world's worst misfortune mounts up fast.[9]

Langland's suggestion that the "worst misfortune mounts up fast" might well be a description of our situation. That a poem like *Piers Plowman* could be written suggests that the poet could still draw on the tradition to show what greed looks like and why it is such a threat to Christians. But it is unclear if that is the case with us. For greed has become the necessary engine to sustain economic growth.[10] We are obligated to want more because if we do not want more then we will put someone out of a job.

For example, in his book *Rediscovering Values: On Wall Street, Main Street, and Your Street*, Jim Wallis calls attention to the adulation of greed by the Wall Street tycoon Gordon Gekko in the movie *Wall Street*. In the midst of the hostile takeover of the fictional company Teldar Paper, Gekko declares, "Greed, for lack of a better word, is good. Greed is right. Greed works. Greed clarifies, cuts through, and captures the essence of the evolutionary spirit. Greed in all its forms, greed for life, money, love, knowledge has marked the upward surge of mankind, and greed will not only save Teldar Paper but that other malfunctioning corporation called the USA."[11]

Gekko's praise of greed, of course, found its most original, elegant, and persuasive form in Bernard Mandeville's *The Fable of the Bees*:

> Vast Numbers throng'd the fruitful Hive;
> Yet those vast Numbers made 'em thrive;
> Millions endeavouring to supply
> Each other's Lust and Vanity
> Thus every Part was full of Vice,
> Yet the whole Mass a Paradise.[12]

9. Langland, *Piers Plowman*, 56–65. Not to be missed is the characterization of covetousness in Passus VI of the poem.

10. Kleinberg calls attention to Adam Smith for transforming the providential hand of God into an ensemble of individual egotisms working by some mysterious ways to produce the good of the collectivity. He quotes Smith: "By pursuing his own interests, he frequently promotes that of society more effectually than when he really intends to promote it." *Seven Deadly Sins*, 110–11.

11. Wallis, *Rediscovering Values*, 45.

12. Mandeville, *Fable of the Bees*, 24. According to Mandeville avarice may be the

From Mandeville's perspective, "frugality is like honesty, a mean starving virtue, that is only fit for small societies of good peaceable men, who are contented to be poor so that they may be easy; but in a large stirring nation you may soon have enough of it."[13] Deirdre McCloskey has tried to qualify Mandeville's account of the necessity of avarice for economic growth by arguing that markets live in communities of virtue for which economists often fail to account.[14] William Schweiker suggests that because "property" is a cultural construction entangled with arrangements for human identity and worth, it may be that what we call "greed" should be better understood as an appropriate desire necessary to sustain market-driven economies.[15]

I am not convinced, however, that McCloskey's and Schweiker's language-transforming proposals to understand greed even in a limited way as a good are a good idea. For example, Alasdair MacIntyre observes that for those shaped by the habits of modern societies it is assumed as a fundamental good that "acquisitiveness is a character trait indispensable to continuous and limitless economic growth." From such a standpoint, it is inconceivable that a systematically lower standard of living can be conceived as an alternative to the economics and politics of

---

"occasion" of many evils, but it is most necessary for a society to flourish. He argues that if you would "render a society of men strong and powerful, you must touch their passions. Divide the land, though there be never so much to spare, and their possessions will make them covetous. Rouse them though but in jest, from their idleness with praises, and pride will set them to work in earnest. Teach them trades and handicrafts, and you'll bring envy and emulation among them . . . Would you have them bold and warlike, turn to military discipline, make good use of their fear, and flatter their vanity with art and assiduity . . . Great wealth and foreign treasure will ever scorn to come among men, unless you'll admit their inseparable companions, avarice and luxury" (95–96).

13. Ibid., 64.

14. McCloskey, "Avarice," 324.

15. Schweiker, "Reconsidering Greed," 259. Schweiker does not mean to suggest that greed is unproblematic but rather to suggest that we need to appreciate how greed inscribes selves into a culture's values but at the same time threatens the bonds that sustain trust in a society. Thus "the paradox is that a commercial culture, through the power of its sign values, can and does foster excessive consumption and thus greed, but in the act of doing so threatens social stability and flourishing. Is it any wonder, then, that in advanced commercial cultures we see the breakdown of concern for the common good both among the wealthy, who consume at an alarming rate, and the poor, who desire that level of consumption? Traditional Christian thought was simply right on this point: greed is a capital vice because it gathers around it other forms of viciousness that undercut the possibility of sustainable social existence" (268).

peculiarly modern societies. For such societies, prices and wages have to be understood to be unrelated so that desert in terms of labor, notions of just price and just wage, makes no sense. Yet a community shaped by the virtues that would make greed a vice "would have to set strict limits to growth insofar as that is necessary to preserve or enhance a distribution of goods according to desert."[16]

That we find it hard to conceive of an alternative to limitless economic growth is an indication of our spiritual condition. It is a condition well understood by the monks who thought the desire for honor and power to be an expression of the felt need to control the world around us so that we might be more godlike. Thus Cassian saw anger as one of the forms greed takes in those who no longer cling to the One alone who can provide stability. Deprived of God, we become self-absorbed, seeking in external goods a satisfaction for our inner emptiness.[17] When those goods fail, we turn on others as well as ourselves as a way to hide the emptiness of our lives.[18]

In *The City of God*, Augustine suggests that the Roman elites indulged in various forms of luxury and illicit pleasures to distract them from the inevitability of death. He observes that "the essential context for ambition is a people corrupted by greed and sensuality. And greed and sensuality in a people is the result of that prosperity which the great Nasica in his wisdom maintained should be guarded against, when he opposed the removal of a great and strong and wealthy enemy state. His intention was that lust should be restrained by fear, and should not issue in debauchery, and that the check on debauchery should stop greed from running riot."[19]

Augustine, according to Robert Dodaro, argued that among the Roman elites, the fear of death, the fear that their lives would not be remembered, meant that they lived in fear of the loss of status and

16. MacIntyre, *Whose Justice*, 112. MacIntyre's suggestion makes clear that a focus on the virtues can have profound social implications. It is often alleged that an ethics of the virtues is at a disadvantage for issues associated with social and political questions, but MacIntyre's observations about the significance of temperance makes clear that that is not the case.

17. Straw, "Gregory," 51.

18. I suspect that there is a close connection between avarice and envy. The latter becomes almost unavoidable in social orders that depend on greed to fuel the engines of "progress."

19. Augustine, *City of God*, 1, 31.

comfort. They were greedy for glory hoping by glory that their lives might have significance. Empire was the means of sustaining status and well-being, but empire also produced an ever-increasing social anxiety about annihilation. As a result, the Romans became overdependent on military force. Dedaro observes that from Augustine's perspective, the Romans were caught in a vicious circle that "linked the threat of annihilation with an ever-growing political and military response to foreign threats, disseminating anxiety throughout the Empire to such an extent that even the inhabitants of Roman Africa are alarmed by the Visigothic assault on Rome."[20]

Of course we may think that the Romans are Romans and we are not. We assume, therefore, that we are not subject to the same death-denying greed that characterized the lives of the Roman pagans. Henry Fairlie, however, has given an account of how greed grips our lives, an account that echoes the suggestion in the book of James that there is a connection between greed and war, that sounds very much like Augustine's characterization of the Romans. Fairlie suggests that we are a people harassed by greed just to the extent that our greed leads us to engage in unsatisfying modes of work so that we may buy things that we have been harassed into believing will satisfy us. We complain of the increased tempo of our lives, but that is a reflection of the economic system we have created. We know, moreover, no other way to keep the system going other than the threat of war. We tolerate the world shaped by our avarice because that world in return temptingly and cunningly makes us believe that there are no alternatives to a world so constituted.[21]

20. Dodaro, *Christ and the Just Society*, 42.

21. Fairlie, *Seven Deadly Sins Today*, 142. Fairlie also observes that avarice is a form of solitude because we are walled off from our neighbors by our possessions. Greed cannot help producing loneliness. Thomas Dumm observes, "What is it that we want? Perhaps it is only the acquisition of more of what we have. In our culture—a civilization of consumption if ever there has been one—the lonely self seeks to possess something to call its own, and ends up by confusing that something with itself. The great drive of capital is to turn everything into a commodity, including the self. In this sense, capitalism may be thought of as a symptom of the lonely self. I do not think we can separate the two—they are conjoined in our epoch. But if the lonely self is in an important sense shaped by the creation of a desire for more, and if this desire in turn gives rise to an anxiety that accompanies the experience of buying and selling, then the anxiety of the lonely self when facing the world of others leads to the deep risk of our selves being bought and sold." *Loneliness*, 52–53.

I do not mean to suggest that it is only with the development of capitalist economic systems that we have lost the ability to recognize greed or, even if we are able to recognize it, think it a moral liability. For example, in a sermon on Luke 16:19–31, Luther observed that the rich and arrogant people of his day no longer heed the warning contained in the story of the rich man and Lazarus. They do not heed because the rich think of themselves as pious and without greed. They are able to do so because vice has been turned into virtue. Greed has come to be viewed as being talented, smart, and a careful steward. Therefore "neither prince nor peasant, nobleman nor average citizen is any longer considered greedy, but only upstanding, the common consensus being that the man who prudently provides for himself is a resourceful person who knows how to take care of himself."[22]

I am sure many of you reading this chapter will not think of yourselves as greedy, especially if you are students. You have, perhaps, not yet become actors in the world of wealth in a manner that might tempt you to be greedy. You are still without possessions so you cannot be greedy. Of course such a view may fail to recognize that to be poor, or at least not rich, is no guarantee that our lives will not be possessed by greed. However, I want to call your attention to a celebrated virtue often commended for students and their teachers that I think exhibits Luther's suggestion that, subtle creatures that we are, we can turn greed into a virtue.

In his important book *Intellectual Appetite: A Theological Grammar*, Paul Griffiths provides a telling account of curiosity.[23] Curiosity has had an interesting history. We may not be able to imagine a world without avarice, but we still think avarice is a vice. According to Griffiths, however, although we think curiosity to be a commendable virtue that scholar and student should try to develop, that has not always been the case. According to Griffiths, prior to modernity, curiosity was universally thought to be a vice. It was so because curiosity was an ordering of the affections, a form of love, by which the knower sought to make that which they knew unique to themselves. The curious desired to create new knowledge in an effort to give them control over that which they knew. By dominating that which they came to know, they could make

---

22. Luther, *Faith and Freedom*, 169.
23. Griffiths, *Intellectual Appetite*.

what they know a private possession. "Curiosity is, then, in brief, *appetite for the ownership of new knowledge*."[24]

The curious seek to know what they do not yet know. As a result, that which they come to know ravishes them by enacting what Griffiths characterizes as a "sequestered intimacy." Griffiths uses the language of "sequestering" to suggest that the curious think that what they have come to know is for their exclusive use. The curious assume that they are masters of what they have come to know. Because they claim that what they know is peculiar to them, they seek as well as create envy in those who do not know what they know.

In a way not unlike Augustine's understanding of the place of the spectacle for the Romans, Griffiths suggests that the curious seek spectacles to distract them from the loneliness that is the necessary result of their desire to possess what they have come to know. The desire for novelty, the desire to have knowledge that I alone can possess, produces a restlessness that "is inflamed rather than assuaged by the spectacles it constructs."[25] Curiosity so understood is the intellectual expression of the greed correlative to an economic system built on the need to have those that make up the system to always want more.

The alternative to curiosity, according to Griffiths, is studiousness. Studiousness, like curiosity, entails an ordering of the affections and is, therefore, a form of love. But the studious do not seek to "sequester, own, possess, or dominate what they hope to know; they want to participate lovingly in it, to respond to it knowingly as gift rather than as potential possession, to treat it as icon rather than as spectacle."[26] For the studious what they know can be loved and contemplated, but not dominated by sequestration. The studious, therefore, accept as a gift what they have come to know, which means they assume that what they know is known in common, making possible a shared life.

The contrast between the curious and the studious will be determined, according to Griffiths, by their willingness or unwillingness to share what they know with others. Whether we are or are not possessed by our possessions can only be determined to the extent that we are ready to give away that which we have. Griffiths associates such a willingness with our willingness to share our knowledge of Christ, just to

24. Ibid., 20.
25. Ibid., 201–2.
26. Ibid., 21.

the extent that the degree to which any of us know Christ and what the gospel is and demands is the "degree to which we must share that knowledge by giving it away."[27]

The studious Christian, therefore, seeks in Griffiths's words a "participatory intimacy driven by wonder and riven by lament" which makes it impossible for them to seek ownership of what they have been given.[28] For Christians believe that all creatures have been brought into being by God out of nothing.[29] Accordingly the studious recognize that only God possesses or owns any creature. Only God, therefore, has the power to sequester any being into privacy or to grant it public display. The sharing of what we know is a form of almsgiving, and is rightly understood not as our giving away what is ours, but rather is making available to others what was God's before we had a use for it.[30]

Greed is rightly called a deadly sin because it kills the possibility of a proper human relation to the Creator. Greed presumes and perpetuates a world of scarcity and want—a world where there is never "enough." But, as Sam Wells argues, a world shaped by scarcity is a world that cannot trust that God has given all that we need; greed prohibits faith. But the contrary is true. Wells reminds us that the problem is not that there is too little in God but there is too much. Overwhelmed by "God's inexhaustible creation, limitless grace, relentless mercy, enduring purpose, fathomless love," we turn away finding such a God "too much to contemplate, assimilate, understand."[31]

27. Ibid., 160.

28. Griffiths identifies three kinds of wonder: (1) the metaphysical wonder of astonished delight that there is anything at all, (2) the wonder that comes from the recognition that we exist and we can be aware of ourselves as existing, and (3) wonder directed at particular creatures such as ladybugs and heavenly bodies (ibid., 127–28). The role of wonder is crucial for Griffiths' account of studiousness because through wonder an intimacy is possible between the knower and the known that is otherwise impossible. That such an intimacy is possible—that is, in the dual good of our knowing something we can know, and something's being known as it is by the knower—is "the vestigial trace of God's knowing act of *creation ex nihilo*" (132).

29. Lance Webb stresses the significance of creation to provide an account of joy, which he takes to be the alternative to avarice. "To glorify God and to enjoy him forever" comes from the recognition that nothing belongs to me, but I belong to Christ. "This is our Sin: that we have upended the order of our Creator and gone out to glorify ourselves and to enjoy things forever." *Conquering the Seven Deadly Sins*, 150.

30. Griffiths, *Intellectual Appetite*, 154.

31. Wells, *God's Companions*, 7.

And so Wells reminds us that it is in the eucharist that we have the prismatic act that makes possible our recognition that God has given us everything we need. The eucharist not only is the proclamation of abundance, but it is the enactment of abundance. In the eucharist we discover that we cannot use Christ up. In the eucharist we discover that the more the body and blood of Christ is shared, the more there is to be shared. The eucharist, therefore, is the way the church learns to understand why generosity rather than greed must and can shape our economic relations.[32]

The good news is that we have been given all we need in order not to be possessed by greed. The good news is that we worship a God who, through our worship of Him, makes it possible for us to recognize that although we may be possessed by greed, through confession and repentance we can be forgiven. Forgiveness, moreover, is the gift of grace that turns our lives of entitlement into lives of humility and gratitude. To learn to be forgiven, to be able to accept the gift of forgiveness without regret, is the condition that makes possible the recognition that all that we have we have through sharing. There is an alternative to a world based on greed. The alternative to the world of greed is a people capable of participating through worship in the love of the Father for the Son through the Spirit.

Bibliography

Augustine, *The City of God*. Translated by Henry Bettenson. Harmondsworth: Penguin, 1972.

Dodaro, Robert. *Christ and the Just Society in the Thought of Augustine*. Cambridge: Cambridge University Press, 2004.

Dumm, Thomas. *Loneliness as a Way of Life*. Cambridge: Harvard University Press, 2008.

Fairlie, Henry. *The Seven Deadly Sins Today*. Notre Dame: University of Notre Dame Press, 1978.

Gorringe, Timothy J. *Capital and the Kingdom: Theological Ethics and Economic Order*. Maryknoll, NY: Orbis, 1994.

Griffiths, Paul. *Intellectual Appetite: A Theological Grammar*. Washington, DC: Catholic University Press, 2009.

Johnson, Kelly. *The Fear of Beggars: Stewardship and Poverty in Christian Ethics*. Grand Rapids: Eerdmans, 2007.

Kleinberg, Aviad. *Seven Deadly Sins: A Very Partial List*. Cambridge: Harvard University Press, 2008.

32. Ibid., 211.

Langland, William. *Piers Plowman: The C Version*. Translated by George Economou. Philadelphia: University of Pennsylvania Press, 1996.

Luther, Martin. *Faith and Freedom: An Invitation to the Writings of Martin Luther*. Preface by Richard Lischer. Edited by John Thornton and Susan Varenne. New York: Vintage, 2002.

McCloskey, Deirdre. "Avarice, Prudence, and the Bourgeois Virtues." In *Having:Property and Possession in Religious and Social Life*, edited by William Schweiker and Charles T. Mathewes, 312–36. Grand Rapids: Eerdmans, 2004.

MacIntyre, Alasdair. *Whose Justice? Which Rationality?* Notre Dame: University of Notre Dame Press, 1988.

Mandeville, Bernard. *The Fable of the Bees and Other Writings*. Edited by E. J. Hundrert. Indianapolis: Hackett, 1997.

May, William. *A Catalogue of Sins: A Contemporary Examination of Christian Conscience*. New York: Holt, Rinehart, & Winston, 1967.

Newhauser, Richard. "*Avaritia* and *Paupertas*: On the Place of the Early Franciscans in the History of Avarice." In *In the Garden of Evil: The Vices and Culture in the Middle Ages*, edited by Richard Newhauser, 324–48. Toronto: Pontifical Institute of Mediaeval Studies, 2005.

———. *The Early History of Greed: The Sin of Avarice in Early Medieval Thought and Literature*. Cambridge: Cambridge University Press, 2000.

———, editor. *In the Garden of Evil: The Vices and Culture in the Middle Ages*. Toronto: Pontifical Institute of Mediaeval Studies, 2005.

Reno, R. R. *Genesis*. Brazos Theological Commentary on the Bible. Grand Rapids: Brazos, 2010.

Rosner, Brian. *Greed and Idolatry: The Origin and Meaning of a Pauline Metaphor*. Grand Rapids: Eerdmans, 2007.

Schweiker, William. "Reconsidering Greed." In *Having: Property and Possession in Religious and Social Life*, 249–71. Grand Rapids: Eerdmans, 2004.

Schweiker, William, and Charles Mathewes, editors. *Having: Property and Possession in Religious and Social Life*. Grand Rapids: Eerdmans, 2004.

Straw, Carole. "Gregory, Cassian, and the Cardinal Vices." In *In the Garden of Evil: The Vices and Culture in the Middle Ages*, edited by Richard Newhauser, 35–58. Toronto: Pontifical Institute of Mediaeval Studies.

Wallis, Jim. *Rediscovering Values: On Wall Street, Main Street, and Your Street*. New York: Simon & Schuster, 2010.

Webb, Lance. *Conquering the Seven Deadly Sins*. New York: Abingdon, 1965.

Wells, Sam. *God's Companions: Reimaging Christian Ethics*. Oxford: Blackwell, 2006.

15

Curiosity

JOHN WEBSTER

I

Christian theological intelligence is exercised in the conflict between the virtue of studiousness and the vice of curiosity. This is because, like all human intellectual acts, theology takes place in the economy of God's reconciling grace, in which ignorance of and opposition to God are being overcome by the instruction of Word and Spirit. The reality of reconciliation, including the reconciliation of reason, is at one and the same time beyond contest and unfinished. Christian theological intelligence has as its ontological and cognitive principle the definitive and perfect utterance of the divine Word—*I am the truth, I have told these things to you*—but the sufficiency of the Word once uttered does not remove the need for intelligence to learn and appropriate the Word's inexhaustible fullness—*When the Spirit of truth comes, he will guide you into all the truth.* But what is meant by learning and appropriation under the Spirit's tutelage? Not, surely, steady accumulation of knowledge by the exercise of skills, but conversion and sanctification, of which the conflict between studiousness and curiosity forms part.

II

Curiosity is to be defined on the basis of studiousness, of which it is a corruption; this, because vices lack any positive independent reality apart from the virtues to which they are opposed, and apart from the natural powers of which they are a misapplication. This axiom, fundamental to a Christian understanding of intelligence and its operations, prevents confusion between Christian prohibition of curiosity and contempt for reason as always and only an instrument of the will. For the latter, the only principle of reason is volitional, the desire to know cloaking the will to power: there is, in effect, no studiousness to be deformed. In Christian understanding, by contrast, curiosity is not nature but defect. The wickedness of intelligence—its complicity in inquisitiveness, idolatry, vanity, and lying—may be very great, but it is not such that it entirely overwhelms and replaces the substance and vocation of creaturely reason. Nature is the condition of possibility for the distortion of nature.

Studiousness and curiosity are active intelligent relations to that which is not known. They are movements of intelligence towards new knowledge, the movements drawing their power from the creaturely appetite to acquire knowledge beyond what is required for the satisfaction of the immediately pressing needs of animal nature. But studiousness and curiosity participate in this movement in differing ways, the one being its well-ordered, temperate enactment, the other its deformation.

Studiousness is a strenuous application of the powers of the creaturely intellect, the end of which is to come to know something for the first time, or to apprehend under a new aspect or with a new interest some object already known. Studiousness is peculiar to embodied rational creatures, and one of the ways in which creaturely intelligence and divine intelligence may be distinguished. God knows all things intuitively and nondiscursively, effortlessly and without accumulation; there is no process of acquisition in divine knowing, no "new" knowledge for the one whose knowledge of himself and of all things is infinite and wholly realized in a comprehensive, single act. Creaturely knowledge, by contrast, is always characterized by coming-to-know. It is discursive, involving an effort of inquiry over time; the powers by which it is moved are restricted in range and duration; the knowledge that even the most studious can acquire is not comprehensive. Further, creaturely intelligence is not self-derived or purely spontaneous, but the exercise of given powers, an exercise that is itself preserved and fortified by a movement beyond itself; but God's intelligence, like his being, is *a se*. God, in short, knows as the uncreated one, whereas creatures know as *creatures*.

Studiousness refers to the activity of the well-ordered creaturely intellect in coming-to-know. Two particular elements of this activity may be picked out as essential. First, studiousness involves earnest, arduous application of the mind; it is not passive or indolent or unfocussed but eager, concentrated, taking pains to acquire knowledge: *studium proprie importat vehementem applicationem mentis ad aliquid*.[1] Second, studiousness is a reflective activity, one whose application is subject to appraisal because governed by standards of excellence. These standards of excellence are both intellectual and moral. Chief among the intellectual standards of excellence is the requirement that studious dedication of mental powers must so relate to the object of study that the integrity of the object is respected as it comes to be known. To come to know is to form a representation of some reality; but that representation must accord with the inherent order of the object: this shape, sound, sequence, conceptual pattern. In this way, studiousness is a contemplative act. Its contemplative character may take the form of dogged resistance to early termination of the movement of intelligence in premature or inadequate representation of the object. Studiousness bears within it an element of discontent; it does not allow itself to enjoy too soon the satisfaction of the desire to know.

What of the moral standards of excellence by which studiousness is governed? Studiousness is inseparable from desire; it is an activity "commanded by appetitive power."[2] It is precisely this that introduces an element of ambivalence into studiousness, because "the studious appetite to discover the truth may be either straight or crooked."[3] From one angle, of course, studiousness is in itself a good, because in a certain way it puts to work the power of our created intellectual nature. Pursuit of new knowledge is *natural*. But there is a further good in studiousness, namely, the application of natural intellectual powers to fitting objects, in due measure and for fitting ends. This brings studiousness within the sphere of moral, not just intellectual, virtue. The enactment of our intellectual nature is a function of desire; but in our fallen condition desire can be disordered, and studiousness distorted into its deviant form, curiosity.

1. Aquinas, *Summa Theologiae* IIaIIae.166.1 resp.
2. Ibid., 166.1 ad 2.
3. Ibid., 167.1 resp.

III

Curiosity results from corruption of intellectual appetite.[4] What makes curiosity vicious is not the intellectual activity of coming-to-know but the corrupt desire that commands the activity: "curiosity does not lie in the knowing precisely but in the appetite and hankering to find out."[5] Most generally described, the elements of curiosity may be set out as follows:

(1) Curiosity applies intellectual powers to improper objects of new knowledge, stretching out to that which lies beyond what is legitimate, and so refusing to consent to the given order, shape, and therefore *limitation* of created intelligence. Curiosity "snap[s] the reins of the prohibition" under the pressure of the desire to know as God knows.[6] This rests on a deep principle of Christian anthropology: there are objects into which human intelligence has the power but not the permission to inquire. The intellect has a given nature and vocation, including a certain scope that may not be transgressed if it is to retain its special glory. Perfect intellect is not intellect unbounded but intellect wholly devoted to that which it has been given to discover.

(2) Curiosity involves the direction of intellectual powers to new knowledge of created realities without reference to their creator. In curiosity, the movement of the mind terminates on corporeal properties of things newly known, without completing its full course by coming to rest in the divine reality that is their principle. In effect, curiosity stops short at created signs, lingering too long over them and not allowing them to steer intelligence to the creator. So Augustine against the Manichees: "[S]ome people, neglecting virtue and ignorant of what God is, and of the majesty of the nature which remains always the same, think that they are engaged in an important business when searching with the greatest inquisitiveness and eagerness into this material mass which we call the world . . . The soul . . . which purposes to keep itself chaste for God must refrain from the desire of vain knowledge like this. For the desire usually produces delusion, so that the soul thinks that nothing exists but what is material."[7] Curiosity, Augustine says elsewhere, is "eating

---

4. On this, see Griffiths, *Intellectual Appetite*.

5. Aquinas, *Summa Theologiae* IIaIIae.167.1 resp.

6. Augustine, *Literal Meaning* 11.41.

7. Augustine, *Morals* 21.

earth," penetrating deep and dark places that are still time-bound and earthly.[8] Or again, in another idiom, curiosity is the "lust of the eyes" (1 John 2:16), so called, Augustine says, because its origin lies in our "appetite for learning," and "the sight is the chief of our senses in the acquisition of knowledge." It is that "vain and curious longing in the soul" that, "cloaked under the name of knowledge and learning" is in reality a greed for "new experiences through the flesh," a disordered "passion for experimenting and knowledge"—flocking to see a lacerated corpse, attending a theatrical spectacle, letting contemplation be distracted by watching a lizard catch flies.[9] Curiosity terminates on *surfaces*.

(3) Curiosity is a deformation of the manner or mode of intelligence, when the movement of coming-to-know takes place inordinately, indiscriminately, and pridefully. (*a*) "Vice can be present from the inordinateness of the appetite and effort to find out."[10] The craving for new knowledge can be so forceful and the satisfaction of coming-to-know so addictive that other goods and legitimate vocations are neglected, limits are transgressed, and intelligence swamped. (*b*) "In how many most minute and contemptible things is our curiosity daily tempted, and who can remember how often we succumb?"[11] Curiosity is indiscriminate intellectual greed, not ordered by right judgments about worthy and unworthy objects of intelligence. What matters to curiosity is the novelty of the object of new knowledge and the excitement accompanying its acquisition, rather than the esteem that the object deserves or the utility of the knowledge of it for pursuit of the human good. "Food that is badly cooked and indigestible induces physical disorders and damages the body instead of nourishing it. In the same way if a glut of knowledge stuffed in the memory, that stomach of the mind, has not been cooked on the fire of love, and transfused and digested by certain skills of the soul, its habits and actions—since, as life and conduct bear witness, the mind is rendered good through its knowledge of good—will not that knowledge be rendered sinful?"[12] (3) Curiosity is entangled with pride, by which it is begotten, and which it in turn begets. Satisfaction of any inflamed appetite expands our pleasure in our powers of acquisition and

8. Augustine, *On Genesis* II.18.27.

9. Augustine, *Confessions* 10.35.

10. Aquinas, *Summa Theologiae* IIaIIae.167.1 resp.

11. Augustine, *Confessions* 10.35.

12. Bernard, *Song of Songs* 36.3.

enjoyment, leading us to view ourselves with gratification as ample, rich, competent beings. Curiosity also does this: the curious, Bernard says, are strangers to the sadness—godly sorrow—that comes from knowledge of God and of ourselves, and their pursuit of knowledge leads only to "self-importance."[13]

(4) Curiosity pursues new knowledge for improper ends: to increase self-esteem by science, to accomplish some evil purpose, to feed prurient appetite by searching out new objects. Acts of intellectual virtue may nevertheless be morally vicious in pursuing unrighteous ends. This is why Bernard, again, presses that fruitful and useful acquisition of new knowledge depends in part upon "the order . . . in which one approaches the object of study"[14]—that is, upon the rightness of the "in order to" element in coming-to-know. Curiosity does not desire to know for the purpose of doing good—to others in charity, to oneself in prudence— and so cannot "avoid the abuse of knowledge."[15]

IV

Christian theology, if it is diligent in pursuing its contemplative and apostolic vocation, and does not content itself with mere study of the phenomena of the Christian religion, is spiritual work. But it is spiritual work undertaken this side of eschatological perfection: like all science, it takes place in the *regio dissimilitudinis*, the "region where likeness to God has been forfeited."[16] Because this is so, theology shares the afflictions of fallen intellect: impotence and sloth, vulnerability to unruly affection, vainglory, idolatry, skepticism; and curiosity, too, is part of the pathos of theology now. The particular ways in which curiosity manifests itself in the work of theology depend upon such things as differing cultural and institutional settings, and the adequacy or inadequacy of the formation of its practitioners. But some general features may be identified (the temptation to provide examples is to be resisted!):

(1) Curiosity may enter when theology is ignorant of the location or situation of its work. Theology takes place in a sphere in which God the teacher is lovingly present to reconciled creatures, summoning the

13. Ibid., 36.2.
14. Ibid., 36.2.
15. Ibid., 36.3.
16. Ibid., 36.4.

intellect to attentiveness and learning. Theology is created intellectual love answering loving divine instruction. Divine instruction initiates, surrounds, and encloses theological intelligence; theological studiousness is the mind's movement within the larger reconciling movement. Theological curiosity detaches the mind from this situation and movement. For the curious, the sphere in which the mind operates is that of spontaneous, not directed, intelligence. In that sphere, the acquisition of new knowledge is an unrestricted good, and submission to tutelage undermines intellectual dignity. Theology can only operate under this regime if it transforms itself into an independent science, one no longer within the *schola revelationis*.

(2) When theological intelligence is overcome by curiosity, it neglects the particular object of theology, and the particular course—*curriculum*—which that object requires theological intelligence to run. Curiosity gives itself to whatever sources of fascination present themselves, especially if they are novel, and it lays great store by improvisation. In theology, curiosity is manifest as a kind of restlessness or instability, where discriminations about what must and what must not be objects of attention do not operate. In acute form, this becomes a species of intellectual promiscuity, driven by addiction to novelty and a compulsion to repeat the experience of discovery.

(3) Curiosity in theology stops short at surfaces, and so inhibits theological intelligence in running toward God. How so? Theology requires mastery of a wide range of historical, textual, and conceptual phenomena. These phenomena are to be understood as signs, mediating divine instruction; to "read" the signs is to be drawn by the signs through the signs, to the divine depth that they indicate. For all its inquisitiveness, curiosity in theology fails to perceive this indicative or ministerial function of the phenomena to which it addresses itself, and instead is absorbed by their natural properties. Further, where theology expects much of analysis of the natural features of the Christian religion, and makes sophisticated use of the disciplines (literary, historical, social scientific) by which analogous features are studied in other fields of inquiry, curiosity is acutely difficult to avoid. The result is the inhibition of theological intelligence, a literary and historical phenomenalism in which "a person strives to know the truth about creatures, without heeding its rightful end, namely knowing about God."[17]

17. Aquinas, *Summa Theologiae* IIaIIae.167.1 resp. For similar criticism of some

(4) Curiosity debases the manner in which theological work is undertaken, causing the theologian to adopt a posture at odds with spiritual vocation. This may involve pride, and a corresponding inattention to creaturely limitation in knowledge; it may involve being inordinately intent on the acquisition of new knowledge; again, it may go along with a vicious individualism in which pursuit of knowledge isolates from the common life of the church and impedes the rule of charity. Within each of these expressions of curiosity is failure to fulfill our intellectual nature as an aspect of conformity to God.

(5) Curiosity disregards the proper ends of theology, which are contemplative and apostolic. Theology is chiefly contemplative; it is a moved activity of the mind that seeks out and clings to God with intense delight; derivatively, theology is apostolic, a work of charity in which contemplated truth is spoken to others, to edify the church, correct error, or persuade unbelief. Curiosity does not pursue these ends, because it is absorbed in the satisfactions of coming-to-know and does not properly attend to the integrity of what is known, or engage in any act of love.

Such is curiosity in theology. How may it be countered?

V

Avoidance of curiosity demands temperance; temperance is a fruit of the Holy Spirit's work of regeneration and sanctification. Restraint, modification, and ordering of desire in the realm of the intellect, as in all spheres of created life, is governed by the biblical axiom, at once metaphysical and moral: "if anyone is in Christ, that person is a new creature; the old has passed away, behold, the new has come . . . All this is from God" (2 Cor 5:17f.). The original and governing principle of created intellect and its operations is the Holy Spirit, whose mission it is to perfect creatures in realizing the divine purpose for them, secured by the reconciling work of the Son in fulfillment of the Father's will. In the Spirit's original work, the intellect is made new; in the Spirit's governing work, the intellect is maintained and directed on its true course. Any account of the virtuous intellect is only as good as its underlying pneumatology. What is required, therefore, is not only rules for the direction of the

---

kinds of literary-historical study of Scripture, see Levering, *Participatory Biblical Exegesis*, and, more generally, T. F. Torrance's insistence on the "depth dimension" of biblical and theological inquiry—see, for example, Torrance, "Epistemological Relevance."

theological mind, but an expansive account of the economy by which it is formed and within which it fulfils its calling.

Curiosity is pervasive and grievous in its effects. Alienated from the life of God, the curious intellect shares the "futility" and "darkened understanding" of the old nature and its "corruption through deceitful lusts" (Eph 4:17f., 22). Because it is ruled by strong desire, curiosity is deeply resistant to correction. Persuasion and catechesis alone are of little permanent effect; they may mitigate the worst excesses of curiosity but are powerless to eradicate its cause. The necessary renewal in the spirit of the mind (Eph 4:23) can be effected by God alone in the person of the Holy Spirit, extending and perfecting the Son's completed work of reconciliation by his own proper work, namely, "the washing of regeneration and renewal in the Holy Spirit" (Titus 3:5). As with creaturely life in its entirety, so with creaturely intellect: "deliverance must be and is by regeneration."[18]

This operation of the Holy Spirit is not simply moral or imperatival but "physical," the realization of the "new nature" (Eph 4:24). By the work of the Holy Spirit which Jesus Christ our Savior pours out "richly" (Titus 3:6), the impotence and enmity of the intellect are decisively countered; desire is redirected; a new principle of intellectual activity is established, and the intellect set upon a new course. In short, there arises within the realm of created intellect an unexpected, indeed astounding, reality, "the new nature which is being renewed in knowledge" (Col 3:10). The restoration and flourishing of created intellect is realized in the double process of mortification and vivification, through which intellectual acts come to conform to their principle and to be fitting to their condition. There must be a putting to death, a putting away, of habits of mind that flow from passion or evil desire (Col 3:5) and a putting on of those movements of the intellect which accord with its new nature. How does this take place in the work of theology?

Theological curiosity is checked and theological studiousness promoted when the intellects of saintly persons are directed to the proper object of theology and to the proper ends of contemplation and edification. In more detail:

(1) Christian theology is an exercise of sanctified studiousness, the work of persons whose intellectual acts are marked by the Spirit's regenerative presence. Such persons are subject to the Spirit's formation,

18. Owen, *Pneumatologia*, 299.

shaped in such a way that they are made capable of responding to the calling of creatures in the matter of knowledge of God. Inhibition of immoderate desire for novelty in knowledge can only happen if practitioners come to see themselves and their work as taking their place within the pedagogy of divine grace. "The grace of God has appeared . . . training us" (Titus 2:11f.). In the missions of Word and Spirit, grace has "appeared," that is, made itself a present and effective reality in created being and time. Thereby, this grace establishes a realm of grace, a space in creaturely life and culture in which salvation—the reconciliation of lost creatures, the renewal of their calling, and the leading of them to completion—is irresistibly at work. By its presence, divine grace "trains"; grace is a divine accomplishment and gift that evokes, enables, and forms creatures. The intellect, too, is embraced by the Spirit's sanctifying work. The double movement of renouncing irreligion and worldly passions and embracing sobriety, uprightness, and godliness (Titus 2:12) extends into the work of reason, including theological reason. Theological intellectual acts are part of "evangelical holiness," the sanctity generated by the gospel's announcement of reconciliation and regeneration.

The saints lack curiosity; but they are eagerly studious, devoted to acquiring the knowledge proffered by divine revelation. In theology, the affections, will, and intellect are "fixed" on the "ways" of God (Ps 119:15), "delighting in" and "cleaving to" the divine testimonies (Ps 119:24), turned from "vanities" (Ps 119:37) in order to "meditate" on the divine law (Ps 119:48), eager to be taught knowledge (Ps 119:66). Such is the studious theological intellect sanctified and schooled by divine grace.

(2) Curiosity falls away as Christian theology directs itself to its singular matter with a definite interest. Christian theology is a comprehensive science that treats of all things (and so offers ample opportunities for the workings of curiosity); but it treats all things under a very specific aspect (this both checks curiosity and quickens studiousness). Theology is not indiscriminately about everything, but about everything in relation to God: *omnia autem pertractantur in sacra doctrina sub ratione Dei.*[19] Moreover, in Christian theology, to treat everything *sub ratione Dei* is to direct the mind to a very particular history—the history of redemption with its center in the missions of the Son and the Spirit, and its ground in the inner divine processions—by which all things are

19. Aquinas, *Summa Theologiae* Ia.1.7 corp.

embraced and shaped. For all the scope of its inquiry, Christian theology is a restricted science, and checking curiosity requires acceptance of the restriction. The apostle's determination "to know nothing . . . except Jesus Christ and him crucified" (1 Cor 2:2) is exemplary of the necessary single-mindedness. This is not to reduce the matter of Christian theology to a few Christological and soteriological topics; indeed, part of the frailty of some modern Protestant theology is unwillingness to venture beyond considering the *beneficia Christi* and reluctance to engage questions of speculative divinity. But though Christian theology has very wide range, it remains a single science, unified by the fact that it considers one matter—infinitely deep, very widely extensive. Curiosity dissipates the theological intellect by giving itself to whatever enchanting objects catch its fancy. Studiousness is intelligence *concentrated*.

(3) Mortification of curiosity happens as theology is directed to its proper end, which is love: love of God who gives himself to be known, and love of the saints and the not-yet-saints by communicating what theology has come to know. Theological coming-to-know does not terminate in the acquisition and storing of knowledge but in its exercise, in adoration of God and edification of others. Curiosity is selfish: like other forms of promiscuity, it is preoccupied with satisfying the appetite for new objects to be consumed or hoarded. The end of studiousness, however, lies beyond itself, in contemplation of God and engagement in apostolic tasks.

VI

To speak of the practice of academic theology in such terms is to court ridicule. Well-seated and prestigious convention detaches intellectual and moral virtue, and does not consider that there are nonnatural principles, moving powers and ends of science—even theological science. It is astonishing that—a few pockets of resistance aside—a good deal of university theology concedes the authority of the convention and adjusts its ambitions and modes of operation accordingly.

Much needs to happen if such a description of theology is to commend itself: fresh willingness to consider the metaphysics and anthropology of *scire per causas*; a measure of freedom from elements of the culture of the research university; deep formation by and loyalty to the Christian gospel; confidence that good theology is a genuine possibility for finite minds. All this, however, depends upon the Spirit's promptings. And so:

> *Creator ineffabilis, qui de thesauris sapientiae tuae tres angelorum hierarchias designasti et eas super caelum empyreum miro ordine collocasti atque universi partes elegantissime distribuisti: Tu, inquam, qui verus fons luminis et sapientiae diceris ac supereminens principium, infundere digneris super intellectus mei tenebras tuae radium claritatis, duplices, in quibus natus sum, a me removens tenebras, peccatum scilicet et ignorantiam. Tu, qui linguas infantium facis disertas, linguam meam erudias atque in labiis meis gratiam tuae benedictionis infundas. Da mihi intelligendi acumen, retinendi capacitatem, addiscendi modum et facilitatem, interpretandi subtilitatem, loquendi gratiam copiosam. Ingressum instruas, progressum dirigas, egressum compleas. Tu, qui es verus Deus et homo, qui vivis et regnas in saecula saeculorum. Amen.*[20]

Bibliography

Aquinas, Thomas. *Summa Theologiae*. Edited by Thomas Gilby. London: Eyre & Spottiswoode, 1964–74.

Augustine. *Confessions*. In *A Select Library of Nicene and Post-Nicene Fathers of the Christian Church*. Vol. 1, *The Confessions and Letters of St. Augustine*, 27–207. New York: Christian Literature Co., 1886.

———. *The Literal Meaning of Genesis*. In *Augustine: On Genesis*, translated by Edmund Hill, edited by John E. Rotelle, 155–506. New York: New City, 2002.

———. *On Genesis: A Refutation of the Manichees*. In *Augustine: On Genesis*, translated by Edmund Hill, edited by John E. Rotelle, 25–104. New York: New City, 2002.

———. *On the Morals of the Catholic Church*. In *A Select Library of Nicene and Post-Nicene Fathers of the Christian Church*. Vol. 4, *The Writings against the Manichaeans and against the Donatists*, 37–64. New York: Christian Literature Co., 1887.

Bernard of Clairvaux. *On the Song of Songs 2*. Translated by Kilian J. Walsh. Kalamazoo: Cistercian Publications, 1976.

Griffiths, Paul. *Intellectual Appetite: A Theological Grammar*. Washington, DC: Catholic University Press, 2009.

Levering, Matthew. *Participatory Biblical Exegesis: A Theology of Biblical Interpretation*. Notre Dame: Notre Dame University Press, 2008.

Owen, John. *Pneumatologia, or, a Discourse Concerning the Holy Spirit* [1674]. In *The Works of John Owen* 3. Edinburgh: Banner of Truth Trust, 1965.

Pius XI, "Studiorum Ducem." *Acta Apostolicae Sedis* 15 (1923) 309–26.

Torrance, Thomas F. "The Epistemological Relevance of the Spirit." In *God and Rationality*. London: Oxford University Press, 1969.

---

20. A prayer before study used by Thomas Aquinas, quoted in Pius XI, "Studiorum ducem," 326.

16

Charity and Human Flourishing

Some Reflections Drawn from Thomas Aquinas

Mark Wynn

Thomas Aquinas has, characteristically, a pretty precise account of the nature of charity or *caritas*. And I shall come to this in due course. But let me begin by taking charity in its somewhat everyday sense—to mean a concern for another person for their own sake, or on account of their own independent reality, and not simply considered as an extension of oneself, nor as a means to the satisfaction of one's own projects. The *Summa Theologiae* is animated, from beginning to close, I am going to argue, by the ideal of charity understood in something like this sense. And this is true, I shall propose, both of Aquinas's choice of themes and of his method.

CHARITY IN ARGUMENT

Anyone who has even the slightest acquaintance with the *Summa* will have been struck by Aquinas's argumentative method. The structure of the text is defined by a certain argumentative procedure: repeatedly, Aquinas poses a question, which he then addresses by, first of all, rehearsing the arguments that might be presented in support of a response that is contrary to the response that he will himself eventually favor. And these counterarguments are typically not just concocted by Aquinas:

they are the views of particular individuals, and Aquinas attributes them to particular scriptural or patristic or philosophical sources. So when applying himself to a given issue, Aquinas routinely begins by heeding the views of other people, and in particular views that are at odds with his own. So the perspective of others is not introduced simply in passing, as an incidental detail to the development of his own account of things; instead, their thoughts are expounded at the very beginning of his consideration of some issue, and it is a clear implication of this method that Aquinas believes that his own answer to a question will need to be judged in terms of its capacity to address the concerns that are represented in these alternative points of view. So here is a first respect in which Aquinas's argumentative method observes the ideal of charity: he heeds the voices of others, and he even gives those voices a kind of priority in his own inquiry, allowing them to set the terms of the debate, and to establish at least implicitly criteria for the adequacy of any answer that might be presented to the question that is under discussion.

Getting ahead of ourselves a little, we might even see in this procedure a concern to adhere to the specifically Christian ideal of love of enemies: Aquinas begins with the views of those who are opposed to him argumentatively. And his method implies that he is willing to meet these others on their own terms: he seeks to show that he can rehearse the arguments of his opponents in terms that they themselves would recognize, and to show that he can formulate the case for their point of view at least as cogently as they are able to do themselves. So this is not just a matter of heeding others' voices, but of seeking out the views of one's opponents, and being careful to "internalize" their views, so that the merits of those views are properly acknowledged. And all this is to be done before one gives any thought to the presentation of one's own perspective. Such an approach to argument is consensual: it does not seek simply to overwhelm the opponent, but to draw them into discussion, by starting with their perspective, formulated in terms that they would recognize, and with the kind of argumentative force that they would acknowledge as proper to their case. Someone who can do these things has earned the right to be heard by their interlocutors, because he has shown a proper respect for the wisdom of others, not presuming to pronounce on an issue until that wisdom, such as it is, has been set out clearly, as a starting point for further reflection.

Moreover, as each question unfolds, it is clear that Aquinas does not treat these alternative views as simply and uninterestingly erroneous. Typically, he attends to them in detail, and, often enough, he shows that he has learned from them and is willing to give some ground to them. The one strategy before all others that enables him to do this is his appeal to distinctions between the senses of key terms. Aquinas's analytical method, which can sometimes seem rather austere, and the mark of an inquiry that is abstractly logical rather than attuned to the demands of properly respectful conversation, is also to be understood, I suggest, as an act of charity. Having stacked up various arguments on one side of his question, the side that he will not in the end endorse, Aquinas then lists, in the "sed contra," an alternative view, and proceeds to provide arguments on behalf of that view, and often he does this by clarifying the senses of key terms. But then, at the close of the question, he returns to the arguments with which he began, and he considers what might be said for them, as well as against them, in the light of his own resolution of the question. So these alternative perspectives have not only the first word but also the last—they frame the debate, providing the criteria of adequacy for any answer to the question that has been set. And crucially, those criteria are not just notional but do real work, as Aquinas examines whether alternative views might after all prove to be true under at least one reading of their key terms. We shall come to an example of this procedure shortly, when we discuss 1a. 27.

This pattern of argument—the formulation of a view contrary to Aquinas's own, the refinement of the senses of key terms, and the observation that some measure of truth can be assigned to the initial view after all, insofar as it is true on one interpretation—is played out over and again in the course of the *Summa*. In our time, philosophical debate of an analytically sophisticated kind seems often enough to be aimed at undermining alternative views—by exposing an equivocation or, in general, a fallacious move in some chain of argument, so that the chain is broken, and the argument's conclusion shown to be unsupported. Aquinas's use of the analytical method is also sophisticated, but its object is fundamentally, I suggest, charitable: if we want, as charitable agents should, to establish whether there is some sense in which a rival view to our own might after all have some claim to truth, then we will need to attend to the range of interpretations of which it admits, and to consider closely, therefore, the various senses that may be assigned to the terms in which it is cast.

Of course, Aquinas is not always so hospitable to his argumentative opponents. He speaks, for example, of "the really stupid thesis of David of Dinant that God was the ultimate unformed matter of things" (1a.3.8)![1] But this is highly uncharacteristic. It is notable that this description of David's view falls in the *responsio* of the question—so here Aquinas is in fact developing his own view, and this alternative view is mentioned just to be set aside, dismissively. But the argumentative discipline that structures each question of the *Summa*, whereby a range of alternative views are rehearsed before we get to the *responsio*, ensures that standardly these other approaches are set out more fully and more carefully, and with a view to allowing their merits, such as they may be, to be displayed to best advantage. Aquinas's handling of David of Dinant's view, under the different conventions that operate within the *responsio*, shows how this mode of argument constitutes a genuine discipline that is at once intellectual and charitable.

Some modern epistemologists have spoken of the "principle of charity," meaning by this that when we interpret others' views, we need to suppose that they are right for the most part, by our lights, because without that assumption we would struggle to assign a determinate sense to their talk.[2] Aquinas is also adhering to a principle of charity, but one that makes more stringent demands of us in our day-to-day interactions with other human beings. His ideal of charity in argument enjoins us to attend closely to what others have to say, and to attend especially to what is said by those who disagree with us; and this ideal requires us to be sure that we can rehearse their point of view, in terms that they would recognize, before we have the presumption to formulate our own for purposes of conversational exchange; and this is an ideal that invites us to seek out as much truth as may be found in alternative views, by searching for, so far as possible, interpretations under which those views turn out to be, at least in significant part, true.

Of course, Aquinas had good reason for proceeding in this way quite apart from his Christian commitment to charity as an ideal of life. The alternative voices to which he is attending are, after all, embedded in the writings of Christian theologians of real authority, or they are taken

1. *David de Dinando qui stultissime posuit Deum esse materiam primum.*
2. See Davidson, "Conceptual Scheme," 196–97.

from Scripture itself, or from the work of Aristotle, who is, for Aquinas, simply "the Philosopher." These are all sources that Aquinas has good reason to take to be truthful under some interpretation. It is also true that Aristotle regularly reviews the perspective of his predecessors, with a view to showing that his own view brings out whatever is truthful in them, and to this extent Aquinas is standing within an already established philosophical mode of inquiry.[3] And it is also true, of course, that the medieval *disputatio* took the form of an exchange of views, where the case on one side of a question was presented and then the case on the other, before the magister's adjudication of the issue. But even allowing for these considerations, Aquinas's procedure is also reasonably taken to be animated by the ideal of Christian charity: we are to make way for the other and to attend to their needs not only practically but also intellectually or argumentatively. And if we are to represent our own view as preferable to that of another, our object should be, fundamentally, to show its superiority by reference to the very argumentative criteria that are operative in our opponent's approach, by showing how our view captures whatever of truth there is in their perspective and more besides.

CHARITY IN SYSTEM

Another feature of the argumentative procedure of the *Summa* that is bound to strike even a beginning reader is of course its massively systematic character. Aquinas sets out the questions that he considers in a clear and systematic sequence, and the articles into which each question is divided ensure that smaller portions of the text are also subject to a determinate order of inquiry. One consequence of this system is that, routinely, the full import of what Aquinas says on a given issue in a given passage in the *Summa* will become fully apparent only as the text unfolds, once we have seen how his handling of this issue, in this instance, is to be nested within some larger intellectual context.

Aquinas's treatment of the notion of "potentiality" provides one example of the need to read the text backwards and forwards in the light of commitments that emerge as the discussion develops. This notion plays a key part in the First Way, of course, where Aquinas argues that change consists in a change from potentiality to actuality, and that change depends upon the agency of something that is, in so far as it effects change,

---

3. See for example Aristotle's procedure in the *Metaphysics*, Book Alpha.

already actual, and that as actual cannot be identified with that which as potential is undergoing change. And he concludes that if change is to admit of an ultimate explanation, an explanation that does not just introduce a further case of something that is liable to change, then we will need to cite some reality that is devoid of any potentiality or fully actual. The argument that Aquinas sets out here is, if we strip out the wider context provided by the *Summa*, no different in intellectual content from Aristotle's argument from motion, which understands change in the same way, and cites the same kinds of consideration in support of the conclusion that there must be a first source of change that is devoid of potentiality.[4]

We have seen that Aquinas begins each question of the *Summa* by setting out various claims with which he will eventually disagree, and that this disagreement sometimes takes the form not of a simple dismissal of other views but, rather, of an attempt to set those views within some more comprehensive account of the issues, which will reveal in what sense they are true, and in what sense false. We might suppose that in 1a.2.3, as he rehearses the First Way, Aquinas is proceeding rather similarly. Here again, he begins with a received view—in this case, the argument from motion that he has inherited from Aristotle. But as the text unfolds in later questions, this view will be set within a wider interpretive context, as the notion of potentiality is gradually reworked. The next crucial step in this scheme arises in 1a.3.4, where Aquinas addresses the question: whether there is in God a composition of essence and existence. Here it becomes clear that even if a creature had always existed, and had never undergone any change, and even if it were immaterial and therefore not naturally susceptible to change, this creature would still exhibit "potentiality" in Aquinas's sense of the term. For such a thing, by virtue of being a creature and not the Creator, would still have received its existence—and we can therefore say that it might not have existed (had the Creator not established it in being) and that its existing involves therefore the actualization of a potentiality (the potentiality of its being rather than not being), even if this potentiality does not come to be realized at any particular time (because the thing has always existed).

Of course, Aristotle does not envisage such a case, so he never gets to consider whether the notion of potentiality might have application in this sort of context. So far from slavishly following a preestablished

4. Aristotle, *Metaphysics*, Book Lambda.

Aristotelian conceptual scheme, Aquinas is here subjecting that scheme to fundamental redefinition, so that it can be used to articulate a distinctively Christian insight, concerning God's role as the source of being. Again, what is striking here is Aquinas's intellectual generosity. He does not just affirm that but for God's agency no creature would exist. Instead, he finds ways of articulating that familiar Christian claim, to which he is already committed independently of his reading of Aristotle, in terms of Aristotelian concepts. So this is an approach that begins with one reading of a key concept—provided by Aristotle, and rehearsed in 1a.2.3—and then extends the sense of the concept, so that it can be used to articulate thoughts that Aristotle himself never entertained (in 1a.3.4). So once more, Aquinas's approach is a case of tradition-constituted inquiry. Here again, his procedure is, at root, intellectually conservative: let us begin with an established view of the physical world and the conditions of its operation, and let us preserve as much of this scheme as we can. But at the same time, he is of course an innovator: his own account does not just recapitulate this tradition, but extends it, by stretching its core categories, so that they can be used to articulate thoughts that were never envisaged, and were not even thinkable, under the old assignment of meanings.

When we get to 1a.27, it becomes clear that there is more still to be said about the notion of potentiality. Here Aquinas continues to say that there is no potentiality in God, but now he adds that there are "processions" in God. Of course, the reader will ask themselves: anything that proceeds surely depends upon that from which it proceeds, so if there is procession in God, then there must be dependence in God, and if dependence then is there not potentiality in the extended sense that was identified in 1a.3.4—for that which depends will surely only be, or only be as it is, granted the activity of that on which it depends, and is its existence, or character, not therefore potential relative to the agency of that on which it depends? Typically, Aquinas does not duck this question by appeal to "mystery" or something of that kind.[5] Throughout, it seems to me, his aim is to clarify the relevant concepts, so as to show at the very least that Christian teaching does not fall demonstrably into contradiction, or more substantively, so that we can see in what sense various claims are true. So at the outset of 1a.27.1,

5. So I am not entirely in agreement with Karen Kilby's characterization of his procedure in this respect in her instructive paper "Aquinas."

Aquinas confronts himself with this objection: "To proceed from another seems incompatible with being the first principle . . . Therefore there is no place for a procession in God."

In due course, in the "ad tertium," Aquinas returns to this objection, and he comments: "To come forth as something external and diverse from a principle is incompatible with being the first principle. But the spiritual coming forth of what is intimate and in no way diverse is included in the very idea of the first principle." Here, the resolution of the issue depends upon drawing a distinction (between two kinds of "coming forth"); so now we can see that the initial objection is after all true under one interpretation, but also that the view it takes is only partial, because it overlooks the possibility of another kind of "coming forth." To cast the point in the terms used in 1a.3.4, I take it that Aquinas is saying that what proceeds in God—in brief, at this point in the discussion, the Son—still exists by nature, even if dependently. Accordingly, the Son does not exhibit the kind of potentiality that would be exhibited by a creature that had always existed, and always existed as changeless. For a creature might not have existed, as its existence is not guaranteed by its nature; and we cannot say similarly of the Son that he might not have existed. Even so, we can clearly affirm of the Son that his existence is relative to the activity of the Father. And this suggests that Thomas's account does allow us to find dependence or possibility in God—providing that we recognize that this dependence does not compromise God's status as self-existent. As long as God is self-existent, then God will be free from potentiality in the extended sense of the term that Aquinas identifies in 1a.3.4. Although Aquinas does not himself proceed in this direction, it seems to me that one could say on this basis that God can be passible, in certain respects, in God's relationship to creatures, providing that we add that this sort of passibility is freely entered into by God, so does not compromise the truth that God exists by nature, and not, ultimately, by virtue of the agency of anything other than God.

Aquinas's handling of the notion of potentiality shows his freedom to rework Aristotle's account in the service of a distinctively Christian conception of the nature of things. Aristotle's concepts are respectfully heeded, they form the starting point of discussion, and in some degree they define the criteria of success in a discussion of this kind, but they are also radicalized, and in Aquinas's hands, they are perfectly pliant to the demands of an alternative rendering of the nature of things.

The systematic quality of Aquinas's discussion discloses another important truth. The *Summa* is intended of course to reveal the nature of the world, and accordingly the articulations that define its structure are intended to map on to the articulations that define the structure of reality. Commentators commonly remark that the architectonic of the *Summa* (its movement from the doctrine of God, into the doctrine of creation, and thence to the doctrine of redemption) reflects the movement of reality itself, as it proceeds from and returns to God.[6] We might also fairly say that the interconnectedness of the various themes of the *Summa*, and the fact that core concepts such as the concept of potentiality are consistently reworked and reapplied to fit contexts that are related but not simply identical to those for which they were at first designed, reveals that reality itself exhibits this same implicate order, so that its character in any one part can only be properly understood once we have set that part within a larger structure. And this in turn reflects the fundamental truth that the world considered as an integral whole was made in order to image the simple God, so that any one of its parts only achieves its fundamental *telos*—of imaging God, so far as it can—by virtue of standing in the right relation to other parts of the created order. So the systematic quality of the *Summa* discloses another important point about charity: our flourishing as God-directed creatures is not a property of individuals only, but of individuals in their holistic context. And accordingly, the requirement to relate ourselves properly to other creatures does not meet us as an alien requirement, which cuts across our possibilities for fulfillment, but instead enjoins us to realize our *telos* so far as we can.[7]

CHARITY IN THE VIRTUES

We have been considering how our success as reasoners, or our flourishing as intellectual creatures, depends upon charity in so far as it depends upon the adoption of an appropriately analytic and systematic method of inquiry. Unsurprisingly, charity is also important for Aquinas when we come to examine, explicitly, the moral life. Aquinas's development of the ideals of the moral life is dependent of course upon his critical

6. See for example Davies, *Thought of Thomas Aquinas*, 21.

7. I explore these themes more fully, and their resonances for an environmental ethic, in Wynn, "Thomas Aquinas."

appropriation of another concept that he has taken from Aristotle—the concept of virtue. Aristotle was interested in the moral virtues—of courage, and justice, and temperance, for example—in so far as they fit us for life in relation to other human beings. Aquinas has the further challenge of thinking about the kinds of virtue that are required if we are to flourish in relation to God. And of course, his Christian forebears have provided him with at least the rudiments of an answer. In general terms, this answer is: we should live according to the ideals of faith, hope, and charity (1 Cor 13). Aquinas also faces a further challenge that was not addressed by Aristotle: Aristotle represents the virtues as the product of a process of habituation, where we become just, for example, by repeatedly doing the just thing, so that doing the just thing becomes habitual, or second nature, to us;[8] but for Aquinas, we need to say more than this, if we are to allow for the role of the divine initiative, or of grace, in sustaining the virtues.

Given these parameters, Aquinas might most simply have said: Aristotle's account is to be topped up by allowing that there are theological virtues—of faith, hope, and charity—virtues that fit us to flourish in relation to God, as well as the moral (and other) virtues that Aristotle described; and these theological virtues (here is a second point of departure from Aristotle) are not "acquired," that is, they do not derive from some process of habituation, but are instead infused, since they owe their origin to the divine initiative. A less charitable thinker might have been content with such a solution. But characteristically, Aquinas wants a more fully integrated, more systemic account, and an account that gives a larger role to the natural order, and a larger role to what his forebears (and preeminently Aristotle) had said about that order.

The central conceptual innovation that allows him to do this is the idea that there are infused moral virtues. He comments that "the theological virtues are enough to shape us to our supernatural end as a start . . . Yet the soul needs also to be equipped by infused virtues in regard to created things, though as subordinate to God" (1a2ae.63.3). This proposal ensures that we do not have simply two ends—the end of proper relationship to God, and the end of proper relationship to creatures—and two sets of virtues, one set fitted to the first end, and another fitted to the second end. To put the point another way, Aquinas is here respecting the traditional Christian conception of charity, by allowing

8. Aristotle, *Nichomachean Ethics*, Book II.

that love of neighbor and love of God cannot be easily prized apart: to fail in the first is to fail in the second. So we cannot suppose that if only we have the theological virtues, then our relationship to God is secured; instead, we must allow that proper relationship to God is conditional upon, and partly consists in, the cultivation of the moral virtues (the virtues concerning our relations with our fellow human beings). The moral virtues, acquired by habituation, remain central to this account—here is Aquinas's acknowledgement of his debt to Aristotle. But once again, Aristotle's picture is set within a wider context, not just by having some further set of ideas (concerning the theological virtues) bolted on to it; instead, it is transformed from within, as we come to see how the moral virtues themselves need to be ordered not only to other human beings, but also to our relationship to God (here we are concerned with "created things as subordinate to God"), and as we come to see how this is only possible in so far as the moral virtues, such as temperance, are not only present in us as acquired, but also as infused.[9]

So here again we see that Aquinas's stance exhibits charity in its regard for the position of his interlocutors; and again we see how the systematic tendencies of his thought issue in a certain conception of charity, one that ties our flourishing in relationship to God to our flourishing in relationship to creatures, so that love of God and love of neighbor are held together inseparably.

Of course, Aquinas also has things to say directly about charity, both the love of God and of neighbor, considered as a theological virtue. One striking feature of his exposition of *caritas* is his suggestion that "charity . . . is not merely love, but friendship" (2a2ae.25.2). He says more exactly that "charity's friendship is based on a fellowship of eternal happiness" (25.10). And when asking whether it is "a necessary part of charity to love our enemies," he notes that in so far "as [our enemies are] capable of eternal happiness, we should love them" (25.9 ad 2). So the love that we owe other human beings has its roots in the fact that we can be related to them as friends in eternal life. This is, it seems to me, a more demanding and more encompassing conception of the ideal of other-regard than the one we find in the standard moral philosophical theories. It is not just that we owe others regard on account of their capacity to feel pleasure and pain, nor that we owe them regard in so far

9. John Inglis provides a helpful account of the interplay between the two sets of moral virtues, acquired and infused, in his essay "Aquinas's Replication."

as they are capable of autonomous choice, or of flourishing in certain ways in this life. A particular human individual may lack the capacity for autonomous choice, and may be so afflicted that there is no realistic prospect of their flourishing under the constraints of this life. Even so, Aquinas would say, we have reason to love them, considered as prospective friends in the life to come. This ideal of love is also deeper than that found in many Christian expositions of the ideal of neighbor love. For example, it is not just that we are called to uphold the interests of our fellow human beings. We could do that while having very little regard for them as individuals. Instead, we are called to see them as friends and commit ourselves to upholding their well-being on the basis of this deeper, even if in many cases still prospective, identification with them.

The theme of charity is also present, naturally, when Aquinas discusses the virtue of faith. He remarks that "faith's act is pointed as to its end towards the will's object, i.e. the good. This good, the end of faith's act, is the divine good, the proper object of charity" (2a2ae.4.3). And he notes that the believing that is characteristic of faith is "an act of the intellect under the impetus of the will" (4.2). So far as there is a conception of Aquinas among intellectuals today, it is probably the view that he was a kind of rationalist who produced various arguments, most famously the five ways, in support of religious belief. But from his stance here, it is clear that the belief that is typical of faith is not the product of some compelling inference; instead, such belief derives from an act of will, where the will is moved in charity by the attractiveness of God. Such a construal of faith invites a radically different conception of "apologetics" from the one that has prevailed in the bulk of philosophical writing on these matters. An apologetics of this kind would take as its first task the need to represent God as a fitting object of charity. So the first concern of such an apologetic would be the question of the divine attractiveness, and God's fittingness to be loved. Here again, while the reader's attention may at first be drawn to the conceptual sophistication of Aquinas's discussion, it is the possibility of an act of love, one in which our flourishing consists, that is the animating *telos* of the whole enterprise.[10]

10. Compare Eleonore Stump's proposal that the under-evidencing of the propositions believed in faith ensures that commitment to God can be grounded in a love of goodness rather than of power: *Aquinas*, 373–74.

CONCLUDING THOUGHTS: CHARITY AND
THE SACRAMENTS

These same charitable concerns are evident in Aquinas's discussion in the third and final part of the *Summa*. Here again, we find that God's agency does not simply displace or render irrelevant the agency of creatures (just as the infused theological virtues, for example, do not displace the need for the acquired moral virtues), while at the same time the agency of creatures is not left untouched, but instead transformed from within (rather as the infused moral virtues draw out the acquired moral virtues). For example, Aquinas comments that the sacraments "touch the body and so produce upon it the sort of effects that are connatural to them as physical entities. But in the very act of doing so they also operate as instruments, producing effects upon the soul in the power of God" (3a.62.1). These twin affirmations tell us once more that the created order is caught up in its integrity into the divine initiative—just as, we might say, Aristotle's thought is caught up in its integrity into the scheme of Christian revelation. Here again is love: God upholds the creature in its integrity, but transforms it from within, by setting it in relation to a goal that is beyond anything for which it is naturally fitted, namely the goal of right relationship to God.

And right relationship to God is itself to be conceived, of course, in terms of charity, or the love of friendship, as Aquinas makes clear when he turns to discuss the eucharist. The idea that "the body of Christ is really and truly in this sacrament" is, he notes, an extension of the idea that in the incarnation God invites us into a relationship of friendship. He comments: "it is the very law of friendship that *friends should live together*, as Aristotle teaches," and this "living together" is possible here and now, he adds, because "he has not left us without his bodily presence in this our pilgrimage, but he joins us to himself in this sacrament in the reality of his body and blood" (3a.75.1). So even when we turn to this most speculative of Aquinas's teachings, concerning the transubstantiation of the elements in the eucharist, we find that his concerns are still fundamentally charitable. This doctrine serves the idea that God's love reaches us here and now, tangibly, as befits a relationship of friendship, in such a way that the natural order is not displaced or rendered irrelevant, but is instead accorded, in its integrity, a new set of divinely oriented possibilities. (See Aquinas's insistence on what might seem a rather fine distinction: the "substance" of the bread and wine is not, he says, "annihilated" but instead "changed into" the body and blood of Christ: 3a.75.3 ad 1.) Here we see Aquinas's "apologetic": the divine attractiveness consists in the fact that God calls us into a new relationship of friendship, with God and with our fellow human beings, and so affirms and extends what we are by nature.

Tim Gorringe's theological writings are defined by their passionate concern for justice and for the ecosystemic integrity of the created order, by their respectful yet transforming engagement with the best secular learning of our time, and by their refusal of any simple dichotomy between the requirements of proper relationship to God and those of proper relationship to creatures. In these matters, he stands squarely within the tradition of Christian reflection that Aquinas epitomizes, and he is, it seems to me, as able and persuasive an exponent of that tradition as any theologian writing today. I count myself fortunate to be able to call him my colleague and, indeed, my friend.

Bibliography

Aquinas, Thomas. *Summa Theologiae*. Edited by Thomas Gilby. London: Eyre & Spottiswoode, 1964–74.

Aristotle. *Ethics*. Translated by H. Tredennick. London: Penguin, 1976.

———. *Metaphysics*. Translated by H. Lawson-Tancred. London: Penguin, 1998.

Davidson, Donald. "On the Very Idea of a Conceptual Scheme." In *Inquiries into Truth and Interpretation*, 183–99. Oxford: Clarendon, 1984.

Davies, Brian. *The Thought of Thomas Aquinas*. Oxford: Clarendon, 1992.

Inglis, John. "Aquinas's Replication of the Acquired Moral Virtues: Rethinking the Standard Philosophical Interpretation of Moral Virtue in Aquinas." *Journal of Religious Ethics* 27 (1999) 3–27.

Kilby, Karen. "Aquinas, the Trinity and the Limits of Understanding." *International Journal of Systematic Theology* 7 (2005) 414–27.

Stump, Eleanore. *Aquinas*. London: Routledge, 2003.

Wynn, Mark. "Thomas Aquinas: Reading the Idea of Dominion in the Light of the Doctrine of Creation." In *Ecological Hermeneutics: Biblical, Historical and Theological Perspectives*, edited by David G. Horrell, Cherryl Hunt, and Christopher Southgate, 154–65. London: T. & T. Clark, 2010.

17

What Are Universities For?

A Christian View

NIGEL BIGGAR

I

One of the most distinctive and attractive features of Tim
Gorringe's theological thinking and writing is its natural openness
to secular inspiration, and therefore the bubbling, eclectic range of material with which it converses. So—to refer to just one of his works, *God's
Theatre: A Theology of Providence*—he cites not only Karl Barth, but also
the theatre director Peter Brook; not only Gerhard von Rad, but also
the philosopher Bertrand Russell; and not only Jon Sobrino, but also
the historian Simon Schama. Closely allied to this creative openness is
Gorringe's characteristic disposition to engage theologically with issues
of secular importance, whether farming, penal practice, social equality,
urban planning, or art—an engagement epitomized in his being one of
all too few theologians who have made time to write for the press.

The essay that follows shares, I think, something of the same spirit.
It concerns a topical issue of importance for the health of society in
general: the *raison d'être* of universities. Further, the bulk of it was first
published in a monthly current affairs periodical and was addressed to

a general readership.[1] It is true that this periodical swings considerably further to the right than Tim Gorringe would ever dream of doing. Still, the essay that it agreed to publish opens with a Marxist's statement, and closes by agreeing with it; and I have reason to suppose that much—if not all—of what comes in between, Tim would applaud.

The theology here is largely implicit. There is an explicit statement of biblical Christianity's affirmation of practical work and of the important contributions to the commonwealth of the social body's less prestigious members. However, there are only allusions to the root of the equal dignity of every human individual in a common responsibility before the one God. Likewise, there is a clear assertion of a variety of nonmaterial human goods, which are no less real for being beyond price. Yet the hinterland claim that there is a given, created, natural order of human flourishing that precedes and frames human choices remains unspoken and unexplained.

The reason for this reticence is not, I think, intimidated embarrassment about religious or metaphysical belief. Nor is it because of a misguided deference to the requirements of a spuriously neutral "secular language" or "public reason." What I have written seeks to make a persuasive argument to a general, plural readership about the proper purpose of universities, and not about the existence or nature of God. It is happy to refer to Scripture or allude to doctrine where that is appropriate, but it does not feel the anxious need to look back over its shoulder to reassure skeptical Christian brethren by proving its theological *bona fides*. There is a time to expose one's theological assumptions to ecclesial testing, but that is not now. Now is a time for an essay in the public expression of Christian intelligence.

II

Comrade Musicians, permit me a few opening remarks on the role of the creative artist in society. In the West, the artist is a mere ornament, victim to market forces. He can be made, or broken, by the vogues of a narrow intellectual elite. Whether he lives or starves depends on how fashionable he is. Freedom is a struggle to survive. *We*—we value our artist. We recognize

---

1. Biggar, "What Are Universities For?" The original version of this essay appeared as an address to Rhodes Scholars at a Trinity Forum conference at Rhodes House, Oxford, on 7 November 2009.

the gift he brings. As any science—any technology—poetry, art are vital to our humanity. Our institutions, therefore, accord the artist proper status. In *our* society he enjoys his rightful place. But with that status comes responsibility. In the West, yes, the artist is free to dabble in abstractions, in sentimental nihilism, in meaninglessness itself. We, the People, demand that you touch us, that you reach into us, that your creations be of meaning to us. In a word, that you *speak*. Have we, in our Soviet music, the beginnings of a failure to speak?

Thus Andrei Zhdanov, Stalin's cultural enforcer, at the Moscow Congress of Composers in 1948. And down there in the audience, about to be denounced for the "hooligan squawkings" of his Ninth Symphony, Dmitri Shostakovich leans over to his neighbor and mutters, "The trouble with Zhdanov is that he's so often right."[2]

Well, half right. Right, that the artist has a public responsibility; wrong, that the responsible artist is always harmonious and upbeat.

Like Zhdanov, today's Western governments are also half right. Right that universities have a public responsibility; wrong that this responsibility amounts to little more than economic responsiveness. Actually, in his less shrunken, fuller conception of public responsibility—if *only* in that—Comrade Zhdanov was rather wiser than our own rulers.

The first occasion on which I unburdened myself in public on the subject of the *raison d'être* of universities was about six years ago, when I was teaching at Trinity College Dublin. I had been asked to preach in the College Chapel at a service to mark the beginning of the academic year.[3] A few months earlier the university had buckled under pressure from Government, and had embarked on a wholesale reorganization in the direction of an allegedly business model of corporate structure. It had done this in the vain hope of appeasing its political masters into reversing the 18 percent cut in core funding that they had suddenly imposed. (And this was while the Celtic Tiger was still purring along very happily—or so it seemed at the time.)

Shortly afterwards the Organisation of Economic Cooperation and Development had published a report on higher education in Ireland.[4]

2. All this, according to the screenplay of Tony Palmer's 1988 film, *Testimony*.

3. On 28 October 2004.

4. OECD, "Review."

Given the nature of the OECD, and given that it compiled its report at the request of Irish government, its recommendations failed to surprise: universities should serve a national economic strategy; they should work harder at the commercial exploitation of scientific and technological research; and they should train students in the intellectual and social skills necessary to meet the needs and opportunities of the labor market.

Against that background I decided to devote my October sermon to reflecting on what universities are for; and when I came to deliver it, I might have been expected—as a member of the Faculty of Arts and Humanities, as an ethicist, and as a clergyman—to wax indignant in moral complaint against government materialism and philistinism. But I resolved not to live down to my stereotype. I decided to distance myself from any whiff of ivory-tower snobbery. After all, Ireland had only very recently emerged out of centuries of relative and humiliating poverty; and the Irish knew better than many Westerners that, whether or not poverty is good for the soul, it really is not a lot of fun; and without the wealth that economic success brings, lots of good and worthwhile things simply cannot get done.

So, no, I did not think then—and I do not think now—that it is inappropriate that Government should ask universities to serve economic goals and to prepare their students for the labor market—that is, for the *nonacademic* work that the vast majority of them will spend most of the rest of their lives doing. I *do* think that economic responsiveness belongs to universities' public responsibility.

We should not idealize or over-moralize universities. Right from their medieval beginnings, they have served private purposes and practical public purposes as well as the sheer *amor scientiae*. For example, the founding of the University of Bologna, which lays dubious claim to be the earliest, was led by market demand. It began with ambitious students appointing professors and monitoring their performance by threatening fines, against which the hapless professors had to put down a deposit![5] The notion that university education should be consumer-led is not a new one.

Moreover, prominent among the original, classic university disciplines was, of course, law, in which both private individuals and public institutions had strong interests. Then as now, individuals wanted to build careers: as Peter of Blois, the twelfth-century poet, former law

5. Rüegg, "Themes," 1:21.

student, and future royal courtier put it: "There are two things that drive men hard to the study of jurisprudence; these are the pursuit of offices and the vain passion for fame."[6] Well, no doubt personal ambition can be distorted by a lust for status and the limelight; but there's nothing wrong as such with individuals wanting to find a social role in which to exercise their talents—and that natural, grassroots desire was undoubtedly one of the inspirations behind the founding of the earliest universities.

But then, as now, there was also top-down inspiration. Popes and bishops needed educated pastors, and they and kings needed educated administrators and lawyers capable of developing and embedding nationwide systems. It is a bit of a puzzle as to why a provincial market town such as Oxford ever came to grow a university in the twelfth century. But one answer is that by the 1180s Oxford had become a seat of the royal administration and of the ecclesiastical courts.[7] Universities have played a public role from the beginning, and they have continued to do so. Since the nineteenth century university professors in many European countries have been part of the civil service; and after 1848 students in Tsarist universities were kitted out in quasi-military uniform.[8]

So the universities were never simply the children of an ivory-tower love of knowledge for knowledge's sake. They were always partly fuelled by practical concerns, whether the concerns of private individuals or of those with public responsibility. But practical concerns as such are not mean and grubby or intellectually untaxing. Law is a very important social institution, which, theologians claim, mirrors the constitution of the cosmos, and on its practice depend important human goods such as social peace, the support of public and private virtue, and justice. The practice of medicine, of course, serves the good of physical health. And the practice of theology serves the good of spiritual and moral health. So there we have three of the four faculties of a typical medieval university—Theology, Law, and Medicine—each of them ordered to educate students in the principles of a practice designed to serve one or more human goods. (If you're wondering about the fourth, the Faculty of Arts, its concern was with developing the verbal, logical, mathematical—and later, general philosophical—understanding basic to studies in the other, higher faculties.)

6. Quoted in ibid., 10.
7. Ibid., 13.
8. Rüegg, "Themes," 3:10.

So our earliest universities were considerably fuelled by practical concerns for certain human and public goods. With the sole exception of medicine, however, they tended to fight shy of technical, or what they called "mechanical," concerns. So no medieval university sported a Faculty of Architecture or a Faculty of Agriculture. Why? I assume that this reflects the infection of medieval Christendom by an Aristotelian disdain for the servile arts—the merely technical skills that slaves, rather than citizens, have to exercise. I say "infection" here because Christianity's Jewish matrix and its own socially humble origins should have immunized it against such class snobbery. Contrast Aristotle with this passage from the Wisdom literature of the Jewish, and then Christian Scriptures: "[The workman and craftsman, the blacksmith and potter:] all these put their trust in their hands and each is skilled at his own craft. A town could not be built without them, there would be no settling, no traveling. But they are not required at the council, they do not hold high rank in the assembly. They do not sit on the judicial bench, and have no grasp of law. They are not remarkable for culture or sound judgement, and are not found among the inventors of maxims. *But they maintain the fabric of the world . . .*" (Sir 38.35–39a). Except in the case of doctors, the medieval university seems to have forgotten this piece of biblical wisdom. And it was only in the post-Reformation, Lutheranized, modern period that the technical sciences began to find a proper home in higher education. So in the mid-nineteenth century the industrialized cities of northern England began to sprout university colleges with close links to local industries. For example, The University of Leeds was heavily oriented to the research and training needs of the textile industry until the latter was decimated in the 1980s. And even a university with an impeccable medieval pedigree such as Glasgow was pleased in 1889 to accept the endowment of a chair of shipbuilding (or "naval architecture," to give it its upwardly mobile title).

Universities have never been simply ivory towers. They have never simply sought knowledge for knowledge's sake. And they have no need to apologize for that. Indeed, I myself harbor doubts about the academic's typical defensive gambit of asserting the intrinsic value of knowledge. It is not that I doubt the intrinsic good of knowledge of the truth. After all, the notion of human beings losing sleep, missing meals, even risking their lives in pursuit of the truth, or in defense of it, is a perfectly familiar one. But some truths are surely rather less valuable than others. There is a truth about the number of times that the surname Biggar appears in the Birmingham telephone directory, and not even I can muster a whole lot of interest in that. It is a truth, of course, but it hardly matters. I am with Comrade Zhdanov on this: as from the artist, so from the academic, an account is needed of why what he does *matters*—and how it matters, how it *speaks*, beyond the realm of his own private fancy.

Such an account is not difficult for natural scientists to render, given the close relationship between the natural sciences on the one hand, and the good of physical health and the means of life-saving or -securing or -enhancing technology. Nor is it very difficult for social and human scientists, given the direct bearing of their disciplines on the psychological health of individuals and the social health of societies.

Explaining why the Arts and Humanities matter, however, is more difficult. Among the doctoral dissertations in the Humanities being examined in Oxford in 2009 was one on the function and status of landscape painting in late-sixteenth and seventeenth-century Rome, another on the Mamluk historiography of the Fatimids, and another titled "Flirting with fame: Byron and his female readers." Now no doubt these topics fascinate those whose hobby it is to study them, but why exactly should they matter to anyone else? And why should public money be spent on them—as opposed to, say, being spent on more helicopters for our hard-pressed troops in Afghanistan? If there is a robust answer, it does not lie immediately to hand—as witness the Arts and Humanities Research Council's strangulated attempts to articulate it in the face of the shamelessly utilitarian "impact agenda" of the late Brown government.[9]

This dismaying inarticulacy is one reason why, six years ago, Britain's then Secretary of State for Education, Charles Clarke, himself a graduate in mathematics and economics, felt no embarrassment in opining that public funding should only support academic subjects of "clear usefulness," saying, "I don't mind there being some medievalists around for ornamental purposes, but there is no reason for the state to pay for them."[10] It is also the reason why in June 2009 Lord Mandelson's delivery of university affairs entirely into the hands of a new Department of Business, Innovation, and Skills provoked no public outcry. And it

---

9. I refer to three documents: the "AHRC Impact Strategy," the "Impact Assessment Position Paper," and "Examples of Economic Impact."

10. "Clarke dismisses medieval historians," *The Guardian*, 9 May 2004. To be fair, Clarke himself denied saying this.

explains why—notwithstanding the fact that David Willetts, the new Minister of State for Universities and Science, has publicly denounced the "bleak" utilitarian view of higher education and asserted its social, civic importance[11]—the new Coalition's Programme for Government only ever mentions universities in connection with "building a strong and innovative economy" and fostering stronger links with industry.[12]

To ask a scholar of history, literature, or theology to explain why what he does *matters* is one thing. To ask that he demonstrate its *usefulness* is quite another. "Usefulness" connotes a shrunken, materialistic, utilitarian understanding of human goods—an understanding that has sunk deep into the Anglo-Saxon mentality. In contemporary colloquial English, when we talk about "goods," we're referring to things such as washing machines and sofas and motorcars and plasma TVs. Up until the modern era, however, the word *goods* encompassed the likes of beauty and justice and friendship and communion with God—meanings that now survive among us only in university departments of moral theology and (to the extent that they follow Aristotle rather than Jeremy Bentham) moral philosophy. Compared to this rich, colorful, and dignifying vision of human flourishing, our modern utilitarian view is pinched, anemic, and degrading. This secularized Protestant perspective is embedded in the fate of other words in the English language. Take for example *otium*, the Latin noun that the medievals used to refer positively to the freedom to reflect, appreciate, and admire: this has come down to us as the disdainful adjective *otiose*—meaning "unemployed," "idle," "sterile." And the medieval word for the basic university course in the liberal rational and public arts of thinking, writing, and persuading—*trivium*—has reached us as "trivial." (I dearly wanted to be able to convert this etymological point into a hat trick by sharing my discovery

11. In an inaugural lecture to the Sheffield University Academy of Public Service on 31 October 2007, David Willetts reckoned the "utilitarian view of higher education [to be] a bleak one," and argued that a university education should be about critical thinking and learning to live with cultural difference and not just about "the practical skills that will aid economic growth"—it "should fit students not just for the workplace but also for society." More recently, in his first keynote speech as Minister for Universities and Science on 20 May 2010, he reaffirmed his earlier view: "there is enormous value in further and higher education which cannot just be captured by utilitarian calculation . . . Too often, politicians have taken the economic value which flows from much academic research and then treated it as the only possible motive for the research. I am not going to make that mistake."

12. *The Coalition*, "31: Universities and Further Education," 31.

that the word for the other half of the medieval liberal arts course—
quadrivium—had given us "drivel." Disappointingly, the Oxford English
Dictionary supplied no hydrogen for that speculative balloon.)

In modern, hard-nosed, utilitarian Anglo-Saxon cultures, it is quite
difficult to get a hearing for the serious worth of anything that cannot
be measured. This is not quite as true in other Western countries. In
Ireland, at least since the late nineteenth century, national identity defined itself over and against the ruthless, materialistic utilitarianism of
the globalizing British Empire.[13] (And if you have read the fine, haunting
novel about Henry James, *The Master*, which was published a few years
ago by one of contemporary Ireland's foremost men of letters, Colm
Toibín, you will notice that he attributes very similar views of Edwardian
Britain to Henry's post-Puritan, New England brother, William.)[14] One
of the extraordinary, concrete public expressions of this Irish resistance
to Anglo-Saxon materialism is that to this day in Ireland, if you can get
yourself registered as an "artist," then you pay no income tax. (Which
might go some way toward explaining why every second person I met
when I was teaching at Trinity College Dublin seemed to be writing and
publishing poetry.) Ireland, then, furnishes some hope that, even in this
day and age, a national society can *publicly* recognize human and social
goods that are beyond measurement.

So while it is difficult in a heavily utilitarian culture such as ours
to make a case for academic activity that does not matter much *economically*, it nevertheless belongs to the moral vocation of university

13. Garvin, *Nationalist Revolutionaries*, chap. 6, "Ideological Themes of Separatist
Nationalism." On p. 125, Garvin quotes Maud Gonne: "England is in decadence. The
men who formerly made her greatness, the men from the country districts, have disappeared, they have been swallowed up by the great black manufacturing cities; they have
been flung into the crucible where gold is made. Today the giants of England are the
giants of finance and the Stock Exchange . . ."

14. Tóibin, *The Master*. On 335, Tóibin has William James address his brother thus:
"The English have no spiritual life, only a material one . . . The only striving is material
striving . . . You do not have in your possession the knowledge which Dickens or George
Eliot or Trollope or Thackeray possessed of the mechanics of English greed. There is no
yearning in England, no crying out for truth." It might be a complete coincidence that
James, a post-Puritan New Englander, shared the view of many late nineteenth-century
Irish nationalists. I note, however, that Tóibin has James's condemnation of English
materialism follow shortly after another passage in which he criticizes England's mis-
management of Ireland (330). I also note that James lived in Boston, a major center of
Irish settlement in the United States. My interpretation assumes, of course, that Tóibin
has not simply invented James's view.

"professors" (in the broad sense of any professional academic) in the Arts and Humanities to do just that. It is a major part of their prophetic responsibility to remember and to articulate what, beyond serving the economy, is the good of studying histories and literatures, religions and cultures, theologies and philosophies, music and drama. Why are these not just trivial, otiose ornaments? Why are they not self-indulgent recreations sponging off the public purse? Why do they matter for human and public flourishing?

These are the questions. So what are the answers? Let me inaugurate two lines of thought. First of all, one valuable gift that the Arts and Humanities make is to introduce us to foreign worlds—worlds made strange by the passage of time; present worlds structured by the peculiar grip of unfamiliar languages; worlds alien to us in their social organization and manners, their religious and philosophical convictions.

Introduction to these foreign worlds confers a substantial benefit: the benefit of distance from our own world, and thereby the freedom to ask questions of it that we could never otherwise have conceived. In foreign worlds, past and present, people see and love and do things differently; and in reflecting upon that difference, it might occur to us from time to time that they see and love and do things *better*.

So, one precious contribution of the Arts and Humanities is their furnishing public discourse with the critical resources of an understanding of foreign worlds, resources vital for social and cultural and moral renewal—a renewal that deserves at least an equal place alongside scientific and technological innovation.

That is my first thought.

My second thought is this: The Arts and Humanities not only introduce us to foreign worlds; they teach us to treat them well. They teach us to read strange and intractable texts with patience and care; to meet alien ideas and practices with humility, docility, and charity; to draw alongside foreign worlds before we set about—as we must—judging them. They train us in the practice of honest dialogue, which respects those distant from us in time or place as potential prophets, who might yet speak a new word about what's true and good and beautiful—about what makes for human flourishing.

A commitment to the truth, humility, a readiness to be taught, patience, carefulness, charity: all of these are moral virtues that inform the intellectual discipline into which the Arts and Humanities induct their students; all of these are moral virtues of which public discourse, whether in the media or in Parliament or in Congress, displays no obvious surplus; all of these are moral virtues without which this country and others may get to become a "knowledge economy," but will not get to become a "wisdom society."

And public decisions that, being unwise, are careless with the truth, arrogant, unteachable, impatient, and uncharitable, will be *bad* decisions—and bad decisions cause real damage to social institutions and the individuals who inhabit them.

What I am saying, then, is that in addition to providing talented individuals with the opportunity to grow their gifts and find a social role to exercise them; in addition to producing qualified applicants for positions in legal practice and in public administration; in addition to training the labor force to staff a high-tech, service-oriented economy; and in addition to generating new scientific knowledge with technological or commercial applications, universities exist to form individuals and citizens in certain virtues—virtues that are not just intellectual, but are also social and political.

Historically, Oxbridge—with its medieval heritage of small college communities and their chapels, and with its tutorial system—has recognized that higher education is properly not just about the communication of information or ideas by lecture, nor just about technical apprenticeship, but about the morally formative influence of tutor on student. It has recognized that this relationship does have a certain pastoral quality to it, that this need not be paternalistic, and that it can develop into equal friendship—as in my experience, and no doubt in Tim Gorringe's too, it not infrequently does.[15] This was certainly the ideal and the practice of John Henry Newman, of whom it was reported that when he was a Tutorial Fellow at Oriel College in the late 1820s, "he cultivated relations [with students], not only of intimacy, but of friendship, and almost of equality."[16] And when he came to found his Catholic University in Dublin, Newman was adamant that its tutors would represent "that union of intellectual and moral influence, the separation of which is the evil of the age."[17]

15. I served as Chaplain and Fellow of Oriel College, Oxford from 1990–99, Tim as Chaplain and Fellow of St John's College, Oxford from 1986–96.

16. Ker, *John Henry Newman*, 38.

17. Ibid., 412.

Well, that separation is even more the evil of the age now. In our present *Zeitgeist*, dominated as it is by a libertarian, atomistic kind of liberalism, the idea that any individual has responsibility for the moral formation of any other—and especially an adult for a late adolescent who is not her own child—is not only implausible but positively suspect. Indeed, if I were to make the suggestion to my academic colleagues that they have a responsibility for the moral formation of their students, I would wager that most of them would meet it with a snort of indignation against such insufferable, Victorian paternalism. And yet, if it is true that university education—especially in the Arts and Humanities—is *not* about the growth of certain intellectual, social, and civic virtues, then it does become very hard to see, I think, why the study of landscape painting or medieval North African history or Byron's reception among women is anything but a private, and rather frivolous indulgence.

Comrade Zhdanov was right. If they do not have a moral vocation, then the Arts and Humanities are doomed to degrade themselves, if not by serving the private whims of cosseted intellectuals, then by trying to justify public investment in terms of their contribution to the tourist and entertainment industries. I hope that such a dismal prospect repels us; but if it does repel us, then it should also move us to turn around and face a sharp question about ourselves and about the culture that we allow to prevail among us: How have we become the kind of people who, presented with the claim that university teachers bear responsibility for the moral formation of their students, would typically snap back, "So who made me my brother's moral keeper?"

Bibliography

AHRC. "AHRC Impact Strategy." n.d. Online: http://www.ahrc.ac.uk/About/Policy/ Documents/impact strategy.pdf.
———."Examples of Economic Impact from AHRC-funded Projects." n.d. (But between 2008 and summer 2009.) Online: http://www.ahrc.ac.uk/FundedResearch/ Documents/Examples of Impact from projects.pdf.
———. "Impact Assessment Position Paper." May 2006. Online: http://www.ahrc.ac.uk/ FundedResearch/Documents/Impact Position Paper.pdf.
Biggar, Nigel. "What Are Universities For?" *Standpoint* 24 (2010) 76–79.
The Coalition: Our Programme for Government. 2010. Online: http://www.cabinetoffice. gov.uk/media/409088/pfg_coalition.pdf.
Garvin, Tom. *Nationalist Revolutionaries in Ireland 1858–1928*. Dublin: Gill & Macmillan, 2005.
Gorringe, Timothy J. *God's Theatre: A Theology of Providence*. London: SCM, 1991.

Ker, Ian. *John Henry Newman: A Biography*. Oxford: Oxford University Press, 1988.

OECD. "Review of National Policies for Education: Review of Higher Education in Ireland." Examiners' Report, EDU/EC (2004) 14. Online: http://www.hea.ie/en/webfm_send/877.

Palmer, Tony, director. *Testimony*. Isolde Films/Channel Four Films, 1988.

Rüegg, Walter. "Themes." In *A History of the University in Europe*, edited by Walter Rüegg. Vol. 1, *Universities in the Middle Ages*, edited by Hilde de Ridder-Symoens, 3–31. Cambridge: Cambridge University Press, 1992.

———. "Themes." In *A History of the University in Europe*. Vol. 3, *Universities in the Nineteenth and Early Twentieth Centuries (1800–1945)*, edited by Walter Rüegg, 3–31. Cambridge: Cambridge University Press, 2004.

Tóibín, Colm. *The Master*. London: Picador, 2005.

Willetts, David. First speech as Minister for Universities and Science, 20 May 2010. Online: http://www.bis.gov.uk/news/speeches/david-willetts-keynote-speech.

———. Inaugural lecture to the Sheffield University Academy of Public Service, 31 October 2007. Online: http://www.davidwilletts.co.uk/2007/10/31/student-experience/.

18

Theology, Happiness, and Public Policy

ADRIAN THATCHER

GOVERNANCE, RELIGION, AND HAPPINESS

Secular theory, having failed spectacularly in its prediction of the demise of religion, now seeks to accommodate it within an overall secular framework. That is why the project *Religion, Justice and Well Being*[1] explored "how governments' promotion of the well-being of its citizens can be achieved in a multi-faith society *where many people's well-being has a significant religious component.* Exactly how should the religious dimension of (some) citizens' well-being shape law, policy, and institutional design?"[2] It was observed that "political debate on religious matters involves higher stakes than ever before." It was thought "unarguable that religion is now a major part of the UK's policy agenda." One of the four aims of the project was "to uncover how Christian, Muslim, Jewish, Hindu, and other religions (and their sub-communities) con-

---

1. This essay brings together two presentations the author gave in a series of projects funded by the Arts and Humanities (AHRC) and Economic and Social Science Research Councils (ESRC), titled *Religion, Justice and Well Being*. The first was given at a colloquium at the University of Wales, Newport, on 25 April 2008; the second at a colloquium at the University of Central Lancashire, on 17 October 2009.

2. *Religion, Justice and Well Being*, emphasis added.

ceive their proper role in policy-making in the UK, and how legislators have responded to this."

There are, of course, assumptions here, prior to any exploration of the territory to be explored. It seems to be supposed (albeit fairly) that everyone wants well-being. (I take "well-being" to be a common synonym for happiness. "Thriving" and "flourishing" have similar meanings, and also convey a sense of the optimization of the human being.) Over time an empirical generalization has become a necessary truth. There is sufficient clarity about well-being for it to be a universal goal or good. There is no longer room for doubt that the promotion of the well-being of citizens is a primary, or even *the* primary task of government.

However, there is a snag in this seemingly straightforward vision of the happiness-aspiring and happiness-producing society. Large numbers of citizens, unreasonably and even truculently, rely on, promote, or include religious beliefs and practices in their quest for well-being. That gives governments a headache. They must be seen to be dealing, but evenhandedly and without prejudice, with this awkward phenomenon: the diverse and persistent religiosity of many of their citizens. Are religious institutions to be dismissed as unreasonable or elevated as partners in the creation of the Big Society?

One possible treatment for this headache, prescribed by the civil servants and their politically correct advisors, and offered for consideration to religious providers of moral and secular goods, was this: place all religious people, and their different traditions, within a common framework suggested by the unanimous pursuit of well-being. In the United Kingdom, this treatment was prescribed by New Labour. Religious people, in seeking God, are really seeking happiness via an unrecommended religious route. This is what they are actually doing, even if they do not know it. If they cannot be deterred, they can at least be contained. Like all moral thinking, which is a means to an end, religious thinking is at root no different. There is also an ancillary advantage in the treatment—a positive side effect. Stubborn religious differences, both within and between diverse religious traditions, are conveniently elided. It is assumed, without argument, that there is a common value, the pursuit of happiness, around which the cooperation of all citizens, religious and secular, may be taken for granted. So effective is this panacea for interreligious disagreement that all citizens, religious and nonreligious, can agree with each other about what finally matters: happiness.

Whereas a century ago a complacent religious liberalism assumed that all religions led to the same God, now its political successor assumes all religions lead to the same end: happiness.

THE RISE AND RISE OF THE HAPPINESS PRINCIPLE

A new coalition government in the UK seems to be taking a different tack. As it massively reduces its spending on welfare, it will instead court and flatter religious people, their traditions and institutions, as partners in the building of the Big Society. Religious people, not just Christians, have good reason to question the elevation of happiness as an ultimate human value, and to reconcile it with the practice of their religion (which Christians call "discipleship").

Of course people will say they want to be happy.[3] Would they ever say they wanted to be *un*happy? Cicero assumed *beati certe omnes esse volumus* (Obviously everyone wants to be happy).[4] But that is Roman thought. The pursuit of happiness is embedded in the Enlightenment, which is one of the reasons why so many contemporary theologians are suspicious of it. By the second half of the eighteenth century, happiness was, and had to be, measurable. The philosophy that measured it was Utilitarianism, and Bentham's "felicific calculus" provided a means.[5] When John Stuart Mill announced a different version of Utilitarianism in 1861, he deliberately called it a "creed," and a "theory of life": "The creed which accepts as the foundation of morals, utility, or the Greatest Happiness Principle, holds that actions are right in proportion as they tend to promote happiness, wrong as they tend to produce the reverse of happiness . . . the theory of life on which this theory of morality is grounded [is] that pleasure, and freedom from pain, are the only things desirable as ends."[6]

While some of the "most estimable" minds have an "inveterate dislike" for the Principle, and "many Stoic, as well as Christian elements required to be included" within it, Mill insists that all rival moral theories are reducible to his own. Love, justice, the virtues, in fact the whole

---

3. Some of the material in this section appeared in an earlier form in Thatcher, "Religion."

4. A sentence from Cicero's lost *Hortensius*, which stirred Augustine to philosophical endeavors (O'Donovan, "Romulus's City," 5).

5. Bentham, *Introduction*, chap. 4.

6. Mill, *Utilitarianism*, chap. 2.

moral universe, point in their contributions to happiness and the avoidance of pain. Indeed Mill thought he had discovered the one universal, moral law, the Greatest Happiness Principle, which was importantly comparable with the discovery of physical laws in the same period.

There is now a vast "happiness literature," sprawling economics, politics, psychology, philosophy, ethnography, psychotherapy, the sociology of institutions and of management, criminology, mental health, and spirituality. A research project, publicly funded,[7] has produced a single volume containing essays on happiness from all these perspectives, in their interactions with theology and religion.[8] The essays (including one from the present author) "explore the religious dimensions to a number of key features of wellbeing, including marriage, crime and rehabilitation, work, inequality, mental health, environment, participation, institutional theory, business and trade."[9]

Happiness is here to stay, fixed in academic research agendas (few of which appear aware of the recent vacuous intellectual history of the topic, or its classical antecedent) and the aspirations of individuals in consumer societies. According to the incontrovertible Richard Layard, the pursuit of happiness is now a "new science."[10] Layard thinks that "many arguments have been brought against this philosophy, but none of them stand up."[11]

HAPPINESS-CRITIQUE

But the Christian tradition, following Augustine, is deeply *wary* of happiness, requiring instead renunciation and charity. Virtue and felicity, taught Augustine, are not credible deities in the Roman pantheon: rather, "they are gifts of the true God," and their connectedness to each other and to God is demonstrated by Augustine's rhetorical question: "Furthermore, where there is virtue and felicity, what need is there to seek anything else? If men are not satisfied with these, what will suffice them? For surely, virtue includes all that ought to be done, felicity all

---

7. The AHRC and the ESRC, funded the project "Promoting Greater Human Wellbeing: Interacting the Happiness Hypothesis and Religion" (2007–2009).

8. Atherton, Steedman, and Graham, *Practices of Happiness*.

9. Ibid., i.

10. Layard, *Happiness*.

11. Ibid., 225.

that ought to be desired."[12] Augustine inveighed against the elevation of happiness over other values, and its separation from "true religion."[13] Rather, he taught, self-denial is a requirement of any Christian disciple.

There is little doubt that a similar polemic against the elevation of happiness, and its separation from virtue and from God in late modern societies, can derive much from Augustine's analyses. The word does not appear in the King James Version of the Bible, showing that at the beginning of the modern period the pursuit of happiness was still over the moral horizon. (When I mentioned during a research colloquium that I had consulted an Authorized Version concordance and found this all-important word missing, I was greeted with laughter, presumably at the thought of a contributor trying to discover what the Bible said about happiness. But my point was a subtler one. In 1611 the pursuit of happiness was not obviously a supreme value, and it may not have occurred to the translators to use it.)

Undergraduate philosophy students have little difficulty in unpicking all this. The difficulties of defining and measuring happiness; the reduction of all moral values to one; the justification for allowing significant amounts of unhappiness and pain for some in pursuing happiness for others; and, notoriously, the inability of agents to calculate the consequences of their actions accurately or, indeed, at all: these are some of the fatal criticisms of the theory. Does anyone believe in consequentialist theories of moral action after the Iraq war? The puzzle is why the theory has persisted given its many flaws. Is it because people *want* to believe it? Does truth cease to matter? Does the theory coincide too well with the aspirations of individuals in capitalist societies for it to be dispensed with? Is the happiness principle a new and successful *meme*,[14] a cultural symbol, replicating itself in the soil of late capitalist, post-Christian moral discourse? Has it successfully eliminated its rivals as they fail to mutate and find favor in advanced secular societies?

Layard's assertion that arguments against the new science do not add up itself receives no supporting argument. It can be taken as self-evident, a necessary truth for all liberal societies to embrace. Like Mill before him, he thinks there are no transcendent sources of happiness worth looking for, although religious instrumentalities may offer some

12. Augustine, *City of God*, 159.

13. Ibid., 163.

14. Dawkins, *Selfish Gene*, 192.

possible help: "there is a range of spiritual practices that help to bring peace of mind, from Buddhist meditation to positive psychology."[15] Religion, chastened, demystified, tolerated, and misrepresented, can rejoice in its new role as an optional provider of therapy for hard-pressed introverts.

Criticisms of the happiness principle are not confined to a few grumpy old theologians. Philip Rieff trenchantly warned, in 1966, that whole capitalist societies were even then being organized as therapeutic cultures, that is, as places where "a sense of well-being has become the end, rather than a by-product of striving after some superior communal end."[16] Where self-actualization beckons, narcissism lurks in its shadow.

Richard Stivers warned that "when religion is associated with happiness it is reduced to the status of a *means* to the end of happiness."[17] He accuses liberal Protestantism of having achieved this transformation by "inverting New Testament teachings about the suffering and rejection that a witness to Christ would necessarily encounter." Alasdair MacIntyre (before his conversion to Catholicism) famously and trenchantly showed why happiness "is indeed a pseudo-concept available for a variety of ideological uses, but no more than that."[18] Thirty years after *After Virtue*, his warning remains timely: "the use of a conceptual fiction in a good cause does not make it any less of a fiction."[19]

More recently, Terry Eagleton locates the pursuit of happiness within the movement away from objective morality to subjective preference, and presses the epistemological question, hugely and willfully neglected, how we know we are happy even when we think we are, warning, "You can . . . be mistaken about whether you are flourishing, and someone else may be more wisely perceptive about the matter than you yourself. This is one important sense in which morality is objective."[20] The prospect of delusion, of "false-consciousness" both in the seeking and the apparent realization of happiness, cannot be eliminated. One might therefore wonder why, given the avalanche of criticisms of happiness like these, it refuses to be buried.

15. Layard, *Happiness*, 230.

16. Rieff, *Triumph*, 261.

17. Stivers, *Culture of Cynicism*, 64, emphasis in original.

18. MacIntyre, *After Virtue*, 62.

19. Ibid.

20. Eagleton, *After Theory*, 129.

HAPPINESS, RIGHTS, AND COMMITMENTS: A NEW MORAL LANGUAGE?

The arrival of happiness and its colonization of human aspiration throws theological thought into various dilemmas. One is about social action; the other is about communication. The first dilemma runs like this: on the one hand, happiness is not the goal of life in Christian faith; on the other hand, the shaping of public policy around, yes, the "delivery" of happiness, has brought about many benefits that coincide very closely with what social theologians want to see. The second dilemma runs like this: on the one hand, if theologians leap on to the happiness bandwagon, do they not connive with their intellectual marginalization? What does that say about the apparent thinness of their sources and traditions? Don't they have any better stories to tell? On the other hand, if they do not utilize the moral and social vocabularies of the secular world, how can they expect to communicate beyond the shrinking linguistic world where the language of theology is still spoken?

These dilemmas are acute. For Christians, happiness is emphatically not the goal of life; nor is their account of right and wrong determined by the fallible calculation of felicific consequences. The meaning of life is rather to be found in the love of God, of one's neighbor, of one's self, and even of one's enemy. Christian theology shares with many social critics a deep misgiving about the value accorded to happiness. Christians are to strive for a worldly holiness, a becoming like God in God's self-gift to the world. They belong to the Body of Christ incarnating itself in the world for the world's sake. They share in the work of God in reconciling the world to Godself, the world, and everything in it. They are citizens of the Reign of God. They believe that God is Spirit, the Giver of Life. Where there is abundant life, there is God the Spirit. Where there is love, there is God. *Ubi caritas, ibi deus est.*

Yet if this hope is more than empty rhetoric there must also be recognition that many secular organizations, which do not use this language, are rigorous in their pursuit of the happiness of people. In my recent theological work around marriage, families, and children, I have come across several areas where theological and secular aspirations for human beings overlap. Here are three: children's happiness; children's rights; and stable marriages.

Layard, chief apostle of the new science of happiness, is also the coauthor (with Judy Dunn) of *A Good Childhood*, a report in the United

Kingdom for the Children's Society, a former Church of England charity. The new science of happiness can be very family- and child-centered. Seven key themes of childhood were explored in the report: "family, friends, lifestyle, values, schooling, mental health and inequality."[21] Religious readers should be careful to distinguish between inattention to a *religious* account of values, and inattention to values, for the report is actually value-rich. Children, the report says, most want and need love and respect, while "[t]he greatest responsibility is on parents. The most important act which two people ever perform is to bring another being into the world. This is an awesome responsibility and, when they have a child, the parents should have a long-term commitment to each other as well as to the welfare of the child."[22] *A Good Childhood* shows how a secular agenda can still be, from a theological point of view, prophetic and transformative. Its impact lies partly in its exposure of the actual but preventable unhappiness of millions of children.

Kathleen Marshall and Paul Parvis have recently defended the rights of children. Rights, in addition to human rights, are assignable to children. They summarize the 1989 United Nations Convention on the Rights of the Child by the "three *Ps*"—"protection—from abuse, neglect, and exploitation; provision—of services to promote survival and development; and participation—in decisions about matters that affect them."[23] They make the case for children's rights overwhelmingly.[24] Of course, rights lack an ultimate rational foundation, and philosophers from Bentham onwards have been able to justify their verdict that they represent "nonsense on stilts." There will always be disagreement about which rights claims are allowable as rights. And an appeal to their rights has not yet halted the enforced enlistment of young boys into African militias, the widespread exploitation of child labor, particularly in India, or the appalling crime of clitoridectomy on millions of young girls, especially in Africa. But these failures of rights provide no reason for failing to endorse them theologically.

There may be some further discussion about how the theological endorsement of children's rights might run. I have suggested that the foundation of children's rights lies with the Christ Child who, while fully

21. Layard and Dunn, *Good Childhood*, xii.

22. Ibid., 155.

23. Marshall and Parvis, *Honouring Children*, 13.

24. Thatcher, *Theology and Families*, 152–66.

God, became a Child.[25] But the best means of endorsement is a separate question. Marshall and Parvis point out that the extent of the acceptance of human rights among governments, politicians, lawyers, and child advocates is very remarkable. The spread of rights language might be considered to be one of the greatest achievements of that most violent of all centuries, an outpouring of hope after the shattering effects of two world wars. There is no other aspirational declaration of comparable influence or scope. Rights language intends the protection of the vulnerable, which alone should secure the support of all Christians. Given the teaching of Jesus about children, how could Christians not come to the conclusion that global organizations such as UNICEF, and local attempts to protect children, are agents of the Reign of God, even unwitting ones, in their transforming work? The teaching of Jesus about the place of children in the Reign of God supports whatever arrangements best assist the thriving of children.[26]

A third example is the extensive empirical research in the United States about the likely happiness-producing consequences of living in particular family forms.[27] Family relationships, family economics, physical health, and emotional health and well-being were examined, and the conclusion repeatedly reached, that lifelong marriage is better for children, for men, for women, and for society, than alternatives to marriage. It was unnecessary to trawl through the standard treatments of happiness to reach an appropriate stipulative definition of happiness in any of these cases, for the evidence was in every case comparative. Outcomes were measured against alternatives in all four areas (and their many sub-areas).

John Witte Jr. was quick to coin the phrase "the health paradigm of marriage," in relation to the results.[28] The study provided empirical confirmation of standard Christian teaching. Its conclusions were "both very new and very old": new because it was validated by empirical secular research, old because "the West has had a long and thick overlapping consensus that marriage is good, does good, and has goods both for the couple and for the children."[29] Marriage need no longer be favored on

25. Ibid., 157–64.

26. Ibid., 127.

27. For the detail, see ibid., 115–26; see also Almond, *Fragmenting Family*.

28. Witte, "Goods and Goals."

29. Ibid., 88.

grounds of social convention, religious teaching, or ideological procla-mation alone. It could be shown independently to provide positive ben-efits for couples, and especially for their children, irrespective of faith or political commitments.

The "health paradigm" of marriage has been regularly reiterated, and the statistics annually updated by the Institute for American Values, whose 2010 report on "The State of Our Unions" bemoans the "retreat from marriage among the moderately educated middle" (*sic*) that "makes the lives of mothers harder and drives fathers further away from fami-lies. It increases the odds that children from Middle America will drop out of high school, end up in trouble with the law, become pregnant as teenagers . . ."[30] Here then is another example of family research yielding strong conclusions that have far-reaching social and moral implications. When religious people (whose record on intact marriages is little better than those with no religious faith) hear that marriage is an indispens-able social institution, they should not content themselves with the re-sponse that they were right all along about marriage being God's will for families. The values at stake are *human* values. The conclusions *should* influence government policy.[31] The research impacts on the present ar-gument because it shows that there are millions of people who commit themselves to each other for life, who are loving, devoted parents of any children they have, and who do all this without the benefit of religious understanding or practice. Their lives are nonetheless belief- and value-laden. In Layard's own words, they *do* "have a long-term commitment to each other as well as to the welfare of the child."

A THEOLOGY OF HAPPINESS?

Can theology make peace with happiness? Can there be a theology of happiness? In answering these questions, Charles Taylor and Tim Gorringe will be our guides.

Taylor finds in Buddhism and Christianity the following similarity: "that the believer . . . is called on to make a profound inner break with the *goals of flourishing* in their own case: they are called on, that is, to detach themselves from their own flourishing, to the point of the extinc-tion of self in one case, or to that of renunciation of human fulfilment

---

30. Institute for American Values, *The State of Our Unions*, xi.

31. Almond, *Fragmenting Family*.

to serve God in the other."[32] However, while Christ clearly renounced human fulfillment, "God wills ordinary human flourishing, and a great part of what is reported in the Gospels consists in Christ making this possible for the people whose afflictions he heals."[33] The history of Christendom reveals a tension between flourishing and renunciation. Prior to secularization and modernity, believers were "called on . . . to detach themselves from their own flourishing." Nowadays "new conditions of belief" exist where this tension changes: "for the first time in history a purely self-sufficient humanism came to be a widely available option . . . a humanism accepting no final goals beyond human flourishing, nor any allegiance to anything else beyond this flourishing."

Once, then, there was almost no option for a person to be a humanist and an agnostic. Now it is the default position. Within these new conditions the tensions between renunciation and fulfillment eases. Believers can both *affirm* human flourishing, while there remains for them "the sense that there is some good higher than, beyond human flourishing." And Christians can still "think of this as agape, the love which God has for us, and which we can partake of through his power."[34] Secularization doesn't make discipleship easier. But it provides an inescapable background where belief in God, now an option only, is pursued (if it is pursued at all): "secularity is a condition in which our experience of and search for fullness occurs; and this is something we all share, believers and unbelievers alike."[35]

The present argument leads toward conclusions already reached by Tim in his discussions of culture and human rights. Whether happiness is a conceptual fiction or what God wills for all God's creatures, belongs to a wider, long-running argument about the relation between Christ and culture. One hundred pages into his argument, Tim summarizes: "theology is concerned with the whole of human endeavour, and not just with a religious segment."[36] Why? Because "[t]he doctrine of creation teaches us this because all things come from God, and nothing is outwith God's sway, and the lordship of Christ in the same way." "[T]here are no autonomous areas of human activity not subject to theological

32. Taylor, *Secular Age*, 17, emphasis added.
33. Ibid.
34. Ibid., 18–19.
35. Ibid., 19.
36. Gorringe, *Furthering Humanity*, 102.

appraisal." And because God the Spirit is the life-enhancing inspiration of all culture: "A theology of culture is at the same time a theology of the Spirit, about God active in the historical process, not a God asleep or unconcerned. If God exists then God acts, and that action must call forth results. The life-affirming aspects of culture, I am arguing, are those results."[37]

And Tim takes a similar position to the one taken here about human rights. Theological, philosophical, secular, and Islamic objections to rights are noted. The distinction between dispensing with human rights and recognizing "that the discourse of human rights is inadequate" is well made.[38] "The theological justification for the language of rights . . . has everything to do with the acceptance of a fundamental human dignity in the name of which we protest the treatment of some groups, or individuals, as effectively subhuman . . . To the extent that the language of liberation is a proper way of construing the witness of Scripture, . . . then 'rights' are implicit in the election of the oppressed as well. *Why* has God elected them? Because God hates injustice, seeks liberation and loves the oppressed."[39] Rights language protects the vulnerable, whether children or adults, and so has an inescapable theological dimension to it.

So how can the critiques of happiness be affirmed in the light of the effective, and potentially prophetic and transformative language of happiness and rights? They remain vital in the struggle against the tendencies in all secular thought to reduce the real to the observable, to reduce knowledge to a narrow empiricism, and to elide the facts of difference into a manageable sameness. The world is now described in a multiplicity of languages. Theological language is the human attempt to witness to the Transcendent and to its breaking into the created world. Its *raison d'être* is the enablement of an account of the world with God the Father as its Creator and Sustainer; God the Son as its Redeemer; and God the Spirit as the Source of all its abundant life. God wills the salvation of all that God has made, and that salvation is broad enough to touch the physical, mental, and emotional health of the beings in God's image. It will inevitably be dismissed by those for whom the Transcendent has no reality. But an incarnational faith celebrates the bursting forth of the

37. Ibid.
38. Ibid., 231.
39. Ibid., 232.

Transcendent into human form and flesh, never again to be confined to abstract thought.

Can theological language be spoken, say, to the health professionals who must understand their professional roles in nonreligious terms? Of course it can. They are themselves the means whereby the divine love is communicated to their clients and patients. They may be surprised to hear this as news, still less as good news, but it is importantly true and deserves to be truthfully said. But without much theological pre-understanding it could not be said at all.

Bibliography

Almond, Brenda. *The Fragmenting Family.* Oxford: Oxford University Press, 2006.

Atherton, John, Ian Steedman, and Elaine Graham, editors. *The Practices of Happiness: Political Economy, Religion and Wellbeing.* London: Routledge, 2010.

Augustine. *City of God.* Harmondsworth: Penguin, 1984.

Bentham, Jeremy. *An Introduction to the Principles of Morals and Legislation.* London: T. Payne, 1789.

Dawkins, Richard. *The Selfish Gene.* 2nd ed. Oxford: Oxford University Press, 1989.

Eagleton, Terry. *After Theory.* London: Allen Lane, 2003.

Gorringe, Timothy J. *Furthering Humanity: A Theology of Culture.* Aldershot: Ashgate, 2004.

Institute for American Values and the University of Virginia. *The State of Our Unions 2010.* Online: http://stateofourunions.org/.

Layard, Richard. *Happiness: Lessons from a New Science.* London: Allen Lane, 2005.

Layard, Richard, and Judy Dunn. *A Good Childhood: Searching for Values in a Competitive Age.* London: Penguin, 2009.

MacIntyre, Alasdair. *After Virtue.* London: Duckworth, 1981.

Marshall, Kathleen, and Paul Parvis. *Honouring Children: The Human Rights of the Child in Christian Perspective.* Edinburgh: Saint Andrew, 2004.

Mill, John Stuart. *Utilitarianism.* Reprinted from *Fraser's Magazine.* London, 1863.

O'Donovan, Oliver. "Romulus's City: The Republic without Justice in Augustine's Political Thought." Paper presented at the annual meeting of the Society for the Study of Theology, Durham, UK, April 2008.

Religion, Justice and Well Being [research project]. 2008. Online: http:// religionjusticewellbeing.wordpress.com/about-the-project/.

Rieff, Philip. *The Triumph of the Therapeutic.* New York: Harper & Row, 1966.

Stivers, Richard. *The Culture of Cynicism: American Morality in Decline.* Oxford: Blackwell, 1994.

Taylor, Charles. *A Secular Age.* Cambridge: Harvard University Press, 2007.

Thatcher, Adrian. "Religion, Family Form and the Question of Happiness." In *Practices of Happiness: Political Economy, Religion and Wellbeing,* edited by John Atherton, Ian Steedman, and Elaine Graham, 148–56. London: Routledge, 2010.

———. *Theology and Families.* Oxford: Blackwell, 2007.

Wall, John, et al., editors. *Marriage, Health, and the Professions: If Marriage Is Good for You, What Does This Mean for Law, Medicine, Ministry, Therapy, and Business?* Grand Rapids: Eerdmans, 2002.

Witte, John, Jr. "The Goods and Goals of Marriage: The Health Paradigm in Historical Perspective." In *Marriage, Health, and the Professions: If Marriage Is Good for You, What Does This Mean for Law, Medicine, Ministry, Therapy, and Business?*, edited by John Wall et al., 49–89. Grand Rapids: Eerdmans, 2002.

19

On Finding Ourselves

Theology, Place, and Human Flourishing

ELAINE GRAHAM

TOPOGRAPHICAL HUMANITY

It is interesting to note that Marshall Berman's famous aphorism about the relentless change of modernity was made in response to the redevelopment of his old neighborhood in New York under the modernist planning of Robert Moses. As familiar streets were redeveloped to make way for urban freeways, Berman observed, "I felt a grief that, I can see now, is endemic to modern life . . . All that is solid melts into air."[1] Berman was quoting from Marx and Engels's observation in *The Communist Manifesto* that the rise of the bourgeoisie was ushering in a new world order of capitalist social relations bent on dislodging older hierarchies and traditions in the name of remorseless change.[2] From his own experience, Berman was noting the very same tendency of modernity to sweep away all feelings of belonging, memory, or value in the face of efficiency and function. Berman's grief is for the loss of more than his physical bearings.

1. Berman, *All That Is Solid*, 295.
2. Marx and Engels, *Communist Manifesto*, 83.

This chapter is about being "lost" and "found," and of the significance of space and place for "finding ourselves"—not just on a grid reference, but as fully human. Tim Gorringe's groundbreaking work on culture and the built environment will inform some of my reflection on this, and in particular his understanding of human nature, and human cultural practice, as a dialectic of the material and the metaphysical. As he argued in his book *Furthering Humanity*, culture "is what we make of the world, materially, intellectually and spiritually . . . In constructing the world materially we interpret it, set values on it."[3]

That is both an elegant summary and affirmation of human creativity—one that for Tim is grounded in the nature of the triune God—and an important synthesis of the worlds of material culture, technology, and the built environment with those of language, story, theorizing, and religion as forms of symbolic cultural practice. For some theologians, such a coupling of "immanence" and "transcendence" speaks powerfully of humanity made in the image of God, since the facility for self-transcendence reflects the transcendence of God.[4]

Tim's work has also been influenced by Henri Lefebvre in taking the "spatial turn" in social theory,[5] whereby place and space are not neutral phenomena but describe the interpretative process by which humans invest meaning in their inhabitation of concrete space. As Tim notes, "To be alive is to write contemporary meanings into our environment."[6] This is an account of what I might term "topographical humanity." The philosopher Jeff Malpas has argued for an understanding of philosophy as "topographical," meaning that to be human is to inhabit place and to reflect on experience in a reflexive and dialectical fashion. "Finding place is thus a matter of *finding ourselves*, and to find ourselves we need first to rethink the question of the nature and significance of place."[7] Space, place, and accounts of human flourishing are closely intertwined in the work of many contemporary social theorists, and it is my intention to consider some of them in order to answer further the question

---

3. Gorringe, *Furthering Humanity*, 5.

4. Hefner, *Technology and Human Becoming*; Graham, *Representations of the Post/Human*.

5. Gorringe, *Built Environment*, 26–36.

6. Ibid., 194.

7. Malpas, "Finding Place," 39.

of where—and how—humanity is understood to find authentic being, especially in the context of urban living.

In his work on urban culture and the built environment, Tim is part of a broader movement in contemporary social theory, geography, urban studies, and theology that reflects what is often known as "the spatial turn."[8] Lefebvre's idea of "the right to the city" articulates a critical theory that fuses experiences of spatial dwelling and political activism as linked forms of human self-realization, and represents a powerful exposition of cultural practice—of world-making and meaning-making—as the arena of self-actualization. The right to the city "aims at pointing to the way in which contemporary urban existence must be transformed to make cities for humans."[9] Space is fundamental to the quest to "find ourselves" as fully human subjects. In the face of alienation wrought by the dominance of global capital, can urban communities "find themselves," spatially, politically, and ontologically?

Other writers have focused on the terminology of "home" and "homeplace" as an antidote to what is regarded as the "dislocation" of much urban experience. But here, we move away from a purely historical materialist version towards one that, in secular and theological work alike, looks to elements such as story, tradition, and spirituality as essential ingredients of physical and existential locatedness.

For his part, Tim would argue that we need an account of human flourishing that is rooted in an account of God—and more specifically, God's self-revelation as Trinity. While Lefebvre's account of human flourishing appears to be about autonomy and self-actualization—self-creativity—a theological account would speak not so much about *finding* as *being found*. But it is not only theologians who would say that the vision of the good city needs to be tempered by factors other than human self-interest. How we find ourselves is ultimately about being placed in relationship—both spatial and cosmological—to a range of "Others" across time, culture, and species, but also to a divine horizon.

THE RIGHT TO THE CITY

At the heart of critical urban theory is the critique of the actually existing city and the unmasking of the ways in which its topog-

8. Soja, "Writing the City Spatially," 50–55.
9. Mendieta, "The City to Come," 444.

raphy has been the result of different economic, political, social and cultural processes that are neither *ad hoc* nor inevitable.[10]

Interest in the "right to the city" in contemporary social theory occurs against a suspicion that global economic trends, centered on neoliberal restructuring, are seeing a shift away from social democratic interventions on the part of the local and national State in favor of the growing power of unelected transnational capital. The impact of such global restructuring, it is argued, is felt most acutely in urban contexts, and it is here that the most concerted analysis of the relationship between global capitalism and urban governance has taken place. As the democratic decision-making and fiscal interventionist powers of elected governments are attenuated in favor of the priorities of global capital, attention has turned to urban citizens' ability to influence the political process; and as an antidote to trends of disenfranchisement and marginalization, commentators have focused on Henri Lefebvre's work as a metaphor for the renewal of the democratic process and as a rallying cry for new social movements campaigning for the empowerment of urban communities.

In *The Right to the City* (1968), Lefebvre regarded urbanization as essential for the rise of capitalism. Space does not constitute the "physical arrangements of things," but "spatial patterns of social action and embodied routine."[11] Lefebvre conceived of a threefold configuration of space: perceived space, conceived space, and lived space.[12] "Perceived" space denotes the objective, physical space experienced in daily life; "conceived" space refers to mental constructions or projections of space, often termed "representations of space." "Lived" space is a kind of synthesis of perceived and conceived space, and represents a person's actual experience of space through strategic action that transcends the other two: a *praxis* of reflexivity, inhabitation, and transformation. Lived space (*le vecu*) is that inhabited by *l'homme totale* or the fully self-actualized person. This is the "third space" of imagination and creativity, of self-expression and resistance, encapsulated in "the Moment," akin to a Romantic expression of a free spirit.[13] Such practices are often the workings of marginalized groups who represent alternative styles of life.

10. Ibid., 442.
11. Shields, "Henri Lefebvre," 212.
12. Lefebvre, *Production of Space*.
13. Shields, "Henri Lefebvre."

It creates a "trialectic" of insurgent relations in which "lived space" defies the conceived space of urban planning and redirects the "perceived space" of banal and overdetermined consciousness.

The production of urban space entails the reproduction of prevailing social relations; material and symbolic interact in producing the conditions of urban space. We can perhaps begin to see how the dialectic of "physical" and "metaphysical" culture begins to emerge in Lefebvre's work, whereby the built environment both embodies and shapes the moral imagination. Social relations are inscribed in space: our imaginaries of space inform social practices that construct the material worlds and topographies that accommodate their inhabitants. Thus, the construction of place, as David Harvey states, is highly dependent on the political economy of capitalism that is "necessarily growth oriented, technologically dynamic, and crisis prone."[14]

Like Lefebvre, Harvey characterizes the quintessential quality of capitalism in its attitude to space and place, in the "tension between place-bound fixity and spatial mobility of capital."[15] Capitalism brings about the total homogenization of space, which results in a sense of placelessness; but not only do city landscapes all look the same, they are denuded of their specific function or even of any continuity with their own history. There is a kind of "forgetting," too, to the economic impact of globalization, which in its drive to construct mass-produced space, completely destroys any sense of authentic place.[16]

Lefebvre repudiates any notion of democratic decision-making resting in the workings of liberal political economy. Rather, the generating source lies in the movements of capital that engender the economic relations that underlie the production of urban space. It is grounded in a particular form of Marxist social analysis in which the appropriation of labor value that generates a surplus sufficient to fuel the capital investment necessary for economic growth is reversed by forms of political agency that are a shorthand for the reclamation of ownership of the means of production. By seizing the "right to the city," citizens have the opportunity to contest the very logic of capitalism. "Since the urban

14. Harvey, *Justice*, 295.
15. Ibid.
16. Ibid., 296.

process is a major channel of surplus use, establishing democratic management over its urban deployment constitutes the right to the city."[17]

For Lefebvre, therefore, "the right to the city is like a cry and a demand . . . a transformed and renewed right to urban life."[18] To assert "the
right to the city" is to claim an agency in relation to the symbolic definitions and material configurations of urban space in which economic
relations are produced and reproduced. For topographical humanity,
social exclusion is "to be deprived access to the space in which we can
be properly human."[19] By contrast, "the right to the city" envisages an
alternative political economy, premised on the restoration or reappropriation of ownership and control of urban space and its surplus value
to its citizen-inhabitants. In the process, a challenge to property rights
strikes at the heart of capitalist political economy itself.

While Lefebvre's broad sweep of analysis may be inspirational, and
has given rise to many campaigns for urban land rights and civic participation, we are still presented with the question of how to construct
concrete strategies for getting from "here" to "there."[20] For a politics
concerned with spatiality, for example, it is unclear as to the specific location of political decision-making within the right to the city. At what
level—local, national, global—does such empowerment take place?
Within conventional liberal democracies, the scale of democratic participation is easily identifiable, generally within a hierarchy of electoral
territories. But in a complex global society, would inhabitants of the city
have the right to determine policies in their place of work as well as
residence; or the corporate decision-making of the property developer
who owns their local shopping mall; or for migrant populations to exercise their "rights" in the affairs of their country of origin? This may give
rise to more flexible, meaningful definitions of democratic participation,
in keeping with more mobile, fluid experiences of the "lived space" of
global cities, but complicates models of political accountability and the
workings of liberal democracy.

It is not easy to conceive of these in the abstract, as critics have
noted. There is a tendency to conflate urban inhabitant with the working
class, presumably as a result of Lefebvre's broadly Marxist analysis. Since

17. Harvey, "Right to the City," 37.
18. Lefebvre, *Writings on Cities*, 158.
19. Mendieta, "City to Come," 446.
20. McCann, "Space."

social and economic antagonism, and conflict over urban space rests on the organization of capitalist social relations, then it is the working class who are to be at the vanguard of the challenge to the capitalist city by means of seizure of the right to the city. But in contemporary global cities, characterized by cultural, ethnic, and religious pluralism as well as economic division, is it not also expedient to challenge "the racist city, the patriarchal city, or the heteronormative city, all of which confront inhabitants in their daily lives"?[21] The politics of identity—not only class, but "race," gender, sexual orientation, dis/ability, generation—will complicate the way we think about and practice the right to the city, not least in situations where straightforward assertion of one set of rights may, potentially, conflict with others.

THE RHETORIC OF HUMAN FLOURISHING

How should we read "the right to the city": as a detailed strategy for transforming municipal governance, or as a form of rhetoric about human agency as the basis of human flourishing? There are some grounds for going with the latter. For David Harvey, the right to the city is more than a process of political empowerment; it is an expression of how freedom to exercise agency in pursuit of self-determination lies at the heart of what makes us fully human. "The right to the city is far more than the individual liberty to access urban resources: it is the right to change ourselves by changing the city."[22]

The humanist thrust of Lefebvre's thought is inescapable. The right to the city is more than a political or legal statement of entitlement, but a manifesto on behalf of human self-determination. It speaks of "substantive moral promises" from the authorities that go beyond specific contractual promises to confer an inherent integrity and dignity to human potential. The right to the city is shorthand for all those social movements "that claim and project spaces in which human [*sic*] can dwell in accordance with the proper upright carriage of dignified human existence."[23]

Lefebvre's Romanticist and existentialist influences may provide further elucidation. The model of human flourishing underpinning the

21. Purcell, "Excavating Lefebvre," 106.
22. Harvey, "Right to the City," 23.
23. Mendieta, "City to Come," 445.

right to the city is one of self-actualization, of the immediacy of purpose and the capacity to act free of external impediment or constraint by un-reasonable authority. In his account of urban life, Lefebvre focused on the immediacy of the everyday (*quotidienneté*) that is corroded by the routines and regulations of modernity and bureaucracy. It is a phenom-enological reality in which we experience the concentration of goods, information, and people. The urban is thus both the place of the banality and conformity of the everyday and the potential site of transformed social relations. "What we make of the world" is no longer, apparently, of our own making, but someone else's; we are deprived of the material re-wards of that labor, but also dispossessed of a moral agency, as creative, self-determining beings. Resistance to this entails capturing moments of illumination, spontaneity, and self-expression.

Much of this would be questioned on theological grounds in terms of its emphasis on human autonomy and perfectibility. Tim would not be convinced by Lefebvre's manifesto's dependence upon a model of hu-man self-actualization. The hubris of secular modernist planning pro-grams rests, he argues, in their belief that perfectibility is possible. Citing Jacques Ellul, he argues, "Cities represent the hubristic attempt to build an ideal place for full human development, equilibrium and virtue, the attempt to construct what God wants to construct, and to put human-kind in the centre, in God's place."[24] Put more prosaically, it embodies the belief that human societies can plan their way to perfection. Citing Reinhold Niebuhr, Gorringe indicts much of twentieth-century urban planning for the heresy of "salvation by bricks."[25]

Similarly, as Clingerman argues, the quest for a *realized* Heaven will always fall short, as "we will be journeying toward a place which is con-structed within our own limitations."[26] Heaven cannot be constructed by human dwelling and building, although this is not to withhold from critical and constructive efforts, since it is "simultaneously an impos-sibility and a necessity, a task never completed but always undertaken in the fulfilment of life . . . Heaven can never be completed by human hands alone. If we think of it to be brought to fruition, Heaven becomes finite. The finite is a place among other places, constructed in the light of the changing narrative of residents and visitors: constitutive building

24. Gorringe, *Built Environment*, 19.
25. Gorringe, "Salvation by Bricks."
26. Clingerman, "Heaven and Earth," 50.

blocks and delimited spaces. To build the infinite, the unthought, and the indescribable is beyond the human condition, at least when this is left to our own devices."[27]

Theologizing about place is thus not so much about a process of human self-discovery but about glimpsing the potential for speaking about God "taking place"[28] amidst the practicalities and specificities of human place. Building Heaven is a task of seeing and interpreting—as Clingerman says, "a *practice* of thinking"—that enables us to find our place; "we build Heaven through the reflexive practice of thinking about how we are emplaced in place, something potentially present in any place wherein we dwell."[29]

In all fairness, then, are we really supposed to see "the right to the city" as a work in progress, "both working slogan and political ideal"?[30] In fact, David Harvey locates Lefebvre's vision within traditions of utopian political thought.[31] Utopia, as simultaneously *outopia* (no-place) and *eutopia* (good place), may not intend to function as a concrete future so much as serve to displace the present, especially when characterized by apathy or fatalism. By implying that all futures are human constructions, such critical social theories function, as Mendieta remarks, to remind us of the constructedness of all social arrangements, however reified they appear, serving as both "seismographs and compasses"[32] for political action.

This does not obviate the need to consider the actual practices and strategies by which greater democratic participation is facilitated; but it does highlight the fact that at the root of such visions is an implicit account of human nature. In asking, "How do we find ourselves?" we are also asking, "What makes us human? What visions of flourishing motivate us?" It is significant to see how many secular writers have turned to a discourse of spirituality as a horizon against which to define the ultimate objectives of urban struggles for justice.

For example, in her work alongside indigenous communities in Australia and Canada, Leonie Sandercock has observed how resistance

27. Ibid.

28. Bergmann, "Making Oneself at Home."

29. Clingerman, "Heaven and Earth," 50.

30. Harvey, "Right to the City," 40.

31. Harvey, *Spaces of Hope.*

32. Mendieta, "City to Come," 446.

to the logic of centralized modernist urban planning expressed itself in opposition to that worldview in the name of alternative, traditional "spiritualities" that prized the sacredness of the land, the continuity of memory, and the fusion of material and metaphysical that they found absent in modernism's functionalist and technocratic progressivism. This alternative approach to the management of space manifested itself in the assertion of alternative methods of orientating oneself to the world: via spirits, gods, myths, and symbols. This was their way of "finding themselves," as people attached by the strings of memory and affinity with their environment and their nonhuman neighbors that they found distressingly absent in modernist city planning.

Social movements for indigenous land rights were profoundly subversive of capitalist conventions of land as private property or commodity.[33] The emphasis within modernist urban planning on rationality, progress, and uniformity has sacrificed ways of dwelling and of understanding place as imbued with memory and meaning. Hence her use of the terminology of "desire" and "spirit" as repressed ways of inhabiting lived, rather than regimented or commodified, space.[34] "The work of urban, social, community, environmental, and even land-use planning is fundamentally a work of hope, the work of organizing hope . . . But where does this hope come from, if not from some kind of faith? . . . The faith at the heart of planning is very simple, it's our faith in humanity, in ourselves as *social* beings, in the presence of the human spirit and the possibility of realizing/bringing into being the best of what it means to be human."[35]

While Sandercock maintains a robustly humanist and nontheistic understanding of human nature, it is apparent that "faith"—not necessarily propositional belief but a vision of that which transcends the immediate and the concrete—is a central part of her scheme. Concepts of memory and tradition, similarly, inform many social theorists in their quest to articulate the values that are carried from one generation to the next and that have a significant impact in shaping cultural and political practices.

Sandercock also deploys spatial terminology to describe the connection between memory and the acquisition of full subjectivity.

33. Sandercock, *Towards Cosmopolis*, 17.

34. Ibid., 4; Gorringe, *Built Environment*, 216–18.

35. Sandercock, "Spirituality and the Urban Professions."

Memory "locates us as part of something bigger than our individual existences, perhaps makes us seem less insignificant, sometimes gives us at least partial answers to questions like 'Who am I?' and 'Why am I like I am?' Memory locates us, as part of a family history, as part of a tribe or community, as a part of city-building and nation-making."[36] The motifs of being heard into speech or becoming visible have been terms used by feminist scholars to describe the passage from object to subject, from hegemony to agency. While feminist theories and theologies have often privileged the language of hearing and seeing more than that of emplacement,[37] the question of how the women's movement has "made space" for women is also relevant here. The division of "public" and "private" has been hugely gendered, and even the concept of the "right to the city" may assume autonomous persons undifferentiated by the markers of gender, dis/ability, race, or age that fails to take account of the ways in which access to public space is a highly contested indicator of social inequality.

In that respect, the Womanist writer bell hooks' evocation of "homeplace" is another interesting fusion of place, meaning, identity, and political agency. hooks describes how in her childhood, "houses belonged to women . . . as places where all that truly mattered in life took place—the warmth and comfort of shelter, the feeding of our bodies, the nurturing of our souls. There we learned dignity, integrity of being; there we learned to have faith."[38] For hooks it was not the public domain of formal politics, but the domestic environment, that served as a key site for articulating a sense of identity for her generation of African-Americans. Black women were their primary mentors, despite having to work long hours for white people, in gendered, low-status jobs servicing white people's domestic spaces—cleaning, washing, cooking, and child care—before coming home. Here, a different dynamic pertained: not a place of enforced servitude but a mustering of the virtues of hospitality

---

36. Sandercock, *Towards Cosmopolis*, 207.

37. "Emplacement" echoes Ricoeur's idea of "emplotment," which relates to the way narrative provides a structure to the various components of a story; emplacement describes the mediation between Lefebvre's trialectic of perceived, conceived, and lived space whereby we construct an account of "our place in place." Clingerman, "Interpreting Heaven and Earth," 47.

38. hooks, *Yearning*, 41–42; see also McKittrick, "bell hooks."

and nurture in order to create "spaces of care and nurturance in the face of the brutal harsh reality of racist oppression, of sexist domination."[39]

This was both a space protected from the pressures of racism, capitalist relations, and derogation of human dignity, but also a sanctuary for the revitalization of alternative visions and practices of citizenship. The domestic sphere, often an ambivalent space for women, is reconceived as what in Lefebvre's terms might be a "third space," of relative freedom to carve out new ways of living, as a space of limited but significant empowerment for Black women. Homeplace was the space in which Black women like hooks' mother could "find herself" and her family, independent of the power of "the white supremacist culture of domination to completely shape and control her psyche and her familial relationships."[40] In roles that appropriated and redirected the demarcations of gender and race, these Black women subverted gendered and racialized expectations about their service role in the economy by making homeplace into a "lived space" "that affirmed our beings, our blackness, our love for one another."[41]

In an era of globalization, social and geographical mobility impacts on our cities as never before: many people are displaced, some as exiles, or in diaspora communities, while others are refugees who have had to leave their homes through persecution or political pressure. It may appear paradoxical, therefore, to see how many writers, including Tim himself,[42] have emphasized the importance of "home" and place in relation to cultural identity. Philip Sheldrake summarizes as follows: "First, 'home' stands for the fact that we persistently need a location where we can pass through the stages of life and become the person we are potentially. Second, we need a place where we can belong to a community. Third, we need a place that offers a fruitful relationship with the natural elements, with plants and animals and with the rhythms of the seasons. Finally, we need a place that offers access to the sacred . . . —perhaps, crucially, relates us to *life itself as sacred*."[43] "Home" is the difference between surviving and dwelling, therefore; and human houses and settlements are designed not only to provide basic shelter and to

---

39. hooks, *Yearning*, 42.

40. Ibid., 46.

41. Ibid.

42. Gorringe, "Shape of the Human Home."

43. Sheldrake, *Spaces for the Sacred*, 10.

meet biological needs but to embody in microcosm a more expansive mapping of the cosmos and humanity's place in it.[44]

Martin Heidegger believed that the purpose of architecture was to provide places of "dwelling" and that this was closely related to the process of finding our place. In an essay titled "Dwelling, Building, Thinking," he speculates on the role of architecture in society.[45] For him, authentic living is premised on the ability to "indwell" one's surroundings, to build in such a way as to foster a harmonious relationship with the rest of creation—the so-called fourfold, which are, according to Heidegger, the earth, the sky, the gods, and our own mortality.[46] Heidegger's classic picture was of the cottage in the Black Forest, designed and located in such a way as to integrate completely with the surrounding environment, and thus expressing its connections to "earth and heaven, divinities and mortals" in the way it combined physical shelter from harsh weather with a place for spiritual dimensions and the memory of the cycles of birth, life, and death that have taken place within its walls.[47] To dwell certainly means a physical locatedness; but it also implies an authentic sense of identity that entails establishing harmony with one's surroundings, an awareness of the interconnectedness of sky, earth, and mortals.

As I have noted elsewhere, Heidegger's comments seem to me to be helpful if we want to put together a practical theology of how to position ourselves in terms of ethical cultural practice.[48] As Young and others—including the theologian Sigurd Bergmann—have noted, this relationship to, between, and within the fourfold is in essence a spatial one: it is about "knowing our place," in terms of humanity configuring its activities of world-building against the horizons or parameters of infinity, transcendence, and nature.[49] To return to Tim's lucid summary of culture as the synthesis of the material and metaphysical: to be authentically human rests in this unique propensity to build and inhabit "worlds" of material objects and those of the imagination. How can the

44. Gorringe, *Built Environment*, 83–86.

45. Heidegger, "Building Dwelling Thinking."

46. Young, "The Fourfold."

47. Heidegger, *Poetry, Language, Thought*; see also Gorringe, *Built Environment*, 84–85.

48. Graham, "Being, Making and Imagining."

49. Young, "The Fourfold"; Bergmann, "Making Oneself at Home."

process of reflection be directed towards informing activities of building that foster the practices of dwelling justly and authentically?

Movements such as Lefebvre's "right to the city" and the evocation of the power of the human imagination to see beyond the immediate and the tangible toward a new world encapsulates the conviction that humanity's capacity to determine its own destiny is not simply a program for political change or urban insurgency. They are deeply moral statements about what it means to be human. Building the good city entails thinking *and* acting differently—against the flow of ideological versions, against the corporate vested interests, in the direction of realizing the practices of participation and reappropriation.

The urban geographer Doreen Massey observed that identity is articulated "not as a claim to a place but as the acknowledgement of the responsibilities that inhere in *being* placed."[50] Whether an explicitly theistic perspective is identified, the business of "finding our place" implies that tradition, memory, and relationships to a range of Others, and not simply the self-actualization of human autonomy, is crucial for human flourishing. "Finding our place" entails more than the basics of subsistence but requires a fundamental way of thinking about what it means to be human and to imagine the conditions conducive for human flourishing. It is also, crucially, about belonging and being at home: matters of physical habitat but, crucially, also about being embedded in more comprehensive webs of meaning, memory, and significance.

Bibliography

Bergmann, Sigurd. "Making Oneself at Home in Environments of Urban Amnesia: Religion and Theology in City Space." *International Journal of Public Theology* 2:1 (2008) 70–97.

Berman, Marshall. *All That Is Solid Melts into Air: The Experience of Modernity.* London: Verso, 1987.

Clingerman, Forrest. "Interpreting Heaven and Earth: The Theological Construction of Nature, Place, and the Built Environment." In *Nature, Space and the Sacred: Transdisciplinary Perspectives*, edited by Sigurd Bergmann et al., 45–54. Burlington, VT: Ashgate, 2009.

Gorringe, Timothy J. *Furthering Humanity: A Theology of Culture.* Aldershot: Ashgate, 2004.

———. "Salvation by Bricks: Theological Reflections on the Planning Process." *International Journal of Public Theology* 2:1 (2008) 119–35.

50. Massey, *World City*, 216.

————. "The Shape of the Human Home: Cities, Global Capital and Ec-clesia." *Political Theology* 2:1 (2000) 80–94.

————. *A Theology of the Built Environment: Justice, Empowerment, Redemption.* Cambridge: Cambridge University Press, 2002.

Graham, Elaine L. "Being, Making and Imagining: Toward a Practical Theology of Technology." *Culture and Religion* 10:2 (2009) 221–36.

————. *Representations of the Post/Human: Monsters, Aliens and Others in Popular Culture.* Manchester: Manchester University Press, 2002.

Graham, Elaine L., and Stephen Lowe. *What Makes a Good City? Public Theology and the Urban Church.* London: DLT, 2009.

Harvey, David. *Justice, Nature and the Geography of Difference.* Oxford: Blackwell, 1996.

————. "The Right to the City." *New Left Review* 53 (2008) 23–40.

————. *Spaces of Hope.* Berkeley: University of California Press, 2000.

Hefner, Philip. *Technology and Human Becoming.* Minneapolis: Fortress, 2003.

Heidegger, Martin. "Building Dwelling Thinking." 1951. In *Basic Writings of Martin Heidegger,* edited by David F. Krell, 343–64. Revised ed. San Francisco: Harper & Row, 1993.

————. *Poetry, Language, Thought.* San Francisco: HarperCollins, 1976.

hooks, bell. *Yearning: Race, Gender, and Cultural Politics.* Toronto: Between the Lines, 1990.

Lefebvre, Henri. *The Production of Space.* Translated by Donald Nicholson-Smith. Oxford: Blackwell, 1991.

————. *Writings on Cities.* Edited and translated by Eleonore Kofman and Elizabeth Lebas. Oxford: Blackwell, 1995.

Malpas, Jeff. "Finding Place: Spatiality, Locality and Subjectivity." In *Philosophies of Place,* edited by Andrew Light and Jonathan M. Smith, 21–43. Philosophy and Geography 3. New York: Rowman & Littlefield, 1998.

Marx, Karl, and Friedrich Engels. *The Communist Manifesto.* Introduction by A. J. P. Taylor. Harmondsworth: Pelican, 1977.

Massey, Doreen. *World City.* Cambridge: Polity, 2007.

McCann, Eugene J. "Space, Citizenship and the Right to the City: A Brief Overview." *GeoJournal* 58 (2002) 77–79.

McKittrick, Katherine. "bell hooks." In *Key Thinkers on Space and Place,* edited by Phil Hubbard et al., 189–94. London: Sage, 2004.

Mendieta, Eduardo. "The City to Come: Critical Urban Theory as Utopian Mapping." *City* 14:4 (2010) 442–47.

Purcell, Mark. "Excavating Lefebvre: The Right to the City and Its Urban Politics of the Inhabitant." *GeoJournal* 58 (2002) 99–108.

Sandercock, Leonie. "Spirituality and the Urban Professions: The Paradox at the Heart of Planning." *Planning Theory and Practice* 7:1 (2006) 65–67.

————. *Towards Cosmopolis: Planning for Multicultural Cities.* New York: John Wiley, 1998.

Sheldrake, Philip. *Spaces for the Sacred.* London: SCM, 2001.

Shields, Rob. "Henri Lefebvre." In *Key Thinkers on Space and Place,* edited by Phil Hubbard et al., 208–13. London: Sage, 2004.

Soja, Edward. "Writing the City Spatially." *City* 7:3 (2003) 261–81.

Young, Julian. "The Fourfold." In *The Cambridge Companion to Heidegger,* edited by Charles B. Grigson, 373–92. Cambridge: Cambridge University Press, 2006.

20

Theological Imagination and Human Flourishing

JEREMY LAW

INTRODUCTION

It was on a Wednesday evening in May 2001 that a small group of us from the Exeter University Theology Department gathered in Tim Gorringe's office to think about connections. We had been charged with producing a document to demonstrate how the individual learning outcomes of our various modules combined to deliver the overall aims of the theology degree program. As the sheet of paper before us took on an ever-greater diagrammatic complexity, Tim was heard to exclaim: "There are more arrows than the Battle of Hastings!" The resulting "Hastings Document," as it was fondly called, seemed to do its job.

In seeking to offer a response to the wonderful range of essays that an unashamed fondness and respect for Tim has elicited, I find myself attempting to produce my own "Hastings Document." What, if anything, beyond the aforesaid fondness and respect, connects these essays together? There is, of course, no one answer to this question. There may, in fact, be an almost limitless array of plausible responses. What I offer below, therefore, is simply what struck me as I read my way through the essays that precede this piece. I hope, learning from Mark Wynn's account of Aquinas, that in charitable fashion I've sought to listen attentively to the voices of others and that my synthesizing attempts do not perpetrate a violent contorting of their intentions towards an alien goal. So, here I am, drinking coffee into the evening and trying to get my arrows to behave.

IMAGINATION

I wish to argue that Tim Gorringe is a theologian of imagination for the sake of the kingdom of God. The attribution of imagination to his work is meant as a profound compliment. I make this explicit because the role of the imagination in theology has long been held to be problematic. John McIntyre traces its ambivalent position to a number of sources. First, the Authorized Version of the Bible, so influential in the English-speaking world, uses "imagination" to translate no less than three different Hebrew and Greek terms; in each case the use is pejorative.[1] Secondly, imagination, while not exhausted by the construction of mental images, falls foul of the "aniconastic" tendency,[2] prevalent especially in the Western church, which privileges imageless thought over pictorial representation. More generally, to admit of imagination in theology would appear to loosen its moorings to what counts as reality and allow it to drift off across a sea of pure human invention and fantasy. What claim then could theology have to *public* attention as the fantasy of the few?

Before advancing further there is a need, therefore, to be clear concerning both what is intended by speaking of the mental faculty of imagination in general and then, more specifically, to articulate what might be its place in theological reflection.

Let us define the faculty of the imagination as the ability to bring to mind that which is not directly and currently present to the senses. As Jean-Paul Sartre suggested, it is the ability to make present that which is currently absent.[3] It is, in Roger Scruton's helpful phrase, "a going beyond what is given."[4] This is not to suggest that the imaginative faculty is an independent power of mind; rather it makes its distinctive contribution

---

1. McIntyre, *Faith, Theology and Imagination*, 5. See, for example, Gen 6:5 and Luke 1:51.

2. Ibid., 6–8.

3. Sartre, *The Imaginary*.

4. Scruton, *Art and Imagination*, 98f.

in concert with perception and reason.[5] This becomes clear if one considers experimental science. The formulation of a hypothesis to be tested by experiment demands an inspired, imaginative leap; but this leap will be grounded in previous observation and rooted in rational sense. One need not, however, make the journey (by imagination!) to the rarefied circumstances of a science laboratory to see the need of imagination operating thus. Its employment in this fashion is an essential function of everyday living.

Both Tim and myself are utility cyclists who use our bikes as transport. The negotiation of traffic from the vulnerable position of two unpowered (or very limited powered) wheels demands an acute sense of anticipation. It requires the mental entertainment of what might happen, in order to provide the protection of a degree of preparedness. Here the imagination makes present to the mind what has not yet occurred. But this is not a process of wild imaginings; its usefulness demands that it be constrained by what might *reasonably* be expected to happen, assisted by accumulated previous experience. Imagination, I suggest, always operates with a combination of *constraint* and *construction* in varying proportions. The interpolation of missing data within a known field of variation mainly concerns constraint. But even the most reckless imaginings of the human mind will not wholly escape being shaped, constrained, by what is already known, even if they proceed by a method of negation of the known.

Imagination then takes its place in relation to the future in the mode of anticipation, but what of its relation to the past and present? As I have defined imagination, clearly memory relies upon its use; it makes present to the mind what is not currently available to the senses. And it does so with the same varying combination of constraint and construction we have just identified. This combination does not arise simply through a deliberate or unintentional attempt to cover creatively over lapses of memory. It is essential to the attempt to render a meaningful account of the past. This latter point becomes clearer if we turn to comprehension of the present, for here too imagination is essential. If it is the case, and I think it must be, that there is no meaning without interpretation, then the mere observation of "facts" is insufficient to produce a coherent account of the world. Rather, such observations require to be placed

5. McIntyre, *Faith, Theology and Imagination*, 89.

within a "horizon of interpretation,"[6] that is, within a cluster of presup-positions about meaning. Only so can they gain significance. Consider trying to guess the identity and purpose of an unknown object. One tries out various "horizons of interpretation" to see which makes most sense: Is it a tool, or a work of art, or a piece of dirt? This "trying out process" requires imagination.

Imagination is invoked in making judgments of value because val-ue depends on interpretation. Imagination is needed for empathy with another (including, and especially, with nonhuman others), creatively standing where the other stands. Motivation towards the achievement of a goal is aided by imaginatively envisioning it. Imagination and the appreciation of humor belong together, for humor often depends upon "seeing" something from a different perspective. The imaginative enter-tainment of alternatives is essential to decision making and planning, thus imagination can change the world. Imagination is what makes us original and grants vision to inspire. In short, imagination is a requisite of human flourishing.

THEOLOGICAL IMAGINATION

The language of salvation is unavoidably a language of protest against the present. It is the expression of a hope that things will be otherwise than they are. In occupying the ground between what is and what is to come, that is to say between the "now and the not yet" of the eschato-logical tension, imagination comes into its own. This is precisely because the imagination can conceive of alternatives to what is presently real. Perhaps the key motif available to a theology that wishes to conceive this saving alternative for the sake of the history of Jesus Christ is that of "the kingdom of God." Thus Mark's Gospel begins with the programmatic announcement of Jesus: "The time is fulfilled, and the kingdom of God is at hand; repent, and believe in the gospel."[7]

In word and deed, in parable as well as in miracle, in words of forgiveness and in table fellowship with outcasts, Jesus does not merely announce the kingdom, he enacts it in anticipatory realization. The king-dom emerges as a transformation of the world, within the world, and for the sake of the world. Jesus' healing miracles, for example, are not so

---

6. Gadamer, *Truth and Method.*

7. Mark 1:15.

much bizarre, inexplicable aberrations of the ordinary, as the emerging lineaments of a new reality that is the fulfillment of the ordinary.[8] The kingdom of God is not about a religious interpretation of the world, nor merely an altered religious consciousness; it is rather this world, in all its concrete particularity and complexity, renewed. The highest realization of the kingdom, however, occurs not in the course of Jesus' historical mission but in Jesus' own person. This is not simply because in the incarnation of the Son made flesh, made matter, the worldly is already inhabited by the divine, it is supremely because in the resurrection of the crucified Jesus, and here alone, matter permanently oversteps the limit of transience and death. Ultimately, as Jürgen Moltmann rightly affirms, the resurrection of Jesus will *entail* the new creation of all that exists.[9] His resurrection is not merely the illustration, ahead of time, of the saving future. Rather it is the anticipation and the source of the resurrection of reality. The new creation equates, thus, with the realization of the kingdom of God to its highest and furthest extent. It is constituted by the transfiguring consummation of creation, purified from sin, death, and every disfiguring negativity, and caught up into conspicuous participation in the loving relations of the Trinitarian being of God.

The realization of the new creation, consequently, lies beyond the bounds of any potentialities immanent in creation. It is not a possibility for the world. It thus lies far beyond human achievement. Its realization is rather the gift of God.[10] Precisely for this reason, it cannot be conceived by rational extrapolation from present trends in the world (which in fact, both for the individual and the current configuration of our universe, seem to point toward annihilation). Rather, the kingdom can only be anticipated by the theological imagination as it is prepared to be *constrained* by what we know of God's gracious action in Christ, yet reach out *constructively* to envisage what consummation might mean for any particular set of circumstances. Anticipation means imaginatively sighting a vector of transformation (of death and resurrection) from

---

8. Cf. Bauckham and Hart, *Hope against Hope*.

9. Moltmann, *Theology of Hope*, 201, 211.

10. Moltmann introduces a very helpful distinction between the historical future and the eschatological future on the basis of two Latin terms. *Futurum* is that future that emerges by the selective realization of the possibilities immanent in the world— future in its commonplace sense. *Adventus* is the future that comes to the world from God, transcending that of which the world is capable. See, for example, *God in Creation*, 132–35; *The Coming of God*, 23–29.

the world we know toward the promised fulfillment of our world in the new creation. In other words, it means risking an account of what, for Christ's sake, the flourishing of life might look like. By so doing, the theological imagination constructs an alternative that calls the present world, the present cultural, political, social, economic, ecological, and gendered world, into radical question. That, as we shall see, is its key power and its public claim. It has a better story to tell than the perpetuation of the *status quo*.

The conviction that the world can be transformed by God leads,[11] in the doctrine of creation, to the world's irreducible dependence upon God from first to last. The notion of *creation ex nihilo* guards against the sense that the world possesses its own independent reason for existence. All is gift. Yet not only is the world contingent in this global sense, its emergent unfolding is contingent too; it is an open process that is not fully determined. That the future need not follow from the projecting of existing trends, that the future need not be a prolongation of the present, means that history can become the arena for action that seeks to anticipate something of what God's kingdom will bring. With God it is always possible to believe that things can be different, better, other than they are. The theological imagination that grasps a sense of the kingdom's content, and so calls the present into question, can thus direct and inspire action in the here and now that, while it cannot lead to the kingdom, can bring about a series of closer representations of what the kingdom will mean. In other words, the theological imagination shapes hopeful action in the service of the flourishing of life in anticipation of God's defeat of every form of death. As Richard Bauckham and Trevor Hart affirm, "Christian faith moves forward toward the realization of God's kingdom in the slipstream of the statements it makes about that kingdom, the new creation of God."[12] And for this "slipstreaming" process the theological imagination is an irreducible essential.

Having sought to defend the usefulness and inescapability of imagination in theology—it is as useful and as inescapable as language itself—is it possible, as a final plank of defense, to ground the legitimacy and status of imagination in the being of God?

---

11. As Gerhard von Rad informs us, notions of creation in the biblical strata stem from the experience of salvation. See *Old Testament Theology*, 136–39.

12. Bauckham and Hart, *Hope against Hope*, 84.

Inspired by Karl Barth's account of God's perfections (more traditionally God's attributes),[13] John McIntyre seeks to legitimate the place of imagination among them. He does so by finding examples of God's imaginative activity within God's activity toward the world (the economic Trinity). Thus he suggests, "God's creative action is consummately imaginative"[14] and can be appreciated in the variegated magnificence of creation. Again, he sees the incarnation as a soteriological strategy of "stunning imaginativeness."[15] However, given the unity of God's being and God's act, which Barth also teaches us, imagination would, for this approach to be consistent, require to be grounded within the life of the immanent Trinity, in God's own self.

Elsewhere[16] I have sought to unfold the loving, perichoretic exchange of the Trinitarian Persons as conversation (as a complement to the mediaeval image of dance). In conversation there is a sharing of the contents of minds as the thoughts of one come to indwell the mind of the other. There is thus a degree of interpenetration, of mutual indwelling. Conversation also suggests an apt relational notion of identity, one of reciprocity and fundamental equality. Moreover, good conversation is a "going beyond what is given"; it is the product of joyful imagination. It is not a matter of listening and repeating, but of a spiraling, creative process that continually opens onto the new. In conversation one is both *constrained* by the other (the response must be appropriate and fitting) yet also free to *construct* afresh, beyond what has been already said. Staying within the orbit of this model of the Trinity as conversation, and building upon the Pauline notion of the Spirit as the power of fellowship,[17] deepened by an Augustinian conception of the Spirit as the "bond of love," might not the Spirit be thus conceived as the "Spirit of Imagination"? Within the life of the immanent Trinity the Spirit is the Person who grounds this creative openness—"the going beyond what is given"—in the relationship of never-ending, loving exploration of the other between Father and Son.

If imagination can be so grounded in the Trinity's own life, then the theological status of imagination is assured. Moreover, the economic

13. See Barth, *Church Dogmatics* 2/1, 322–677.

14. McIntyre, *Faith, Theology and Imagination*, 50.

15. Ibid., 54.

16. Law, "Unfolding Conversation," 145–49.

17. 2 Cor 13:14.

expression of imagination in the *opera Trinitatis ad extra* finds its transcendent ground. In the "imaginative" calling the universe to be and in its redemptive transformation to become the kingdom (the new creation) there pertains a fundamental coherence between God's act and being. When the Spirit inspires the prophetic imagination of an Isaiah or a Jeremiah, when the Spirit drives forward Jesus' enactment of the kingdom (as presented especially in the Synoptic Gospels), and when the Spirit works today to inspire the imagination of the church,[18] the Spirit enables in time what is rooted in the Spirit's eternal Trinitarian identity. Consequently, the use of the theological imagination in service of the kingdom of God, unfolded above, is a most fitting way in which the theologian actualizes her or his identity as "in the image of God."

Having sketched the outline contours of the theological imagination, I now wish to turn to the offerings of this volume's contributors to fill in its content with more depth and detail.

CREATING ALTERNATIVES

Where does one go, asks Walter Brueggemann, to "think outside the box" of a totalizing ideology? In his sights is the economic ideology of neoliberalism and the appalling social, and we may add environmental, consequences of its logic of the accumulation of surplus value. When one is repeatedly told "about the practical impossibility of alternative[s] to the 'facts on the ground,'" where does one go to gain perspective? One turns, he suggests, "to the Hebrew Bible and to the odd, inexplicable 'voice' that speaks in that enigmatic, unsettled, unsettling tradition." One turns to the prophetic imagination that via theological performance is able to "deabsolutize" the dominant claim by, "*acts of imagination* that expose the imagination of the [prevailing] regime as faulty, inadequate, and eventually false." This, incidentally, is precisely how Francesca Stavrakopoulou bids us reread Gen 2–3; it is "not so much a myth about creation . . . it is a story about preventing the king from becoming like a god."

Brueggemann directs us to other texts. He invites us to read Mic 4:1–5 as an imaginative evocation of a new future invoked by God's promise for a failed and destroyed city, a galvanizing alternative to motivate action. Likewise Isa 65:17–25, which sees Jerusalem as a place for the unbounded flourishing of life set in the midst of a "new heavens and

18. Cf. Gorringe, *Built Environment*, 5, 48.

a new earth," should be read as an imaginative alternative set against, "an urban economy engaged in self-destruction through its limitless greed." Thus in circumstances where human flourishing is compromised and undercut, and we can begin to believe that this is just the way things have to be, the prophetic imagination makes uncompromised flourishing chooseable again. "The work of the poem [in Isa 65:17–25] is to break the totalism of that idolatry of greed, not to deliver the listener into a panacea, but into a context where alternatives are chooseable."

Rachel Muers rereading of Hos 13 and 14 belongs to the same dynamic. Hosea 13 is seen to afford a vision of the destruction of human life, and the sources on which it depends, as a consequence of a false attempt to create security apart from reliance on God. Military might and purely technical solutions to the ecological crisis—as equally "the works of our hands" (Hos 14:3)—are perceived to fall into the seduction of self-help. By contrast, and as an invitation to repentance, Hos 14 holds out the vision of the flourishing of life as a promise of unconditional divine love. Thus, the prophetic imagination of the all-inclusive shalom of God, "exposes and shatters the destructive illusions that hold people and societies captive."

What these authors demonstrate is that the products of prophetic imagination can be reinhabited, reread, in order that the vision of a saving alternative they hold out may, in turn, direct and empower our contemporary imagination of what is possible in the company of God—of the God, we may add, who brings creation out of nothing and raises the dead.[19] In the perspective of the transcendent future of the new creation, Micah, Isaiah, and Hosea become our contemporaries as we look from our different vantage points towards the same kingdom of God. It is the ability of the imagination to "go beyond what is given" that renders this dynamic conceivable. And thus the theological imagination can challenge the present through its offer of a "counter-hegemony."[20]

Further examples of just this challenge are offered by a number of the contributors to this volume. Hauerwas' "taxonomy of greed" serves the purpose, among others, of challenging a view of greed as a necessary evolutionary force of progress that justifies its place in economic practice. And, in his defense of the public place of the Arts and Humanities (and thus of theology) in the academy, Nigel Biggar suggests that one

19. Cf. Gorringe, *Furthering Humanity*, 266.
20. Cf. ibid., 262.

of the essential tasks of such disciplines, not replicated elsewhere, is to introduce us to "foreign worlds" as questioning alternatives to the present. They offer, "distance from our own world, and thereby the freedom to ask questions of it that we could never otherwise have conceived."

Imagination when operating on a grand scale produces the notion of utopia. Elaine Graham helps us understand this concept aright. In the Marxist tradition at least, a utopian dream is not a distracting fantasy, unconnected to the "real world." Rather utopia is "simultaneously *outopia* (no-place) and *eutopia* (good place)" and its intention is not "to function as a concrete future so much as to serve to displace the present, especially when characterized by apathy and fatalism." Utopia may be appropriated theologically to inspire the notion of a "permanent revolution" that outruns every conceivable historical future, allowing no compromising reconciliation with the present.[21] In this sense the kingdom of God may be understood as the fundamental utopian concept with which theology has to wrestle. Beneath this overarching vision, and as a dialectical expansion of it, Graham reminds us that theology has much to learn from alternative sources of displacing utopias. Thus in bell hooks' "homeplace," domestic space irrupts into public dialogue as the source of an alternative vision of citizenship and as a space of empowerment through which a sense of "dwelling" usurps merely "surviving."

It is not just the reading of Scripture that enables imaginative "thinking outside the box." The practice of the Christian community can be just as effective, as Mike Higton's analysis of the eucharistic center of Tim's theology demonstrates. "Do this in remembrance of me," as a re-entry into the whole pattern of Jesus' table fellowship, enacts a powerful set of interlocking questions of the *status quo*. The participant is brought within the orbit of God's unconditional welcome, to an experience of the primacy of grace. And for Tim grace is "the most politically far reaching of all Christian doctrines. If creation is grace . . . then self-evidently life is not there to appropriate the benefits for myself, to hoard things over against others. The only response to grace . . . is gratitude, which politically means the struggle for social justice."[22] Consequently, as Higton unfolds, the Eucharist constitutes a summons to "live against the grain of the present world order." It is a practice that constitutes a "seedbed

---

21. Thus, for example, Leonardo Boff's use of the doctrine of the Trinity in *Trinity and Society*.

22. Gorringe, *Built Environment*, 20.

of political imagination and creativity," the centerpiece of the church as "a school in which we discover (or should be discovering) that 'another world is possible.'"

We cannot conclude this section, on theological imagination as the source of creative alternative perspective, without also learning from David Horrell and Louise Lawrence that an essential element of the very alternative that imagination holds out to us is precisely in contradistinction to prevailing Christian practice, including the interpretation of Scripture. What happens when what was once taken as "good news" becomes bad news for nonhuman creation and for Deaf culture respectively? Thus in service of "an ecological reformation of Christianity" called for by James Nash, Horrell desires to reread Paul in the interest of questioning "the deeply entrenched anthropocentrism of the Christian tradition with its sense of human uniqueness." He finds instead, in the "metamoral" norms of Paul's ethics, that is, in the requirements of corporate solidarity and other-regard, a way in which to underscore the significance of all creation. And Lawrence, for her part, attempts to de-center a hearing-dominated reading of Matthew's Gospel by voicing an alternative perspective that clears the way for reception of the Gospel by members of the Deaf community on their own terms. The community for which Matthew's Gospel was written is not so different, it seems, from contemporary Deaf culture.

REVALUING THE PRESENT

Here we revisit the inescapable role of the imagination in interpretation described earlier. Clearly, a revaluation constitutes the provision of an alternative value, so what follows in this portion of our reflections is very closely related to the preceding section. In order to interpret, however, one must first see, and to really "see" what is there, one must risk interpretation. Zöe Bennett helps us here with her account of John Ruskin, a man of preeminent commitment to "good seeing." As Ruskin remarks: "To see clearly is poetry, prophecy, and religion,—all in one." While he confined his seeing to the production of *Modern Painting* (1860), all was well; but when he turned that same penetrating gaze to the political economy of his day just a short while later in *Unto this Last* (1862), his former admirers, disturbed by the implications of what he saw (in the now "masculine" world of production) accused him of being a "preaching governess." Where others saw only the tough and necessary realities of the pursuit of economic gain, he, with biblically shaped imagination, saw deeper: "There is no wealth but life." It was a vision that, as Bennett informs us, was to inspire the imaginations of Mahatma Gandhi, the originators of the British Labour Party, and Martin Luther King Jr. to work for the "furthering of humanity"—for life in all its fullness.

In his examination of greed, Hauerwas reminds us "that our very ability to name sins is a theological achievement . . . Accordingly a community must exist that makes possible the identification of the subtlety of sin." When consumer virtue suggests that it is our civic and economic duty to seek and possess "more," that greed is necessary to save jobs, even for life to flourish, then we need theological imagination to revalue greed as a refusal of grace. "In the Eucharist we discover that we cannot use God up" with the implication that generosity rather than greed must be allowed to shape our economic relations. Only in generosity do we reflect the Trinitarian life of God in which we are called to participate.

Theological revaluation is not always a case of direct opposition to existing values. Thus Adrian Thatcher worries about how to assess the pursuit of happiness, which, while not yet the Gospel—this has some tough things to say about self-renunciation and other-regarding charity that make the quest for self-actualization (happiness) look rather narcissistic—has, nevertheless, as an orientating point for public policy, "brought about many benefits that coincide very closely with what social theologians want to see." Thatcher's way out of any simplistic either/or of the gospel over against contemporary culture, is to argue, following Charles Taylor and Tim Gorringe, that Christian theology can affirm human happiness as far as it goes, but needs to say more. By way of its affirmation and extension, the desire for happiness must be set within the more encompassing story of God's love for us in Christ that seeks the consummation of everything good in creation. There is a strong parallel to be found here with Aquinas's solution to the relationship between the cardinal and theological virtues relayed by Mark Wynn. There too we find the paradigm of affirmation and extension, and on the same basis: "love of neighbor and love of God cannot be easily prized apart." Rather, the latter needs to be allowed to transfigure and deepen the former. In the exercise of theological imagination, consummation turns out to be both a rubric of *constraint* and an invitation to *construction*, to a reaching out beyond the given for what is not yet given (construction), yet always for the sake of the already given (constraint).

A beautiful example of theological revaluation is provided in Wynn's account of Aquinas. In moral philosophy the notion of other-regard is usually justified on the basis of the capacity of the other to feel pain and pleasure, or on the basis that the other constitutes an autonomous center of choice. But Aquinas offers us, "a more demanding and more encompassing conception." Rather, "the love that we owe other human beings [including our enemies] has its roots in the fact that we can be related to them as friends in eternal life." What Aquinas offers, therefore, in the encounter with another is the theologically imaginative concept of "prospective friends." To act thus is to privilege the practice of charity that lies at the heart of the kingdom of God.

What underscores the vital role of imaginative revaluation is Paul Fiddes' observation that today a person's quest is not so much for the scientifically verifiable, for assured certainty, as "for stories that make sense of the world, and that convince by their power of explanation." Here Christianity has something enticingly distinctive to offer, a better story to live by. The church that seeks to live within a relationship of covenant with God, a covenant ultimately rooted in the Trinity's own covenantal relationships, finds meaning in "the supreme metanarrative: the story that God goes out from God's self on mission, in the openness to the future that is the power of the Spirit." Here is a theological model forged through imagination (in response to God's self-revelation) to lead meaning-making imagination toward the fountainhead of life: creation matters to highest reality.

BODILY IMAGINATION

The exercise of theological imagination is always situated. There is no transcendent vantage point from which it might operate with universal applicability. As with every mental function, it is inseparable from the body. When one imagines, it is always from a *particular* time, social location, geographical and cultural position. Human flesh is gendered, has a given sexual orientation and racial identity; the imagination is implicated in all this. And that is why, if one is to escape a default normalization of the parochial, there is an urgent need to be receptive to the insights of others who complement our "*Sitz im Leben.*" We need the charity epitomized by Aquinas's argumentative method in which, "he heeds the voices of others, and he even gives those voices a kind of priority in his own inquiry." The perspective of the other can both refine and stretch our own imagination; theology must always be a dialogical affair.

Lawrence forces those of us who can hear to listen to the Deaf, to be open to the views of a marginalized cultural-linguistic minority. Horrell insists that we consider what it would mean for an ecological theology to "place intrinsic moral value . . . on the nonhuman creation, *for its own sake*."[23] And Dhyanchard Carr wishes us to attend to, "the not so well known background to the story of the tragedy that befell the Tamils of Sri Lanka in the . . . early part of 2009." He also desires that we view these historical events from the perspective of a theological imagination that rightly disturbs a notion of easy providence, one more suited to the affluent West. Carr distinguishes two communities on the basis of his reading of Gen 4. On the one hand there is the community of Cain, in which he includes himself and presumably almost all who read this volume, "those of us who in spite of our unworthiness enjoy God's providential protection and care." On the other hand there is the community of Abel, those who suffer the appalling consequences of the actions of others, those we might say who suffer history rather than determine history. Inspired by Gorringe's conviction that the atonement is not only a once-for-all event completed at Calvary but rather "it is Calvary made real in human history through the Holy Spirit,"[24] Carr offers an arresting reappraisal of the meaning of recent Tamil suffering. In the light of the Jesus who cries out on the cross in solidarity with all the victims of history's openness—the same crucified Jesus who also speaks the word of forgiveness to all who are complicit in the creation of such victims—the undeserved suffering of the Tamil community must be seen as vicarious. The suffering community of Abel becomes the agent of forgiving redemption for the community of Cain. In an imaginative reversal of appearances, when it comes to who holds the initiative in the theological arena of grace, it is the community of Cain that unexpectedly becomes the passive party.

Duncan Forrester's account of the attempt to take the Christianity of the Scottish Enlightenment into India, as a catalyst of national reform, also serves as a warning of the difficulty we face, despite our best intentions, in being truly open to the other. Thus he comments, "although Duff and his colleagues professed that their own role was modest and

23. Emphasis added.

24. Gorringe, *God's Theatre*, 101.

temporary [that change could only be carried through by an indigenous 'Indian Luther'], in practice they contradicted their own theories refusing equality of status to their converts." In consequence, the missionaries were not prepared to hear the range of astute observations offered by the converts concerning the form of Christianity they received. What is the difference between caste distinctions and denominational rivalries, particularly in the refusal of communion? How does a message of equality in Christ square with the apparent racial superiority shown by some missionaries? And, most seriously for our purposes, there was no openness to the emergence of an indigenous theological imagination that wished to demonstrate Christianity as the fulfillment of the Vedic tradition so that being a Christian need not mean inevitable alienation from Indian culture.

If the exercise of imagination is always situated, then what of the effects of the built environment that Tim has so convincingly put on the theological map? If imagination responds to imagination, and we human beings need to "find ourselves" in space, as Graham persuades us, then the environment in which we imagine matters. This assertion gains credence from Graham Ward's thesis that *On Religion: Speeches to Its Cultured Despisers*—which provoked an epochal shift in theology—would not have come about without Schleiermacher's exposure to the city of Berlin. "Even intelligence needs stimulating and nurturing [and the] city was now a new vibrant experience for Schleiermacher." Berlin provided both the connectedness, and the sense of entry (via the Brandenburg Gate) into the emergence of the new, to provoke hitherto unexperienced forms of dialogue and social interaction. The *salon* mediated public and private space affording a form of "free sociality" that Schleiermacher experienced as "paradise." "Thus the city as a work of art, and the moral and spiritual life of its citizens as a work of art [via the *salon*], each impacts upon, and makes possible, the other." Schleiermacher's mind becomes the locus for the realization of such possibility. The result is the imaginative originality of *Gefühl* as a theological category, which Graham further expounds as a "feeling of dwelling." A theology of reciprocal relationality thus emerges from the experience of reciprocal relationality that the city of Berlin made possible. As Gorringe affirms, the built environment both shapes and is shaped by theological imagination: "If "event" is the final word when it comes to God [learning from Barth], then "imagination" is for the built environment [learning from Marx]."[25] Thus he also affirms, "[p]rofound, creative grace filled spiritualities produce profound grace filled environments; banal, impoverished, alienated spiritualities produce alienating environments."[26] Imagination counts.

THE PRACTICAL INSTANTIATION OF IMAGINATION

The theological imagination leads to action. This is gloriously demonstrated in Christopher Rowland's contribution. He introduces us to Gerrard Winstanley who, spade in hand, begins to dig the common land of George Hill in Surrey as a prophetic enactment of his theological conviction that the earth is a "common treasury." "Learning from Barth," says Tim Gorringe, "I take it for granted that for the theologian ethics and dogmatics cannot be separated."[27] Consequently there can be, "no theological assertion without its ethical correlate."[28] As Winstanley illustrates, it is the theological imagination that mediates this correlation. But it is, perhaps, the martyr that reveals this truth to the highest degree. The martyr requires a very particular commitment to an end not yet seen, but as yet only imaginatively grasped. John de Gruchy's account of Dietrich Bonhoeffer, as a saint and martyr who challenges our customary understanding of the religious life, reveals someone who, in the end, is prepared to die not as a witness to being "religious in a particular way" but rather as a testament to "the human being Christ creates in us." His collision course with dehumanizing Nazism was thus inevitable, and his death was both a protest on behalf of, and a promise of, a truly human future.

More prosaically, but no less counter-culturally, the church lived as covenant is a profound instantiation of the theological imagination. Not simply because it seeks to demonstrate an aspect of God's life as Trinity in anticipation of God's coming kingdom, but, as Fiddes unfolds, because it is an inherent attempt to live with the openness of the world. Unlike a contract "where the conditions are set out before entering it . . . a covenant . . . is a 'walking together in ways known *and to be known.*'" In other words, it is a way of living together that leaves room for imaginative flexibility in response to an unfolding world. Church then, at its

25. Gorringe, *Built Environment*, 48.

26. Ibid., 24.

27. Ibid., 2.

28. Ibid., 4.

best, has the potential to be a public performance of theology. And such performance is found in Ruskin's appeal to the imagination of his audience through his writing. In Ruskin's art, Bennett finds an answer to her own question: "how are the fruits of . . . theological reflection to be made to do the work we want them to do in the public world?"

THE "ESCHATOLOGICAL PROVISO"

For me, one of the best clues to appreciating how Tim's theology functions is given in his meticulously careful analysis of Karl Barth's Tambach lecture of September 1919.[29] Taking Ragaz's place at the last minute, Barth addresses a conference of German religious socialists at a time of considerable upheaval and political unrest in Germany. Avoiding all quietism, Barth also calls into question the notion of historical revolution by the radicalizing notion of "God's revolution." Tim summarizes the essence of the Lecture thus: "The God who is the revolution beyond all revolutions is at work in all reality [contra the narrow focus of the religious socialists]. Our task is to share in *this* movement."[30] The movement of God, which lies beyond every political or religious movement, is revealed in the resurrection of Jesus as "the revolution of life against the unbounded power of death." Consequently, "[t]he Wholly Other God—itself resisting all secularization, all mere being put to use and hyphenated—drives us with compelling power to look for a basic, ultimate, original correlation between our life and that wholly other life."[31] Hopes for social change, even and most especially by revolution, cannot be identified with the kingdom of God, but they may nevertheless participate in the kingdom of God that precedes all revolutions. This, I believe, is Tim's position too. Theology has, for the sake of the God revealed in Jesus Christ and the sending of the Spirit, no other choice but to be radically committed to the perfecting of every aspect of creation. But human action thus motivated, while it may serve the flourishing of life, can never deliver the kingdom of God, which, because it involves the forgiveness of sins and the resurrection of the dead, always outstrips human possibility. Thus human action, even as it orientates itself with respect to God's kingdom, always stands under the "eschatological

29. For the account that follows, see Gorringe, *Karl Barth*, 48–52.

30. Ibid., 49.

31. Quoted at ibid., 50.

proviso."[32] And the manner in which we seek to share in God's movement, the way in which we seek to participate in God's revolution, is by the exercise of the theological imagination that connects the "not yet" to the "here and now" as anticipatory constructions of the desired future.

There is much to be said for the "hermeneutic of immediacy" practiced by John Ruskin, which "is like the verbal equivalent of what Stanley Spencer does in his paintings of Cookham, superimposing . . . the resurrection on Cookham churchyard." There is great rhetorical power in Winstanley's reading of the Parousia as the perfect society for the present. But in collapsing the eschatological tension they ultimately sell God's "permanent revolution" short. The theological imagination must not be prematurely brought to equilibrium with the reality that is already given; it thrives within a horizon that is forever stretching away toward a transcendent future that only God can achieve. Its essence is "to go beyond what is given." In this way the theological imagination escapes the temptation of mere curiosity that John Webster forcibly brings to our attention, the temptation to "terminate on surfaces," and instead enacts the virtue of studiousness in its unremitting desire to strain after what God will finally mean for the world.

CONCLUSION

Tim Gorringe is a theologian of imagination for the sake of the kingdom of God. That is the inner secret of the worldly relevance yet Christian identity his work offers. But the imagination is not an independent power. It works, as we saw at the outset, in inseparable partnership with perception and reason. Imagination must thus be chastened by experience and theological logic. Imagination without theology is blind, but theology without imagination is dead; worse it could easily become a religious endorsement of the *status quo*. What then is theology's public claim? It is only right that we should leave the last word to Tim: "Theology contributes, alongside philosophy, literature and the rest, by providing space for reflection [from which constructive action springs], by testing our dreams."[33]

32. Cf. Gorringe, *Furthering Humanity*, 19, 266.

33. Ibid., 263.

Bibliography

Barth, Karl. *Church Dogmatics* 2/1. Edinburgh: T. & T. Clark, 1957.

Bauckham, Richard, and Trevor Hart. *Hope against Hope*. London: DLT, 1999.

Boff, Leonardo. *Trinity and Society*. Translated by P. Burns. Maryknoll, NY: Orbis, 1988.

Gadamer, Hans-Georg. *Truth and Method*. London: Sheed & Ward, 1975.

Gorringe, Timothy J. *Furthering Humanity: A Theology of Culture*. Aldershot: Ashgate, 2004.

———. *God's Theatre: A Theology of Providence*. London: SCM, 1991.

———. *Karl Barth: Against Hegemony*. Oxford: Oxford University Press, 1999.

———. *A Theology of the Built Environment: Justice, Empowerment, Redemption*. Cambridge: Cambridge University Press, 2002.

Law, Jeremy T. "Unfolding Conversation: A Theological Reflection on the Evolution of the Brain/Mind in *Homo Sapiens*." In *Theology, Evolution and the Mind*, edited by Neil Spurway, 130–54. Newcastle upon Tyne: Cambridge Scholars Publishing, 2009.

Moltmann, Jürgen. *The Coming of God: Christian Eschatology*. Translated by M. Kohl. London: SCM, 1996.

———. *God in Creation: An Ecological Doctrine of Creation*. Translated by M. Kohl. London: SCM, 1985.

———. *Theology of Hope: On the Ground and Implications of a Christian Eschatology*. Translated by J. W. Leitch. London: SCM, 1967.

McIntyre, John. *Faith, Theology and Imagination*. Edinburgh: Handsel, 1987.

Rad, Gerhard von. *Old Testament Theology*. Vol. 1. Translated by D. M. G. Stalker. London: SCM, 1975.

Sartre, Jean-Paul. *The Imaginary: A Phenomenological Psychology of the Imagination*. Abingdon: Routledge, 2010.

Scruton, Roger. *Art and Imagination*. London: Methuen, 1974.

Select Bibliography of the Works of Timothy J. Gorringe

BOOKS

Redeeming Time: Atonement through Education. London: DLT, 1986.

Love's Sign: Reflections on the Eucharist. Madurai: Tamil Nadu Theological Seminary, 1986.

Discerning Spirit: A Theology of Revelation. London: SCM, 1990.

God's Theatre: A Theology of Providence. London: SCM, 1991.

Capital and the Kingdom: Theological Ethics and Economic Order. Maryknoll, NY: Orbis, 1994.

Alan Ecclestone: Priest as Revolutionary. Sheffield: Cairns, 1994.

God's Just Vengeance: Crime, Violence and the Rhetoric of Salvation. Cambridge: Cambridge University Press, 1996.

The Sign of Love: Reflections on the Eucharist. London: SPCK, 1997.

Karl Barth: Against Hegemony. Oxford: Clarendon, 1999.

Fair Shares: Ethics and the Global Economy. London: Thames & Hudson, 1999.

Salvation. London: Epworth, 2000.

The Education of Desire: Towards a Theology of the Senses. London: SCM, 2001.

A Theology of the Built Environment: Justice, Empowerment, Redemption. Cambridge: Cambridge University Press, 2002.

Furthering Humanity: A Theology of Culture. Aldershot: Ashgate, 2004.

Crime. London: SPCK, 2004.

Harvest: Food, Farming and the Churches. London: SPCK, 2006.

The Common Good and the Global Emergency: God and the Built Environment. Cambridge: Cambridge University Press, 2010.

Earthly Visions: Theology and the Challenges of Art. New Haven: Yale University Press, 2011.

ARTICLES

"In Defense of the Identification: Scripture as Word Of God." *Scottish Journal of Theology* 32:4 (1979) 303–18.

"Evangelism and Incarnation." *Indian Journal of Theology* 30:2 (1981) 69–97.

"On Not Doing 'Western' Theology." *Indian Journal of Theology* 32:3–4 (1983) 63–69.

"Title and Metaphor in Christology." *Expository Times* 95:1 (1983) 8–12.

"Job and the Pharisees." *Interpretation* 40:1 (1986) 17–28.

"Not Assumed is Not Healed: The Homoousion and Liberation Theology." *Scottish Journal of Theology* 38:4 (1985) 481–90.

"'Amen, Komm Herr Jesus': Eucharistie, Eschatologie und die Option fur die Armen in Zum Gespräch mit angelsächsischer Theologie." *Evangelische Theologie* 50:1 (1990) 26–39.

"Sacred Space: Traditions in Conflict." *Church Building Magazine* 23 (1992) 3–6.

"The Heart of the Matter." *Church Building Magazine* 26 (1993) 3–6.

"Categories for a Theology of Communication." *Arasaradi Journal of Theological Reflection* 6 (1993) 10–18.

"Choosing Life." *Arasaradi Journal of Theological Reflection* 7 (1994) 49–55.

"Rembrandt's Religious Art." *Theology* 98:1 (1995) 15–19.

"The Church Teaches . . ." *Expository Times* 107:7 (1996) 196–201.

"Authority, Plebs and Patricians." Review of Oliver O'Donovan's *The Desire of the Nations. Studies in Christian Ethics* 11:2 (1998) 24–29.

"Theological Table Talk: Kitsch and the Task of Theology." *Theology Today* 56:2 (1999) 229–34.

"Figuring the Resurrection: Botticelli as a Teacher of the Church." *Theology Today* 55:4 (1999) 571–77.

"The Shape of the Human Home: Cities, Global Capital and Ec-clesia." *Political Theology* 2:1 (2000) 80–94.

"Can Bankers be Saved?" *Studies in Christian Ethics* 14:1 (2001) 17–33.

(with E. J. Wibberley) "Agriculture in Rural and International Economy: Theological Reflections and Practical Consequences." *Journal of the Royal Agricultural Society of England* 163 (2002) 149–56.

"The Prisoner as Scapegoat: Some Sceptical Remarks on Present Penal Policy." *Journal of Offender Rehabilitation* 35:3–4 (2002) 243–51.

"The Case for a Pre-Emptive Strike and So Forth . . ." *Political Theology* 5:2 (2004) 215–18.

(with Ken McPhail and Rob Gray) "Accounting and Theology, an Introduction: Initiating a Dialogue between Immediacy and Eternity." *Accounting, Auditing & Accountability Journal* 17:3 (2004) 320–26.

"Town Planning: A Theological Imperative?" *Journal of Theology for Southern Africa* 123 (2005) 16–28.

"Violence: Is There a Civilizing Process? Does the Gospel Play any Role in it?" *Contact* 145 (2005) 21–32.

(with Ken McPhail and Rob Gray) "Crossing the Great Divide: Critiquing the Sacred Secular Dichotomy in Accounting Research." *Accounting, Auditing & Accountability Journal* 18:2 (2005) 185–88.

"Farming in a Post-Carbon World." *Crucible* (2007) 35–41.

"Reflections on the Good Pub Guide." *Theology* 111:4 (2008) 243–50.

"Salvation by Bricks: Theological Reflections on the Planning Process." *International Journal of Public Theology* 2:1 (2008) 119–35.

"Living Toward a Vision: Cities, the Common Good, and the Christian Imagination." *The Anglican Theological Review* 91:4 (2009) 521–37.

"Idolatry and Redemption: Economics in Biblical Perspective." *Political Theology* 11:3 (2010) 367–82.

BOOK CHAPTERS

"Sacraments." In *The Religion of the Incarnation: Essays in Commemoration of Lux Mundi,* edited by Robert Morgan, 158–71. Bristol: Trinity, 1989.

"After Christianity?" In *Christianity for the Twenty-First Century,* edited by Philip Esler, 261–74. Edinburgh: T. & T. Clark, 1998.

"The Parish Church and the Ecological Movement." In *Small is Cosmic: Millennial Issues in Parochial Perspective,* edited by Edward Bailey, 117–24. Bristol: Winterbourne, 1998.

"Political Readings of Scripture." In *The Cambridge Companion to Biblical Interpretation,* edited by John Barton, 67–80. Cambridge: Cambridge University Press, 1998.

"Property." In *Christian Ethics: An Introduction,* edited by Bernard Hoose, 173–85. London: Cassell, 1998.

"Eschatology and Political Radicalism: The Example of Karl Barth and Jürgen Moltmann." In *God Will Be All in All: The Eschatology of Jürgen Moltmann,* edited by Richard Bauckham, 87–114. Edinburgh: T. & T. Clark, 1999.

"Liberation Ethics." In *The Cambridge Companion to Christian Ethics,* edited by Robin Gill, 125–37. Cambridge: Cambridge University Press, 2001.

"Karl Barth and Liberal Theology." In *The Future of Liberal Theology,* edited by Mark Chapman, 163–69. Aldershot: Ashgate, 2002.

"To a Dancing God." In *Moving Forms of Theology: Faith Talk's Changing Contexts,* edited by Israel Selvanayagam, ch.14. Delhi: ISPCK, 2002.

"The Bible and Subversion." In *Bible and Practice,* edited by Christopher Rowland and John J. Vincent, 44–50. Sheffield: Urban Theology Unit, 2002.

"Invoking: Globalization and Power." In *The Blackwell Companion to Christian Ethics,* edited by Stanley Hauerwas and Samuel Wells, 346–59. Oxford: Blackwell, 2003.

"Atonement." In *The Blackwell Companion to Political Theology,* edited by Peter Scott and William T. Cavanaugh, 363–76. Oxford: Blackwell, 2003.

"Gandhi and the Christian Community." In *Indian Critiques of Gandhi,* edited by Harold Coward, 153–70. Albany: State University of New York, 2003.

"Culture and Barbarism: Karl Barth amongst the Students of Culture." In *Conversing with Barth,* edited by Mike Higton and John C. McDowell, 40–52. Aldershot: Ashgate, 2004.

"Terrorism: Some Theological Reflections." In *The Twenty-First Century Confronts Its Gods: Globalization, Technology, and War,* edited by David J. Hawkin, 111–28. Albany: State University of New York Press, 2004.

"Slouching towards Jerusalem: Achieving Human Equality." In *Public Theology for the Twenty-First Century: Essays in Honour of Duncan B. Forrester,* edited by William F. Storrar and Andrew R. Morton, 315–30. Edinburgh: T. & T. Clark, 2004.

"The Principalities and Powers: A Framework for Thinking about Globalization." In *Globalization and the Good,* edited by Peter Heslam, 79–93. London: SPCK, 2004.

"Politics." In *The Blackwell Companion to the Bible and Culture,* edited by John F. A. Sawyer, 414–31. Oxford: Blackwell, 2006.

"Parvulus: The Idea of the Little Child in Medieval Preaching and Commentary." In *Generationen im Kloster: Jugend und Alter in der mittelalterlichen vita religiosa* [*Generations in the Cloister: Youth and Age in Medieval Religious Life*], edited by Sabine von Heusinger and Annette Kehnel, 65–74. Berlin: Lit Verlag, 2008.

"Aesthetics and the Built Environment." In *Theological Aesthetics after Von Balthasar*, edited by Oleg V. Bychkov and James Fodor, 216–33. Aldershot: Ashgate, 2008.

"Rethinking 'Migration' and 'Mission.'" In *Mission and Migration*, edited by Stephen Spencer, 159–72. Derby: Cliff College Publishing, 2008.

"The Transforming Power of the Cross." In *Perspectives on the Passion: Encountering the Bible through the Arts*, edited by Christine E. Joynes, 42–52. Aldershot: Ashgate, 2008.

"Ewangelia i kara [Gospel and punishment]." In *Kara W Nauce I Kulturze*, edited by Jarosław Utrat-Milecki, 146–66. Warsaw: University of Warsaw, 2009.

"Crime, Punishment and Atonement: Karl Barth on the Death of Christ." In *Commanding Grace: Studies in Karl Barth's Ethics*, edited by Daniel L. Migliore, 137–61. Grand Rapids: Eerdmans, 2010.

"The Decline of Nature: Natural Theology, Theology of Nature and the Built Environment." In *Without Nature? A New Condition for Theology*, edited by David Albertson and Cabell King, 203–20. New York: Fordham University Press, 2010.

"Keeping the Commandments: The Meaning of Sustainable Countryside." In *Ecological Hermeneutics: Biblical, Historical and Theological Perspectives*, edited by David G. Horrell, Cherryl Hunt, Christopher Southgate, and Francesca Stavrakopoulou, 283–94. London: T. & T. Clark, 2010.

"The Use of Scripture in Dialectical Theology." In *The New Cambridge History of the Bible: From 1750 to the Present*, edited by John Riches. Cambridge: Cambridge University Press, forthcoming.

SHORT EXPOSITORY PIECES

"A Zealot Option Rejected (Luke 12:13–14)." *Expository Times* 98:9 (1987) 267–70.

"Numbers: Chapter 11." *Expository Times* 117:1 (2005) 12–14.

"Numbers 13–14." *Expository Times* 117:5 (2006) 182–84.

"Numbers 15." *Expository Times* 117:8 (2006) 316–18.

"Three Texts about Moses: Numbers 12, 16 and 20." *Expository Times* 118:4 (2007) 177–79.

"Sermon on Luke 12:32–40." *Expository Times* 118:10 (2007) 497–98.

"23rd December: Advent 4: Isaiah 7:10–16; Romans 1:1–7; Matthew 1:18–25." *Expository Times* 119:2 (2007) 83–84.

"16th March: Sixth Sunday in Lent—Palm Sunday: Isaiah 50:4–9; Philippians 2:5–11; Matthew 21:1–11." *Expository Times* 119:5 (2008) 236–37.

"1st February: 4th after Epiphany: Deuteronomy 18:15–20; 1 Corinthians 8:1–13; Mark 1:21–28." *Expository Times* 120:4 (2009) 181–82.

"16th August: Proper 15: David's Big Ideas: 1 Kings 2:10–12; 3:3–14; Ephesians 5:15–20; John 6:51–58." *Expository Times* 120:10 (2009) 498–99.

DICTIONARY ARTICLES

"Pneumatology." In *The Blackwell Encyclopedia of Modern Christian Thought*, edited by Alister E. McGrath. Oxford: Blackwell, 1995.

"Christian Socialism," "Usury," and "Providence." In *Dictionary of Ethics, Theology and Society*, edited by Paul Barry Clarke and Andrew Linzey. London: Routledge, 1995.

"Alan Ecclestone," "Contextual Theology," and "Punishment." In *The Oxford Companion to Christian Thought*, edited by Alistair Mason and Hugh Pyper. Oxford: Oxford University Press, 2000.

"Cross, Salvation, Redemption." In *New Dictionary of Pastoral Studies*, edited by Wesley Carr. London: SPCK, 2002.

"Utopia," and "Liberation Theology." In *The Palgrave Dictionary of Transnational History*, edited by Akira Iriye and Pierre-Yves Saunier. London: Palgrave, 2007.

OTHER

Debt and Mission, USPG Thinking Mission pamphlet 27. 1996.

"Foreword." In *Faiths and Faithfulness: Pluralism, Dialogue and Mission in the Work of Kenneth Cragg and Lesslie Newbigin*, by Nicholas J. Wood. Milton Keynes: Paternoster, 2009.

Index

305